HISTORIC NATIVE PEOPLES OF TEXAS

HISTORIC
NATIVE PEOPLES
OF TEXAS

BY WILLIAM C. FOSTER

Foreword by Alston V. Thoms

 UNIVERSITY OF TEXAS PRESS, AUSTIN

Requests for permission to reproduce material from this work should be sent to:
        Permissions
        University of Texas Press
        P.O. Box 7819
        Austin, TX 78713-7819
        www.utexas.edu/utpress/about/bpermission.html

LIBRARY OF CONGRESS CATALOGING-IN-PUBLICATION DATA
Foster, William C., 1928–
  Historic native peoples of Texas / by William C. Foster ; foreword by Alston V.
Thoms. — 1st ed.
     p.   cm.
  Includes bibliographical references and index.
  ISBN 978-0-292-71792-3 (cl. : alk. paper) — ISBN 978-0-292-71793-0 (pbk. : alk. paper)
    1. Indians of North America—Texas—History—Sources.   2. Texas—History—
Sources. I. Title.
E78.T4F67 2008
976.4'0497—dc22

                            2007043191

TO THOMAS N. CAMPBELL

CONTENTS

FOREWORD

Alston V. Thoms

Texas, by virtue of its size and geographical setting, is an exceptionally informative place from which to examine Native American lifeways and history on a continental scale. It lies at the intersection of topographically complex and expansive forest, grassland, and desert habitats that encompass much of the continent. To understand and contemplate salient characteristics of Texas' ecological and cultural complexity, at any time during the last 15,000 years, is to simultaneously acquire significant knowledge about North America's southern tier. Said differently, Texas is a microcosm of native America's hunting, fishing, gathering, farming, and networking lifeways. That microcosmic trend continues into the present, albeit with more people in an evermore technologically complex world.

In *Historic Native Peoples of Texas,* William C. Foster provides us with an unprecedented opportunity to learn in considerable detail about Indian lifeways during the initial rounds of European exploration in south-central North America. This ethnohistoric saga is based on observations made by more than forty chroniclers who accompanied twenty-five major Spanish expeditions throughout the state and several French forays along the coast and into the northeastern part of the state. The accounts begin with Cabeza de Vaca's narrative of the failed Narváez expedition on Galveston Island in 1528 and end in 1722 with the establishment, in the Pineywoods, of the first capital of the Spanish Colonial province of Texas.

For archaeologists, anthropologists, historians, students, and other interested readers, this book provides historical snapshots of Texas' ever-changing indigenous landscape and its diversity of hunter-gatherer and horticultural lifeways prior to European military dominance and sustained colonization. Regardless of their shortcomings, these perspectives provide our most historically accurate views of the Native peoples of Texas. It is nonetheless important to recognize that climatic changes were well underway and Texas' cultural landscape was in a state of flux during the late 1400s and early 1500s, decades before the arrival of Spanish explorers.

Foster is an eminently respected historian who brings together in the present book a substantial body of information about Texas' Indian people that was otherwise embedded in his previous, well-researched books about seventeenth- and eighteenth-century Texas. To that already impressive body of data he added ethnohistoric information derived from all the known sixteenth-century explorers' accounts. *Historic Native Peoples of Texas* includes discussions of well over two hundred Indian groups whose homelands were within eight designated culture areas. Foster's culture areas are derived from the perspectives of the chroniclers of the times. They are delimited primarily by the distribution of culturally related groups who tended to be at peace with one another and frequently formed alliances against groups in adjacent culture areas. These areas do not coincide with ethnographically defined culture areas in southern North America—Plains, Southeast, and Southwest—that extend into Texas, although they may be seen as sub-areas thereof. Given Foster's decidedly ethnohistoric perspective, it is not surprising that his culture areas bear little resemblance to the state's archaeological regions, which tend to approximate ecological zones.

During the early historic era, Texas was more densely populated by surprisingly diverse groups in comparison to the "tribes" of the nineteenth century, including the Apache, Caddo, Comanche, Karankawa, Tonkawa, and Wichita. As a testament to the state's ever changing cultural landscape it is worth pointing out that, of this list of resident tribes in the nineteenth century, only the Caddo and Karankawa had truly ancient roots in Texas. Apaches arrived sometime in the fifteenth century, not long before the Spaniards, and the Wichita, Tonkawa, and Comanche arrived more than a century later. As one who teaches undergraduate and graduate courses at Texas A&M University in Native American and Texas Indian cultures, I am well aware of the broad patterns and many intricacies of native lifeways. From my decidedly ecological perspective—and as an archeologist with almost forty years of fieldwork and ethnohistorical research in the state—it is readily apparent that Texas epitomizes the concepts of Native American cultural diversity, continuity, change, and survival through the millennia. Nonetheless, in reading earlier drafts of *Historic Natives Peoples of Texas* I encountered "new" ethnohistoric information that is certainly pertinent to my own archaeological and anthropological research.

What contributed substantially to Texas' multicultural character were interregional and intra-continental travel corridors that traversed the state for millennia. Native guides led virtually all of the European expeditions into Texas along these routes. Major east-west travel corridors connected Caddo and other communities of mound-building farmers in eastern North America with farmers in New Mexico and other parts of the American Southwest who lived in permanent fortified towns. A major trailway system along Texas' Coastal Plain, known archaeologically as the Gilmore Corridor and historically as the *Caminos Reales,* linked state-level groups in central Mexico with chiefdoms in the Mississippi River basin and beyond. It was probably along these pathways, more than 2,000 years ago, that corn, and later beans, from Mexico were introduced to sedentary hunter-gatherers in the American Southeast.

Foster employs the word "cosmopolitan" in reference to the well-traveled and geographically knowledgeable Texas Indians. He also uses that term in conjunction with inter-band, multilingual encampments and trade fairs held throughout the state. In doing so, he calls attention to the humanity and ingenuity of these people, as he does elsewhere in this book. For example, he notes that prominent ethnolinguists argue that American Indian sign language may have originated somewhere on the Texas Coastal Plain. He presses the point of indigenous humanity by placing religious practices of Texas Indians into a global context. And he routinely calls upon archaeological data to demonstrate the millennia-old roots of the cosmopolitan nature and humanity of Texas Indians.

Historic Native Peoples of Texas pays considerable attention to the fact that the Little Ice Age occurred during the sixteenth and seventeenth centuries. The food-resource productivity of Texas' vast landscape was enhanced, perhaps substantially, as a result of increased precipitation and cooler weather, especially in the drier regions of the state. Of course climatic changes led to significant alteration of demographic and sociopolitical landscapes. This was especially the case when changes in the density and distribution of key food resources were accompanied by widespread depopulation and a punctuated introduction of new technologies. Foster's chroniclers found themselves in the very midst of profound changes that resonated globally.

As Elizabeth John wrote in her seminal ethno-diplomatic history entitled *Storms Brewed in Other Men's Worlds: The Confrontation of Indians, Spanish, and French in the Southwest, 1540–1795* (University of Nebraska Press, 1975), major demographic, technological, and socio-cultural changes were well underway by the late sixteenth century and continued throughout the seventeenth century. These changes set into play a centuries-long arms race among indigenous populations well beyond Texas. This arms race was triggered by the introduction of Spanish horses, metal, and guns to Pueblo Indians in the upper Rio Grande Valley of New Mexico and to Hispanized Indians in northern Mexico. During the late 1500s, Pueblo farmers allied with Spanish newcomers against bands of Apache who lived by hunting, gathering, and raiding their towns and farmsteads. Direct trading was established with Apache groups on rare occasions when the Pueblos and Spaniards sought peaceful relationships. More commonly, Apache warriors forcibly expropriated horses, metal, and guns from their Spanish and Pueblo neighbors.

The arms race disproportionately benefited the Apaches who used horses, metal, and, to a lesser degree, guns to increase their military dominance and facilitate their expansion into central Texas. That expansion, already underway in the late "prehistoric" era, further displaced indigenous groups southward and brought them into armed conflict with Hispanic settlers on New Spain's frontier in northern Mexico. Native peoples, known geographically as Coahuiltecans, whose homelands were in south Texas and northeast Mexico, needed horses, metal, and guns to thwart both the northward expanding Hispanic populations and the southward expanding Apaches. Their raids on Hispanic settlements during the mid 1600s prompted the Spanish to mount punitive expeditions into south Texas. By the late 1600s, other native fighting forces throughout Texas, including Caddos in the Pineywoods and Jumanos in the deserts and mountains of far-west Texas, were also mounted, carried metal weapons, and, occasionally, bore firearms as well.

Foster's primary interest is to reflect how the native peoples of Texas lived in what he calls their "natural state." The accounts compiled by chroniclers of the Narváez, Coronado, and de Soto/Moscoso expeditions in the mid 1500s certainly contain our best insights into native lifeways before they were profoundly impacted by Europeans. It is also clear that ethnohistoric information extracted from accounts of second-round expeditions during the late 1600s and early 1700s do not equally reflect the late "prehistoric" state of affairs in Texas. By then, depopulation from European diseases, slave raiding, and warfare by the Spanish and Indian allies had significantly altered pre-Hispanic cultural landscapes and land-use patterns.

To meet the principal objective of *Historic Native Peoples of Texas*— a synthesis of information complied by competent chroniclers who witnessed first hand Native peoples *throughout Texas*—Foster necessarily included ethnohistoric information from seventeenth- and early eighteenth-century Spanish and French expeditions. To restrict his study to ostensibly more authentic mid-sixteenth-century accounts of Indian lifeways would effectively limit the geographic and cultural scope to narrow pathways followed by a few expeditions into the vastness of south-central North America. With its two-century-long temporal scope, Foster's ethnohistoric synthesis is vastly more comprehensive in terms of the state's ecological and cultural diversity and hence of far greater utility to scholars, students, and other interested readers. This book is indeed a major component of the late twentieth and early twenty-first century historiographies and ethnographies that place Texas at the forefront of Native American studies. Its humanistic perspective and synthesis of ethnohistorical research will be valued for generations to come.

PREFACE

Spanish and French diary accounts of sixteenth- and seventeenth-century expeditions into Texas provide the early primary sources of information relating to the historic Native peoples of the state. European chroniclers preparing the diaries and journals were highly competent scribes who recorded daily the compass directions followed and the number of leagues traveled. Chroniclers also noted the names and lifeways of the Indian groups encountered and the fauna and flora observed.

The original diary accounts were handwritten in sixteenth- or seventeenth-century Spanish or French, utilizing military or clerical terminology, symbols, and abbreviations of the period. Today the services of specially trained professional Spanish and French translators of manuscript documents are required to meet the needs of most contemporary American scholars.

During the past decade, academic presses in Texas have published over twenty new or fresh English translations of diary and journal accounts of early European expeditions into Texas. These recent translations were prepared by professional translators with highly competent editors who often had available several copies or versions of the original diary manuscript. The published translations generally include an introduction that gives a comprehensive historical context to the expeditions, full and informative annotations, and accurate expedition route maps prepared by skilled cartographers.

The recent publication of this unprecedented number of English translations of accounts of early European expeditions into Texas provides an excellent opportunity to present a fresh, comprehensive overview of the historic Native peoples of Texas.

As indicated in the present study, the historic Indians of Texas followed a wide diversity of lifestyles and cultural patterns during the study period, ca. AD 1528 to 1722. Caddoan farmers in the piney woods of northeast Texas were successful horticulturists and mound builders in the tradition of the American peoples of the Southeast. In far West Texas, many Native groups were associated with the Pueblo agriculturists of the American Southwest and with tribes south of the border deep into Mexico. Most Native groups in Central and South Texas followed a hunter-gatherer lifestyle like their ancient ancestors who first settled North America.

Although the lifestyles of Texas Indians differed across the state, all Texas Native groups, both sedentary and nomadic, shared a cosmopolitan disposition to engage in broad networks of interaction and trade. From the present study we find that during the historic period Texas Indians served as the pivotal central link connecting Pueblo and other Indian groups in the American Southwest with late Mississippian and other cultural centers in the Southeast.

To compare historic and prehistoric cultural patterns of the Native peoples of Texas from an anthropological and archeological perspective and also to strengthen the overall study, I invited Alston V. Thoms to review and comment on the manuscript and to prepare the foreword. Alston Thoms is an associate professor in the Department of Anthropology at Texas A&M University and one of the most distinguished academic and field archeologists in Texas. Professor Thoms presently teaches courses on the prehistoric Native population of North America and the Native peoples of Texas. The present work would not have been published without the knowledgeable contributions and guiding hand of Alston Thoms.

I would like to express my deep appreciation also to the two highly competent archeologists, Stephen L. Black and Mariah F. Wade, who served as readers of my original manuscript for the University of Texas Press. Stephen Black is editor of the highly acclaimed educational Web site Texas Beyond History (www.texasbeyondhistory.net), associated with the Texas Archeological Research Laboratory at the University of Texas at Austin. Mariah Wade is an assistant professor in the Department of Anthropology at the University of Texas at Austin. It is most appropriate that Mariah Wade served as a reader of my manuscript because her supervising professor during her studies in the Department of Anthropology at the University of Texas was Thomas N. Campbell, to whom this work is dedicated. Thomas Campbell was the principal reader of *Spanish Expeditions into Texas, 1689–1768,* my first book published by the University of Texas Press.

Others made valuable contributions to the present study. Molly O'Halloran expertly prepared the special area maps, and Reeda Peel created the major illustrations. Dorcas Baumgartner assisted with her computer and editorial skills and with her continuing personal support. Gary E. McKee conducted research on numerous subjects associated with the present work and edited, reviewed, and updated each of the numerous versions of the present manuscript. To him I owe my most profound expression of gratitude.

Before he passed away last year, Jack Jackson, at my request, read and commented on the introduction to the present work. Jack reviewed and commented on all or parts of every manuscript that I prepared for publication during the past decade. I am pleased that this manuscript is no exception.

For over a decade I have been guided and encouraged in my research and writing by my special friend Theresa May, the assistant director and editor-in-chief of the University of Texas Press. Theresa has been patient with me throughout the past eight years, relying only on my word that, for her, I would eventually complete my study of the historic Native peoples of Texas. And now, thanks to Theresa, it is done.

HISTORIC NATIVE PEOPLES OF TEXAS

INTRODUCTION

There is today no consensus among scientists as to precisely when modern *Homo sapiens* first arrived in North and South America. Most archeologists, however, agree that the initial arrival occurred more than 12,000 years ago and that early settlers probably came in multiple waves, and perhaps by sea as well as overland. Anthropologists also agree that early human immigrants to the Americas brought with them their sophisticated lithic and hunting technologies, their spiritual world view, and other core cultural traits.[1] To give an anthropological and archeological perspective to the study of the historic Native peoples of Texas, we will review briefly how these cultural traits persisted or changed from the first hunter-gatherers in North America to the historic Native peoples of Texas.[2]

The contemporary American anthropologist Thomas D. Dillehay describes the cultural traits that were brought to the Americas by modern *H. sapiens*. Dillehay writes that "we must view the settlement of the Americas as an integral part of a worldwide human social and cognitive explosion that first took off some 40,000 years ago."[3] Dillehay adds that "these people explored new continents and brought with them the basic cultural foundation of early American culture."[4]

Paul Ehrlich, Richard Klein, and Ian Tattersall identify several specific cultural traits that the first settlers brought to the New World. Klein writes that modern *H. sapiens* hunters fashioned a spear or dart thrower (an atlatl) that substantially increased the accuracy, range, and force of the projectile.[5] Modern *H. sapiens* hunters had domesticated dogs and fashioned grooved net sinkers and blades struck from cylindrical flint cores.[6] They were also the first mariners to cross the open ocean.

Significantly, modern *H. sapiens* crafted 30,000 years ago not only bone spear and dart points but also bone musical instruments. In their

1

assessment of the new cultural life of modern *H. sapiens,* Tattersall and Schwartz reference a site in the French Pyrenees dated to ca. 32,000 years ago from which a set of bone flutes was recovered.[7] They were perhaps the first musicians, although the Neanderthal may have devised an earlier form of music on their own.

Another cultural feature initiated by the new *H. sapiens* is found in their artistic work and expressions. Beginning in about 30,000 BP, modern humans began painting black and red images of prehistoric animals and abstract forms on recessed walls of rock shelters in Europe and on the walls of deep caves and caverns.[8] One of the most impressive displays of modern *H. sapiens* art is found at the cave of Chauvet in southern France. Dated to ca. 35,000 years ago, the images include a wealth of skillfully drawn figurative and nonfigurative subjects—mammoth, leopards, owls, plus abstract geometric sequences of red dots.[9]

Modern humans in Europe and western Asia dressed up wearing carefully designed, nonutilitarian objects such as microdrilled tubular ivory beads and zoomorphic pendants for personal adornment.[10] A triple human burial in modern Russia dated to ca. 29,000 years ago includes beads sewn into the clothes of the deceased. The one adult had 3,000 beads fashioned of mammoth ivory; the boy's clothing had over 5,000 beads, and the girl's had even more.[11]

Modern *H. sapiens* buried their dead with elaborate grave goods, which some anthropologists interpret as a belief in a spiritual world and in life after death. In an apparent attempt to preserve the human remains, modern *H. sapiens* spread red ocher (an impure reddish iron ore) over the body.[12] The European archeologist Juan Luis Arsuaga points out that red ocher has excellent antibacterial qualities, and thus it may have been used by modern *H. sapiens* and earlier by Neanderthal and *Homo Erectus* to protect the integrity of the body.

During the Last Glacial Maximum (the coldest period of the last Ice Age), which occurred ca. 18,000 to 20,000 years ago, the Arctic ice sheet in North America covered most of Canada and the Great Lakes region and glaciers expanded throughout the Rockies. Scientists project that this climatically forced accumulation of water, held in the form of ice and snow in higher latitudes and higher elevations, reduced global sea levels by 400 feet or more below present levels.[13] After the Last Glacial Maximum, glaciers in North America (and Europe) receded and the Arctic ice sheet began to melt and retreat.

12,000 BC

Before the beginning of the relatively warmer Archaic period, early settlers had dispersed throughout North and South America. Early modern *H. sapiens,* called Paleo-Indians or Clovis people, first appeared in Texas as big and small game hunters and gatherers of plant food. The projected date for the arrival of Clovis people in Texas is based in part on artifacts recovered by archeologists in the 1920s and 1930s at sites in West Texas and New Mexico where Clovis spear points were found associated with the remains of megafauna such as mammoth and now-extinct large bison (*Bison antiqus*).[14]

During the early Holocene, the natural environment in North America changed dramatically from that known during the late Pleistocene. On the Great Plains the conifer forests gave way to grassy prairies. Yet other species of trees and cacti, including pine, cedar, oak, pecan, cypress, mesquite, and prickly pear, thrived 10,000 years ago in parts of East and Central Texas.[15]

Many species of the largest mammals in North America became extinct during the early Archaic period.[16] Between ca. 10,000 and 8,000 BC, the heavily hunted mammoth and mastodon disappeared from the landscape, probably because of the abrupt warming climatic change and perhaps as a result of the sudden threat of a previously unknown predator, the modern *H. sapiens* hunter. Although the demise of the American mastodon and mammoth was important, the extinction of the North American horse and camel during the same warming period was perhaps of greater importance. The horse and camel were domesticated in the Middle East and Europe with significant cultural and survival consequences for the human population in the Old World. But in North America no comparable large animals were domesticated.

Bison also changed during the warming period of the early Holocene years. The bulky long-horned and long-haired *Bison antiqus* became extinct while the smaller *Bison bison* survived with a lighter and slimmer frame and shorter horns and hair.[17] Likewise, the large dire wolf expired and the smaller gray wolf was the replacement. The lion-sized saber-toothed tiger also became extinct, and the range of the smaller modern-day jaguar expanded. Large versions of several other large mammals, including the archaic bighorn sheep, the oversized javelina (peccary), and the large armadillo, downsized to the lighter and smaller versions known today.[18]

According to a recent study of the wildlife population in Texas and the Southwest during the late Pleistocene and early Holocene, several smaller species of wildlife known today were present in Texas 10,000 or more years ago.[19] These include deer, pronghorn antelope, jackrabbit, small cottontail rabbit, wild turkey, vultures, and the roadrunner, all of which survived in about their present size from the late Pleistocene into historic times.[20]

Tim Flannery gives special attention to the spectacular array of the cat species (*Felid*) that roamed the North American continent at the end of the last Ice Age. The researcher identifies the felids as the jaguar, cougar, ocelot, lynx, bobcat, jaguarundi, and margay. Flannery writes that "this spectacular array of felids [in North America], 13,000 years ago, exceeds anything seen elsewhere in the world."[21] Noting the continuity, current-day zoologists report that the same seven species of large cats that were in North America during the close of the last Ice Age are still found today in parts of South Texas, the Trans-Pecos, and northern Mexico.[22] Climatic and other environmental changes over the past ten millennia have apparently altered the range and population density of the cats, but several species have found niches in which to survive.

7000 BC

As global warming continued, modern *H. sapiens* made another major break from the lifeways of previous hominid. Until about 7000 BC, all species of humans had survived in the same basic manner, as mobile hunters, fishermen, and foragers. Other large mammal species had survived and still survive in a similar manner, primarily as either carnivores or grazing (or browsing) herbivores.

Suddenly (in geologic time) and globally, modern *H. sapiens* altered this million-year-old hominid pattern of living as hunter-gatherers and, for the first time, began to collect and cultivate preferred seed of useful plants and to harvest, process, and store edible plant products. This revolutionary change to the domestication of plants by modern *H. sapiens* occurred almost simultaneously (within a period of three millennia) in areas around the globe—in the Middle East, southern China, and Mesoamerica.[23] The domestication of draft animals followed soon thereafter, but not in North America.

The agricultural revolution expanded during the rapidly warming Altithermal period between ca. 5000 and 2000 BC and led eventually to new, more complex sedentary human lifestyles with heavily populated agricultural communities, monumental architecture, social stratification, and dramatically new social institutions.[24] As on other continents, the new sedentary agricultural centers were concentrated first in the warmer tropical zone of North America. The domestication of crops together with the construction of earthen mounds first appeared in North America ca. 2500 BC on the Yucatan Peninsula, in south-central Mexico, and in Huasteca, an area only 150 miles south of the lower Rio Grande.

While advanced agricultural production emerged in Mesoamerica during the Middle Archaic period, significant cultural changes were also occurring at the same time in the Temperate Zone of North American. During this warming period, sedentary or semisedentary Native people in northern Louisiana constructed a dozen or more multiple mound complexes, some with connecting elevated terraces around large open plazas as large as three football fields across.[25] Archeologists project that the subsistence base of the Middle Archaic Louisiana mound builders rested not on agriculture (as in Mexico) but rather on the abundant local aquatic and riverine resources along an ancient course of the Arkansas River.

Louisiana mound builders were also collectors of useful plants, including goosefoot (*Chenopodium*) and other cultigens that were domesticated later during the Woodland period in the Southeast. These early mound builders in Louisiana and Mississippi also fashioned beautifully sculptured plummets for fishing or hunting, and they crafted microdrilled cylindrical chert and red jasper zoomorphic beads.[26] In the recently discovered mound works of these Middle Archaic engineers, artists, and emergent horticulturists we find some of the earliest evidence of the vibrant culture that emerged later in the Eastern Woodlands and on the lower Mississippi.

During the Late Archaic in the American Southwest, sedentary or semisedentary horticultural settlements arose. Recent studies indicate that domesticated maize and amaranth were cultivated in northwest Chihuahua, a short distance (ca. fifty miles) south of the New Mexico border.[27] The introduction of the bow and arrow and ceramics across much of Texas in ca. AD 600 to 800 marks the end of the Archaic period and the beginning of the Prehistoric period.

But the major agricultural revolution with accompanying large sedentary cultural centers, monumental architecture, long-distance trade patterns, and tropical cultigens did not spread broadly northward into Texas and across the Temperate Zone of the American Southwest and Southeast until the early Medieval Warm period beginning in ca. AD 900.[28]

AD 900

Between ca. AD 900 and 1200, the population of the Native peoples in North America increased rapidly, and for the first time numerous large and small horticultural settlements emerged or greatly intensified in parts of the lower Temperate Zone across the American Southwest and Southeast.[29] Small villages or towns with populations of less than 2,000 and two larger metropolitan areas with populations that may have exceeded 30,000 became established as regional agricultural, ceremonial, and political centers.[30] These small and large politically and religiously stratified population centers were located near or on the floodplain of major rivers, and their economic viability depended partly on favorable climatic conditions that permitted the annual production and storage of substantial surpluses of maize, beans, squash, and local domesticates.

During this classic period of Native North American culture, highly skilled Native architects, engineers, and artisans constructed monumental public earthworks and massive stoneworks, and Native artists painted delicately figured polychrome ceramic artwork.[31] For example, construction workers at Cahokia, a large metropolitan area on the middle Mississippi River, built the largest earthen mound in North America, which exceeded one hundred feet in height. At Chaco Canyon in northeastern New Mexico, workers constructed extensive stone storehouses and other structures up to four stories high. The massive stone masonry structure at Pueblo Bonito at Chaco Canyon had over 600 rooms.[32]

At Paquimé on the Río Casas Grandes about eighty miles below the New Mexico–Chihuahua border, Native workers built adobe brick apartments and other structures up to seven stories high.[33] The water system that provided flowing fresh underground spring water to the apartment complex at Paquimé and also river water to adjacent fields was the most sophisticated in Mesoamerica.[34] In the Mimbres Valley about 120 miles north of Paquimé in southwestern New Mexico, Mimbreno artists painted spectacular and imaginative geometric and figurative forms on ceramic pieces that touch and delight us today.[35]

At Cahokia, Chaco Canyon, Casas Grandes, and the Davis site in East Texas, skilled Native astronomers, engineers, and craftsmen built sophisticated facilities designed to conduct astronomical observations.[36] These facilities permitted the scientific measurement of the movement of the sun, moon, and stars. Readings from the facilities were interpreted by Indian astronomers to mark the turn of the seasons. But perhaps more importantly, the astronomical readings gave confidence to the Native people that their buildings, culture, and lives were aligned in harmony with higher celestial powers.

During this classic period of Native American culture, well-defined long-distance networks of interaction, which first developed during the Archaic, spanned the North American continent.[37] Native populations on the northwest coast of Mexico and the Gulf of California were connected by trade routes that carried literally millions of marine shells over 500 miles directly to Casas Grandes and to communities in Arizona and New Mexico. Archeologists have confirmed that the copper metallurgy and a cast copper bell technology known at Casas Grandes (but unknown in the Mississippian Southeast) originated on the Pacific coast of Peru and Mexico.

In turn, merchants in Casas Grandes traded directly with La Junta de los Ríos people and their friends in West Texas. Scarlet macaw feathers, cast copper bells, blue and white cotton blankets, shell beads, and turquoise pendants were traded from Casas Grandes. Again, in turn, it appears that tribes residing or stationed near La Junta annually sent trade delegations and hunting parties over 500 miles farther east to modern-day Tamaulipas on the Gulf of Mexico and to the Hasinai in East Texas.

Farther east, Caddo Indians in East Texas were related closely by culture and trade to Cahokia and, we know later, to the Acansa and Taensa Indians on the Mississippi. The Mississippian cultural tradition and interaction sphere extended across the Southeast to the Atlantic coast.

The classic period of North American Native culture flourished for several centuries; some cultural centers continued well into the sixteenth century before beginning to decline. Anthropologists offer different explanations for the collapse of Native cultures across the continent at the close of the classic period. Researchers frequently mention the negative effects of the Little Ice Age on horticultural activities in the higher latitudes and elevations. In his recent (2005) study of the collapse of cultures and of why societies fail or succeed, Jared Diamond describes the climatic change in the Northern Hemisphere as follows:

> Between AD 800 and 1300, ice cores tell us that the climate in Greenland [and the Northern Hemisphere] was relatively mild, similar to Greenland's weather today or even slightly warmer. Those mild centuries are termed the Medieval Warm Period. Around 1300, though, the climate began to get cooler and more variable from year to year, ushering in a cold period termed the Little Ice Age that lasted into the 1800s.[38]

In his recent studies (1999, 2003) of climatic change and the evidence of increased conflict and warfare in the Southwest, Steven A. LeBlanc of Harvard University agrees with Diamond's assessment of climatic change and its effect on horticulture during the past 1,100 years. LeBlanc writes the following: "The Medieval Warm Period came to an end around 1200, and not long thereafter the first signs of the Little Ice Age were seen in Europe. Famine was recorded in England in 1317 as crops did not mature due to the cold. I believe the same thing happened in North America."[39]

This climatic change to colder weather and shorter growing seasons threatened marginal horticultural communities in the higher elevations and higher latitudes of the Temperate Zone of North America.[40] It appears that the cold and deep snow brought by the Little Ice Age may have prompted large bison herds on the Great Plains to drift southward into the warmer, richer, and wetter Southern Plains. The increased precipitation turned the comparatively dry and sometimes xeric and barren

Southern Plains of South Texas and parts of the Chihuahuan Desert in northern Mexico into rich, deep grassy prairies that invited bison herds to extend their range to the Texas Gulf Coast, northern Coahuila, and northwest Chihuahua.[41]

By the time the first Spanish explorers visited Texas (1528–1543), the major cultural centers such as Cahokia, Chaco Canyon, and Casas Grandes had all faded. But, as De Soto discovered, some strong Mississippian-style horticultural chiefdoms were still dominant throughout parts of the Southeast and into Arkansas and East Texas. At the same time, Pueblo people continued to flourish on the Rio Grande and Pecos River in New Mexico, despite the colder climatic conditions as confirmed by sixteenth-century Spanish chroniclers.

AD 1500

By ca. AD 1500, Plains Indians were also on the move, following the drifting bison herds south to warmer latitudes and more grass on the extended Southern Plains. To add to the cultural mix, diversity, and conflict, large semisedentary tribes from southern Coahuila and Chihuahua in Mexico, including the Toboso, Tepeguan, Salinero, and many of their allies, sent scouts and hunting parties north 400 miles or more in search of bison on the plains of Southwest and Central Texas.

This book picks up the documentary history of the Native peoples of Texas with the landing of the Spanish explorer Cabeza de Vaca on the central Texas coast in 1528. Whereas the pre-Columbian history of the Americas is based primarily on the physical record studied by anthropologists, archeologists, paleontologists, paleozoologists, climatologists, and other specialists, the documentary history of the Native peoples of the state is based primarily on ethnographic and ecological information found in the earliest European expedition accounts. These written expedition diaries were prepared by officially designated and competent chroniclers who encountered and reported firsthand on the Native peoples of Texas in their natural state. European chroniclers also reported on weather conditions and the species of plants and animals observed. The historic Native peoples of Texas were either hunter-gatherers or horticulturists, so reports on climatic conditions and the range and concentrations of wild plants and animals constitute critical information for understanding the lifeways and behavior of the Native population in the state.

This work focuses on and describes as accurately as possible the Texas Native population encountered on Spanish and French expeditions into Texas in the sixteenth, seventeenth, and early eighteenth centuries. The ethnohistoric material is organized around certain themes, particularly a study of the patterns of subsistence, settlement, and long-distance inter-action networks between Texas tribes and other Native groups within and beyond the present state borders. Because the historic Indians of Texas were cosmopolitan and had interregional networks of interaction, the geographic scope of this study extends far beyond the state bound-aries into areas as far south as Monterrey and Durango in Mexico, as far west as the Mexican state of Sonora and Arizona, as far north as central Kansas and Missouri, and eastward beyond the Mississippi Valley. An understanding of the historic Native peoples of Texas requires a map that includes the Southeast, the American Southwest, the Southern Plains, and northern Mexico.

Our study ends in 1722 with the closing of the period of major ex-plorations in Texas, the establishment of the first capital of the province of Texas, and the commencement of the Hispanic colonization period. However, in some regions of the state, such as the southeast, Spanish and French explorations continued for several decades after Spanish coloni-zation was well under way in other parts of the state. After the period of major exploration, information about Native Americans in Texas sel-dom reflects how Indians lived in their natural state, which is the pri-mary interest of the study. We should note here, perhaps, that our focus on how the Native peoples of Texas lived at the time of first European contact implies that only limited attention is given to the relationships between Texas Native groups and the Spanish and French authorities or the Catholic Church.

European expedition diaries were usually written by military and clerical chroniclers who were assigned the duty of maintaining an official daily record of the journey. Spanish and French government officials and the Catholic Church depended upon the accuracy of the information provided by expedition diarists to formulate policy for the conquest of the new lands and conversion of the Native people.

Official chroniclers on expeditions into Texas were generally well-educated scribes who understood the importance of preparing an accu-rate daily written account of the journey. Accounts usually included the direction the party had taken, the number of leagues traveled, a name identification and description of rivers crossed and prominent land forms observed, the location and size of bison herds and other wild fauna and flora seen, as well as information on the Native populations encountered. Indians who served as expedition guides were used as in-terpreters to communicate with different tribes, often using a common sign language.

Confidence in the accuracy of the information found in the expedi-tion diaries is substantially enhanced when both the government and

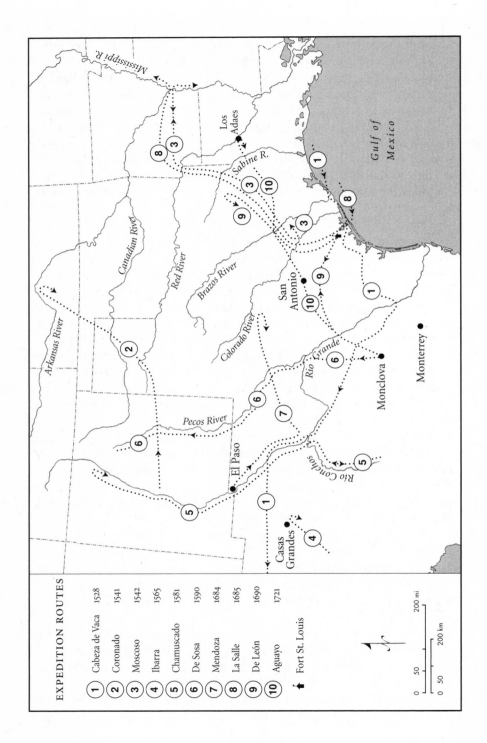

EXPEDITION ROUTES

①	Cabeza de Vaca	1528
②	Coronado	1541
③	Moscoso	1542
④	Ibarra	1565
⑤	Chamuscado	1581
⑥	De Sosa	1590
⑦	Mendoza	1684
⑧	La Salle	1685
⑨	De León	1690
⑩	Aguayo	1721
⚓	Fort St. Louis	

MAP 0.1

the church assigned independent diarists to maintain separate records of the same trip. Confidence in projecting the route of an expedition is also strengthened when several successive trips were conducted along the same route over a short period of time. This occurred, for example, when a Spanish expedition from Parral marched down the Mexican Río Conchos and up the Rio Grande to New Mexico in 1581, and a second expedition was dispatched over the same route a year later. A French expedition marched from Matagorda Bay to the Hasinai Indian villages in East Texas in 1686, and the next year a second French expedition followed this same route. Four Spanish expeditions marched from Monclova, Mexico, into Texas between 1689 and 1693 using the same or similar routes and the identical crossing areas when fording the Rio Grande, Guadalupe, Colorado, and Brazos Rivers.

This study reviews information from over thirty Spanish and French expeditions or limited excursions that crossed into Texas, and on each journey one or more chroniclers provide significant firsthand ethnohistoric information on the Native peoples encountered.

Between 1528 and 1543, three major Spanish expeditions or remnants thereof visited the central Texas coast, the Big Bend in West Texas, the Texas Panhandle, and East Texas. Specifically, Cabeza de Vaca lived for about six years on or near the central Texas coast and in 1535 continued his journey west to visit South Texas and the La Junta de los Ríos people on the Rio Grande in West Texas.[42] Cabeza de Vaca's party followed the Rio Grande upriver to a point about fifty miles below modern El Paso and then traveled west across the Chihuahuan basin and range toward the Casas Grandes river valley and the Pacific. In 1541 Coronado marched across the Texas Panhandle on his expedition from New Mexico to visit Quivira in Kansas and crossed the Panhandle again on his return.[43] In 1542 Luis de Moscoso visited the Hasinai Caddo and other Caddoan tribes in northeast Texas, sent scouts to the lower Colorado River, and the following year sailed westward, landing on the Texas Gulf Coast on his voyage to Mexico.[44]

During the second half of the sixteenth century, Spain initiated five expeditions into the American Southwest and the Trans-Pecos region of West Texas. The first was initiated in 1565, when Francisco de Ibarra marched up the west coast of Mexico, crossed the high Sierra Madre Occidental, and explored northwestern Chihuahua as far north as the Río Casas Grandes, about 150 miles west of El Paso.[45] Along the Casas Grandes, Ibarra's troops camped near the abandoned ancient city that the diarist Baltasar de Obregón called Paquimé. Ibarra's troops found evidence of bison in the area and encountered the Texas plains tribe that

Ibarra called the Querecho. About twenty-four years earlier, Coronado had met bison hunters called the Querecho about 500 miles to the north in the Texas Panhandle.

Spanish authorities sent two small but important expeditions from southern Chihuahua down the Río Conchos and up the Rio Grande in West Texas to New Mexico during the period 1581–1583.[46] In 1590 Castaño de Sosa's large expedition, the first authorized to colonize New Mexico, crossed West Texas following the Pecos River.[47] In 1598 Don Juan de Oñate crossed the western tip of Texas near El Paso on the second colonizing expedition to New Mexico.[48] Later that year, Oñate's lieutenant, Vicente de Zaldívar, marched his troops onto the Southern Plains near the present-day Texas–New Mexico border to secure bison meat for the winter.[49] Three years later, Oñate himself led an expedition across the Texas Panhandle following Coronado's earlier path.[50]

The close of the sixteenth century and the first half of the seventeenth century is marked by the appearance of important regional historical treatises dealing with northern New Spain, including Texas. In 1620 Fray Juan de Montoya wrote a *relación*, or account, of the discovery of New Mexico, which includes informed comments on the Native population and on Spanish expeditions across West Texas to New Mexico in the late 1500s.[51]

In 1630 Fray Alonso de Benavides composed his *Memorial*, or account, of the history of New Mexico that includes very significant ethnographic information on Native cultures on the western boundary of Texas in the first quarter of the seventeenth century.[52] In 1644 Fray Andrés Pérez de Ribas authored an account of his earlier travels and missionary work in northern Mexico, including Chihuahua and Coahuila. Ribas describes in sympathetic detail the Indian cultures on the southern boundary of Texas.[53]

In 1650 Captain Alonso de León (the elder) completed his history of Nuevo León and northern Coahuila, focusing on the period 1620 to 1650.[54] Many of the Native tribes described by De León spent as much time in South Texas as in modern-day northern Mexico. Juan Bautista Chapa, the explorer, scholar, and close friend of Alonso de León, wrote his history of northeastern Mexico and Texas covering the period 1630 to 1690.[55] In reviewing the history of Nuevo León and Texas, both De León and Chapa provide graphic accounts of the serious depopulation of Native peoples as a result of European-introduced highly contagious diseases.

During the second half of the seventeenth century, a new wave of Spanish and French expeditions explored Texas. A large Spanish military expedition was sent from Monterrey, Mexico, across the Rio Grande into South Texas in 1665 to punish the Cacaxles Indians for their raids on Spanish communities and ranches in Mexico.[56] In 1675 Fernando del Bosque led Spanish troops and missionaries from northern Mexico into South Texas to explore the area and pacify the Native groups.[57] Nine years later Juan Domínguez de Mendoza crossed the Trans-Pecos region from El Paso for the purpose of meeting East Texas and South Texas tribes on common ground in the Hill Country of Central Texas.[58]

In 1685 the French explorer Robert Cavelier, Sieur de La Salle, landed on the central Texas coast and established a fort and colony. The French establishment, called Fort St. Louis, survived for about four years near the shores of modern-day Matagorda Bay. We have several journals describing Native encounters and the flora and fauna near the French post and detailed diary accounts of the 1686 and 1687 French explorations from the bay area to East Texas and beyond.[59]

In response to La Salle's French threat, the Spanish government authorized between 1689 and 1693 four substantial overland military expeditions into south-central and East Texas from Coahuila, Mexico. Governor Alonso de León (the younger) led major expeditions to Texas in 1689 and 1690.[60] Governor Domingo Terán de los Ríos commanded the 1691–1692 expedition,[61] and Governor Salinas Varona led the resupply expedition to support a failing Catholic mission in East Texas in 1693.[62]

Soon after Salinas Varona returned to Monclova, the Hasinai Caddo drove the Catholic fathers out of Texas just as the Pueblo Indians had revolted against and driven the Spaniards from New Mexico thirteen years earlier. Although a Spanish expedition was sent in 1709 to reopen the Caddo frontier to Spanish troops and Catholic priests,[63] the effort proved unsuccessful, and Texas remained Indian country.

Spain was unable to reestablish friendly relations with the Hasinai Caddo until 1716. In that year Captain Diego Ramón and the very able and experienced priest Isidro Espinosa led a small company of troops and a few colonists to East Texas to establish several forts and missions.[64] Two more large Spanish expeditions followed from Coahuila in 1718 and 1721.[65] The 1721–1722 expedition, led by Governor Marqués de San Miguel de Aguayo, established the first capital of the province of the Tejas at the small Spanish community of Los Adaes near the Red River in present-day Louisiana. During the same period (1719–1722), French authorities dispatched envoys to establish contacts among Indian groups in northeast Texas and along the Texas coast.

The documentary accounts related to these early Spanish and French expeditions and the regional histories covering the study area provide a rich body of firsthand ethnohistoric and environmental information that is the basis of this overview of the historic Indian population of Texas.

For the purposes of this study, the state of Texas is divided into eight Indian Study Areas (see Map 0.2), which correspond to the eight chapters in this book. As will be noted in more detail in each chapter, the boundaries of the Study Areas generally identify different ethnographic regions that have shared cultural traits—the eastern and western sections of the central coastal plains (Areas I and II), the Karankawa country of the coastal bend (Area III), South Texas (Area IV), the Trans-Pecos (Area V), the High Plains and Hill Country (Area VI), Caddoan East Texas (Area VII), and the upper Gulf Coast (Area VIII).

Each chapter is followed by a chapter supplement that includes an alphabetical list of the names of the Indian tribes and bands reported in that Study Area. Each entry in the supplement includes variants in the name of the tribe, the name of the diarist reporting the meeting,

MAP 0.2
EIGHT NATIVE STUDY AREAS
OF TEXAS

the date of the encounter, and where the tribe was seen or reported (by county where possible). Entries also include the names of tribes encountered with the named entry tribe and the suspected homeland of visiting groups. A total of over 400 named tribes and bands are included in the eight supplements.

The study also includes two appendices, which record early Spanish and French expedition reports of both wild and domesticated flora and fauna observed in Texas and adjacent areas. The plant and animal tables list alphabetically the species of plant or animal reported, the diarist who reported the sighting, the date of the report, and the geographic location of the species. Paleontological information is included on some mammal species. It is hoped that the information will prove helpful to zoologists and botanists in projecting the range and density of population of specific plants and animals during the study period. Moreover, there may be general public interest in understanding whether animals and plants known today were present in Texas 500 or 5,000 years ago.

The present seems to me to be a particularly appropriate and favorable time to prepare an overview of the early historic Indian population of Texas because during the past decade an unprecedented number of significant documentary and archeological studies have been published detailing the early European exploration of Texas, northern Mexico, the American Southwest, and the Southeast. These publications include no fewer than twenty new or fresh English translations of early accounts of Spanish and French expeditions into Texas that previously had been overlooked or were in need of a fresh translation with full annotations.

The following are several examples of Spanish and French expedition diary translations and archeological overviews recently published by the academic press in Texas and cited in the study. In 2002 the University of Texas Press published a fully annotated English translation of Cabeza de Vaca's account of the Narváez expedition and his journey across the continent from 1526 to 1536.[66] The same volume includes a translation of the report of the expedition and journey prepared by the highly acclaimed chronicler Oviedo y Valdez. The following year, the same press published a fully annotated translation of the diary of the 1675 Bosque expedition and of the 1683–1684 Mendoza expedition across Texas.[67] And the University of Texas Press in 1997 released the publication of an English translation of Captain Alonso de León's 1686 and 1687 expedition diaries and Juan Bautista Chapa's own account of De León's 1689 and 1690 expeditions into Texas.[68]

In 2005 Southern Methodist University Press published *Documents of the Coronado Expedition, 1539–1542.*[69] The William P. Clements Center for Southwest Studies published in 1999 the Spanish texts of Vicente de

Zaldívar's 1598 expedition from New Mexico to the Southern Plains[70] and released in 2002 a critical edition of the several Spanish texts of Mendoza's 1683–1684 Texas expedition.[71]

The Texas State Historical Association in 1995 released *Imaginary Kingdom,* which contains both Pedro de Rivera's 1727 expedition diary to Los Adaes and the recently discovered personal diary of the Marqués de Rubí written during his inspection tour of colonial Texas in the 1760s.[72] In 1998 the association published the first English translation of Henri Joutel's unabridged journal of La Salle's expedition to Texas (1684–1687)[73] and five years later, in 2003, published the most complete diary account of La Salle's 1682 expedition on the Mississippi River.[74]

In 1993 the *Southwestern Historical Quarterly,* published by the Texas State Historical Association, issued the first English translation of Governor Salinas Varona's 1693 expedition diary to Texas.[75] More recently, in 2006, the *Southwestern Historical Quarterly* published a fresh translation of the Domingo Ramón diary of the 1716 Spanish expedition into Texas; significantly, the editor adds that it is her intention to provide soon a fresh annotated translation of the diary of Fray Isidro de Espinosa from the same 1716 expedition.[76]

In addition, during the past ten years, numerous new archeological excavation reports, site-specific studies, and archeological overviews in Texas have been published. The most comprehensive and significant recent archeological overview of Texas, entitled *The Prehistory of Texas,* was released by Texas A&M University Press in 2004.[77]

During the past decade numerous detailed site-specific archeological studies have been published by the Center for Big Bend Studies at Sul Ross University in Alpine, by the University of Texas Press, by Texas A&M University Press, and by or for several agencies of the State of Texas, including the Texas Archeological Research Laboratory, the Texas Department of Transportation, the Texas Parks and Wildlife Department, and the Texas Historical Commission.

The archeological studies cited in the present work give a broader context and an added perspective to the documentary accounts. The studies provide much needed physical evidence to correct and help interpret information found in the expedition diary accounts. But there is much left to be done in the archives and the field.

With this background, we will turn to our study of the historic Native peoples of Texas.

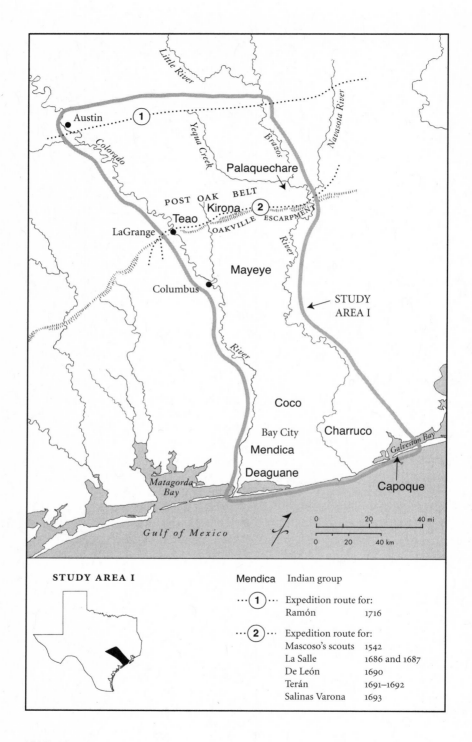

STUDY AREA I

Mendica   Indian group

···①···   Expedition route for:
           Ramón   1716

···②···   Expedition route for:
           Mascoso's scouts   1542
           La Salle   1686 and 1687
           De León   1690
           Terán   1691–1692
           Salinas Varona   1693

MAP 1.1

1 BETWEEN THE LOWER BRAZOS AND THE LOWER COLORADO RIVERS

STUDY AREA I

The country covered in Study Area I includes that between the lower Brazos River basin and the lower Colorado River (see Map 1.1). The area stretches north from the central Gulf Coast about 140 miles to include parts of the Oakville Escarpment and the Post Oak Belt, which run generally southwest-northeast parallel to the coastline. The raised Oakville Escarpment (with elevations up to 500 feet) is a prominent geologic feature that parallels the Post Oak Belt across the northern part of the area. The coastal lands can be characterized as prairies divided by wooded areas concentrated along the major rivers that run northwest to southeast. The region includes all or parts of fourteen counties: Galveston, Brazoria, Matagorda, Fort Bend, Wharton, Waller, Austin, Colorado, Washington, Fayette, Burleson, Lee, Bastrop, and Travis.

The boundaries of Area I are established for purposes of this study on the basis of comments made by local Indians to French or Spanish chroniclers. An Orcoquiza Indian chieftain identified the eastern boundary of the area. The chieftain told Captain Joachín de Orobio y Basterra that the Orcoquiza Indians living along the lower Trinity River occupied the area east of the lower Brazos River basin (in Area VIII) and the Coco and other Indians lived west of the Brazos (in Area I).[1]

A local Cantona tribal leader identified the western boundary. The Cantona told the French chronicler Henri Joutel that the lower Colorado was a boundary river that served to separate tribes living to the west of the river (in Area II) from tribes living to the east (in Area I).[2] Both Spanish and French diarists identified the northwest boundary as the Apache-occupied Blackland Prairies and Hill Country north and west of the Post Oak Belt.[3] The northern boundary runs from near Austin to Bryan and then following the Brazos River southward downriver to Brazoria County and on to the southern end of Galveston Island.

Several small rivers and large creeks flow into the Gulf of Mexico from drainage areas between the lower Brazos and Colorado Rivers. Oyster Creek enters the Gulf a few miles east of the Brazos River. The creek flows from northern Fort Bend County about three to five miles east of the Brazos southward to the Gulf. Caney Creek flows into the Gulf about three miles east of the northeast tip of present-day Matagorda Bay. The San Bernard River, which enters the Gulf about ten miles west of the mouth of the Brazos, drains parts of Brazoria, Colorado, and Austin Counties. Cummins Creek is the only large tributary on the lower Colorado that enters the river from the east; the creek flows southward from Fayette County and joins the Colorado near Columbus. Yegua Creek flows eastward into the Brazos River about twelve miles west of the junction of the Brazos and the Navasota Rivers.

The Oakville Escarpment crosses the northern part of Area I between Fayette and Washington Counties. This geologic structure forms the uplift and more open higher elevations and served as a platform for the central leg of a long-distance trade route that ran between northeastern Mexico and East Texas. The distinct high hill and bluff on the Colorado today called Monument Hill was first named Jesus, Maria y Joseph de Buena Vista by Alonso de León in 1690 and was called Maria by nineteenth-century Anglo settlers. The high bluff is a significant landform associated with the Oakville Escarpment, which crosses the Colorado River in central Fayette County.

The most densely wooded section in Area I is the Post Oak Belt, which runs north of the Oakville Escarpment. The Post Oak Belt crosses the Colorado River a few miles north of La Grange. This thirty- to fifty-mile-wide belt is an extremely dense growth of closely spaced post oak, blackjack, and hickory interlaced with grapevines, chaparral, and other thick thorny brush and vines. Spanish diarists called it the Monte Grande. The customary crossing areas on the lower Colorado and Brazos Rivers and other physiographic and ethnographic information are marked on Map 1.1.

Between 1528 and 1721, two French explorations and six Spanish overland expeditions visited Area I. With each journey, one or more written accounts were prepared that recorded encounters with the Native population. These expedition diaries, journals, and other related documents compose the earliest written primary sources that record Texas flora and fauna, identify Native Texas tribes by name, and describe the location and spheres of interaction of the Native population in Area I.

In summary, Álvar Núñez Cabeza de Vaca, the treasurer on the Spanish expedition led by Pánfilo de Narváez, spent about five years (between 1528 and 1533) along and inland from the central Texas coast, principally in Area I.[4] Luis de Moscoso assumed command of the Hernando de Soto expedition after De Soto died, and his scouts visited the northern part of Area I in the summer of 1542; Moscoso landed along the coast of Area I in the summer of 1543 on the party's voyage from the Mississippi to Pánuco, a Spanish port city on the northern Gulf Coast of Mexico.[5]

The French explorer Robert Cavelier, Sieur de La Salle, crossed Area I first in 1686 and again in 1687, traveling on both explorations between Fort St. Louis on the Gulf Coast and the homeland of the Hasinai Caddo Indians in East Texas.[6] The northern part of Area I was visited by Governor Alonso de León in 1690,[7] Governor Domingo Terán de los Ríos in 1691–1692,[8] Governor Gregorio de Salinas Varona in 1693,[9] and Fray Isidro de Espinosa in 1709.[10] Spanish and French documents prepared on each expedition conducted between 1528 and 1709 will be reviewed in detail to highlight relevant ethnographic and ecological information. Documents related to the Spanish expeditions of 1716, 1718, and 1721–1722 also include limited but important information relating to Area I.

Sixteenth- and Seventeenth-Century Spanish and French Expeditions

In early November 1528, Álvar Núñez Cabeza de Vaca and his companions from the Pánfilo de Narváez expedition drifted westward along the Texas coast off Area I.[11] A storm tossed their small float ashore near the southwest tip of Galveston Island. After Cabeza de Vaca's party recovered from the turbulent landing, the Spaniards located fresh water, built a fire, and cooked maize that they had brought with them from Florida. Lope de Oviedo, one of Cabeza de Vaca's closest companions, climbed a nearby tree to survey the surrounding country. Lope could see that the party was on an island and that the area had been disturbed by large hooved animals, perhaps bison. Lope also found a footpath that he followed for about a mile to an unoccupied Indian campground from which he took an earthen pot, a small dog, and some fish. Soon after he returned to his own camp, about 200 Indians, called Capoque by Cabeza de Vaca, appeared armed with bow and arrow. In a friendly manner, the Natives began to communicate with the Spaniards by hand signs. The Capoque returned the following day to bring food, including fish and roots, and later that day the Indians invited the Spaniards to their encampment and to stay with them.

A few days after Cabeza de Vaca landed on Galveston Island, a second boat from the Narváez expedition, one captained by Andrés Dorantes and Alonso del Castillo, landed about four miles up the island from the Capoque camp. Dorantes' party became associated with another Indian tribe or band called the Han, who spoke a language that was different from the one spoken by the Capoque. Cabeza de Vaca adds that the Han, who lived on the opposite end of Galveston Island, also had a separate family lineage from the Capoque. This information suggests that the small independent bands of Indians in Texas may have been basically extensions of family-related groups.

After the Dorantes party landed, the November weather turned sharply colder. With scant clothing and limited shelter, the Spaniards began to weaken and many died from the severe cold, leaving only fifteen survivors out of the eighty who had landed. In describing the severity of the cold, Fernández de Oviedo y Valdez writes that fish in the bay were found frozen. As mentioned in the Introduction, the Narváez expedition was undertaken during the 500-year climatic period called the Little Ice Age, and the weather was much colder and more mesic than we know today.

Soon after the Spaniards arrived, about half the population of the Capoque community died from a stomach illness. The Capoque thought initially that the Spaniards had intentionally brought the misfortune to them, but when the Indians realized that many Spaniards were also dying, the Indians concluded that the visitors were innocent.

At this point in his narrative, Cabeza de Vaca describes the Capoque and their relationship with other tribes. He writes that the Capoque were tall and well built. The men had their nipples and lower lip perforated with pieces of cane. All the men were naked, but the women covered parts of their bodies with moss. Girls dressed in deerskins. Cabeza de Vaca says that the Capoque moved every three or four days and did not plant crops. Their huts were covered with a matting and were often constructed on a bed of oyster shells. They usually slept wrapped in an animal skin on the shell floor.

Cabeza de Vaca says that the Capoque generally buried the dead, but they cremated the shaman (their only nominal leader) during a ritual celebration and dance. We recall from the Introduction that modern *H. sapiens* in western Eurasia were some of the earliest hominid to bury their dead with extravagant and useful grave goods, suggesting a belief in a life hereafter. Cabeza de Vaca writes that the powdered bones of the shaman were mixed with water and the mixture drunk when the tribe celebrated the first anniversary of the shaman's death.

Each male Capoque had only one wife, but the shaman was permitted two or three. The woman recovered the game or fish taken by her husband and delivered the food to her father's hut. Cabeza de Vaca adds that these marriage customs prevailed "from this island for more than fifty leagues [ca. 130 miles] inland."[12] This comment is significant because it is an indication of how far inland from the coast Cabeza de Vaca traveled. The author also says that, as a trader, he covered laterally over 130 miles along the coastline. Thus, Cabeza de Vaca's trading region covered most of Area I, which suggests that the Caddo in East Texas may have been aware of the Spaniard's presence.

Cabeza de Vaca also describes the annual migration of the Capoque from their island homeland to the mainland. The tribe remained on the island from October to March, eating principally roots dug from beneath the water and fish caught or otherwise taken in traps. The Indians moved by canoe to the bay shore in March and April, adding oysters to their diet, and in May they moved to the mainland to hunt deer and pick berries. Cabeza de Vaca adds that May was the month when the Natives continuously danced and celebrated. The Capoque stayed on the mainland for about four months, until September, according to the chronicler Oviedo.

The Spaniards remained with their respective Indian hosts, the Capoque and the Han, from November 1528 until May of the following year when Dorantes, Castillo, and ten companions decided to continue on their westward journey along the Texas coast toward Pánuco, leaving Cabeza de Vaca and Lope de Oviedo with local Indians. Cabeza de Vaca wrote that he remained with the Capoque for about eighteen months, probably until the spring of 1530.

Fortunately, the account by Oviedo y Valdez, which is based in part on notes taken from Dorantes' later testimony, records the movement of the Dorantes party from Galveston Island westward down the Texas coast, giving the number of leagues that Dorantes traveled between the rivers and large creeks that the party had to cross where the streams entered the Gulf.[13] This geographic record of Dorantes' measured line of march given in Spanish leagues is important in helping identify the island on which the Spaniards landed, the rivers crossed moving west along the coast, and the location of the Native tribes identified by Cabeza de Vaca.

Oviedo writes that local Indians first led Dorantes' party across the narrow bay separating the island from the mainland. Indian guides traveled with Dorantes down the coast westward about five miles to a stream that they crossed with difficulty in rafts that they constructed. The party continued along the coast another eight miles to a very large river that emptied and spread fresh water far into the gulf. During this river crossing, the force of the river current carried one of Dorantes' rafts far into the gulf and two of his men drowned. The remaining Spaniards continued along the coast another ten miles to a third stream and, after crossing it, continued another fifteen miles to a fourth river or creek. Here friendly Indians from the opposite or west side of the stream crossed the water and carried the Spaniards back across the fourth stream in a canoe.

The next day, the Dorantes party proceeded to follow along the coast (probably along the gulf side of Matagorda Peninsula) and, after traveling four days, arrived at the mouth of Matagorda Bay, a body of water that Dorantes recognized as Espiritu Santo. The coastline and bay were described by Dorantes as follows: "This bay was wide, and makes a point toward the part [in the direction of] Pánuco, which comes out to the sea almost a fourth of a league, with some cliffs of white sand. [These are] large, which reasonably ought to appear from afar in the sea, and for this [reason] they suspected that this was the river of Espiritu Santo."[14]

Based on Oviedo y Valdez's account, the island on which the Spaniards initially landed is projected to be either present-day Galveston Island or San Louis Island (southwest of Galveston Island), the first stream crossed by Dorantes was Oyster Creek, the second and largest stream was the Brazos River, the third stream was San Bernard Creek, the fourth was Caney Creek, and the sandy point described as extending into the Gulf was the entrance to Matagorda Bay, called Pass Cavallo. At that time, the Colorado River flowed into northern Matagorda Bay and was not crossed by Dorantes. The establishment of the location of the island on which Cabeza de Vaca landed and the number of leagues traveled along the Dorantes coastal route also suggests that the Spanish chroniclers may have been employing the customary Spanish league of 2.6 miles.

After the Dorantes party departed San Louis Island or the lower tip of Galveston Island, Cabeza de Vaca remained on the island until the spring of 1530 when he moved to the mainland to live with the Charruco Indians, who resided in a heavily wooded area probably associated with the lower Brazos.

During the period 1530 to 1534, while waiting for his friend Lope de Oviedo to depart with him, Cabeza de Vaca developed an active trade network operating primarily within Area I. Cabeza de Vaca's statement that the marriage customs of the coastal Indians prevailed for more than 130 miles inland suggests that he traveled and was familiar with tribes living at least as far inland from the coast as the junction of the Brazos and Navasota Rivers. As will be noted later, trade visits to an area 130 or more miles inland may possibly have put Cabeza de Vaca in contact with visiting hunters from the East Texas Caddoan tribes but probably not to the Hasinai homeland. Cabeza de Vaca adds that he did not travel to trade during the winter months because the bitter cold kept the Native population of this area in hibernation.

Cabeza de Vaca writes that he traded Native coastal export items, such as cones and other pieces of sea snail, conchs used for cutting, sea-beads, and a fruit like a bean that the Indians valued very highly, using it for a medicine and for a ritual beverage in their dances and festivities. He brought back from the interior to the coastal Indians animal skins, hard canes for arrows, flint for arrowheads, with sinews and cement to attach them, tassels of deer hair, which the Indians dyed red, and red ocher, which the Natives rubbed on their faces.[15] In the Introduction, I mentioned the use of red ocher by modern *H. sapiens* ca. 30,000 years ago and Neanderthal even earlier to paint their own bodies and to sprinkle on the body of the deceased before burial.

Although Cabeza de Vaca does not disclose where he first saw bison, he writes that he saw them on several occasions and notes that bison were plentiful and attracted distant hunters who had bison hides to trade. As noted later, Spanish chroniclers encountered bison hunters from northern Mexico and the Plains near the lower Colorado. After spending almost five years along the lower Brazos basin and inland throughout his trade area, Cabeza de Vaca and his companion Lope de Oviedo in 1533 moved together southwest from the Charruco Indians to stay for a short visit with a small tribe or band called the Deaguane, who lived along the coast between the Charruco and Matagorda Bay. The author writes that the Mendica Indians lived inland from the Deaguane.

Cabeza de Vaca reports that while he was with the Deaguane, the Quevene Indians (probably a Karankawan band from the Matagorda Bay area) attacked the Deaguane encampment at midnight, killing three Indians and wounding many others. In retaliation, the Deaguane attacked a Quevene village early the following morning, killing five of the enemy. Apparently the distance traveled from the Deaguane camp to the Quevene was covered in about four to six hours or less. This projected distance of twenty or thirty miles traveled in four to six hours is consistent with the projection that the Deaguane lived in eastern Matagorda County east of the Colorado River and that the Quevene was a Matagorda Bay tribe associated with the Karankawa.

These raids between the Deaguane and Quevene are one of the few occasions involving bloody warfare that Cabeza de Vaca describes between close Indian neighbors. This report suggests that the Colorado River represented some form of tribal boundary that separated the Matagorda Bay Quevene in Area III from their enemy the Deaguane, who lived a short distance northeast of the bay area and east of the Colorado River in Area I.[16] Therefore, the eastern boundary of the Karankawa may have been near the Colorado River, as projected by Robert A. Ricklis. It is also significant that Cabeza de Vaca reports that the warfare was brought to a truce by a delegation of Quevene women who visited the Deaguane to obtain peace soon after the exchange of attacks.

A short time later, Deaguane guides escorted Cabeza de Vaca and his companion Lope de Oviedo farther down the coast to a bay that Cabeza de Vaca (like Dorantes before him) identified as "Espiritu Santo," or present Matagorda Bay. Moving westward along Matagorda Peninsula the two Spaniards and the Deaguane women who served as guides met the Quevene. This report probably places the Quevene in Calhoun County on the western shore of Matagorda Bay in the Karankawa territory of Area III. The Quevene admitted that earlier they had killed three of Dorantes' comrades, and they then threatened to kill Cabeza de Vaca and Lope. This threat frightened Lope into returning eastward back up the coast with the Deaguane women, leaving Cabeza de Vaca alone. We have no further word regarding Lope who, after living over four years with the Native people near the Texas coast, was perhaps fully acculturated.

Although the feisty and mean-spirited Quevene frightened Lope into returning up the coast, Cabeza de Vaca remained in the bay area in Area III with the Quevene for a brief time. His travels westward into Area III conclude Cabeza de Vaca's report on the Indians living in Area I, as the Matagorda Bay Indians will be considered later.

Despite the clear identification by Cabeza de Vaca of the relative location of the Capoque, Charruco, Deaguane, and Mendica Indian tribes, writers have often incorrectly located the Native groups. Although it has not been possible to equate convincingly the Charruco, Deaguane, or Mendica with any tribes named in subsequent Spanish or French expedition accounts, some anthropologists have tentatively equated the Capoque with the Coco, a tribe identified in the general area by several Spanish expedition diarists. This issue is developed later in the chapter as more information on the Coco is analyzed from late sixteenth- and seventeenth-century Spanish documents.

In 1542, about eight years after Cabeza de Vaca departed Area I and moved westward into Area III, the Spanish expedition leader Luis de Moscoso and his men visited eastern and south-central regions of Texas. These Spaniards were hearty members of the Hernando de Soto expedition, which had landed initially in Florida three years earlier. Moscoso had accepted command of the expedition after De Soto died earlier that year. Moscoso's troops marched into East Texas, probably as far as the homeland of the Hasinai Caddo on San Pedro Creek in Houston County. Among the Hasinai the Spaniards found evidence of interaction and trade with the Native people of northern Mexico and the American

Southwest. The foreign trade items included turquoise and cotton goods, which the Hasinai said originated from Native people living in the direction where Christians lived, meaning probably the Spaniards who resided to the southwest.[17] This report suggests that a Native trade network crossed Area I to connect the East Texas Caddo and the Native peoples of the Southwest and northern Mexico.

Although Moscoso sent a scouting party to the southwest and across Area I to the Colorado River, or a short distance beyond, the troops found no maize, and Moscoso returned to a winter campsite on the Mississippi. In 1543 Moscoso's men constructed several large and serviceable boats (referred to as brigantines) and sailed down the Mississippi and westward along the Texas Gulf Coast toward present-day Tampico near the mouth of the Río Pánuco.

Spanish accounts of Moscoso's trip along the Texas coast are not sufficiently detailed to permit any confident identification of the party's specific location along the route, but the record of Moscoso's Texas coastal journey is nevertheless relevant to the present study. According to one chronicler known as "the Gentleman from Elvas," Moscoso's men entered the Gulf of Mexico from the mouth of the Mississippi on July 18, 1543. The Spaniards followed the shoreline westward, staying always within sight of land and coasting under sail or by rowing. As fresh water was needed every few days, the brigantines were frequently beached or anchored at suitable locations along the Texas coast.

Although the Gentleman from Elvas does not mention any encounter with coastal Natives after leaving the Mississippi, another chronicler on the journey, Garcilaso de la Vega, the Inca, describes meeting Indians at a location where the Spaniards beached their boats for about eight days to fish and apply the natural black bitumen, or tar, found on shore to repair leaks in the boats.[18] The location, which was near a large waterfowl nesting area, was reached after having sailed westward about sixteen days from the mouth of the Mississippi. Garcilaso describes the area as having "four or five islets not far from the mainland" and a beach with large trees and no undergrowth. Garcilaso explained that the black pitch had worked up from the floor of the gulf from an underwater source or fountain. To soften the tar for application to the boats, the Spaniards used cooked fat prepared for the voyage from the slaughtered hogs that had followed the troops from their initial Florida landing.

According to Garcilaso, during the eight-day stopover while Moscoso's boats were repaired, eight Indians armed with bows and arrows exchanged their locally grown maize for deerskins that the Spaniards had brought with them from the Mississippi. This form of exchange was repeated on two other days before the Spaniards departed.

Charles Hudson, a respected authority on the De Soto–Moscoso expedition route, suggests that Moscoso probably met the Indians near Galveston Bay.[19] Hudson adds that the Moscoso party "possibly sailed through San Luis Pass at the southern end of Galveston Island,"[20] near the boundary line separating Areas I and VIII. It appears that the Spaniards may have visited both Areas I and VIII. In support of his conclusions, Hudson notes that Moscoso's chroniclers refer to the tar or pitch found on the beach as "copei" and adds that on the De Soto Map, a location identified as "point de copei" is sited west of the Mississippi and east of a river identified as the "Madelena" on the central Texas coast.[21]

Apparently the Moscoso party continued to stop at locations along the Texas coast west of Point de Copei. Garcilaso reports that the men had nothing to eat except the maize they had secured from the Texas Indians and that the men needed to go ashore frequently to hunt for shellfish and to fish for several days.

Hudson estimates that Moscoso's party passed the mouth of the Río de las Palmas (present-day Río Soto la Marina) on September 8, 1543, and that their first boat entered the Río de Pánuco two days later. As no gold or silver treasure was found on the De Soto–Moscoso four-year expedition, the Spanish government lost interest in the northern Gulf Coast, and European explorers did not return to the central Texas coast until the French arrived 142 years after Moscoso's men had departed.

1600s

In 1682 the French explorer Robert Cavelier, Sieur de La Salle, canoed from the Great Lakes region down the Mississippi River to the Gulf of Mexico and claimed the Mississippi River and its drainage areas for France.[22] To secure and possibly to expand the French claim to the Mississippi, the king of France, Louis XIV, authorized La Salle to lead a maritime expedition from France in 1684 to establish a military post and settlement near the mouth of the Mississippi. Apparently, by a navigational miscalculation made while sailing across the Gulf of Mexico, La Salle missed the mouth of the Mississippi and sighted land first in Louisiana about one hundred miles to the west of the mouth of the river. La Salle then sailed father westward to the present-day central Texas coast.

Henri Joutel, the expedition's most competent diarist, writes that on January 13, 1685, La Salle was aboard the storeship *Aimable* in a calm, drifting slowly with the currents toward land in about thirty feet of water at a latitude of 28° 59'.[23] This sighting (which is considered reasonably accurate) places La Salle and Joutel off the coast of Area I, a few miles west of the location where Cabeza de Vaca and his companions had landed in 1528 and near the location that Moscoso and his men had visited for eight days in 1543. La Salle directed Joutel to take two shallops (or shipboats) and a small number of armed men who were aboard the *Aimable* and on the smaller ship *La Belle* to search for fresh water on shore.

According to Joutel, as his party rowed toward the beach, they saw twenty to thirty Indians moving along the beach toward them. However, the rough surf near the beach forced Joutel to anchor offshore. When the Indians saw that the boats had stopped, they signaled the Frenchmen to come ashore and held up animal skins apparently for trade. Seeing that Joutel's party was not moving toward the shore, the Indians then held in the air their bows, which they lowered to the ground indicating peaceful intentions. Joutel answered by tying his handkerchief to the end of a musket and waving it like a flag, signaling the Indians to swim out to the boats.

The Indians deliberated a short time before nine members of the band entered the water, but the swells started to draw them under. The Natives seemed unaccustomed to swimming in the deep Gulf waters, although subsequent reports indicate the coastal Natives were excellent swimmers in the calmer waters of the bays and rivers. The Indians returned to shore and located on the beach a large log that they carried to the water. After launching the log, the men aligned themselves along its length, supporting themselves with one arm on the log and stroking the water with the other.

When the Indians arrived on board the *Aimable,* La Salle gave them tobacco to smoke and something to eat and drink. The Natives expressed gratitude using signs and seemed at ease, except the rocking of the boat caused them some queasiness. To La Salle's disappointment, the Indians were unable to speak any of the Native languages of the Great Lakes region known to him. When they were shown the sheep, pigs, chickens, and the hide of a cow that the Frenchmen had killed aboard the ship, the Indian visitors made signs indicating that they had all of these animals where they lived. Actually, however, the Natives had no domesticated animals except the dog. Toward evening La Salle gave each Indian a knife and a string of glass beads and asked Joutel to return the Natives to land. The Indians swam to shore from Joutel's boat, leaving without any record of their tribal identity. This was the first written account of Native residents of Area I recorded since Moscoso's trip in 1543, 142 years earlier.

The following day, January 14, Joutel and other members of La Salle's party aboard the *Aimable* saw twenty bison on the shoreline, the first bison Joutel had ever seen. La Salle had seen and hunted bison on the 1682 discovery expedition down the Mississippi.[24] On the 15th, La Salle's party saw more bison and deer along the coast of Area I. But by the 16th,

La Salle's ship had sailed westward beyond Area I, and Joutel gives no further comments on Indians in Area I at that time.

La Salle's party in 1685 landed near the mouth of Matagorda Bay and made their way into the bay area and inland from the bay about twelve miles to establish a French post called Fort St. Louis on the right bank of Garcitas Creek in modern Victoria County. During the remainder of 1685, La Salle and his troops spread out to explore the surrounding area and to search westward toward Mexico. Spanish documents indicate that La Salle's men scouted over 250 miles west of the fort and visited the Cibola Indians near the junction of the Pecos River and the Rio Grande. During this time and throughout 1686, La Salle kept Henri Joutel, his senior officer, at the fort as post commander.

In early 1686 La Salle decided to explore northeast of the post for the Mississippi River, his ultimate destination. The French priest Anastase Douay prepared the only reliable account of La Salle's 1686 overland expedition.[25] The expedition left the fort in Area III, crossed Area II and the Colorado River, and entered the northern part of Area I in Fayette County. The priest describes La Salle's journey from Matagorda Bay across Area II to the shallow hard-bottom ford on the Colorado that was the principal Indian and bison river crossing connecting Area I and Area II.

Soon after leaving the ford and entering Area I, the small French party, numbering about twenty, encountered a local Native tribe that Douay called Biskatronge and that provided La Salle with guides for the journey farther east. Several days later the Frenchmen encountered a second large tribe; this one Douay called Kirona. La Salle stopped for a few days to visit with these Native people because they were so different from the Natives he had encountered near the bay. Unlike the coastal Indians, the Kirona were part-time farmers. Douay says that they grew maize. Moreover, the Kirona told La Salle that they had traveled to meet with Spaniards living to the southwest, perhaps the Spanish priests stationed near La Junta de los Ríos in West Texas. When La Salle reached the East Texas Caddo a few weeks later, he met Jumano Indians from West Texas, which tends to confirm the statement made by the Kirona to Douay and the interaction of Native people in East and West Texas at the time.

After leaving the Kirona, La Salle continued eastward to the customary crossing of the Brazos near its junction with the Navasota River. The Frenchmen called the Brazos River "the River of Misfortune" because La Salle almost lost his life in a canoe accident while crossing the large river. Here the French party leaves Area I and moves northeastward toward the East Texas Caddo in Area VII. On the return trip to the bay, the Frenchmen named the Colorado River the "Maligne" because a large alligator attacked and killed one of La Salle's servants who was attempting to swim across the boundary river separating Areas I and II.

On La Salle's 1687 expedition in search of the Mississippi, Joutel accompanied La Salle, and Joutel's account offers the most comprehensive list and description of Area I Indian tribes written by any European. On the 1687 trip, La Salle and his party of twenty men, which included Joutel, Abbé Jean Cavelier (La Salle's brother), and again the priest Douay, departed the French post on Garcitas Creek on January 13, and by February 2 the party had reached the west bank of the Colorado River at the same crossing area that La Salle had used the year before. Joutel writes that just before reaching the crossing, La Salle's men recovered, from the hollow of a tree, strings of glass trade beads and some maize that La Salle had left the year before, anticipating that he would return to the same traditional fording area.

While constructing a boat to use in crossing the flooded Colorado River (the first large river the party forded after leaving the bay area), a group of unidentified Indians (in Area II) provided Joutel with a list of the names of twenty-two tribes that lived across the river to the north and east (in Area I). The local Indians reported to Joutel that the Cenis (the western Hasinai Caddo), as well as the other twenty-two named tribes, occupied the area east of the Maligne, or present-day Colorado River. The Indians who provided the list of tribes added the significant comment that the Colorado was a boundary river and that normally tribes living to the west of the river did not cross it except when going to war.[26]

Joutel's list of twenty-two named tribes does not include the names (or a variant of the names) of the Capoque, Han, Charruco, Deaguane, or Mendica—the five tribes that Cabeza de Vaca reported near the coast in southern Area I in the early 1530s. But significantly it does include the Meghey (Mayeye), a tribe reported repeatedly in northern Area I by subsequent Spanish diarists.

After La Salle crossed the Colorado and into Area I in Fayette County on February 9, his party moved slowly a few miles across a grassy prairie (probably an extension of present-day Rabb's Prairie) to hunt bison for two days. The party then continued along a bison trail eastward to a creek that La Salle had named Dure on his 1686 trip. This stream was likely Cummins Creek. At this point, La Salle's party was within a few miles of the archeological site called the Cummins Creek Mine site, which was the subject of a 1991 archeological study and report by Steven M. Kotter and several associates and contributors. The report suggests that periodically between ca. AD 600 and 1480 hunters from West Texas had established temporary bison hunting and processing camps in the area.[27] The party turned sharply northwest along the east bank of the creek, avoiding the denser center of "a great forest" (the Post Oak Belt). La Salle, who had been guided through the same area the year before by local Indians, was following a creek (Cummins Creek?) that cut through the thick woods, along a trail that was near the route followed by subsequent Spanish expeditions.

Along his route across Area I, Joutel reported hunting bison, deer (or pronghorn antelope), turkey, and bear. On February 16, the party found a village of fifty huts of Indians called Teao located in western Washington County. The Teao huts were larger than the huts that Joutel described west of the Colorado near Buckner's Creek in Area II and much larger than those near the bay in Area III. Assuming the Teao huts accommodated about eight to ten occupants, the camp population might have been 400 to 500 residents.

The Teao acknowledged that they (like the Kirona) had visited the Spaniards living to the southwest. The Teao added that they were friends of the Hasinai and Jumano, whom La Salle had visited in East Texas the year before. The Teao identified by name the Ayano and Cannohatino as their enemies. This reference to the Cannohatino indicates that Joutel considered the "Cannohatino," whom the Teao identified, to be a tribe different from the "Kannehouan" (or Cantona?), whom Joutel had included in the list he had prepared with great care a week earlier.

An elder in the Teao village told La Salle by signs that three Frenchmen were living with the Hasinai. This surprised La Salle. The fact that the Teao in western Washington County knew what was happening over one hundred miles northeast in present-day eastern Houston County suggests that an active communication system of some form existed between the two allies, the Teao and the Hasinai. The Teao had several horses and traded a large roan to La Salle. They also mentioned favorably their friends the Ebahumo, whom La Salle had met a few weeks earlier in Area II over one hundred miles to the southwest.

After this meeting with the friendly Teao, La Salle continued traveling generally eastward toward the lower Brazos River crossing area located near the junction of the Navasota and Brazos Rivers. During the next few days the French party met several local Indian hunters who identified themselves as Palaquechare. Their village or encampment was located in central Washington County, a few leagues west of the modern city of Brenham. The Palaquechare told Joutel that they also had accompanied the Jumano westward to visit the Spaniards and had obtained horses from the Jumano.[28] This statement represents one of the few firsthand accounts confirming that the Jumano were directly responsible for securing Spanish horses for Central Texas hunter-gatherer tribes as well as for the Hasinai. Joutel writes that from the words spoken by the Pala-quechare La Salle was convinced that they were a part of the Caddoan confederation.

In another surprising disclosure, the Palaquechare told Joutel that they planted corn and beans when conditions permitted. This statement tends to confirm the information received from Moscoso's expedition accounts and Douay's report that some of the Native people in northern Area I were part-time horticulturists. The Palaquechare said that they would plant maize when they found a favorable place where they could remain for some time. However, they added that their enemies would occasionally drive them from their corn fields. In effect, the tribe ex-plained to Joutel that as an emerging horticultural group they were not strong enough militarily to defend their own agricultural products in the field.[29]

The Palaquechare said that they were preparing to go to war with their enemy who lived toward the east and added significantly that their enemy had flat heads and planted maize. The statement that their enemy lived to the east, were known as Flatheads, and were maize farmers in-dicated to La Salle that the Palaquechare were preparing to fight some of the Flathead tribes whom he had met in 1682 on the lower Mississippi.[30] Joutel later met a young Caddo who had escaped from Chickasaw cap-ture. Thus, the enemy may have been the Chickasaw who at the time were well-known slave hunters operating west of the Mississippi.[31] This report suggests that hunter-gatherer tribes in Area I may have been at war with tribes residing about 350 miles to the east on the east side of the Mississippi but, at the same time, were close allies with tribes living over 500 miles to the west in the Trans-Pecos.

The Palaquechare and a small Hasinai party hunting in the area nearby provided La Salle with guides to escort the Frenchmen to the Brazos ford located several miles below the customary crossing near the junction of the Brazos and Navasota Rivers. La Salle recognized one Hasinai as the man from whom he had received by trade a horse that he still had with him. The Hasinai hunting party, which included about fifteen men, were living in four or five huts, apparently smaller units than the huts occupied by the Teao. Along the route to the Brazos, Joutel found excellent build-ing stone, a reference that helps confirm the route through the Brenham area, famous today for its construction stone.

On March 5 La Salle's party reached the first of several very steep ravines that emptied into the Brazos River from the west. These deep but short ravines or creeks are marked on the current USGS map *Austin NH 14-6* and are near the archeological location called the Allens Creek site.[32] Joutel notes that near the Brazos there were large mulberry trees and that the Indians used mulberry bark to make rope as well as in the construction of their huts.

Joutel refers to the Brazos River as the Canoe River, and his description of La Salle's unfortunate and dangerous crossing of the large and swift river in 1686 makes clear that he was speaking of the same large river that Douay in 1686 called the Misfortune River. The fact that Joutel describes the Canoe River as being larger than the Maligne is crucial information, confirming that the Maligne is the relatively smaller present-day Colorado, that the Canoe is the larger Brazos, and that the much smaller upper Trinity is the River of the Cenis. The arrival of La Salle's party at the Brazos crossing area concludes Joutel's report on the Native people in Area I.

As referenced in the Introduction, the Spanish viceroy directed the governor of Coahuila, Alonso de León, to lead an overland expedition in 1689 from Monclova, the capital of Coahuila, to search for La Salle's fort, thought then to be located somewhere on the central Texas coast.[33] De León did not enter Area I on his 1689 expedition, but he did locate the French fort near Matagorda Bay in Area III.

On his second expedition to Texas, conducted the following year,[34] De León forded the Colorado River and moved into Area I at the same shallow bison and Indian crossing that La Salle had used in 1686 and 1687. The governor waited a short distance east of the crossing area for a Hasinai guide. After a short wait, some Hasinai hunters approached him and agreed to escort the Spanish party from the Colorado eastward across Area I to the Brazos River. After crossing the Brazos, De León moved northward beyond Area I following La Salle's route to the Hasinai villages on present-day San Pedro Creek in eastern Houston County. The governor records encountering only several Hasinai hunting camps with bison and deer meat and wild turkey in his trips through Area I. When Governor Domingo Terán de los Ríos crossed Area I in 1691 and again in 1692 along the same route, he did not report encountering any Indians,[35] and when Governor Salinas Varona followed the same route in 1693,[36] no report was given of any encounter with Indians in Area I.

1700S

There are no known records of European expeditions into Area I between 1693 and 1709 when Fray Isidro de Espinosa and his small party crossed the Colorado near the junction of Onion Creek and the Colorado and moved into Area I a few miles east of present-day Austin.[37] Espinosa had followed De León's route and used the same fording areas on the Rio Grande, the Nueces, and the Frio, but his party had turned north after crossing the Frio to move toward the present San Antonio area rather than continuing eastward toward Matagorda Bay.

From the San Antonio area, Espinosa's party proceeded northeast into Area II and the open prairie along the southern skirt of the Balcones Escarpment in Comal and Hays Counties to cross the Colorado north of the Post Oak Belt and above the mouth of present-day Onion Creek. At this point, Espinosa's party is within about ten to fifteen miles of the archeological site called the Middle Onion Creek Valley site.[38] Although Espinosa mentions no bison along his route between the Rio Grande and the Colorado, he reports that his party used a bison crossing to ford the Colorado and that bison herds were seen on both sides of the river. Pecan trees, poplar, and wild grape were growing along the riverbanks.

About fifteen miles east of the Colorado in Area I, Espinosa's party encountered a friendly encampment of about 2,000 Indians, several of whom were mounted. Most of the encampment was composed of Yo-juane, but there were Simaoma and Tusonibi as well. Thomas N. Campbell has identified the primary homeland of the three tribes.[39] According to Campbell, the Simaoma were from northeastern Mexico and the Tusonibi and Yojuane were residents of the Red River area of northeast Texas and Oklahoma. Campbell concludes that all three tribes were non-resident immigrants who had been forced by either the Apache or the Spaniards to move into Area I from their traditional areas of residence.

It should be noted that eighteen years earlier, Terán had reported meeting about 3,000 Jumano and other Trans-Pecos Natives in the same general area. During that earlier meeting in 1691, the Trans-Pecos tribes, whose leaders only were mounted, identified themselves as annual visitors (not immigrants) engaged in hunting bison and trading with local tribes and with Hasinai Caddo. In 1709 Espinosa also reports that the leader of the Yojuane was very concerned about a possible attack by his enemies, the Apache Indians, who he said occupied the nearby area to the west and northwest of the upper Colorado crossing area.

The historic records suggest that at the time of Espinosa's expedition, the Simaoma were not new immigrants to the area, as suggested by Thomas Campbell, but were more likely visitors engaged in hunting and trading. In 1693 Governor Salinas Varona had encountered the same Simaoma people in Fayette County about fifty miles downstream from where Espinosa in 1709 met the tribe. At the time of the earlier 1693 encounter, the Simaoma (and Mescal Indians from northern Mexico) were meeting with local Toho west of the Colorado. The visiting Simaoma were likely trading with the local Toho Indians and engaged in hunting bison near the lower crossing of the Colorado in Fayette County.

The second tribe met by Espinosa was the Yojuane. Campbell considers the Yojuane a Tonkawan people who, in the eighteenth century, ranged in eastern Central Texas from the Colorado east of Austin north to the Red River. The Yojuane were mentioned also in the 1727 Spanish expedition account of Brigadier Pedro de Rivera in association with the Ervipiame, Coco, and Mayeye (Meghey), all known Area I tribes in the 1720s. Espinosa's identification of the Tusonibi (the third tribe met by Espinosa) is the only known expedition reference to the tribe, so there appears to be no present basis in any Spanish expedition record to conclude that the tribe was either local to the area or a nonresident.

Although no European expeditions entered Area I between 1709 and 1716, a large Spanish expedition, led by Captain Domingo Ramón and Fray Isidro Félix de Espinosa from Coahuila, crossed the northwestern corner of Area I in 1716 to colonize East Texas.[40] By this time, however, Native life along the expedition routes had been seriously disturbed by both the increased Spanish pressure from the south and from Apache encroachment from the northwest.

On April 27, 1716, Ramón and Espinosa (who led the 1709 expedition to the Colorado River) left the customary Rio Grande crossing area moving northeast. The expedition plan was to follow the route Espinosa had used earlier to the Colorado and then to find a new route farther northeast to the homeland of the Hasinai in East Texas.

On May 14, the expedition party crossed the upper San Antonio River, according to the separate accounts maintained by Ramón and Espinosa. They record no meetings with local Native people in the open area between the upper San Antonio and the lower Colorado, but both record numerous Indian encounters in the heavily wooded areas between the Colorado and Brazos river crossing areas. Espinosa (whose account usually includes more detailed ethnographic information than Ramón's), records that on May 30 the Spaniards, guided by a Payaya Indian, met a small group of six Ervipiame and Mescal Indians. About ten days later (June 10), Espinosa writes that the party encountered more Ervipiame and some Mesquite, Ticmam, and (significantly) one Hasinai Caddo. Ramón adds that some Indians were on horseback while others walked. These Indians escorted Espinosa and Ramón to a very large Native encampment of perhaps 2,000 Indians located about eighteen miles to the northeast.

This large assemblage of several different tribes included (according to Espinosa) the Pamaya, Payaya, Cantona, Mixcal, Xarame, and Sijame. Ramón waived the usual prohibition against trade with the Native population, and Spanish troops spent the following day in active exchange for animal skins with the Indians gathered. Espinosa's party crossed the Brazos River on June 15 and moved on northeast beyond Area I into Area VII.

The 1718 Spanish expedition was led by Governor Martín de Alarcón, whose party crossed the Colorado and entered Area I near present-day Columbus on its march to East Texas. Immediately after crossing the river, Alarcón met a group of five refugee tribes—the Emet, Toho, Sana, Curmicai, and Hugugan—whose homeland was west of the Colorado River in Area II. These Native groups were seeking Spanish and Caddoan protection from the advancing and aggressive Apache. The tribes asked the Spaniards for help to return to their homeland west of the river. After offering some limited assistance, Governor Alarcón proceeded with Hasinai guides across Area I and toward East Texas.

In 1721, when Governor Aguayo led his expedition into Area I from the Colorado crossing used by Espinosa in 1709 and 1716, the governor marched northward rather than eastward into Area I and crossed the Brazos near modern-day Waco rather than the modern Bryan area.

Conclusions

The Native people living in Area I were primarily hunters, fishermen, and gatherers. But there is evidence from multiple sources that some of the people, perhaps those living in the eastern sector closer to the Caddo, were part-time horticulturists. Despite the characterization of being primarily hunters and gatherers, the Native people of Area I were engaged in substantial and continuous interaction with neighbors residing hundreds of miles from Area I during both the historic and late prehistoric periods.

The Native tribes living in western Area I said that they had visited Spanish priests or posts in West Texas and northern Mexico and traded regularly with Native people in the Southwest. Native people in the eastern part of Area I said that they were at war with an enemy living to the east called the Flatheads. The Flatheads cultivated maize, and La Salle thought they were one of the tribes he had encountered on the lower Mississippi on his discovery expedition in 1682—such as the slave-raiding Chickasaw whom La Salle had met. Area I tribes also traded regularly with the friendly Hasinai Caddo who lived northeast of Area I. Although it seems that Area I Native people had no permanent settlements, they were nevertheless very cosmopolitan.

Spanish and French chroniclers over a period of about 200 years, from the 1520s to the 1720s, recorded the names of over fifty tribes or bands residing or visiting Area I. An alphabetical list of the named groups is found in the supplement following this chapter, and the geographical location of the resident tribes is indicated on Map 1.1.

Of the fifty-four named tribes or bands identified by expedition chroniclers in Area I between 1528 and 1722, only about thirteen tribes appear to be local tribes or bands whose homeland was in Area I. These include five tribes along the coast named in Cabeza de Vaca's and Oviedo's accounts, five tribes in the northern part of the area named in the French accounts of Douay and Joutel, and three tribes named by later Spanish expedition chroniclers. The geographic location of these tribes is marked on Map 1.1.

Of the forty-one tribes that are not confidently identified as local resident tribes of Area I, twenty-one are named by Joutel as residents in an unspecified region in northeast Fayette County. Thus, we have included the tribes named by Joutel as Area I tribes without having further information.

Of the remaining twenty tribes identified as probably nonresidents, the visiting tribe most frequently identified in the area is the Hasinai Caddo. We know from French and Spanish accounts that Area I served as an Hasinai hunting preserve, and the numerous citings of Hasinai hunting parties encountered in the area supports this understanding.

The second notable characteristic of nonresident tribes found in Area I follows from the fact that the northern part of Area I was, in part, Caddo hunting territory. It therefore represented an area that afforded Hasinai allies some temporary refuge from the constantly approaching Apache from the northwest.

During the latter part of the study period, Spanish expeditions encountered two large shared encampments of visiting tribes ten miles or less from the Colorado River within Area I. The first was encountered in 1716 near the Brazos River crossing; the second was recorded in 1718 on the lower Colorado River near present-day Columbus.

The first large encampment in 1716 included at least ten tribes, primarily from Areas II and IV to the west of Area I. The large encampment of visitors encountered in 1718 included five tribes from Area II. The tribes specifically asked the Spanish for protection from the Apache so that they could return to their homeland to the west in Area II. As noted earlier, by the second decade of the eighteenth century, Spanish expedition accounts record only limited ethnographic information on how Texas Indians lived in their natural state. Being chased and uprooted by an aggressive enemy was not a new and previously unknown threat for local Indians in Central Texas. The new factor was that this aggressive enemy, the Apache, were mounted on Spanish ponies and had modern Spanish weapons, which local tribes often did not.

BETWEEN THE LOWER BRAZOS AND THE LOWER COLORADO RIVERS

This chapter supplement lists alphabetically the names of Indian tribes and bands reported in diary accounts and associated expedition documents referenced in the Area I study. Some entries identify local Area I Native groups; others identify nonlocal groups that were reported in Area I on temporary visits to hunt, trade, or raid. The narrow objective of the supplement is to locate geographically as precisely as possible (usually by county) where the tribe or band was observed. Entries also include the name of the expedition leader or diarist who recorded the encounter and the date of the event, unless otherwise indicated.

On the La Salle 1687 expedition through Area I, Henri Joutel prepared a list of the names of tribes or bands that a local Indian leader said lived to the east of the Colorado River crossing, presumably in northern Area I. As this report by Joutel is the only reference made to most of the named tribes and the precise location of the tribe in Area I is uncertain, the entries below include only a brief comment that the tribe was one that Joutel listed as living immediately to the east of the customary Colorado River crossing in Fayette County.

The following documentary sources are among the works consulted in preparing the supplement: Alex D. Krieger, *We Came Naked and Barefoot: The Journey of Cabeza de Vaca across North America*; Lawrence A. Clayton, Vernon James Knight Jr., and Edward C. Moore, eds., *The De Soto Chronicles: The Expedition of Hernando De Soto to North America in 1539–1543*; Isaac J. Cox, ed., *The Journeys of René Robert Cavelier, Sieur de La Salle*; William C. Foster, ed., *The La Salle Expedition to Texas: The Journal of Henri Joutel, 1684–1687*; Herbert E. Bolton, ed., *Spanish Exploration in the Southwest, 1542–1706*; William C. Foster, *Spanish Expeditions into Texas, 1689–1768*; Thomas N. Campbell, "Espinosa, Olivares, and the Colorado Indians, 1709," *Sayersville Historical Association Bulletin* 3 (1983): 2–16.

1. Ahouergomahe. Joutel included the Ahouergomahe in a listing of twenty-two tribes that lived in the northern part of Area I.
2. Akehouen. Joutel included the Akehouen in a listing of twenty-two tribes that lived in northern Area I.
3. Arhau. Joutel included the Arhau in a listing of twenty-two tribes that lived in northern Area I.
4. Biskatronge. Several days after La Salle crossed the Colorado in Fayette County and entered Area I on his 1686 trip to the Hasinai Caddo, the friar Anastase Douay reported meeting the Biskatronge,

also called the "weepers" because they cried for a quarter of an hour after meeting the Frenchmen.

5. Caddo (Hasinai, Cenis). Joutel reported in mid-February 1687 that the Cenis (Hasinai) were hunting in the area east of the Colorado River crossing in Area I. On February 22, Joutel recorded meeting another small Hasinai hunting party in Area I in east-central Washington County. Subsequently, members of the Hasinai party served as guides for Joutel's party on the trip into Area VII from the Brazos to the principal Hasinai Caddo village in Houston County.

On May 4 and 5, 1690, De León found members of a Hasinai hunting party in Area I about five leagues east of the customary crossing of the Colorado River in Fayette County. On June 23, 1693, Salinas Varona met Hasinai near the same traditional crossing area west of the Colorado. In June 1716 Espinosa met a Hasinai hunting party in western Brazos County and encountered a Caddoan farming community in western Grimes County. Aguayo met a Hasinai party between the Navasota and the Trinity Rivers in Leon County on July 15, 1721.

6. Cantona (Kannehouan?). Joutel encountered a leader of a local tribe ("Les Kannehouan") in Fayette County a few miles west of the traditional crossing of the Colorado on La Salle's 1687 journey toward the Mississippi River. It is thought that the Kannehouan and the Cantona may be the same because the Cantona were met at the same location near the Colorado River crossing in June 1690 and again in 1691, 1692, and 1693.

7. Capoque. Cabeza de Vaca reported that the Capoque lived on the island upon which he first landed in Texas in November 1528. The island was probably Galveston Island or nearby St. Joseph Island. Some authorities consider the Capoque to be the same tribe as the Coco, but this has not been demonstrated.

8. Charruco. Cabeza de Vaca reported that the Charruco lived in the woods on the mainland opposite the island upon which he first landed. The tribe probably lived in the wooded area near the lower Brazos in Brazoria County. Cabeza de Vaca lived with the Charruco after living a year and a half with the Capoque.

9. Chaumene. Joutel included the Chaumene in a listing of twenty-two tribes that lived north of the Colorado River crossing in Area I.

10. Coco. On March 6, 1746, Captain Joachín de Orobio y Basterra reported that the chief of the Bidai Indians described for him the boundaries of the Indian tribes in the southern part of Area I. The Bidai chief said that the Orcoquiza occupied the area from the Neches River on the east to a western boundary area halfway between the

Trinity and the Brazos (primarily in Area VIII.) The chief added that the Coco lived to the west of the Brazos along the coast and farther inland in Area I. Earlier Spanish documents suggest that the Coco visited and possibly also occupied part of central Area II. On April 21 and 22, 1768, Fray Solís described the north-central part of Area I as "Coco Indian country." Although the Coco may have ranged into central Area II, it appears that their homeland was primarily along the coast and inland in Area I. Some writers consider the Coco to be the same as Cabeza de Vaca's Capoque, but this is not certain.

11. Curmicai. On September 30, 1718, Alarcón met the Curmicai and four other tribes in Area I near Cummins Creek in Columbus County. As there appears to be no further documentary reference to the tribe, the homeland of the Curmicai remains uncertain.

12. Deaguane (Aguene, Deguene). Cabeza de Vaca reported that the Deaguane guided Lope de Oviedo back up the Texas coast away from the Quevene, with whom he stayed only for a few days. The tribe probably lived along the coast east of the Colorado River in eastern Matagorda County. The tribe was a coastal neighbor to, but enemy of, the Quevene.

13. Emet. On September 30, 1718, Alarcón met a group of five tribes, including the Emet, in Area I a few leagues west of the Colorado River in Colorado County. De León's 1689 encounter with the Emet in De-Witt County and in Lavaca County suggests that the Emet considered Area II as their primary homeland.

14. Exepiahoke. Joutel included the Exepiahoke in a listing of twenty-two tribes that lived in Area I.

15. Flathead. Joutel wrote that the Palaquechare told La Salle that they were prepared to go to war against the Flatheads, who the Palaquechare said lived to the east (toward the Mississippi River) and planted maize. La Salle interpreted the comments to imply that the Area I tribe was going with its allies the Caddo to fight the Flatheads that he had visited on the lower Mississippi in 1684. Specifically, the Flatheads may refer to the Chickasaw, who were called Flatheads by La Salle's chroniclers and who were engaged at the time in widespread raiding west of the Mississippi River for the English slave trade.

16. Hugugan. On September 30, 1718, Alarcón met a very large shared encampment of five tribes, including the Hugugan, in Area I in Colorado County near Cummins Creek. This is the only recorded sighting of a tribe by that name. As there is no other reference to the Hugugan, the question of whether the homeland of the Hugugan was Area I or otherwise remains unresolved.

17. Jumano (Chouman). On February 20, 1687, the Palaquechare in

Area I told La Salle that they were friends of the Jumano, who had visited them in Area I and whom the Palaquechare had visited in West Texas. Other Spanish reports indicate that the Jumano annually visited the Hasinai in East Texas as well as other local allies en route, including tribes in Area I.

18. Kabaye. Joutel included the Kabaye in a listing of twenty-two tribes that lived in Area I. Thomas Campbell suggests that the Kabaye may have been the same tribe as the Cava, who were recorded in Spanish expedition documents. This is unclear because the Cava were repeatedly reported in Spanish expedition accounts but only in Area II.

19. Kemahopiheim. Joutel included the Kemahopiheim in a listing of twenty-two tribes that lived in Area I.

20. Keremen. Joutel included the Keremen in a listing of twenty-two tribes that lived in Area I.

21. Kiabaha. Joutel included the Kiabaha in a listing of twenty-two tribes that lived in Area I.

22. Kirona. Douay wrote that La Salle met the Kirona on his march east between the Colorado and the Brazos Rivers in 1686. Douay reported that the tribe gave them ears of corn and told them that the tribe knew "whites" who lived toward the west.

23. Koienkahe. Joutel included the Koienkahe in a listing of twenty-two tribes that lived in Area I.

24. Komkome (Konkone). Joutel included the Komkome in a listing of twenty-two tribes that lived in Area I. Campbell notes that the Komkome (called Konkone) were not the same as the Tonkawa, as assumed by some writers.

25. Korimen. Joutel included the Korimen in a listing of twenty-two tribes that lived in Area I.

26. Kouyam. Joutel included the Kouyam in a listing of twenty-two tribes that lived in Area I. Campbell notes the similarity in the names Kouyam and Kouan, both of which are cited in French documents associated with La Salle's expedition to Texas.

27. Mayeye (Meghey). Joutel wrote that the Mayeye lived northeast of the Colorado River, probably in the northern part of Area I. The Mayeye were frequently reported in northern and central Area I by Spanish diarists. Alarcón met the Mayeye in eastern Colorado County on September 29 and 30, 1718. Rivera met the tribe in Burleson County on August 28, 1727. Rubí saw the Mayeye in northern Area I on September 2, 1767. Solís met them in Burleson County on April 25, 1768. Campbell writes that it is generally agreed that Joutel's Meghey were the same as the Spanish Mayeye and that they lived between the Colorado and the Brazos (in Area I).

28. Mendica. Cabeza de Vaca wrote that the Mendica lived inland from the coastal Deaguane, probably in northeast Matagorda County and eastern Wharton County.

29. Meraquaman. Joutel included the Meraquaman in a list of twenty-two tribes that lived in Area I.

30. Mesquite (Mezquite). On June 10, 1716, Espinosa met some members of the tribe gathered in or near the northwest boundary of Area I with the Yeripiama, Ticmam, and a Caddo Indian in Burleson County about seven leagues west of the customary crossing of the Brazos. Three days later, the Espinosa party met a group of up to 2,000 Indians composed of those met on June 10 plus the Pamaya, Payaya, Cantona, Mixcal, Xarame, and Sijame. Earlier on the same expedition, Espinosa had met a lone Mesquite traveling in the opposite direction (southwest) along the customary route between the Rio Grande crossing and the San Antonio area.

On May 31, 1715, Don Juan Antonio de Trasviña y Retis reported visiting a pueblo called El Mesquite on the Río Conchos about four leagues upstream from La Junta, and in his summary Retis repeated that he had renamed the pueblo of the Mesquites. In his 1727 description of Chihuahua, Álvarez Barreiro (Rivera's engineer) reported that Mezquite were living in that province. Campbell notes that Spanish documents refer to Mesquite living both in Coahuila and near La Junta and that the relationship between the two groups is unknown.

31. Mixcal (Mescal). The tribe was encountered in northern Coahuila by De León in 1689 and later by Terán in 1691. On May 26, 1693, Salinas reported the Mescal in Fayette County near the customary crossing of the Colorado, and about six weeks later on his return to Monclova he met members of the tribe at the Rio Grande crossing in Maverick County.

On May 30, 1716, Espinosa met six "Mescales and Yeripiamos" in Area I in Burleson County. One was a convert from the mission San Juan Bautista. About a week later, Espinosa met several members of the tribe again near the customary crossing of the Brazos. The Mixcal are considered residents of northern Coahuila.

32. Ointemarhen. Joutel included the Ointemarhen in a listing of twenty-two tribes that lived in Area I.

33. Omenaosse. Joutel included the Omenaosse in a listing of twenty-two tribes that lived in the northern part of Area I.

34. Palaquechare (Palaquesson, Palakea, Alakea). On February 20, 1687, Joutel met the Palaquechare in Area I in west-central Washington County. Based on their language and accent, La Salle thought

that the Palaquechare were members of the Caddoan confederacy. Campbell interprets the evidence to suggest that the Palaquechare were Caddoans. Douay wrote on the same journey that the French party encountered the "Palaquesson" soon after crossing the Colorado River. He reports only that the tribe had ten villages and were allies of the Spaniards. Abbé Cavelier reports on the same 1687 expedition that the party encountered the "Palakea or Alakea" in Area I. Campbell equates Douay's Palaquesson and Cavelier's Palakea with Joutel's Palaquechare but mislocates the tribe as probably residing between the Brazos and Trinity Rivers in Area VII rather than between the Colorado and the Brazos Rivers in Area I, as I project.

35. Palona. On La Salle's march across Area I on his 1687 trip to East Texas, Douay wrote that the French party met the Palona and that the tribe was living near the Taraha, Tyakappan, and Palaquesson. Although Joutel did not mention the tribe by the same name, Abbé Cavelier also wrote that the French expedition party met the Palona in Area I.

36. Pamaya (Pamai). On June 13, 1716, Espinosa and Ramón met a large group of about 500 to 2,000 Indians, including the Pamaya, in Area I near the Brazos River crossing in Burleson County. The tribe had been encountered on Spanish expeditions earlier outside Area I. On May 27, 1691, Massanet reported meeting the Pamaya (called Pamai) at the present-day Arroyo Salado, which runs northward into the Rio Grande in northern Coahuila. On April 11 and 12, 1709, Espinosa met the Pamaya along with the Pampopa on the Medina River in Bexar County. Campbell places the tribe's residential area between the Rio Grande in Maverick County and the Bexar County area. The tribe is not considered to be native to Area I.

37. Payaya. On June 13, 1716, Espinosa met members of the Payaya near the customary crossing of the middle Brazos in Burleson County. However, Spanish diarists had recorded several earlier meetings with the tribe to the southwest. On June 13, 1691, Terán met members of the tribe in the San Antonio area. On July 1 and 2, 1693, Salinas found the Payaya near San Antonio in Bexar County. On April 11 and 12, 1709, Espinosa met members of the tribe near San Antonio. On April 9 and 10, 1717, the French merchant and traveler François Derbanne saw the tribe ("Paillaille") in Area II about twelve miles west of the Colorado River in Travis County. The tribe is not considered to be native to Area I, but rather a resident of Areas II and IV.

38. Quevene. In 1534 Cabeza de Vaca wrote that the Quevene raided an

encampment of their neighbors the Deaguane at a location in Matagorda County. The tribe is generally considered Karankawan.

39. Quouan. Joutel included the Quouan in a listing of twenty-two tribes that lived in Area I.

40. Sana (Xana). On September 30, 1718, Alarcón met the Sana (Xana) in a shared encampment with the Emet, Toho, Huyugan, and Curmicai in Area I about ten miles east of the Colorado River near Cummins Creek in eastern Colorado County. The tribes asked Alarcón to establish a mission for them near the Guadalupe River in Gonzales County. Earlier, Spanish diarists had repeatedly reported the Sana to the west of Area I. In 1690 De León encountered the Sana in Area II, and in 1693 Salinas had two meetings with the tribe in Area II. The Sana are considered to be native to Area II. According to the historian Juan Bautista Chapa, the Frenchman Jean Géry claimed that the Sana were loyal to him and to France.

41. Sijame. On June 13, 1716, Espinosa and Ramón encountered the large (500- to 2,000-member) Ranchería Grande tribes, including the Sijame, in Area I near the customary Brazos River crossing in Burleson County. Earlier, on April 13, 1709, Espinosa had met the tribe near San Pedro Springs in Bexar County. Rivera reported that in 1727 the Sijame were residents of Coahuila. It appears that the Sijame were not native residents of Area I.

42. Simaoma (Siamomo, Simomo). Espinosa met the Simomo in Area I in eastern Travis County on April 19, 1709. Salinas Varona had earlier encountered the Simaoma a few leagues west of the Colorado River crossing area on May 26 and again on June 24, 1693. Campbell considers the Simomo as residents of the Monterrey area and to be the same as the Simaoma.

43. Spichehat. Joutel wrote that the Spichehat lived northeast of the Colorado River crossing in Area I.

44. Taraha. On La Salle's 1687 trip to the Hasinai Caddo in East Texas, Douay wrote that La Salle's party met the Taraha in Area I, having marched north-northeast from Cummins Creek. Douay reported only that the tribe lived near villages of the Tyakappan and Palona and had horses.

45. Teao. Joutel reported that the tribe was met by the La Salle party at a Teao encampment located in western Washington County on February 16, 1687. The Teao told Joutel that they were allies of the Trans-Pecos Jumano and the East Texas Caddo. As Joutel included the Tohaha in his listing of tribes living west of the Colorado River and a few days later he named the Teao as a tribe living east of the

Colorado, it seems very unlikely that the Tohaha and the Teao were the same tribe, as suggested by Campbell. It seems particularly unlikely that the two tribes are the same in light of Joutel's added specific comment that La Salle's party had never heard the tribal name Teao before meeting the tribe. For purposes of this study, the Teao and the Tohaha are considered separate tribes, the former a resident of Area I and the latter a resident of Area II.

46. Tehauremet. Joutel included the Tehauremet in a listing of twenty-two tribes that lived in Area I.

47. Teheaman. Joutel included the Teheaman in a listing of twenty-two tribes that lived in Area I.

48. Telamene. Joutel included the Telamene in a listing of twenty-two tribes that lived in Area I.

49. Timamera (Timamar, Ticmamar, Ticamar). On June 10, 1716, Espinosa met the Ticmamar with one Hasinai and several Mesquite and Ervipiame in Area I east of the customary Brazos crossing in Burleson County. In 1767 Nicolás de Lafora, the engineer on Rubí's expedition, reported that the tribe (Timamar) was living in Coahuila. The primary residential area of the tribe was probably northern Coahuila.

50. Toho. On September 30, 1718, Alarcón met the Toho with their allies the Sana and Emet in Area I near modern-day Columbus in Columbus County. Earlier the Toho had been reported on several occasions in Area II. In 1689 De León met the Toho west of the Colorado River in Lavaca County and saw them in Fayette and Colorado Counties in 1690. In 1693 Salinas reported meeting the Toho, Mescal, and Simaoma in southwest Fayette County in Area II. The Toho are considered residents of Area II. The Frenchman Géry claimed that the Toho were loyal to him and to France.

51. Tusonibi. On April 19 and 20, 1709, Espinosa met the Tusonibi, who were with the Simaoma and Yojane in Area I on Wilbarger Creek in Travis County. Apparently this encounter with the Tusonibi was the only one recorded on a Spanish expedition into Texas. As there is no conclusive evidence in expedition documents to indicate whether the tribe was local to the area, a visiting tribe, or an immigrant, we leave the question open. Campbell identified the "homeland" of the Tusonibi as northeastern Mexico along with their allies the Simaoma.

52. Tyakappan (Ticapana). On La Salle's 1687 march northeast from Fort St. Louis to visit the Caddo in East Texas, Douay wrote that the French party met the Tyakappan in Area I after marching east from the Colorado River. The tribe was residing near the Palona and Pala-

quesson. Although Joutel did not mention the tribe by name, Abbé Cavelier met a tribe in the same area called the Ticapana.

53. Xarame. On June 13, 1716, Espinosa recorded meeting the Xarame at a large settlement known as Ranchería Grande west of the customary crossing of the Brazos River in Burleson County. Seven years earlier, on April 8, 1709, Espinosa had met the Xarame with members of the Pacuasin tribe on the Leona River in Frio County. Campbell suggests that their traditional range extended from the Nueces and Frio Rivers southwest into northeastern Coahuila. Area I does not appear to be the native homeland of the Xarame.

54. Yeripiama (Ervipiame, Yurbipame). On May 30, 1716, Espinosa with Ramón met the Yeripiama and Mescal near Big Brushy Creek in Area I in Williamson County and met them again on June 10 in Burleson County. The Yurbipame had been encountered earlier on the 1675 Bosque expedition that marched into South Texas, perhaps in Maverick County in Area IV. The tribe is not considered a resident of Area I.

55. Yojuane (Jojane). On April 19 and 20, 1709, Espinosa met with the Yojuane in Area I in eastern Travis County. The tribe was a part of a gathering of about 2,000 Indians that included the Simaoma and Tusonibi. In April 1768 (about sixty years later), Solís reported that the Jojane were living with the Coco, Tonkawa, and Mayeye in Area I near the Brazos River in Burleson County. Campbell considers the Yojuane a Tonkawan people who originated from the Red River area in North Texas.

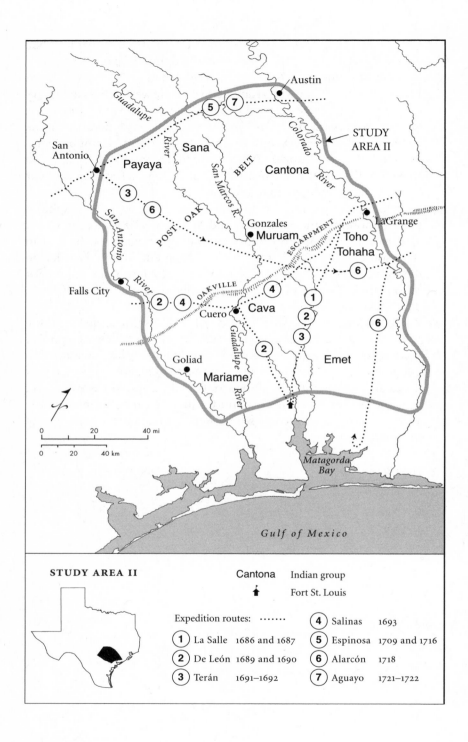

STUDY
AREA II

Austin

San
Antonio

Sana

Payaya

Guadalupe River

San Marcos R.

BELT

Cantona

Colorado River

LaGrange

POST OAK

Gonzales
Muruam

ESCARPMENT

Toho
Tohaha

San Antonio River

Falls City

OAKVILLE

Cava
Cuero

Salinas 1693

Emet

Goliad

Mariame

Guadalupe River

Matagorda
Bay

Gulf of Mexico

0   20   40 mi
0   20   40 km

STUDY AREA II

Cantona   Indian group

🛡 Fort St. Louis

Expedition routes: ·······

① La Salle   1686 and 1687

② De León   1689 and 1690

③ Terán   1691–1692

④ Salinas   1693

⑤ Espinosa   1709 and 1716

⑥ Alarcón   1718

⑦ Aguayo   1721–1722

MAP 2.1

2

BETWEEN THE LOWER COLORADO AND THE SAN ANTONIO RIVERS

STUDY AREA II

During the study period, Study Area II was a bountiful open country, rich in both natural flora and fauna and was the homeland of dozens of small hunter-gatherer tribes and bands. The eastern boundary of Area II is the lower Colorado River, which local Indians considered a boundary river (see Map 2.1). The San Antonio River serves as the western boundary of Area II. Fray Damián Massanet wrote that the Indians living between the San Antonio River and the lower Colorado River spoke many languages and often communicated with each other and with visitors by hand signs. The observation by local Indians and Massanet that the San Antonio River on the west and the Colorado River on the east were Indian cultural borders is supported by Spanish and French accounts reviewed in this chapter.

Although Area II is one of the smallest of the study areas, it is distinctive in its physiographical and cultural contrast with adjoining areas. The northern boundary of Area II is generally coterminous with the southern rim of the Balcones Escarpment and the southern range of the Apache during the study period. In the late seventeenth century, the Post Oak Belt (called the Monte del Diablo by the Spanish), which runs southwest-northeast through Guadalupe, Caldwell, and Bastrop Counties in Area II, served as a barrier of thick post oak, cacti, and tangled heavy mustang grape vines that tended to keep the large mounted Apache bands in the Hill Country in Area VI to the north and west of Area II. However, by the second decade of the eighteenth century, local Area II Native groups living south of the Post Oak Belt in Gonzales, DeWitt, and Lavaca Counties were aware of the Apache pressure.

The southern border of Area II is marked along a cultural line that separated Area II tribes from the coastal Karankawa Indians, who traditionally remained close to the bay islands and shoreline (in Area III) but who ventured inland perhaps up to thirty or forty miles in the spring and summer to hunt bison and smaller game. This southern boundary line will be delineated with more precision in the following chapter, covering Area III, in which several recent studies will be reviewed that indicate a more precise range of the Karankawa bands or tribes.

Area II includes all or part of twenty counties—Travis, Hays, Comal, Bexar, Wilson, Guadalupe, Gonzales, Caldwell, Fayette, Bastrop, Colorado, Wharton, Matagorda, Lavaca, Karnes, DeWitt, Victoria, Goliad, Refugio, and Jackson.

The southern coastal plains, which are a part of Area II, are drained by a number of large rivers with heavily wooded areas of live oak, post oak, pecan, cottonwood, and cypress along the riverbanks. During the study period, the winters were much colder and precipitation was much heavier than we know today. The coastal prairie was frequently flooded and boggy during the winter, making long-distance movement difficult during those months. An ancient Indian trail, later called the lower Camino Real, ran along the Oakville Escarpment between the San Antonio River near the present-day Conquista Crossing about three miles upriver from Falls City in Karnes County and the Colorado ford near La Grange in central Fayette County. A second Indian route (called the upper Camino Real) ran between present-day San Antonio and the Colorado River crossing near the junction of Onion Creek and the Colorado.

Between the lower Colorado River and the San Antonio River, several smaller rivers and creeks flow as tributaries into the Guadalupe or discharge directly into the coastal bays. The San Marcos River (fed by the Blanco River) joins the Guadalupe in Gonzales County; the Medina flows into the upper San Antonio River; and the Lavaca and Navidad Rivers join in Jackson County and flow into Matagorda Bay. Buckner's Creek is a significant Fayette County stream that originates in Area II and flows into the Colorado downriver from the customary fording location and several miles upriver from the high bluff called Monument Hill today. Garcitas Creek in Victoria County runs directly into Matagorda Bay.

The Oakville Escarpment and the Post Oak Belt cross the northern part of Area II running southwest-northeast. The escarpment crosses the Guadalupe near the Gonzales-DeWitt county line and intersects the Colorado River near the customary fording area of the Colorado in Fayette County. The Post Oak Belt, a twenty- to thirty-mile-wide forested savanna of dense mixed post oak, blackjack, hackberry, and hickory, is a few miles north of and runs generally parallel to the Oakville

Escarpment through northern Gonzales and Fayette Counties. South of the Post Oak Belt is the high ground of the Oakville Escarpment, which formed the raised geologic platform and more open terrain conducive to long-distance travel between points in northeastern Mexico and northeast Texas.

High precipitation experienced during the Little Ice Age suggests that the Post Oak Belt was even more dense than we know it today. During the study period, the open prairies were covered with tall and lush grasses, and the rivers and water courses carried much larger volumes of water and more aquatic resources than are found today. This rich environment served as a magnet attracting large and small game animals and long-distance foreign Native hunters from outside Area II. In the late seventeenth century, and probably for several centuries earlier, large bison herds remained in Area II throughout most of the year,[1] and other large mammals such as cougar, bear, antelope, and deer were present in substantial numbers.

The mesic-hydric climate during the study period influenced the density and range of the Native population in Area II, as it did the flora and fauna. The abundance of bison attracted long-distance hunters and traders from throughout the Southern Plains, the Trans-Pecos, and northern Mexico. The heavier snows and colder conditions on the High Plains during the Little Ice Age may also have driven bison herds farther south. The exceptionally cold climatic conditions in the Rocky Mountains and on the High Plains during the Little Ice Age (ca. AD 1350–1850) is documented by climatologists who write that during the Little Ice Age glaciers in the Rockies expanded significantly and became larger that at any time during the previous 10,000 years.[2] In the 1680s and 1690s bison were reported to the southwest of Area II into northern Coahuila and Chihuahua in Mexico, an area that today could not sustain bison herds or even support herds of sheep or goats.

Historians and archeologists often have been confused about the identity of Area II rivers, which were given different French and Spanish names in the sixteenth, seventeenth, and eighteenth centuries, and about the location of Indian tribes and expedition routes in Area II. For example, many contemporary historians and anthropologists mistakenly assume that the river called the "Maligne" by French chroniclers was the Brazos River rather than the Colorado.[3] A careful cross-document analysis of Spanish and French expedition diaries and journals will permit these geographical conflicts over the names used for Texas rivers to be resolved with substantial confidence.

Between 1529 and 1709 elements of at least six Spanish and two French expeditions crossed Area II. While Cabeza de Vaca and his companion Lope de Oviedo remained in Area I, other members of the Narváez expedition, including Andrés Dorantes, traveled southwestward down the Texas coast in 1529 into Area III and soon thereafter into Area II.[4] Cabeza de Vaca did not follow and meet his companions in Area II until 1533. After Cabeza de Vaca's party escaped from the Area II Indians and traveled farther south into Area IV in 1535, no European expedition entered Area II for about 150 years, although the Texas Gulf coastal area was officially claimed by Spain during this period.

In 1685 the French explorer Robert Cavelier, Sieur de La Salle, landed near Matagorda Bay (in Area III) and established a colony and fort on Garcitas Creek in present-day Victoria County.[5] During the following two years, La Salle and his men crossed Area II (in 1686 and again in 1687) on long-distance overland expeditions to locate the Mississippi River. In early 1689 Spanish officials in Chihuahua (then Nueva Vizcaya) heard from Jumano and Cibola Indians who had traveled through Area II that La Salle's post on the coast in Area III had been destroyed by local Indians. At the time that the Indian reports were being received in Chihuahua, General Alonso de León was commencing an overland expedition from Coahuila in northeastern Mexico to find La Salle's colony. The Spanish general visited Area II on both his 1689 and 1690 expeditions. Following De León, General Domingo Terán in 1691 visited Area II, and his captain, Francisco Martínez, made a side expedition through Area II to rescue (or perhaps just to secure) two young French boys and a teenage girl. Governor Salinas Varona returned to Area II in 1693, and the priest Isidro de Espinosa in 1709.[6] Accounts of these expeditions will be reviewed in detail to identify by name and to locate and describe Native tribes encountered in Area II during the early historic period.

Between 1709 and 1716, no Spanish expeditions were dispatched through Area II to East Texas because the Hasinai Caddo remained resistant to any overtures by the Spanish government or the Catholic Church. But by 1716 the situation had changed, and the priest Isidro de Espinosa with Captain Domingo Ramón led a Spanish expedition across the Rio Grande, through San Antonio and the northern part of Area II, to East Texas. The 1716 expedition was followed by a second Spanish expedition in 1718 and a third in 1720–1721.[7] By the time these expeditions occurred, however, the Native population in South, Central, and northeast Texas had been so disrupted by Spanish and French incursions that expedition accounts offer limited information on the natural lifeways of the Native population. Nevertheless, the three eighteenth-century expeditions through Area II will be reviewed briefly with comments regarding the location and movement of specific tribes.

Sixteenth- and Seventeenth-Century Spanish and French Expedition Documents

In June 1533 several Deguene women escorted Cabeza de Vaca and his companion Lope de Oviedo westward along the Matagorda Peninsula on the central Texas coast from Area I into Area III.[8] Andrés Dorantes (who had landed on the Texas coast with Cabeza de Vaca) and other survivors of the Pánfilo Narváez expedition had moved westward down the coastline in the same direction toward Pánuco four years earlier. The few Spaniards who had survived were then living as slaves with different Texas coastal tribes or bands.

When Cabeza de Vaca and his Deguene women guides first met the local Matagorda Bay Indians, called Quevene, the Spaniard inquired about his friends Dorantes and the other companions who had earlier traveled down the coast. Quite brashly the Quevene boasted that they had killed several of Cabeza de Vaca's friends, and they threatened Cabeza de Vaca by pressing an arrow into his chest over his heart. This threat was sufficient to frighten Oviedo into turning around and returning eastward, accompanied by the Deguene women. Cabeza de Vaca remained for only a short time in the Matagorda Bay area. Within a few weeks he was able to escape from the Quevene and move inland into Area II to live with the Mariame Indians, who resided near the "River of Nuts" (probably the lower Guadalupe River).

Cabeza de Vaca and the historian Oviedo y Valdez both describe the Indians in Area II, and it appears that the Mariame and Yguase lived inland from the Quevene about thirty miles or more from the coast. The Mariame moved frequently to hunt deer, other small game, and occasionally bison. The Mariame made robes, shields, and footwear from bison skins. According to Cabeza de Vaca, the Mariame were not just geographically separated from the Quevene but were physically smaller than the coastal tribe and spoke a different language. William Newcomb equates the Mariame with the Muruame, a tribe encountered in eastern Gonzales County in 1693 by Governor Salinas Varona, but Thomas Campbell argues against such an identification. I agree with Campbell because the Muruame were located over eighty miles north of the homeland of the Mariame. Cabeza de Vaca said the Yguase lived west of the Mariame, probably in Goliad and Refugio Counties.

Whereas Henri Joutel in the 1680s writes that bison were always present near the French fort located north of Matagorda Bay in Area III, Cabeza de Vaca reports that during his six-year stay inland from the coast, mostly in Area I, he saw bison and ate bison meat only on three occasions. But he writes that the bison came from the north to the Gulf coastal area and roamed over the land for more than 1,000 miles inland. Significantly, Cabeza de Vaca adds that the Native people who followed the bison herds traded in bison hides and skins. This is the first written report that visiting hunting parties from the Plains regularly traveled to the central Texas coast to hunt bison and to trade bison skins with local tribes. Subsequent Spanish and French accounts confirm this report, and we learn the identity of some of the tribes that followed the bison herds into the coastal area of the Southern Plains.

The unusually dry conditions in South Texas described by Cabeza de Vaca suggest that annual rainfall at that time was below the present average for Area II. It certainly represents an anomaly during the Little Ice Age, although all long-term warming or cooling climatic periods are interrupted for short-term periods. The short-term drought is confirmed subsequently in Cabeza de Vaca's 1535 report from the Big Bend in West Texas in which the La Junta Natives complained that because they had experienced a drought during the previous several years, they would be unable to plant corn until they had another good rain, which was expected.

Nevertheless, during most of the 200-year period from 1500 to 1700, the grass prairie lands of Area II attracted large bison herds and numerous bison hunters from far distant areas. In addition, numerous tribes moved into the Guadalupe Valley in the fall to pick pecans and hunt deer, as Cabeza de Vaca reported. According to Cabeza de Vaca, tribes that traveled to the lower Guadalupe were so numerous that much of the game near the river had been frightened away. More specifically, Cabeza de Vaca wrote that the Susola Indians living near the coast southwest of Area II traveled up to seventy-five miles to gather pecans on the lower Guadalupe River.

But in the early 1530s, the central Texas coastal area was not bountiful; times were hard. According to Cabeza de Vaca, food was very scarce. Cabeza de Vaca writes that the Natives at that time lived on small rodents, snakes, and snails, and sometimes they went several days without food. Alligators, fish, clams, and other aquatic resources were found in the rivers, but the inland tribes living in Area II seldom sought tidal food resources, upon which their coastal neighbors the Karankawa relied. Pottery was evidently not made by the Mariame, and bows were acquired by trade with the Avavare, who lived about eighty miles to the south in Area IV.

Cabeza de Vaca tells that in the fall of each year the local Mariame traveled southwestward out of Area II along an inland route following the contour of the coast to large prickly pear fields to feast on the cactus fruit, called tuna, and to trade and mix with tribes from the lower Nueces

River area. It was on such a journey to the prickly pear fields, apparently located several miles west of modern Corpus Christi in Area IV, that Cabeza de Vaca and three of his companions made their escape out of Area II and across South Texas toward Mexico.

About eight years after Cabeza de Vaca moved southwest out of Area II toward northeastern Mexico, the De Soto–Moscoso expedition visited the East Texas Hasinai Caddo.[9] Moscoso dispatched an advance party from the Hasinai villages in East Texas to scout the area to the southwest (toward the Colorado River and Area II). After riding ten days, the scouting party reached a large river called the "Daycao," which most commentators have identified (and I think correctly) as the Colorado River. The fact that the Hasinai told Moscoso that they hunted deer throughout the area up to the Daycao but not beyond further suggests that the Daycao was the Colorado River because, as Henri Joutel reported, the Native groups considered the Colorado as a boundary river during the study period (and perhaps for centuries earlier), separating Hasinai hunters from hunting parties west of the river. After crossing the Daycao, Moscoso's scouts found that no maize was cultivated by the small itinerant tribes to the southwest. When the scouts reported that no maize was available beyond the Daycao, the Spaniards turned around and returned to the Mississippi.

Frenchmen Arrive

No other European left a record describing the Native population between the lower Colorado and the San Antonio Rivers until Robert Cavelier, Sieur de La Salle, and his colonists landed on the central Texas coast in early 1685, about 140 years after Moscoso's expedition departed East Texas. Comments on tribes living in Area II were recorded by several members of La Salle's party, including Henri Joutel, the priest Anastase Douay, and Abbé Cavelier. However, Joutel's journal account is the most significant and reliable record of La Salle's expedition to Texas and of the Native populations in particular.[10] Many studies of the Indians of Texas would have benefited substantially from consulting these important French sources.

Joutel records in an unusually deliberate manner the lifeways of the Indians of Central Texas, including their alliances. He frequently notes the size of Indian huts and how the huts were constructed, what the Natives ate, the identity of tribal allies and enemies, where tribes traveled to trade, hunt, and go to war, whether named Indian nations raised crops or used pottery, how Natives constructed and propelled dugout canoes, and how Natives dressed. Joutel took special care to assure the accuracy of his reports; for example, when an Indian informant named nineteen tribes living in Area II, Joutel wrote down the name of each tribe and three days later returned to his Indian source to read back the names he had written down in order to check the accuracy of his understanding of each tribal name.

As Joutel was post commander at Fort St. Louis in 1685 and 1686 while La Salle and most of his troops were away from the post on explorations, his early observations and comments on the local environment and Native life concentrate on events that occurred near the fort itself (located in Area III) and will be covered in the next chapter. But Joutel offers extensive observations about the Indians in Area II in his diary account of his journey with La Salle from the bay area to East Texas in 1687. Joutel, Abbé Cavelier, Douay, Pierre Talon, and Pierre Meunier (all of whom prepared commentaries or gave statements regarding La Salle's expedition to Texas) were all included in La Salle's party that left Fort St. Louis on January 12, 1687, in an attempt to obtain relief in Canada for La Salle's colony on the Texas coast.

On the fifth day out, La Salle's party moved into Area II, having marched north-northwest about forty miles from the bay during the previous four days. On the fifth day the French party passed an abandoned Indian encampment area where there were an estimated 300 hut pole frames (the hide coverings likely having been removed by the Native occupants and transported for use at the next campground). Although some authorities suggest that Texas coastal Natives moved both the pole structure and the hide covers (as did the Plains Indians), several expedition accounts report finding abandoned encampments with only the skeleton pole structure left intact.[11] As these itinerant hunters and gatherers revisited preferred and well-located campground sites, the pole structures remained available for possible use later. Joutel apparently assumed from the size of the pole structure itself that each hut accommodated four or five occupants, and he estimated the population of the abandoned Indian camp at 1,000 to 1,200 individuals. Joutel's estimate of the number of occupants for each Indian hut in Area II is generally in line with comparable projections made by subsequent Spanish diarists.

About fifty miles north of the French post, in northern Jackson County, La Salle encountered an Indian tribe or band that Joutel called Ebahamo. Joutel's comments on this tribe are surprising in several respects. First, the group included one member who was Caddoan or who at least spoke the Caddoan language. La Salle, who spoke several Indian languages, had become familiar with the Caddoan language during his stay with the Hasinai the year before. This was unexpected by Joutel because the Hasinai Caddo homeland in present-day Houston County lay approximately 150 miles northeast of the Ebahamo camp. Subsequent accounts from Spanish sources, however, also report very strong Caddo influence throughout Areas I and II, and the Ebahamo confirmed to Joutel that they were close allies of the East Texas Caddo. The strong influence of the Hasinai Caddo on the Native people in Area I was mentioned in the previous chapter.

The Ebahamo was a well-traveled cosmopolitan tribe, although the members were hunters and gatherers who cultivated no crops. The Ebahamo had visited Spanish communities that were a ten-day journey west of Area II. Joutel writes that Indians could travel about 200 French leagues (or about 480 miles) in ten days, or an average of about 48 miles a day. Joutel's estimate is consistent with the travel time reported by the Cibola and Jumano, who traveled annually from the Big Bend area to south-central Texas and with the distance traveled daily by the Emet runner-messenger who in 1689 carried De León's message to the Frenchmen in East Texas. This effort would involve a daily rapid walking pace of four miles an hour for twelve hours. During the summer months at the latitude of Area II, a traveler would have at least sixteen hours of daylight.

These comments regarding visits by South Texas Natives to Spanish outposts in northern Mexico are similar to travel reports given by several tribes in Area I that mentioned that they also were allies of the Ebahamo. The Ebahamo even detailed that on the trip west to visit the Spaniards there were four large rivers to cross (perhaps referring to the Guadalupe, San Antonio, Nueces, and Rio Grande) and that bison were plentiful along the way until the last few days. The Ebahamo, who had round shields made of bison hide, said that they were going to fight an unnamed enemy living to the northwest (perhaps the Apache in southern Area VI). This cosmopolitan propensity reminds us that the ancestors of the historic Native peoples of Texas were the cosmopolitan, geographically aggressive modern *H. sapiens* who first settled North America.

According to Joutel, the Ebahamo used the distinct hand sign of "hooking their fingers" to express friendship with the Frenchmen.[12] An authority on American Indian signs, W. P. Clark, writes that the Indian sign language gesture of friendship was to "link index fingers in front of body."[13] Elaine Costello writes that to make the American Sign Language (ASL) gesture for friendship "hook the bent right index finger over the bent left index finger."[14] It is curious that Costello and many other authorities on the history of ASL often ignore the numerous parallels between Indian sign language and contemporary ASL and the contributions made by Indian sign language to the important modern method of human discourse by the use of hand signs.[15]

Linguists specializing in North American Indian languages have concluded that the Indian sign language probably originated on the South-

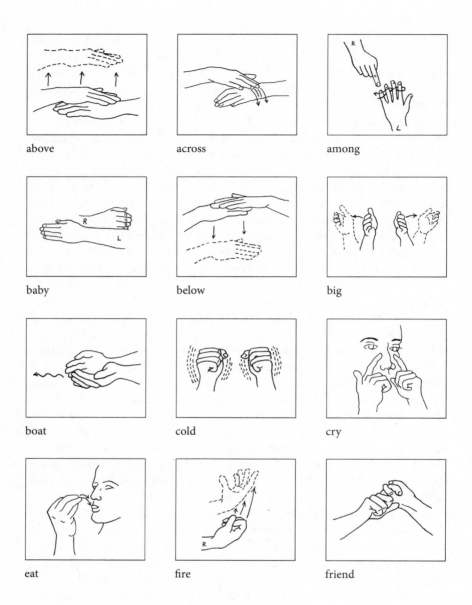

above   across   among

baby   below   big

boat   cold   cry

eat   fire   friend

FIGURE 2.1   NATIVE AMERICAN HAND SIGNS

ern Plains of the Texas Gulf Coast, possibly in Area II. It appears that the numerous local Area II tribes (perhaps numbering up to a hundred or more) may have jointly with the bison hunters and traders from the Plains made a significant and lasting cultural contribution in the form of an original nonspeech communication system of broad application and use.[16]

By the end of January, La Salle's party had reached a very large tributary creek of the Colorado River. Joutel describes the stream (probably Buckner's Creek) as the swiftest they had seen and says that its flow was adequate for the operation of a water mill. In approaching the creek, La Salle spotted an Indian village of about twenty-five huts, which Joutel describes as oven-shaped, larger structures than the ones he had seen on the coast. These larger huts were covered not with reed mats (as were some Indian huts on the coast) but with carefully scraped, dried, and greased bison skins. Joutel estimates that there were up to eighteen occupants in each of the larger huts. This suggests an encampment of about 450 residents.

The camp elders told La Salle that they had heard that his party was marching northeast to visit the Caddo and therefore they knew La Salle would pass near their campsite, which they had positioned close to the junction of the large creek (Buckner's Creek) and river (the Colorado). This comment by the Indian leader is significant because local Indians had directed La Salle and his party in 1686 (and later directed Spanish expedition leaders) to the same flat, shallow, hard-rock fording area (today called the Ripples), located on the Colorado in Fayette County about five miles upstream from the modern city of La Grange. The Indians anticipated where La Salle would cross the river; it would be at this natural, convenient, and safe customary crossing area that had been used probably for centuries, or perhaps millennia, by Indians and bison herds as well. During the late seventeenth century, this same crossing on the Colorado was used by La Salle in 1686 and 1687 and by Spanish expeditions in 1690, 1691, and 1693 (see Map 2.1).

Like the Ebahamo earlier, this friendly tribe escorted La Salle and some of his men to their chief's hut, where finely dressed bison skins were spread out on the ground for La Salle to sit upon. Smoked and fresh meats were served to the Frenchmen. The tribe had only two horses, and both were needed by them as pack animals. Therefore, the elders denied La Salle's offer to obtain the horses by trade. The Ebahamo encountered earlier apparently had no horses. But the Indians exchanged large leather straps and packs made of bison skin for French items. The Frenchmen used the long straps to secure loads and to serve as girths on the horses that he had obtained from the Hasinai the year before.

La Salle's party proceeded from the large creek for about four miles across a wide prairie (probably modern-day Rabb's Prairie) to the Colorado River, which Joutel described as being about the size of the Seine River at his hometown of Rouen in northern France. La Salle and his men remained for about two weeks at the riverside camp, constructing a boat to transport the expedition party and supplies across the swollen river. During this time, Joutel met some friendly but unidentified Indians who provided him with a list of the names of nineteen tribes that lived in Area II west of the lower Colorado. The Natives said that the Colorado was a boundary river that they and their neighbors on the west side crossed only when they were going to war with an enemy living to the east. The comment again suggests that the local Native population, the East Texas Hasinai, and Trans-Pecos tribes had clearly understood territorial hunting boundaries and close, although unwritten, alliances. The comment about crossing the Colorado only to fight an enemy to the east also suggests that local tribes were at times engaged in fighting the "Flatheads," who were likely the enemies of the Caddo living east of the Mississippi.

The local Indians told Joutel that they moved frequently and did not plant crops. They added that most of their neighbors and allies were also roving bands living off fishing and hunting, sometimes driving bison herds back and forth to each other. A statement made by the Indians that their tribe was allied with forty-five other local tribes suggests again that many tribes living in Area II had intertribal alliances that permitted them to live together peaceably. The local Indians said that some of their enemies lived to the southwest (perhaps referring to the coastal Karankawa) and other enemies lived to the east (perhaps a reference to the "Flatheads" or other Indians living near the Mississippi River).

The Indians gave Joutel the following list of names of tribes living west and northwest of the Colorado in Area II:[17] Les Kannehouan, Piechar, Chancre, Peissaquo, Panequo, Kuasse, Coyabegux, Orcan, Peinhoum, Tohaha, Petao, Tserabocherete, Onapiem, Piohum, Tohau, Pechir, Petsare, Serecoutcha, and Tsepcoen.

From the whole of Joutel's record it appears that the Indians who gave him this descriptive report and the list of tribal names in Area II were most likely the tribe first named in the list and only tribal name capitalized by Joutel, "Les Kannehouan." It also appears that this may have been the same tribe that Spanish writers called Cantona, a tribe that frequently turned up near the same Colorado crossing in Area II according to subsequent Spanish expedition journals.

Joutel writes that different tribes visited their camp each day on the Colorado, and each one communicated in its own language or dialect.

HISTORIC NATIVE PEOPLES OF TEXAS

This report is confirmed later by Fray Massanet and other Spanish writers who commented on the numerous Indian tribes and different languages spoken in Area II. A recent linguistic study suggests, however, that several tribes living in Area II spoke the same language. LeRoy Johnson and Thomas H. Campbell report that the Sana, Cava, Mesquite, Emet, Toho, Sijame, and Manam all spoke Sanan.[18] According to Campbell and Johnson, the eastern Sanan linguistic area was in Area II on the inland coastal plain, east and southeast of the Edwards Plateau and north of Matagorda Bay in the last decades of the seventeenth century.

Joutel offered other comments about the Native people he met in Area II. He wrote that he did not notice that the Indians had any formal religion but that they acknowledged something great above, pointing to the sky. The Indians, he said, were usually nude "except for the women who cover their nudity." During the winter, all put on soft dressed skins for protection from the cold.

Joutel reports that Natives living near the Colorado used earthenware pottery to cook meat and roots. The archeologist Robert A. Ricklis suggests that ceramics first became commonly used on the central Texas coast in about AD 1250–1300.[19] Archeologists have dubbed the local pottery type Leon Plain, which is an undecorated vessel tempered with crushed bone. According to Ricklis, cooking vessels recovered from archeological excavations in the area often have a residue of bison bone fat, mesquite bean grease, and deer bone fat.

Joutel also reports that local Indians had baskets woven of reeds or rushes and domesticated dogs with straight ears and muzzles like foxes. In summary, the chronicler observed that these "vagabond, roving people" do not have ways that are cruel, but "a good watch is required for fear of surprise." After the extended visit with tribes near the river crossing, La Salle proceeded to cross the Colorado and moved outside Area II.

Spanish Explorers Return

News of La Salle's colony on the Texas coast shocked Spanish officials into dispatching a series of marine and overland expeditions to locate the French fort. One of the early overland reconnaissance efforts conducted to obtain information about the French colony was dispatched from Parral, capital of Nueva Vizcaya, located over 500 miles west of Matagorda Bay. The Spanish governor of Nueva Vizcaya requested that a search of the Texas coast be made by the Jumano and Cibola Indians who had earlier reported several meetings on the Rio Grande with curious, unidentified, but armed Europeans, assumed by the Spaniards to be La Salle's men. Knowing that Trans-Pecos tribes conducted annual excursions to trade and hunt bison in Area II, the governor and Captain

Juan de Retana requested Juan Sabeata, the chieftain of the Jumano and Cibola, to lead an Indian scouting party from the Big Bend to investigate the Gulf coastal area where the French colony was thought to be located.[20]

In response to the governor's request, a small group of Jumano and Cibola Indians in the late fall of 1688 rode eastward from the Big Bend into the South Texas plains to "the river that has nuts," which was probably the Guadalupe River. Upon their return, two Cibola leaders testified at Parral in April 1689 that the French fort was found deserted and that they had seen only some destroyed guns and a few cannon at the site (in Area III). At two Indian villages in the nearby hills (probably the rolling hills along the Guadalupe in the southern part of Area II), the witnesses said they found local Indians celebrating the massacre of the French colonists. One Indian was described as dressed in a black friar's cloak; other Indians had French books and were dressed in French clothing.

Guadalupe Valley Indians who were celebrating and dancing claimed that they had joined the coastal Indians in destroying the French settlement.[21] It thus appears that Fort St. Louis was destroyed not by Karankawa alone, but in a joint attack that included other Area II tribes, such as the Emet and Cava and possibly the Toho and Tohaha. As the Jumano and Cibola scouts had come to the bay area only to gather information on the location and condition of the French post, the Indian scouting party returned to Parral with this information, delaying only long enough to visit their allies the Hasinai in East Texas.

By the time the governor in Parral received word of the destruction of the French fort in April 1689, Governor Alonso de León had departed Monclova, Coahuila, on an overland expedition to the bay area to search for La Salle. With two local Indian guides and a captured French soldier named Jean Géry, De León's expedition marched across the Rio Grande, Nueces, and San Antonio Rivers to a ford on the lower Guadalupe (later called Vado del Gobernador) in DeWitt County. On this occasion, Governor De León named the river the Guadalupe in honor of the patron saint of his expedition, the Blessed Virgin of Guadalupe.

On the first day's march toward the fort area from east of the Guadalupe River, Spanish troops found an encampment of Cava and Emet Indians in the nearby rolling wooded hills. The tribes were preparing to move and had loaded packs of bison hides on the backs of fourteen dogs in the manner of Plains Indians. At the camp, Fray Massanet saw a large young Indian wearing a black Recollet friar's cloak apparently taken during the massacre at the French fort. Massanet's description of the camp and the Indian wearing the clerical cape suggests that De León's party may have visited the same encampment that the Cibola and Jumano scouts had found several months earlier, where they also reported seeing a local Indian wearing a black Franciscan robe.

The Cava and Emet told De León that several days earlier a number of Frenchmen and Hasinai Indians had stopped by their camp on their way back to East Texas from a visit to the destroyed French fort. However, the Cava and Emet did not tell the Spaniards of any participation in the destruction of the French settlement, which they had bragged about several months earlier to the Jumano and Cibola visitors. The Cava and Emet said (with the Frenchman Géry serving as interpreter) that the attack on Fort St. Louis had occurred three months earlier, or in mid-January 1689. If we assume that these Indians participated in the attack, as evidence suggests, this probably represents the only firsthand account giving a projected date when Fort St. Louis was destroyed.

With local Cava and Emet guides, De León's party delayed their journey to the fort and followed the route of the Hasinai and Frenchmen northward to an encampment of Tohaha and Toho Indians near the present-day city of Yoakum. Again Géry served as the interpreter. The Pacpul and Quem guides brought by De León from Coahuila knew the route from Coahuila to the bay on the central Texas coast and to the French post, but they were not conversant in the local languages. In this Indian camp the Spaniards saw more loot from the French fort, including French clothes and a Bible. De León estimated the population of the village at over 250. The evidence further suggests that several tribes in Area II may have participated in the attack on Fort St. Louis along with the Karankawa.

The following morning, De León continued moving northward in Area II in search of the Frenchmen. By afternoon De León's party had reached an encampment of Emet Indians in either western Fayette County or eastern Lavaca County. According to De León, this Emet village received the Frenchman Jean Géry with open arms and demonstrations of affection celebrating Géry's return to them. Apparently, under orders from La Salle several years earlier, Géry had met, endeared himself to, learned the language of, and gained the loyalty of this Emet band as well as of other tribes in Area II. It seems apparent that Géry was known favorably by the Emet, Cava, Toho, and Tohaha tribes in Area II and that these tribes spoke a language familiar to Géry. The Frenchman had testified earlier to Spanish authorities in Mexico that he had "subdued" or made allies with many tribes in the area of the French fort before moving to the middle Rio Grande to do the same.

The Emet reported that the Hasinai and Frenchmen had passed through their camp several days before De León's arrival and had crossed the nearby large swollen river (probably the Colorado River). De León then decided to return to his troops, who were waiting near the Guadalupe, and to proceed from there to the French fort near the bay. Before leaving the Emet encampment, however, De León sent by Native courier a letter requesting the Frenchmen in East Texas to return and surrender to him. The governor dispatched the note via a local Emet runner who said that he knew well the customary route (which ran about 200 miles northeastward) to the principal Hasinai villages in Houston County.

Once the Emet courier departed on his run to the Caddo, De León and his men turned back south toward the Guadalupe as word had been received that the horse remuda at the base camp had stampeded and over one hundred horses were missing. De León reports that unidentified Indians from different local encampments near the Guadalupe cooperated with Spanish troops in a joint search effort to recover the horses. After the second day, most of the horses had been gathered, and a missing Spanish soldier was also returned, to De León's surprise, guided by several friendly local Indians.

The following day, with an added Cava guide, De León proceeded southeast from the base camp near the Guadalupe and out of Area II to the deserted French post on Garcitas Creek in Area III. Indians had destroyed most of the fort, leaving broken equipment, torn books, and the remains of several bodies. Juan Bautista Chapa writes a haunting description of the location and the devastation of the fort, and notes the return of the Emet courier, but these subjects will be developed more fully in the following chapter on Area III, covering the central Gulf coastal tribes. After leaving the bay, De León's troops returned to the earlier base camp near Vado del Gobernador on the Guadalupe in DeWitt County.

At the Guadalupe crossing area near modern-day Cuero, De León met with the Frenchmen and several Hasinai Indian escorts who, as requested in De León's message, had returned to Area II. After interrogating the two French captives, De León prepared to return to Monclova and told the visiting Hasinai goodbye, expecting the Indians to leave. But, as Chapa relates, the Hasinai chieftain refused to be the first to leave the camp because he considered the Guadalupe River valley Indian country and would formally remain at the site until the Spanish visitors departed first. Although the Hasinai invited De León to return the next year, the chieftain insisted on remaining on the bank of the Guadalupe River and signaling goodbye to the Spanish visitors as they departed and disappeared to the southwest.

As the Hasinai captain had invited the Spaniards to return the following year and to establish a presence in East Texas, De León and Massanet returned to Vado del Gobernador and revisited the desolate French fort in early 1690. On the 1690 march into Area II, De León reported searching for but failing to locate any Indians along the route to the Colorado crossing. After fording the Colorado River at the customary crossing in Fayette County and leaving Area II, De León and Massanet visited the Hasinai in East Texas and established a mission.

Later that year, after visiting the Hasinai and returning westward into Area II, De León found a large shared encampment of Area II Indians, including the Tohaha, Cantona, Sana, and Cava. The local Natives reported that the Indians at the bay (the Karankawa) were holding several French children captive, so De León assembled a small unit of soldiers and local Indian guides to visit the bay area and recover the children. The main camp proceeded southwest to camp near Vado del Gobernador. On the week-long trip across Area II from the Colorado to the bay, the Spanish party traversed the same area that La Salle had crossed in 1686 and again in 1687 between the same two locations—the customary Colorado crossing area in Fayette County and the French post on Garcitas Creek in Victoria County.

On La Salle's last trip in 1687, the French party passed six separate Indian camps along the one-hundred-mile line of march from the bay area moving northward to the Colorado crossing. On his five-day trip moving southward in 1690, De León visited five Indian encampments along the same hundred-mile trek between the two locations. De León first visited a village of Toho and later a Coco Indian camp. De León had met with Toho in DeWitt County the year before. The Coco ("Cooc"), who were encountered about one hundred miles north of the bay shore, have been identified mistakenly as a Karankawan band by some writers.[22]

In Jackson County De León found a large encampment of over 3,000 Naaman and a camp of Caisquetebana. The Naaman and Caisquetebana Indians had not been reported earlier by either Spanish or French chroniclers. Thomas Campbell suggests that the Naaman may be the same tribe that later was identified as the Aranama, who also lived in the southern part of Area II. There is no other reference to the Caisquetebana by that name, or a similar one, in either French or Spanish accounts of tribes in Area II.

In Area III the governor engaged in a fire fight to recover three French children from the Karankawa Indians who were camped at the head of San Antonio Bay. After the encounter at the bay, De León's party reported no other Indians in Area II as he marched up the Guadalupe to join the main camp and crossed the river near Cuero to return to Coahuila.

De León's initial diary account of the 1690 expedition was prepared on the Rio Grande and sent forward to the viceroy before the return to Monclova and the completion of the expedition. That version of his diary does not name any Indian tribes encountered on the trip. However, De León revised and expanded his original diary account with a more thorough and complete report that adds, among other new materials, the tribal names of the Indians recorded on the journey.[23]

In September 1690, after De León and his party had returned to Mexico, Massanet wrote a letter to the viceroy in which he named the Indian tribes he found in South and Central Texas and identified their customary residential area.[24] The priest wrote that eight tribes lived near the Guadalupe River (in Area II): the Tohaha, Toho, Emet, Cava, Sana, Panasiu, Apasam, and Manam. Massanet (with De León) had encountered the Tohaha, Toho, Emet, Cava, and Sana in Area II on the 1689 and 1690 expeditions. Joutel also includes the Tohaha and Toho among the tribes living in Area II. In his list of tribes loyal to him, Jean Géry names the Cava and Emet. The Panasiu named by Massanet may have been the same tribe as the Panequo, a tribe that Joutel lists as living in Area II.

Massanet's Apasam may have been the same tribe that the priest identified the following year (1691) as the Apaysi on the Frio River in Frio County. The Manam are not named in any other Spanish or French source, but the name could have been confused with the Naaman, who were residents of Area II. According to Massanet, the Chaguantapan and Muruam also lived in central Area II closer to the Colorado. The Muruam were subsequently reported by Salinas Varona in Area II.

On his 1691 expedition, Governor Terán followed De León's route from Monclova northward but crossed the San Antonio River into Area II west of the modern-day city of San Antonio rather than farther downstream in Karnes County, where De León had crossed the river in 1689 and 1690. Terán used friendly Payaya Indians as guides in Area II on his march eastward across Comal and Hays Counties. When he reached the San Marcos River near its headwaters, he called it the Guadalupe because at that time it had not been separately named and was known only as a branch of the Guadalupe. Near the San Marcos River, Terán's party found an Indian trade ground and a large shared encampment of from 2,000 to 3,000 Indians. Both Terán and Massanet give interesting but different accounts of this important encounter. As the two accounts are dissimilar in significant respects (such as the names of the tribes at the shared encampment), both versions of the meeting will be reviewed.[25]

According to Governor Terán, there were about 2,000 Jumano, Cibola, Casqueza, Cantona, and Mandone Indians in the large camp. The tribes showed Terán formal *patents* from the governors of Chihuahua and New Mexico. This was the first expedition report from Central Texas of Indians holding formal documents (*patents*) issued by Spanish governors authorizing them to occupy Spanish-claimed lands. Terán described the Indian leaders as brave and haughty.

As mentioned, Massanet's story differs from Terán's in several respects. First, Massanet estimated that in the shared encampment there were about 3,000 Indians and names the Jumano, Cibola, Cantona, Chalome, Catqueza, and Chaymaya. The priest reports that many Indians rode horses and their leaders were mounted on saddles with stirrups. Massanet identifies the Jumano, Cibola, and Chaymaya as residents of the Big Bend and northern Mexico; he adds that they were neighbors of the Salinero Indians in southern Chihuahua and of the Apache. The Spaniards knew the Salinero very well because the tribe and their neighbors the Tobosco occupied large parts of Coahuila and Chihuahua east and south of Parral and along the Río Conchos. The two tribes frequently raided Spanish posts and settlements in Chihuahua to steal horses and slaves. Both tribes had been reported earlier in the Edwards Plateau area in reports from the 1684 Mendoza expedition. These visiting tribes in Area II, some of whom were over 400 miles from their homeland, held captive five local Muruam boys who, according to Massanet, lived on the Guadalupe.

Massanet added an interesting comment suggesting that the Muruam lived at peace with the Indians living near the coast, probably referring to the Karankawa. According to the historical record, the East Texas Hasinai and the coastal Karankawa were enemies, and the Hasinai and West Texas Jumano were very close allies. These relationships may explain why the Jumano would hold young Muruam boys as captives. As allies of the coastal Karankawa, the Muruam were probably the enemy of the Jumano, Cibola, and Hasinai. This assessment of the relationship between local tribes in Area II is supported by the fact that the Karankawa and Muruam were never reported in shared camps with other Area II tribes or with visiting West Texas or Hasinai tribes. Like the Karankawa, the Muruam were feisty and aggressive toward the Spaniards who visited their homeland in Area II.

From the San Marcos River, Terán and Massanet marched eastward to the lower Colorado in Bastrop County and downriver to Fayette County, where they camped for three weeks in Area II while Captain Francisco Martínez with a small company of men rode south to Matagorda Bay to recover three remaining French youths thought to be held by the coastal Indians and to meet a cavalry company that had been dispatched by ship to join the governor's forces. Captain Martínez kept a diary of his march to the bay from Terán's temporary encampment on the Colorado, located about fifteen miles upriver from the customary crossing of the Colorado.[26] Martínez describes the capture of two French boys in Area III but does not identify by name any Area II tribe encountered on his line of march. Martínez also reports that the young French teenage girl was not recovered because she was being held elsewhere by Indians residing somewhere inland.

Martínez writes that the coastal Natives demanded horses in exchange for the two young French boys and that the Indians used signs and smoke signals to communicate with the Spaniards and with each other. In his 1768 comments on the large number of Native languages that were spoken in Central Texas, Fray Gaspar José de Solís writes that the different Indian tribes in Area II frequently communicated among themselves and with outside groups by the use of hand signs. Solís adds that Catholic priests from central Mexico received instruction in the use of Indian sign language before arriving to serve in Texas.[27] As mentioned, modern linguists have concluded that Indian sign language may have originated among the numerous tribes in the central Texas coastal area and spread with the assistance of Plains Indians throughout the Midwest. Soon after Martínez returned to the base camp on the Colorado, Terán's party marched northeastward out of Area II. Although Terán crossed Area II on three other occasions in 1691 and 1692, the governor did not record by name or further describe any other Area II tribe.

In early May 1693, Governor Salinas Varona led an expedition across South Texas following De León's 1689 and 1690 route rather than Terán's trek through San Antonio. The purpose of his trip was to resupply the beleaguered Catholic mission in East Texas. Salinas gives a full account of the names and locations of the tribes he found on his line of march through Area II. Near Coleto Creek, a tributary to the Guadalupe in De-Witt County, the governor encountered a band of armed Jumano and Toboso. Earlier, near the Rio Grande crossing, some Pacuache Indians had warned Salinas that warriors from these two tribes from northern Mexico and West Texas planned to intercept his party as it marched toward the customary Colorado crossing. The mounted Jumano and Toboso appeared hostile to Salinas; the warriors were painted red and carried oval leather shields. Although Salinas captured and released several Indians, no direct attack on the Salinas convoy was attempted by the Indians.

Near the Colorado, as Salinas continued northward through Area II, the governor met a group of Sana Indians who informed him that the Simaoma, Mescal, and Toho Indians were gathered at Tres Cruces, a location about twenty miles southwest of the Colorado crossing area. The Sana had been seen in the same area by De León in 1690 in a shared encampment with the Tohaha, Cantona, and Cava. This was the first reported meeting with the Simaoma but they would be seen again. Both De León and Terán earlier reported meeting the Mescal at the Rio Grande crossing called Paso de Francia in Area IV, so the Mescal were perhaps visiting with the local Toho and Sana to hunt, trade, or for other social purposes. It is unlikely that the Mescal were migrating to the Colorado crossing area, as the tribe was seen again by Salinas near the Rio Grande about six weeks later.

Another tribe from the Nueces and Rio Grande, the Cacaxtle, greeted Salinas near the river crossing. The Cacaxtle was a well-known South Texas tribe that had raided Spanish frontier communities and ranches in Nuevo León for horses and slaves as far south as Monterrey in the mid-seventeenth century. Although the Cacaxtle were the target of Spanish retaliatory expeditions into Texas in 1663 and 1665, the large tribe obviously was not exterminated. Salinas had met the tribe earlier on his expedition when he crossed the Rio Grande on May 9. The Cacaxtle appear to have been in the Colorado crossing area to meet other tribes to trade or hunt rather than with any intention of immigrating.

When Salinas returned to the same Colorado crossing on June 23, after visiting the Hasinai and the Catholic mission, he was met on the west bank of the river (in Area II) by Cantona, Jumano, and a small band of other Hasinai Indians. This shared encampment in which the local Cantona were hosting the Hasinai visitors from East Texas and the Trans-Pecos Jumano is reminiscent of Terán's 1691 meeting on the San Marcos with the Cantona, Jumano, and other West Texas tribes that had earlier visited the Hasinai in East Texas. About eight miles west of the Colorado, Salinas met other Hasinai and the Simaoma, who were camped together. Presumably the purpose of this meeting was again for trade rather than to hunt together because the Caddo bison-hunting grounds did not extend west of the Colorado.

Nearby, in western Fayette County, a band of Sana greeted Salinas, and a few leagues beyond, some Cacquite were camped. Salinas asked the Cacquite for a guide to direct him back to the Frio River crossing by way of the present-day San Antonio area, which Terán had visited in 1691 but Salinas had not seen. The Cacquite (who may have been the same tribe that Terán had called "Casqueza" and Massanet "Catqueza" in 1691 on the San Marcos River) provided Salinas with an extremely competent guide who was also fluent in Spanish. It should be noted that the captain of the Casqueza (or Cacquite) met by Terán and Massanet in 1691 also spoke Spanish. Salinas's guide may have been the same Indian leader from Parral called Tomas, mentioned by Chapa and by Jumano witnesses in testimony at Parral. Regardless of the resolution of the questions surrounding the identity of Tomas, the Cacquite guide proved very competent. As the Cacquite were later reported living in Coahuila, it appears that they, like the Jumano, Hasinai, Simaoma, and Mescal, were visitors in Area II engaged in hunting, trading, and socializing rather than in immigrating.

From Fayette County the Salinas expedition party with the Cacquite guide first traveled about ten miles westward to Peach Creek in Gonzales County, where a very hostile band of Muruam Indians were encountered. Salinas described the meeting with the testy Muruam warriors (who numbered over one hundred) as so tense that he required his men to remain on guard and mounted wearing their coats of mail. The Muruam arrived at Salinas's camp in the afternoon and by nine o'clock that night Spanish troops were unable to drive the Indian visitors out of the campgrounds. The defiant Muruam were able to steal four horses from the Spanish remuda. The hostile encounter with the Muruam in Area II is in contrast to the basically friendly reception the Spaniards and French usually received from local tribes in Area II and is similar to the antagonistic encounters the French and Spanish forces often had with the Karankawa. This was the last Indian encounter recorded by Salinas before he crossed the Guadalupe and San Antonio Rivers moving west and out of Area II.

1700S

In 1709 Fray Isidro de Espinosa, Fray Antonio de Olivares, and Captain Pedro de Aguirre led a small expedition party from the San Juan Bautista presidio and mission on the Rio Grande northeastward following Terán's route to the San Antonio area where the party engaged a mounted Pampopa as a guide. Near San Antonio Espinosa found a gathering of more than 500 Siupan, Chaularame (or Xarame), and Sijame, all from Coahuila. The Spanish party crossed the Guadalupe near modern New Braunfels moving northeast.

Employing a Sana Indian as a scout, Espinosa's party visited the present-day San Marcos area and then followed Onion Creek downstream to the Colorado River and the crossing of the river frequently used by bison and Native people. No Indians were reported between the Guadalupe and the Colorado in Area II, but a few leagues east of the Colorado in Area I, Espinosa met the Yojuane, Simaoma, and Tusonibi. The Indians reported that the Caddo were still living in their own country (east of the Trinity) and had not moved to the Colorado, as the Spaniards had been told. But Espinosa specifically confirmed what Spanish diarists had earlier reported, namely that Hasinai hunting parties frequently hunted bison and deer up to the east bank of the Colorado. This comment is also consistent with Joutel's report that the Colorado served as a boundary river. This encounter was covered in the previous chapter on Area I.

Espinosa's 1709 account includes valuable information about Native life in Central Texas in the early 1700s and about local wild animals and plants. Although Espinosa's party had not seen any bison or even any tracks of bison along the route from the Rio Grande to Area II, the party found large herds near the Onion Creek crossing area on the Colorado. The priest describes how Area II Natives utilized many parts of the bison. He writes that the hump on the bison extended from the neck to the rump and that the meat was superior in lightness and taste to the loin of fine Castilian beef. The priest noted later that there had been large herds of bison in Nuevo León but that Spanish settlers depleted the herds, taking only the bison tongue and tallow.[28]

On the return trip, Espinosa again identified no native tribes in the northern prairie area of Area II, which stretched along the route between the Balcones Escarpment on the north and the Post Oak Belt on the south. But he did identify wildlife in the area, including bear, cougar, jaguar, and fox.

After Espinosa's expedition party returned to Coahuila in 1709, no Spanish expeditions were dispatched through San Antonio and Area II for another seven years. But between 1716 and 1721, three large colonizing expeditions crossed Area II en route to East Texas and ultimately Louisiana to establish the new capital of the territory.[29] As these expeditions were conducted for the purpose of colonizing previously explored areas in Texas rather than to explore new territory and investigate unknown areas and Native peoples, only limited new ethnographic information is made available in the diary accounts of the subsequent journeys. Nevertheless, each of the three expeditions through Area II will be reviewed briefly and the new ethnographic information will be noted.

When Espinosa reached the Colorado River in 1709, local Indians advised the priest that the Catholic Church and Spaniards were still unwelcome in the Hasinai homeland. However, perhaps with increased French pressure and colonization on the lower Mississippi, this situation had changed by 1716. In the spring of that year, Espinosa returned to Texas following the route to the Colorado that he had taken northeast from the Rio Grande seven years earlier.

Near San Antonio (in Area II), the priest and his party secured a Payaya guide to lead the party across the northern part of Area II below the Balcones Escarpment to the Colorado crossing near the mouth of

Onion Creek. No Indian tribes were reported during the eighty-mile, eight-day trip. After crossing the Colorado and entering Area I, Espinosa and Ramón were in country new to them. The Spanish party located guides and several Hasinai to assist them on their trip farther east and beyond Area II.

Two years later, when Governor Alarcón departed San Antonio to march with his troops to East Texas, the governor's party used three Hasinai guides to lead the Spaniards first to Matagorda Bay and then north to the crossing on the Colorado River near present-day Columbus. Among the few Indian tribes encountered en route (in Area III) was a Karankawan band. This encounter will be covered in the following chapter.

When Governor Aguayo first marched into San Antonio in 1721, he secured the services of a highly regarded Indian leader called Captain Juan Rodríguez from the Ranchería Grande encampment. The Indian captain led Aguayo's party across northern Area II along the route first used by Espinosa in 1709. Although no Indian tribes or bison were encountered en route through Area II, the Spanish party began seeing large herds of bison on the open prairies north of the Colorado crossing in Area VI. Rather than crossing the Brazos at the customary ford near the junction of the Little Brazos, Captain Rodríguez led the party northward deeper into Area VI, a territory recognized as Apache hunting grounds. The captain assured Aguayo that the Apache would not attack a large military convoy of the size accompanying Aguayo. When the party was near present-day Waco, the Spanish force crossed the Brazos and turned eastward. Large herds of bison were seen and hunted, but Apache warriors never appeared. By this time, Aguayo was in Area VI, well beyond the northern boundary of Area II.

As mentioned, subsequent Spanish expedition documents in the mid-1700s offer little new on how Texas Natives lived in their Native state, but the documents provided significant information on Texas flora and fauna.

Conclusions

Spanish and French sixteenth- and seventeenth-century documentary accounts name and identify the location of over fifty Indian tribes encountered or reported in Area II. The named tribes are listed alphabetically in the supplement at the end of the chapter. In addition to the names and variants of the names of the resident and nonresident tribes identified in Area II, the list notes the county area in which the tribe was reported, the source and date of the report, the names of other tribes found in shared encampments, the tribal names of any identified friends or enemies of the tribe, and, if the tribe is a nonresident of Area II, the principal residential area of the tribe.

Map 2.1 indicates the major trade routes through Area II, the Spanish and French expedition routes, and the location of Indian trade grounds and the archeological sites mentioned in the chapter. Cabeza de Vaca named three specific tribes that resided or visited Area II, La Salle's chroniclers (primarily Joutel) listed over twenty, and late seventeenth-century and early eighteenth-century Spanish accounts identified over twenty more.

The historic record confirms that both East Texas Caddo and West Texas tribes annually visited Area II and that Native people from these widely diverse cultures exerted substantial influence over local Area II tribes. But the record shows that Area II hunter-gatherer tribes themselves were cosmopolitan. They traveled eastward to visit with the Caddo. Toward the west, Area II tribes traveled to the Trans-Pecos and to northeastern Mexico. These extensive regional patterns of interaction, spanning 600 miles or more west to east, the multiple mixed, large shared encampments of several thousand Indians, and the territorial hunting and political alliances with Caddoan and Trans-Pecos tribes indicate that Area II Indians, although hunter-gatherer tribes, had a complex social organization. The degree of complexity is reflected in the fact that contemporary Indian linguists, including Ives Goddard, credit these hunter-gatherers with the origin of Indian sign language employed so widely in Area II and other parts of Texas and the Great Plains.

In sum, it appears that the relatively abundant animal and plant resources available in the open and hospitable terrain in Area II attracted tribes from the mountainous and more arid desert areas to the west and southwest and from the more densely wooded area to the east and northeast. Thus, the soil, terrain, and climatic conditions and the associated natural resource attractions in Area II encouraged economic and cultural interaction between the hunter-gatherer Indians of Area II and the tribes from the American Southwest and the Southeast.

SUPPLEMENT: STUDY AREA II
BETWEEN THE LOWER COLORADO AND THE SAN ANTONIO RIVERS

This chapter supplement lists alphabetically the names of Indian tribes or bands reported in expedition accounts referenced in the Area II study. Entries include both Native groups that were residents of Area II and nonresident tribal groups that were reported visiting the area for purposes of trading, raiding, or hunting. The principal objective of the supplement is to locate geographically as precisely as possible (by county where possible) where each Native group was encountered. Entries include the name of the leader or diarists on the expedition and the date of the encounter.

The following documentary sources are among those consulted in preparing the supplement: Alex D. Krieger, *We Came Naked and Barefoot: The Journey of Cabeza de Vaca across North America;* William C. Foster, ed., *The La Salle Expedition to Texas: The Journal of Henri Joutel, 1685–1687;* Isaac J. Cox, *The Journeys of René Robert Cavelier, Sieur de La Salle;* William C. Foster, *Spanish Expeditions into Texas, 1689–1768;* and William W. Newcomb Jr., "Historic Indians of Central Texas," *Bulletin of the Texas Archeological Society* 64 (1993): 1–63. Citations to Thomas N. Campbell's comments are found in entries of specifically named Indian tribes in Ron Tyler et al., eds., *The New Handbook of Texas.*

In his diary account of La Salle's 1687 journey to visit the Hasinai Caddo, Henri Joutel listed nineteen tribes that were residents of the northern part of Area II. The tribes listed by Joutel are included below with only a source note indicating that the tribe was identified by Joutel as living in northern Area II.

1. Anachorema. The friar Anastase Douay wrote that La Salle's party in early January 1687 met the Anachorema near the Lavaca River after traveling northeast four days from Fort St. Louis. Joutel did not give a name to the tribe met on this occasion, but he did describe the encounter.

2. Aname (Anami, Aranama?). In 1718 Governor Alarcón met "the entire nation of the Aname" near the modern city of Columbus in Area II. The large tribe had come in search of Alarcón to request that he establish a mission for them near Garcitas Creek. Thomas Campbell writes that Aname is probably a variant of Aranama.

3. Apache. In 1717 the French trader François Derbanne reported that a band of about sixty Apache attacked his commercial expedition in Area II between the Colorado and San Marcos Rivers. In 1721 Juan Antonio de la Peña, Aguayo's diarist, described the Hill Country west of Austin as Apache country.

4. Apasam (Apayxam). In 1690 Massanet identified the Apasam as one of eight tribes that lived near the Guadalupe River. No further reference has been found to the tribe.

5. Aranama (Aname? Naaman?). If Aname is a variant of Aranama (as accepted by Campbell), Alarcón met the tribe in Colorado County in Area II in 1718, and if Naaman is another variant of Aranama (as suggested by Campbell), De León met the large friendly tribe in the

same part of Area II in 1690. In 1727 Rivera reported that the Aranama were living in Victoria and DeWitt Counties. Subsequently, the tribe was reported in Area II by Rubí and Solís.

6. Cacaxtle. Salinas Varona met five Cacaxtle Indians near the customary crossing area of the Colorado in Fayette County on May 27, 1693. Salinas identified the hilly range east of Hondo Creek in Area IV as the Cacaxtle homeland. Campbell suggests that their homeland in the 1600s was in the area of present La Salle and Macmillan Counties in Area IV. The Cacaxtle are not considered permanent residents of Area II.

7. Caddo (Hasinai, Cenis, Tejas). Joutel did not record meeting any Caddo or Cenis in Area II, but did note their influence with an Area II tribe, the Ebahamo. Joutel indicated that the Cenis considered the lands east of the Colorado River in Area I as their hunting ground and available for occupation and use, but that the Colorado River represented the western boundary of Caddo hunting territory. Governor Salinas Varona and other Spanish expedition diarists recorded numerous visits by the Tejas or Western Caddo into Area II.

8. Caisquetebana. De León reported meeting the Caisquetebana in Area II on the upper Arenosa Creek in June 1690. Four members of the tribe served as guides for De León's party and led the Spaniard to the Cascosi (Karankawan) encampment at the head of San Antonio Bay, the area in which three of the Talon children were held.

9. Cantona (Kannehouan?). Joutel wrote that the prominent tribe "Les Kannehouan" lived west and northwest of the customary crossing of the lower Colorado in Fayette County, as did the Cantona, according to Spanish expedition diarists. Campbell raises the question as to whether "Kanohatinos" and the Cantona were the same tribe. Spanish diarists recorded meeting the Cantona on the upper San Marcos River and on repeated occasions near the lower Colorado crossing area, where Joutel met the Kannehouan.

10. Catqueza (Casquesa). In 1691 Terán and Massanet both reported that the Catqueza, along with the Jumano, Cibola, and other West Texas tribes, were encountered a few leagues west of the San Marcos River in Hays County. Terán added that some of the 2,000 Indians at the large encampment were from Chihuahua and had *patents* from the governor permitting them to occupy Spanish lands. Massanet was particularly impressed with the leader of the Catqueza, whom the priest called Captain Tomas. Tomas was conversant in several Aztec dialects and in Spanish. In 1693 Salinas encountered in Area II a large encampment of Saquita who provided him with a guide who

was fluent in Spanish. The knowledgeable Saquita guide led Salinas along a new route from the Colorado westward through the San Antonio area and southwest toward the Rio Grande. For purposes of this study, the Catqueza and Saquita are considered the same tribe whose homeland was northern Mexico.

11. Cava (Saba?). In 1684 Mendoza listed the Sabas as a tribe he was to meet along with the Hasinai Caddo. Massanet met the Cava in De-Witt County in Area II on April 16, 1689; the tribe was in a shared encampment with the Emet near Irish Creek in DeWitt County. De León met them again that year near the customary crossing on the Colorado River. There appears to be no connection between the Cava reported by the Spanish in Area II and the Kebaye listed by Joutel in Area I.

12. Chaguantapan. In Massanet's 1690 letter to the viceroy, he reported that the Chaguantapan lived in Area II, closer to the Colorado than to the Guadalupe River.

13. Chalome. In 1691 Massanet reported meeting the Chalome (along with the Jumano, Cibola, and Catqueza) near the headwaters of the San Marcos River. The Chalome are identified as one of the tribes from the Trans-Pecos.

14. Chancre. Joutel listed the Chancre as one of the nineteen tribes that lived west of the customary Colorado River crossing in Fayette County.

15. Chaymaya. In 1691 Massanet identified the Chaymaya as a visiting tribe at a shared encampment near the headwaters of the San Marcos River. Massanet stated that the homeland of the tribe was on the Rio Grande near the homeland of the Jumano and Cibola.

16. Cibola. A Cibola chieftain testified in early 1689 in Parral that annually the tribe visited Area II to trade and hunt. The Cibola were highly mobile bison hunters whose homeland was between the lower Pecos River and La Junta on the Rio Grande. In June 1691 Terán and Massanet reported meeting the Cibola and other West Texas tribes near the San Marcos River. Massanet commented that the Cibola and Jumano were enemies of the Apache and friends of the Salinero, who resided primarily in southern Coahuila.

17. Coyabsqux. Joutel listed the Coyabsqux as one of the nineteen tribes that lived west of the customary Colorado River crossing in Fayette County.

18. Ebahamo. Joutel with La Salle met the Ebahamo on January 21 and 22, 1687, on the upper Navidad River near the present Colorado County line. The Ebahamo, a band of hunter-gatherers, indicated

by signs that they were allies of the western Caddo and many tribes in Area II. Members of the tribe had visited the Spaniards, who they said lived ten days' journey (ca. 500 miles) to the west. Significantly, they added that bison were found all along the route southwest except for the last day or two. One of their members spoke Caddoan. On February 16 on the same journey, Joutel reported meeting the Teao, who indicated that they were friends of the Ebahamo.

19. Emet (Emot). Massanet reported that the De León expedition party in 1689 met the Emet (with the Cava) on or near Irish Creek in De-Witt County. The Frenchman Jean Géry told Chapa that the Emet (Emot) were loyal to him.

20. Jumano (Choumay, Chouman). In January 1689 the Jumano chieftain Sabeata testified in Parral that he and his people lived near La Junta on the Rio Grande and annually traveled to hunt bison and engage in trade fairs with local Indians in Area II and with the Hasinai. Joutel wrote that the Jumano were allies of the Caddo and many tribes in Area II, including the Ebahamo. Pierre Talon, who lived with the Caddo and their allies from 1687 to 1690, testified that the Jumano were peaceful and that many members spoke Spanish.

21. Kannehouan (Cantona?). Joutel wrote that the Kannehouan were one of nineteen tribes that lived in Area II toward the west and northwest of the crossing area on the Colorado River. Campbell raises the question of whether the Kanohatino and Cantona were the same tribe, but I suspect that the Kannehouan and Cantona were the same tribe.

22. Kuasse. Joutel listed the Kuasse as one of the nineteen tribes that lived in Area II west of the customary Colorado River crossing in Fayette County.

23. Manam. In a 1690 letter to the viceroy, Massanet listed the Manam as a tribe living near the lower Guadalupe River.

24. Mariame. Cabeza de Vaca lived with the Mariame for about a year and a half after leaving the Texas coastal tribes in Area I. The Mariame lived on the lower Guadalupe, principally along the river between southern Victoria County and northern DeWitt County. Oviedo y Valdez also described the Mariame based on statements by Dorantes, who lived with the tribe for about four years. According to Oviedo, who carefully recorded the distance and direction traveled, the Mariame and some of their friends moved each summer more than one hundred miles south to eat tuna. As noted by Campbell, a movement southward one hundred miles from the Guadalupe in central DeWitt County places the Mariame on the lower Nueces

in the area near the county line between San Patricio and Nueces Counties. During their seasonal migration, the Mariame remained on the lower Nueces for about two months to feast on tuna and to trade with tribes local to the Nueces and other tribes visiting the area from their homeland farther south, closer to the Rio Grande. This annual gathering of tribes appears to have been generally peaceful, although the Avegato were considered enemies of the Mariame.

25. Mescal. De León (in 1690), Terán (in 1691), and Salinas (in 1693) met the Mescal near the customary crossing of the Rio Grande in Area IV. However, Salinas also reported the tribe in Area II near the La Grange crossing in 1693. In 1716 Espinosa recorded the Mescal between the Colorado and the Brazos in Burleson County.

26. Muruam (Muruame). In June 1691 with Terán's expedition, Massanet reported that Terán traded horses with the Jumano for the release of five Muruam youths and that the Muruam lived in Area II on the Guadalupe. A similar report on the residential location of the Muruam is found in Massanet's 1690 letter to the viceroy and in Salinas's encounter with the tribe in Gonzales County in 1693.

27. Naaman. De León recorded encountering an exceptionally large and friendly gathering of Naaman (numbering about 3,000) in Area II on the lower Lavaca River in Jackson County. Campbell suggests that the Naaman may have been the same as the Aranama.

28. Onapiem. The only reference to the tribe was made by Joutel who listed the Onapiem as one of nineteen tribes that lived in Area II west of the customary Colorado River crossing in Fayette County.

29. Orcan. Joutel listed the Orcan as one of the nineteen tribes that lived west of the customary Colorado River crossing in Fayette County.

30. Pacpul. Massanet reported that the chief of the Pacpul, a tribe resident in Coahuila, served as a guide through Area II on De León's 1689 expedition.

31. Panasiu. In Massanet's letter to the viceroy dated September 1690, the priest listed the Panasiu as one of the tribes that lived in Area II near the Guadalupe River. No further reference has been found to the tribe.

32. Panequo. Joutel listed the Panequo as one of the nineteen tribes that lived west of the customary Colorado River crossing in Fayette County.

33. Payaya (Paillaille?). Payaya guides were used by Terán in 1691 to lead his expedition from present-day San Antonio to the San Marcos River. In 1693 Salinas and in 1709 Espinosa also found the Payaya in the San Antonio region. In 1717 the Frenchman Derbanne found

78

some "Paillaille" in Area II about twelve miles west of the Colorado. For purposes of this study, the Payaya are considered Area II residents.

34. Pechin. Joutel listed the Pechin as one of the nineteen tribes that lived in Area II west of the customary Colorado River crossing in Fayette County.

35. Peinhoun. Joutel listed the Peinhoun as one of the nineteen tribes that lived in Area II west of the customary Colorado River crossing in Fayette County.

36. Peissaquo. Joutel listed the Peissaquo as one of the nineteen tribes that lived in Area II west of the customary Colorado River crossing in Fayette County.

37. Petao. Joutel listed the Petao as one of the nineteen tribes that lived in Area II west of the customary Colorado River crossing in Fayette County. By mistake, Pierre Margry duplicated Joutel's Petao by adding the tribal name Petaro.

38. Petsane. Joutel listed the Petsane as one of the nineteen tribes that lived in Area II west of the customary Colorado River crossing in Fayette County.

39. Piechar. Joutel listed the Piechar as one of the nineteen tribes that lived in Area II west of the customary Colorado River crossing in Fayette County.

40. Piohum. Joutel listed the Piohum as one of the nineteen tribes that lived in Area II west of the customary Colorado River crossing in Fayette County.

41. Quansatinno (Kanoatinoa, Quanoatinno, Canohatino). Both Douay and Abbé Cavelier mentioned the tribe living near the Colorado in Area II. Douay reported that the Quanoatinno were at war with the Spanish and with the Hasinai Caddo. Joutel also noted that the Canohatino were enemies of the Caddo.

42. Quara (Kourara). Douay reported that on La Salle's 1687 expedition to East Texas, their party met the Quara and the Anachorema together near the "First Cane River" (the Lavaca River), probably in central Jackson County. Apparently Abbé Cavelier referred to the same tribe as the Kourara. Joutel only mentioned meeting an unidentified tribe near the Lavaca in 1687.

43. Quem. Massanet reported that a member of the Quem tribe told him at Mission Caldera in Coahuila that he had visited Area II and the French post near Matagorda Bay searching for his wife. Subsequently the Quem served as a guide on De León's 1689 expedition. Chapa gave a more comprehensive account of the Quem guide, who

had earlier traveled to the French settlement. Chapa added that the Quem was the one who had guided De León all the way to the bay because he knew the land very well.

44. Sana. De León in 1690 and Salinas in 1693 met the Sana in Area II, near the Colorado crossing area in Fayette County.

45. Serecoutcha. Joutel listed the Serecoutcha as one of the nineteen tribes that lived in Area II west of the customary Colorado River crossing in Fayette County.

46. Simaoma (Sinaoma, Simomo). Salinas met the Simaoma in Area II in a shared encampment with Mescal and local Toho on May 26, 1693, near Tres Cruces, a location about twelve miles south-southwest of the customary crossing of the Colorado in Fayette County. He also met the Simaoma in a shared camp with the Hasinai near the same location in Area II on his return trip. In 1709 Espinosa reported the Simaoma (Simomo) in Area I a few leagues east of the Colorado crossing in a shared encampment with the Tusonibi and Yojuane. Campbell considers the Simaoma native to northeastern Coahuila and Area IV north of the Rio Grande.

47. Susola. Cabeza de Vaca geographically placed the principal residence of the Susola near the Avavare on the lower Nueces. The tribe was apparently one of many that traveled annually up to eighty miles to the Guadalupe River in Area II to pick pecans in season.

48. Tacame. In 1727 Rivera listed the Tacame as residents of Area II living near the Espíritu Santo presidio on the Guadalupe, but he described the tribe as not being directly related to the nearby mission. Campbell places the primary residence of the Tacame in the early eighteenth century in Area IV south and west of the San Antonio River.

49. Tamerlouan (Paouite). The testimony of the Talon brothers is the only presently known source of information regarding the Tamerlouan. The Talons reported that the Tamerlouan (like the coastal Clamcoet) were cruel and made war on La Salle because he had taken their canoes. The brothers added that the Tamerlouan lived farther inland from the seashore. Pierre Talon, who lived for a time with the Toho, an ally of the Hasinai Caddo, fought with the Toho against the Tamerlouans, also called Paouites, according to the Talons. It is unclear from the Talon testimony as to whether the Tamerlouans resided in Area II or only visited the area from their homeland in Area III.

50. Toboso. In 1693 Salinas encountered some aggressive Jumano and Toboso in Area II in DeWitt County. The Toboso were residents of Chihuahua east of the Río Conchos.

51. Tohaha. Joutel listed the Tohaha as one of the nineteen tribes that lived in Area II west of the customary Colorado River crossing in Fayette County. De León reported the tribe in Area II in 1689 and 1690.

52. Toho (Tohau). Joutel listed the Toho (Tohau) as one of the nineteen tribes that lived in Area II west of the customary Colorado River crossing in Fayette County. De León met the Toho in Area II in 1689 and 1690.

53. Tserabocherete. Joutel listed the Tserabocherete as one of the nineteen tribes that lived in Area II west of the customary Colorado River crossing in Fayette County.

54. Tseperen. Joutel listed the Tseperen as one of the nineteen tribes that lived in Area II west of the customary Colorado River crossing in Fayette County.

55. Yguase (Yguaze). Oviedo y Valdez wrote that Castillo and Estevanico lived with the Yguaze, who were neighbors of the Mariame and were culturally similar to the Mariame. The tribe was principally located inland, southwest of the Mariame, probably in northern Refugio and Goliad Counties. Although their homeland was adjacent to Area II, the Yguaze, like other neighboring tribes, visited the Guadalupe River basin each fall in search of pecans.

56. Yojuane (Yojane). Espinosa met the Yojuane in Travis County near Wilbarger Creek on April 19 and 20, 1709.

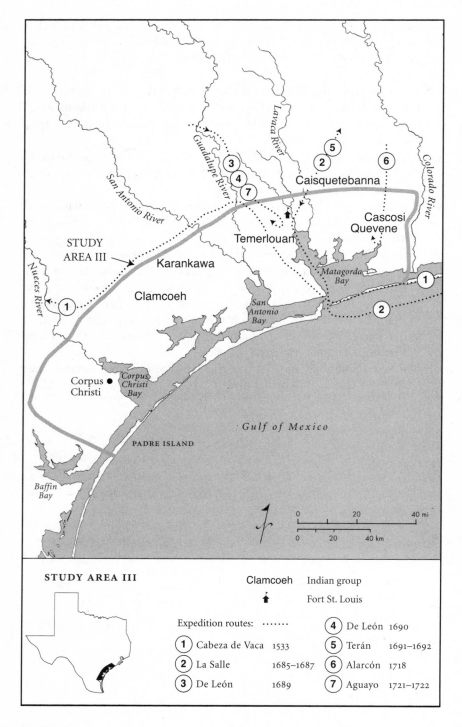

STUDY
AREA III →

Karankawa

Clamcoeh

Corpus ● Christi

Corpus Christi Bay

Guadalupe River

San Antonio River

Nueces River

Lavaca River

Colorado River

Caisquetebanna

Cascosi Quevene

Temerlouan

Matagorda Bay

San Antonio Bay

PADRE ISLAND

Baffin Bay

Gulf of Mexico

0   20   40 mi

0   20   40 km

STUDY AREA III

Clamcoeh   Indian group

🔺   Fort St. Louis

Expedition routes: ·······

① Cabeza de Vaca 1533

② La Salle 1685–1687

③ De León 1689

④ De León 1690

⑤ Terán 1691–1692

⑥ Alarcón 1718

⑦ Aguayo 1721–1722

MAP 3.1

3 ♠ THE CENTRAL TEXAS COAST

STUDY AREA III

Study Area III was the primary residence of the central Texas coastal people currently referred to as the Karankawa (see Map 3.1). The Colorado River forms the eastern boundary of Area III; the northern shoreline of Baffin Bay is the southern boundary. Area III extends about twenty to thirty miles inland from the bending coastline, although the coastal residents may have hunted occasionally up to forty miles inland. The geographic area included in Area III is similar to that identified by Robert A. Ricklis as the Texas Central Coast in his study of the central coastal cultural area.[1] Ricklis demonstrates that during the period AD 1000 to 1500 the central coastal cultural area can be established on the basis of the distribution of distinctive artifacts. According to Ricklis, the eastern limit of the Rockport pottery, with its asphaltum or bitumen surface treatment, was the Colorado River delta area. As reviewed in this chapter, the historic record supports the same geographic boundaries for Area III.

Area III includes all or part of the following Texas counties: Matagorda, Jackson, Victoria, Refugio, San Patricio, Nueces, Aransas, Kleberg, and Calhoun. An early documentary use of the term Karankawa (Carancaguaze) to identify the Indians of the central Texas coast is found in the Spanish explorer and diarist Pedro de Rivera's 1727 diary.[2] Subsequently the Spanish engineer and diarist Nicolás de Lafora on the 1767 expedition of the Marqués de Rubí uses the same name for the coastal Indians.[3]

Customarily the Karankawa remained near the bays and shoreline in the fall and winter, moving out into the prairies and venturing upstream along the heavily wooded banks of the rivers and creeks that emptied into the bays. The Gulf waters served as an effective physical boundary because the shallow-draft dugout canoes constructed by Texas coastal Indians were not serviceable in the open waters of the Gulf of Mexico.

As the Karankawa generally remained within the same coastal area, the general location of the tribes and separate bands is more certain than the location of Area I and II tribes, which were more numerous and cosmopolitan. I should add, however, that the historic record indicates that the Karankawa did travel inland over 200 miles northeast from the coast to northeast Texas to engage their enemies the Caddo and perhaps the so-called Flathead Indians farther east.

The area of Karankawa occupation included Matagorda Bay northeast to the Colorado River; the upper Lavaca Bay area, fed directly by the Navidad and Lavaca Rivers; the outlying Matagorda Peninsula; Matagorda Island, lying farther south; the Guadalupe Bay and San Antonio Bay areas, into which the Guadalupe and San Antonio Rivers drain; Copano Bay, fed by the Mission River; Aransas Bay; San Jose Island; Mustang Island; Corpus Christi Bay at the mouth of the Nueces River system; and south to Baffin Bay.

Unlike the numerous and diverse tribes reported in Areas I and II, there was a relatively small number of central coastal tribes or bands living in Area III, perhaps as few as four or five named bands. The Coco, who were encountered primarily east of the Colorado River, frequently ranged up to 150 miles inland and were often found in shared encampments with inland tribes unassociated with the Karankawa. For purposes of this study, the Coco are considered an Area I tribe and not a traditional Karankawan coastal tribe.

Apparently all central coastal people spoke the same language, today called Karankawan. Although some linguists have attempted to demonstrate that Karankawan was related to the language spoken by Carib Indians of the West Indies, most authorities have not accepted the connection.

Between 1527 and 1700, four Spanish expeditions and one French maritime expedition visited Area III. Between 1700 and 1750, two additional Spanish overland expeditions and a second French maritime expedition visited the area. Andrés Dorantes, a leader on the 1526 Narváez expedition, was probably the first European to visit Area III (in 1529) along with several companions who were moving westward along the Texas coast. Five years later, Dorantes's friend, Cabeza de Vaca, followed the same coastal route westward into Area III. After Cabeza de Vaca's visit, no European expeditions recorded a visit to Area III until Robert Cavelier, Sieur de La Salle, landed on the central Texas coast in 1685 to establish his fort and colony on Garcitas Creek in Area III.

In search of La Salle, Governor Alonso de León of Coahuila led the first overland visit to Area III in 1689, and the governor returned in 1690. In 1691 and 1692 General Domingo Terán and Captain Francisco

Martínez, serving under Terán, visited Area III. In addition, in the early 1700s, the Spanish governor Martín de Alarcón and the Marqués de San Miguel de Aguayo visited the Matagorda Bay area on their expeditions to Texas, and in 1720 the Frenchman Jean Béranger visited Aransas Pass in Area III by ship.

Review of Sixteenth- and Seventeenth-Century Spanish and French Expedition Documents

According to his own account, Cabeza de Vaca traveled down the Texas coast from a point near Galveston Island to Matagorda Bay and into Area III in the fall of 1534.[4] Cabeza de Vaca identified by name two coastal tribes, the Doguene and Quevene, who lived between the Brazos River and lower Matagorda Bay. He encountered the Doguene in Area I several miles east of Matagorda Bay but gives limited information about the tribe. The Quevene lived in Area III, farther southwest along the coast, principally on the southwest side of Matagorda Bay, called the Bay of Espiritu Santo by Cabeza de Vaca. At the time of Cabeza de Vaca's visit to the area, and perhaps for decades earlier, the Doguene and the Quevene were at war.[5] On his trip along the coast, Cabeza de Vaca was visiting the Doguene camp when the Quevene attacked and killed three tribesmen and wounded others. Early the next morning, the Doguene retaliated by traveling westward to the homeland of the Quevene and killing five Quevene and wounding many others. This hostile relationship between the Quevene on Matagorda Bay and their neighbors to the east suggests that the eastern cultural boundary of the Matagorda Bay Indians was near the Colorado River during the early 1500s. This boundary generally coincides with the location of the northeastern boundary of the Karankawa identified by Robert Ricklis.[6]

When he first met the Quevene, Cabeza de Vaca inquired about his Spanish comrades who had worked their way westward along the coast about five years earlier. The Quevene told him that members of their tribe had murdered three of the Spaniards because the captives had left one Indian family to live with another. When asked how the surviving Spaniards were living, the Indians said that they were treated like slaves. To demonstrate how the other Spaniards were treated, the Quevene began slapping Cabeza de Vaca and his friend Lope de Oviedo and pressed an arrow point into Cabeza de Vaca's chest saying that they might kill him as they had killed his friends.

A short time later, when a visiting band of Mariame came to gather pecans at a nearby river (probably the Guadalupe), Cabeza de Vaca slipped away from the Quevene and joined the Mariame to live in Area II. At that time, the Mariame were holding Cabeza de Vaca's friend, Andrés

Dorantes, and the two Spaniards lived as slaves in Area II until they were able to escape in 1535.

Dorantes had also visited and lived with the Quevene in Area III a short time before escaping to live with the Mariame. Dorantes said that while in the services of the Quevene, he had been severely abused and had fled more than fifty miles to a river where the Mariame lived (in Area II). Cabeza de Vaca's account gives no further information on the range of the Quevene, and his life with the Mariame was covered in the previous chapter.

Although the men from Moscoso's command probably visited the coastal barrier islands in Area III on their 1543 voyage along the Texas coast to Pánuco, the historical record of the Moscoso trip along the coast is not sufficiently detailed to provide information on native coastal people in Area III.[7]

The French Arrive

The next recorded accounts of Europeans visiting Area III are found in the chronicles of La Salle's 1685 expedition to the Texas Gulf Coast.[8] On January 14, 1685, La Salle's two ships, the *Aimable* and the *Belle,* were located at 28° 51' north latitude several miles east of the Area III coastline. As La Salle continued to sail west for another three hours, his chronicler, Henri Joutel, reported seeing deer and a herd of bison. La Salle and members of his present party, who had been with him also on his 1682 discovery expedition down the Mississippi (including Gabriel Minime, Sieur de Barbier, and the priest Zénobe Membré), had seen and killed bison on that exploration. But for most of the French soldiers and colonist, this was their first sighting of bison.

The French party continued to see more Indians and bison along Matagorda Peninsula in Area III as the two ships sailed farther south-west. On January 16 the party arrived at the entrance to Matagorda Bay, later called Pass Cavallo by the Spaniards. Joutel noted the distinctive high sand cliffs or mounds near the northern tip of Matagorda Island and cited the location at 28° 20' north latitude, a projection reasonably close to the mark. Joutel's comments describing the distinctive sand mounds south of the mouth of Matagorda Bay are very similar to the description of the area made about 150 years earlier by Oviedo.[9] The description also fits the landscape at the entrance to Matagorda Bay today.

On January 17 La Salle continued to sail westward beyond Matagorda Bay to the southern tip of Matagorda Island, where La Salle, Joutel, and some of the troops landed. During a search for fresh water, which was successful, the men killed several deer and over 100 other unidentified game animals. In early February Joutel and La Salle's nephew, Crevel

Morenger, marched a company of about 130 men back up the length of Matagorda Island toward Matagorda Bay. At the same time, La Salle turned his three vessels about and sailed offshore in the same easterly direction.

During the ten-day, eighty-mile hike up the coastline, the Frenchmen encountered no Natives, but the troops located numerous water holes that had been dug in the sand by local Indians, Native tracks indicating their recent presence, and campsites where Indians had made fires.

On February 14 La Salle landed near Pass Cavallo, and five days later Joutel records La Salle's first encounter with Matagorda Bay Indians, whom the expedition member Pierre Meunier later identified as the Cauquesi (or Caucosi). When La Salle sent a detail of soldiers to secure a log for use in building a canoe, a large party of Indians suddenly appeared before the detail. The soldiers, stricken with terror, raced back to inform La Salle that the local Natives had captured several soldiers. La Salle quickly gathered a number of armed men and proceeded to investigate. When he arrived at the scene and saw that the Indians were advancing directly toward him, La Salle urged his men to continue their advance, marching to a drumbeat. The Indians started to turn and run, so La Salle ordered several men (including Joutel) to lay down their arms, and La Salle did the same. The natives followed suit and came up to La Salle with the Frenchmen they were holding captive.

Joutel describes the friendly gestures that the natives made—rubbing their hands on their own chests (over their hearts) and then rubbing their hands over the chests and arms of the Frenchmen. This meant, according to Joutel, that they were pleased to see the Frenchmen, who responded by repeating the same form of greeting to the Indians. In March 1682 La Salle had received the same form of gestures of affection from the friendly Acansa Indians on the Mississippi when he departed their village on his discovery expedition to the Gulf.

La Salle and the Texas coastal Indians communicated by the use of signs, but when the Frenchmen vocalized a word or two, the Indians replied with deep guttural sounds. The natives also made a clucking sound with their tongue, according to Joutel, similar to that made by Frenchmen giving directions to a horse.

After the animated greetings were over, La Salle returned to the French camp accompanied by several of the Indian leaders. Four soldiers remained with the large group of Indians. At camp, after offering the Indian leaders food and drink, La Salle asked them about the location of the Mississippi River. They knew nothing, indicating by signs that inland there was good hunting for bison. When the Indians were ready to leave his camp, La Salle gave them hatchets and knives and, along with Joutel and others, conducted the Indians back to the place where the French soldiers had been left. In the meantime, however, the Indians had taken the four soldiers to their own camp about four miles away. Therefore, La Salle and his men were forced to continue their march to recover these soldiers at the Indian camp.

Joutel writes that the large Indian camp visited included about fifty huts covered with reed mats and bison hides. It was located on a point of the bayshore. Joutel adds that the huts were built with poles bent like staves of a barrel and looked like large ovens. Based on the number and size of the huts, the village was probably occupied by 200 to 300 Indians. The women wore only animal skins from their waists to their knees and had markings (probably tattoos) on their faces. Most men were naked, but several had a deerskin slung over their back. Joutel admired the way the women placed one foot on the head of a dolphin and quickly cut up the marine mammal using a sharp piece of flint as a knife. The village also had about forty large and small dugout canoes.

La Salle told the coastal Indians that he was looking for a large river, and he named the tribes that he had visited on the lower Mississippi. When La Salle made a sign that he had met some Indians with flat heads, an old Indian used signs to indicate that he was familiar with the Indians who had flat heads and demonstrated with a bow that he and his people had gone to war with them. These "Flathead" Indians may have been some tribe on the lower Mississippi whom La Salle's party had encountered and called Flathead in 1682. We should also note that the Palaquechare Indians in Area I also reported to Joutel and La Salle that they were going to war with the Flatheads. After securing his four soldiers, La Salle returned to base camp.

Several weeks later, realizing that more canoes were needed, La Salle dispatched several men to secure canoes from local Indians. During negotiations at a nearby Indian camp, the soldiers saw that the Indians had acquired pieces of iron and blankets from a nearby grounded French cargo ship. Indian women were wearing the French cloth as skirts. After receiving this report, La Salle ordered his nephew Morenger to return to the Indian camp and demand canoes in exchange for the French goods taken. Instead the Frenchmen frightened the Indians into abandoning their camp, leaving behind a few blankets, animal skins, and canoes. The soldiers seized the goods, including the Indian canoes, which they tried to paddle back to their camp.

The Frenchmen, however, immediately ran into problems trying to return to camp in the Indian canoes. There were no oars to paddle the canoes, and the Frenchmen did not know how to punt the canoes with the long poles used by the Indians. Unable to propel or steer the canoes, the soldiers decided to spend the night near the bayshore not far from the Indians' recently abandoned camp. As it was a cold night, the small French party lit a fire and posted a sentry; everyone, including the sentry, went to sleep.

Meanwhile, the Indians returned to their camp, found that the Frenchmen had taken their canoes, blankets, and animal skins, and assumed that war had been declared. Seeking revenge, the Indians tracked the party and found the fire and sleeping Frenchmen. Under cover of darkness, the Natives attacked, using clubs and peppering the campsite with arrows. Joutel adds that immediately before the attack, the Indians uttered their usual cry or whoop. This same form of war cry La Salle's men had heard on more than one occasion on the lower Mississippi in 1682. Morenger and several others returned the fire, and the war was on, a conflict that continued to destabilize the French colony during the next four years.

The next day La Salle learned that two of his best men had been killed in the Indian attack and that two others, including his nephew Morenger, were seriously wounded. Although the Frenchmen were concerned that the arrows that had stuck the two wounded men had been poisoned (as were the arrows used by some natives in the Caribbean Islands), this was not the case. There is no known report of poisoned arrows being used by tribes living near Matagorda Bay. Joutel wrote that after the scrape, the Indians moved farther inland from the bay entrance and La Salle forbade anyone from having any dealings with the local Indians. When natives thereafter sought a meeting, the Frenchmen fired gunshots in the air to turn them away.

In the late summer of 1686 La Salle returned to Area III from an unsuccessful expedition in search of the Mississippi with word that he had met and lived for a time with the Cenis (the Hasinai Caddo), who had supplied him with horses, corn, and beans. The exact date of La Salle's return is not recorded by Joutel, but presumably it was in the late summer because Joutel notes that the heat was so unbearable that La Salle decided to wait until the cooler months to explore again.

During La Salle's stay at the post in late 1686, he recognized that hostilities with the local Native population had continued despite his earlier raid on their villages. For example, in the fall of 1686, a band of Indians was encountered by Lieutenant Barbier, La Salle's Indian guide Nika, and eight other men on a hunting trip near the post. Seeing that there were only a few Frenchmen in the hunting party, the Indians attacked and then retreated with one of their number wounded or killed. A few days later, ten Indians ambushed and killed a soldier near the stockade.

In early January 1687 La Salle left the fort on his last journey—this time taking both Joutel and the priest Douay with him. Joutel maintained a daily account on this trip, including notes on the direction and number of leagues traveled each day. With Douay's account also available, the complementary records permit us to plot with confidence La Salle's route on contemporary large-scale topographical maps. After La Salle's men departed the bay, only about twenty soldiers and colonists, including seven women and girls, remained at the post.

On the second day out (January 13), Joutel reports several large herds of bison and other game. Earlier Joutel had reported 5,000 to 6,000 bison in herds only a few miles north of the post. La Salle crossed the Lavaca River about twelve miles north of the bay and only a few miles above the convergence of the Navidad and Lavaca Rivers. The party camped that evening about a mile east of the Lavaca. Joutel says that a very large (but unspecified) number of Natives had camped in the area a few days before La Salle's visit. Joutel's comment was based on his count of the number of pole hut structures that the Natives had left. It should be emphasized that only limited information is available for use in estimating the population of Indian tribes and that information such as the number and size of Indian huts in a deserted Indian encampment is critical information in estimating encampment populations.

The next day (January 14), La Salle saw a lone Indian on foot, closely following a moving herd of bison, and the leader directed a soldier to mount a pack horse and capture the Native. When the horseman rode up, the Indian stopped and followed the mounted Frenchman's directions to turn back toward La Salle's party. The Native was visibly fearful, and for good reason; as Joutel comments, normally when an Indian fell into the hands of an enemy, "no mercy is given." Although some members of the expedition party wanted to kill the captive, La Salle treated him with kindness, mindful of the vulnerability of the few colonists remaining at the post and the vengeful nature of the Natives. La Salle told the Indian that he wanted no more war and asked the Indian to sit by the warm fire and smoke with him. The Indian did this but continued to tremble. The Indian told La Salle by the use of signs that earlier some Frenchmen had fired shots at him near the mouth of the Lavaca River. The Frenchmen gave the Native some small gifts and then signaled that he could resume his hunt. Joutel says that members of his party admired the manner in which the captive took his leave—moving very slowly and deliberately at first, until he was out of range, and then doubling his pace.

Soon thereafter the expedition party was surprised by a number of Natives advancing toward them. Acting quickly, La Salle placed his gun on the ground and moved toward them, motioning them to come forward. The Indian leader moved toward La Salle and for the first time

Joutel describes briefly the physique of the coastal natives as very fine, adding that they "seemed quite human." Caresses and strokes were exchanged, as the Frenchmen and Natives had done when La Salle first landed on the coast.

After smoking with the visitors, La Salle told them he wanted peace and distributed gifts. While the soldiers prepared a brush barricade around the evening camp, fourteen other Indians slowly approached the camp. These visitors said that they had heard the news that the Frenchmen were no longer making war and they approved of the peace proposal. After offering the Natives something to smoke and some small exchange items, La Salle asked them to leave, pointing out that they were ready for sleep. At this time La Salle's party was about fifteen to twenty miles north of the bay area, near the northern boundary of Area III. The next Indian encounter occurred farther north in Area II, beyond the coverage of this chapter.

The Frenchmen Pierre Talon and his younger brother Jean-Baptiste provide additional information about the coastal Indians and the fauna and flora in Area III.[10] These observations were recorded in testimony that the brothers gave in France in 1698. During the interrogation, the Talon brothers name two tribes that were at war with La Salle: the Clamcoeh, who the boys say almost never left the seashore, and the Temerlouan, who lived a short distance north of the bay. The brothers add that La Salle's men had taken the canoes of the Temerlouan and that the theft of the canoes incited the war. If the Temerlouan had canoes on or near the bay area, the tribe was probably affiliated in some way with the tribe currently called the Karankawa.

The boys say that the inland area north of Area III was populated with numerous small tribes, each with its own name and language, and the tribes were often at war. The boys observe that the mild climate contributed to the Natives' longevity and good health. Using medicinal herbs, which were plentiful, the Indians cured any illness and healed wounds. The Clamcoeh are described as being much more cruel and barbaric than the Caddo, and, unlike the Caddo, they had no fixed village location. The Clamcoeh quickly erected their huts using two forked branches and a stick crossbar that they covered with prepared bison skins.

The coastal natives, according to the young Frenchmen, were natural clowns and buffoons, given to drunkenness, dancing, and singing. For musical instruments, they scraped a notched stick or rasp with another stick and shook gourds filled with pebbles. These instruments are similar to those played by Indians from the Rio Grande to the Mississippi, as will be noted later.

The Talons said that the Clamcoeh were well built and that a deformed child was killed and buried immediately. The healthy child was tattooed. The boys say that the natives used French pins and needles for tattooing them. Both Talon boys emphasize that they spoke the language of the tribe with whom they lived and could communicate easily by signs with other Indian tribes who spoke different languages.

One of the most astonishing and revealing stories that Jean tells about his captors involves a daring raid that the Clamcoeh conducted against a band of Caddo in East Texas. According to Jean, the Matagorda Bay Indians traveled by canoe from their homeland on the western shore of Matagorda Bay to a large river farther east, probably the Colorado River. Here the tribe left in hiding the French captive children along with the aged, women, and young Indian children while the warriors executed a raid against a band of East Texas Caddo called the "Ayenni."

After six weeks, the Clamcoeh returned to the lower Colorado with several horses, forty to fifty scalps, and thirty to forty slaves—several of whom were eaten at a feast celebrating the victory. As Jean's brother Pierre was staying with the Hasinai at the time of the raid, he was able to confirm that the raid occurred and that captives were taken.

Jean's story represents the only known firsthand observation by a European of ceremonial cannibalism by the Karankawa. There were, as will be noted, other firsthand accounts of ceremonial cannibalism in other study areas, in Mexico, and on the Mississippi. The story also confirms the deep animosity that existed between the Area III bands and the Caddo and the fact that the coastal Indians were sufficiently familiar with the country over 200 miles northeast of the bay to execute such a successful military strike in the heartland of the Caddo.

Spaniards Return

This review of early French accounts of Area III Indians concludes with the testimony of the Talon brothers. Documents prepared in connection with Spanish expeditions that entered Area III in response to the French threat will now be reviewed. One of the important Spanish maritime expeditions entered Area III in the spring of 1687, a few months after La Salle undertook his final overland expedition, while Fort St. Louis was still occupied by French colonists.

In late December 1686 Spanish authorities dispatched two ships to search for La Salle's settlement, thought to be located somewhere on the central Gulf Coast. Juan Enríquez Barroto, the pilot of Captain Martín Rívas's ship, the *Piragua*, maintained a diary of the trip.[11] The ships sailed northward from Veracruz along the present-day Tamaulipas coastline, where local Indians were captured and taken aboard to serve as interpreters. On March 14, 1687, Enríquez records that the two ships visited three Indian camps near the mouth of the Rio Grande. About a week later (March 20), the expedition party apparently reached modern-day Corpus Christi Bay, where a number of unidentified Indians on the nearby sand dunes greeted the Spaniards. Most of the Indians were bald ("Pelones"), but the captured translator could not speak their language.

On April 3 the Spanish ships reached latitude 28° 23' north and the entrance to Matagorda Bay; the next day Enríquez records finding the remains of La Salle's ship, the *Belle*. Two days later the diarist reports a serious encounter with the coastal Natives on the northeast shore of Matagorda Bay. Initially the Spaniards were received in a friendly manner, although the Natives asked the visitors to disarm, and then the Indians conducted an inspection, searching under the Spaniards' coats for pistols or cutlasses. Again the Tamaulipan interpreters were of no help, and communication was conducted by signs.

The coastal bay Indians were distrustful and refused an invitation to board the Spanish ships. When the Indians saw more Spanish soldiers approaching, they returned to their nearby encampment after taking a Spanish ensign captive. A fight ensued in which the Spaniards attempted to capture an Indian, but they could not subdue the Native because he was "of great statute and very robust." The Indian whom the Spaniards attempted to capture wielded his knife and wounded three soldiers with it before he summoned help from other Indians, who arrived on the scene shooting arrows. When Spanish reinforcements arrived, muskets blazing, the Indians fled with several of their men wounded.

After this hostile encounter, the Spanish ships remained at the bay (unmindful of the nearby French colony) until the wind was favorable for sailing back into Gulf waters. On April 12, 1687, the ships continued along the central Texas coast beyond the boundary of Area III.

In late 1688 Juan Isidro de Pardiñas, the governor of Chihuahua in Parral, requested the Cibola and Jumano Indians living near La Junta to investigate the coastal area where the tribes annually traveled in the spring and summer to hunt and trade.[12] The Natives were to report on the location and condition of the new French colony. During this scouting expedition for the Spanish governor, the Cibola visited Area III and found the destroyed Fort St. Louis. From the report of the investigation, it is clear that the Cibola (and probably the Jumano) had visited Area III previously, but no coastal Indians were encountered by the Cibola in Area III.

In the spring of 1689 Governor Alonso de León of Coahuila commanded the first Spanish overland expedition from northern Mexico to enter Area III.[13] De León arrived at the bay a few months after the post had been raided by local Indians. The Frenchman Jean Géry, who had been captured by the Spaniards near the Rio Grande a year earlier, helped guide the Spanish troops to the French fort and from the fort overland to the entrance of the bay. According to his own testimony, Géry had landed on the Texas coast with La Salle. Soon after their arrival, La Salle commissioned Géry to make friends with and pacify the tribes living to the north and the west of the bay area. Géry was therefore familiar with the tribes living north of the bay in Area II, and he was also familiar with the tribes living to the southwest near the Rio Grande in Area IV. In addition to Géry, two Indians from Coahuila, one a Pacpul and the second a Quem, were also employed as guides. Both Indian guides proved to be very familiar with the route from the Rio Grande to Area III.

On his 1689 trip to the bay, Governor De León visited several Indian camps located sixty to eighty miles inland from the bay area, but the governor does not report any encounter with Area II Natives near the fort. On his 1690 expedition, De León returned to the bay before visiting the Caddo Indians in East Texas, but again the governor reports no contact with Natives in the area. The governor visited the area again on his return trip from the Caddo in June 1690 to rescue three Talon children from the coastal tribe that he called the Cascosi.[14]

De León writes that on June 20, 1690, the day before reaching the Cascosi encampment where the children were being held, he traveled about twenty-five miles southward toward the bay area. During that day, the Spanish party encountered in the southern part of Area II the friendly Caisquetebanna, and this tribe provided guides to lead the Spaniards to the coastal Indians holding the French children in Area III. As the Caisquetebanna were camped more than thirty miles north of the upper bay area, it is likely that they were culturally and linguistically unassociated with the coastal Indians. De León crossed the "Arroyo of the French" (present-day Garcitas Creek), passing the old French fort area. Then he camped on a small creek a short distance southwest of the stream that the Indians called Canoe Creek, probably present-day Placedo Creek.

The following morning (June 21), De León met two Indians, presumably Karankawa, on horseback riding north. The mounted Indians turned around and guided the Spaniards to the Indian encampment where Marie-Madeleine, Robert, and Lucien Talon were held. De León writes that the camp was on the headland of a small bay, probably San Antonio Bay. An argument with the Indians ensued, and a fight erupted. The Indians began to shoot arrows, wounding two horses; De León's men killed four Indians and wounded another two. De León then withdrew with the three French children to the campsite that he had occupied the night before. The next day, with the young French girl and her two younger brothers, De León's party rode hard until dark, covering over thirty miles across present-day Chicolete Prairie along the left bank of the Guadalupe. This put them beyond the customary residential range of the coastal Indians and out of Area III. At the Guadalupe crossing in Area II, De León met the main body of his expedition and proceeded back to Monclova.

The following year, the Spanish government dispatched another expedition from Monclova to the East Texas mission field. This force was led by Governor Domingo Terán de los Ríos and included the veteran priest Damián Massanet.[15] One objective of Governor Terán's 1691 expedition to Texas was to recover from the coastal Indians the remaining French children who were being held captive—two boys and a young teenage girl. One source of information about the French girl was Jacques Grollet, who had testified to Alonso de León that the coastal Indians had told him that a young girl and three boys were being held.

Terán's party included Captain Francisco Martínez, who had served with De León the year before on the trip to the bay to capture the first three French children. The governor's party also included the captured Frenchman Pierre Meunier, now serving as a guide and interpreter. When Terán reached Area II and the Colorado River in early July, Captain Martínez and a detachment of twenty men were dispatched to the bay to recover the remaining French boys and young French girl and to rendezvous at the bay with Captain Gregorio de Salinas Varona, who was in command of a contingent of fifty additional troops. Salinas and his men were scheduled to arrive at the bay by ship. Although the Martínez diary does not add any new tribal names to those known to live in the coastal area, the captain's account of his route confirms a number of significant place-names and geographic locations, and his comments on the disposition of the French girl are of special interest.[16]

As Martínez had been with De León in 1690, he knew the crossing area of the Colorado River in present-day Fayette County and could identify with ease the distinctive high bluff near the crossing. De León had named it Jesús María y Joseph Buena Vista, and today it is known as Monument Hill. Martínez reported camping near "Buena Vista" on the first day out, July 3, after traveling about eighteen miles along the west bank of the Colorado. The party continued riding southward toward the bay for the next three days, but Martínez does not report encountering any Indians en route. On July 6 Martínez crossed the Lavaca River, which he called the Cane River.

On the 7th, after traveling another thirteen miles south of the Lavaca, the party crossed Garcitas Creek, called "Frenchmen's Creek" by Martínez. This distance and direction traveled southward between the Lavaca River and Garcitas Creek is consistent with the distance given by Joutel when La Salle's party left the French post on Garcitas Creek in early 1687 marching northward to the Lavaca River. The information is also consistent with the distance and direction given by De León moving southward in 1690 when he crossed first the Lavaca and then "Frenchmen's Creek" on his way to recover the first three French children. Two leagues down Garcitas Creek, Martínez found the location of the old French fort and saw a lone Indian whom Meunier brought back to the Spaniards' camp. The local Indian said, through Meunier, acting as interpreter, that he was from the bay and had held the young French girl (Marie-Madeleine Talon) before she was rescued the previous year. Martínez found no remaining signs of French occupation at the former location of the fort. The same local Indian told Martínez that he was holding one of the remaining French boys but that he was prepared to return the boy the next day.

The following day, Martínez moved his camp and large remuda of horses to secure a fresher supply of water. The water in Garcitas Creek near the former French post was brackish, unfit for continued consumption by either humans or horses. Earlier, when the small French community was located there, the Frenchmen received a freshwater supply from a nearby spring, but Martínez moved about four miles southeast to a small creek that had an associated large pond of fresh water.

On the 9th, Martínez proceeded to a bayshore location near the Indian village where the three Talon children had been rescued in 1690. There Meunier spoke with local Indians who were sending smoke signals and preparing to depart. Martínez, through Meunier, asked the natives to return the remaining two French boys and the young French girl and offered them horses in exchange. The Indians responded that they did not have either the French boys or the young girl with them, but that they would give notice of the offer to Indians in nearby camps. When Martínez returned to his base camp, he was told that an Indian had visited the camp and informed them that the following day he would return with one of the French boys. The Native asked the Frenchmen to meet him at a location on the bayshore about two miles from Martínez's camp. He also gave a soldier two arrow points and a small piece of bison skin to so inform Martínez.

The following day (the 10th), Martínez, Meunier, and several soldiers went to the appointed location where they met several Indians whom they had seen the day before. The Spaniards were successful in recovering only one of the two French boys, Jean Talon. Three of the Indians at the meeting returned to the Spanish camp with Martínez to obtain a horse and a few other gifts. But Martínez held one of the Indians as a hostage at camp, and the other two were told that their companion would be released only when the other boy and the teenage girl were surrendered.

Two days later the Indians returned with the second French boy, Eustache Bréman, but they said that there were no other French captives in the bay area and that the young girl had moved inland beyond their control.

With the two French boys, Martínez then proceeded to retrace his tracks toward the Colorado, but he left the bay without the young French girl and without word from Captain Salinas Varona. When Terán later visited the bay area on the same expedition, he did not report any Indian encounters in Area III.

1700S

After Terán's expedition, no Spanish or French troops entered Area III until 1718, when Governor Martín de Alarcón visited Tres Palacios Bay in the eastern section of Area III.[17] The first coastal Indians encountered by Alarcón were called Caocose (Cascosi); they quickly dove into the bay and swam across a half-mile-wide cove. The following day Alarcón met other Caocose who were friendlier. These coastal Natives arrived in a large canoe that accommodated sixteen men, women, and children. Gifts of clothing and tobacco made by the Spaniards were exchanged for the Indians' dried fish. Soon after the meeting, Alarcón returned to the northeast and beyond Area III.

In the summer of 1720 a French naval expedition visited Area III and reported on the inhabitants. This expedition was led by a French naval captain, Jean Béranger.[18] Béranger sailed from New Orleans westward along the Texas coast beyond Matagorda Bay (called St. Bernard Bay) to Aransas Bay northeast of Corpus Christi. The captain spent over a week in the Aransas Bay area trading with the local Indians. Asphalt balls found near the water were used to repair his ship. He records that the Natives did not cultivate any crops but rather were dependent on local marine resources. He describes the Indians as tall and shapely with a handsome countenance. Some men were over six feet in height. Béranger visited a Native community center that he calls a market town populated with over 500 residents. But he says that they had no chief.

The captain writes that he also visited "a small permanent village of about a dozen large, quite round huts."[19] Here he noticed the use of mulberry tree bark to make rope. The village was used as a storage depot for dried fish to be consumed the following winter. It appeared to Béranger that these Indians seldom ventured far inland, where he says their enemies lived.

At the close of the week, the French vessel left the area to return eastward to the Mississippi. While Captain Béranger was visiting Aransas Bay, Governor San Miguel de Aguayo was preparing to lead his Spanish troops from Monclova to East Texas, which the French then held. In 1721 Aguayo successfully pushed the French out of East Texas and back east of the Red River in Louisiana. By January 1722 Governor Aguayo was back in San Antonio, preparing to visit Area III and to construct a Spanish fort on the site of the former French post of Fort St. Louis.[20] Although the governor's efforts to construct the fort were successful, the diary account of the governor's inspection visits provide no significant new ethnographic information regarding the Area III Native population.

Archeological and Anthropological Studies

In addition to the ethnographic record found in expedition diaries and associated primary documents, a very competent late nineteenth-century anthropological study of the central Texas coastal Indians is available. This study was prepared in 1891 by Albert S. Gatschet for the Peabody Museum of American Archaeology and Ethnology.[21] Gatschet's study includes essays prepared by Charles A. Hammond of Massachusetts and by Alice W. Oliver, a "well-educated" resident of Matagorda Bay. Hammond describes, among other subjects, the construction and use of Karankawa dugout canoes. Hammond writes that the coastal Indians poled or punted canoes by employing the pole while standing on the stern. Hammond also describes how the Karankawa constructed huts with slender fifteen- to eighteen-foot willow poles bent toward the center and secured at the top with straps of deerskin. The huts were covered with deerskins or with the skin of a bear, wildcat, or panther.

Oliver writes that Karankawa men were tall and strongly built but with slender hands and feet. They were not dark, and many had delicate features. The women were short and stout. The men wore a waistcloth and a blanket or skin thrown over one shoulder. They spoke a guttural language. They also communicated by sending smoke signals from small fires at night or during the day. These comments confirm several of the observations of the coastal Indians recorded by Henri Joutel.

Oliver describes three musical instruments used by the Indians— a large gourd filled with small stones, a notched rasp, and a flute. The Mississippi and Southwest Indians played these same instruments plus drums made of skins stretched over earthen vessels, but Oliver does not mention the use of a drum.

Two archeological overviews recently conducted in the San Antonio Bay and Matagorda Bay areas also help interpret the historic record compiled by La Salle's chroniclers and Spanish diarists. The first is a cultural resource investigation of the San Antonio Bay area where the Cascosi (Karankawa) Indians released three Talon children to Governor De León in 1690.[22]

The overview was prepared in 1992 by Richard A. Weinstein and his associates. This work includes a study of the paleogeography of the lower Guadalupe River and San Antonio Bay region. In contrast to the site-specific Blue Bayou study, Weinstein's review involves primarily a synthesis and an assessment of a large number of sites previously excavated in the limited geographic area and thus is similar in coverage to an archeological overview.

One site given attention by Weinstein and his associates that is of special interest is identified as 41CL2, which is located in Area III on a small cove that the Guadalupe River flows into before entering San Antonio Bay. The Indian encampment visited to recover French children by De León in 1690 and by Martínez in 1691 was located in the same area, near the head of San Antonio Bay. The investigator and his associates conclude that the location served as a principal Indian encampment area on San Antonio Bay during the period AD 700 to 1700 and perhaps thereafter. The study assessed numerous artifacts, including Indian pottery, arrowheads, and faunal remains, that suggest the site was occupied by traditional coastal tribes. Thus, according to this archeological study, coastal Indians' use and occupation of the upper San Antonio Bay area occurred during the prehistoric period dating from at least as early as AD 700.

Another archeological study that contributes to the interpretation of the historical accounts of the Matagorda Bay Indians was also prepared by Richard A. Weinstein and his associates.[23] Published in 1994, two years after the first study was released, this work presents a regional assessment of the lower Lavaca River, including the area in which the Navidad and Lavaca Rivers converge. The project did not include the Garcitas Creek area (the location of La Salle's settlement), but it did include areas where Joutel, Douay, De León, and Martínez reported seeing Matagorda Bay Indians in Area III. On his 1686 and 1687 expeditions to the northeast, La Salle also crossed the lower Lavaca, and Joutel reported that bison were frequently hunted by both the French colonists and local Indians in the same area.

The 1994 archeological study is significant in several respects. First, it confirms that the same aboriginal ceramic composition and design features are found in both the San Antonio Bay area and the lower Lavaca River area. Second, the tabulation of faunal remains analyzed in the study from sites along the lower Lavaca match the description of wildlife near the bay as reported by Joutel, indicating that some species reported by French chroniclers had been present in the bay area for several centuries or more. Both the archeological study and Joutel's report indicate the prehistoric and historic presence of bison, deer, rabbits, squirrels, box and soft-shell turtles, lizards, rats, mice, viperous snakes, turkey, grouse, quail, ducks, geese, swans, gar, catfish, and flounder.

Conclusions

A review of historical sources indicates that the central Texas coastal Indian today referred to as Karankawa resided in a coastal area that extended from the eastern Matagorda Bay area in Matagorda County south and westward to northern Baffin Bay in Kleberg County. During the historic period, French and Spanish writers identified by name at least eighteen tribes that either resided in or visited the study area. These tribes are listed alphabetically in the supplement at the end of this chapter.

Ethnohistorians have attempted to determine whether these tribes identified by name by Cabeza de Vaca and by La Salle's chroniclers were the same tribes as those identified by similar or slightly different names in other seventeenth- and eighteenth-century documents. No attempt has been made here to clarify this subject. It should be noted, however, that the name Karankawa is a relatively recent one, a collective tribal name that emerged in the eighteenth century. It is appropriate that a common name was given to the tribes and bands living together in Area III because the natives shared a common and distinctive cultural heritage and a language that may date to the first centuries of the first millennium AD or earlier.

The Karankawa may have considered the Muruame as friends and later the Apache as at least a temporary ally when the Karankawa revolted at the original site of the La Bahía mission. The record is also clear that the Karankawa were bitter enemies of the Caddo. Although the historical record suggests that the Karankawa remained near the central Texas coastal area, their raid on the East Texas Caddo reported by Jean Talon indicates that the tribe was knowledgeable of the country to the north and east for at least 200 miles. This raid and a comment made by the old warrior that he had fought the Flatheads suggest that the Karankawa, like other Texas Indian tribes, were more cosmopolitan than many historians have suggested.

The report by Béranger and the archeological study of the residential site at the head of San Antonio Bay both suggest that the central Texas coastal Indians may have occupied substantial community areas even though they were not horticultural. An abundance of local seafood resources may have offered this alternative lifestyle to some members.

This chapter supplement lists alphabetically the names of Indian tribes or bands reported in diary accounts referenced in the Area III study. Some entries identify Native groups that were residents of Area III, but other entries name foreign tribes who were reported visiting the area for purposes of trading or hunting. The principal objective of the supplement is to locate geographically as precisely as possible (usually by county) where the Native group was encountered. Entries also include the name of the leader or diarist on the expedition and the date of the encounter.

The following sources were consulted in the compilation of this supplement: Alex D. Krieger, *We Came Naked and Barefoot: The Journey of Cabeza de Vaca across North America;* Juan Bautista Chapa, *Texas and Northeastern Mexico, 1630–1690;* Herbert E. Bolton, ed., *Spanish Exploration in the Southwest, 1542–1706;* William C. Foster, ed., *Spanish Expeditions into Texas, 1689–1768;* Isaac J. Cox, ed., *The Journeys of René Robert Cavelier, Sieur de La Salle;* Robert S. Weddle, *La Salle, the Mississippi, and the Gulf: Three Primary Documents;* and William C. Foster, ed., *The La Salle Expedition to Texas: The Journal of Henri Joutel, 1684–1687.*

1. Apache. In 1724 Governor Fernando Pérez reported from the presidio on Garcitas Creek in Area III that the Apache had visited the nearby mission Indians at La Bahía and had joined them in revolt. The local Area III Indians identified at the mission included the Cujane, Coapite (Guapite), and Karankawa.

2. Ayennis (Hasinai?). Jean Talon reports that captive slaves from a western Caddo band called Ayennis were returned to Area III as a result of the successful raid by the Karankawa, who at the time were also holding him and a second French boy as captives. In 1718 a Hasinai guide was used to direct Alarcón's party into Area III where they encountered the Caocose (Cascosi).

3. Bahamo. Douay identified the Bahamo as neighbors at Fort St. Louis and as a wandering tribe with whom La Salle was at war. Douay wrote that on the first day's march from Fort St. Louis in January 1687, La Salle's party met the Bahamo, who were en route to war with a tribe called the Erigoanna. La Salle offered a peaceful alliance with the Bahamo. This report is consistent with the account by Joutel, who also reported (but did not identify by name) that a local bay-area tribe was encountered soon after leaving the post on the 1687 expedition.

Joutel said that La Salle's 1687 expedition departed the fort on January 12; two days later (according to Douay) the party met the Bahamo and the Quinet in Jackson County about nineteen miles northeast of the French post. On January 21 La Salle met, according to Joutel, the Ebahamo, who were friends of the Caddo and the Jumano. The encounter with the Ebahamo occurred about fifty-five miles north of the bay area in Area II. Although some current writers consider the Ebahamo and Bahamo to be the same tribe, Joutel and Douay clearly did not.

4. Caisquetebanna. De León wrote that when his expedition party approached the bay area (and Area III) in June 1690 after visiting the Hasinai, the friendly Caisquetebanna in Lavaca County provided guides to lead him to the Karankawa (called "Cascosis" by De León), who held three French children. After arriving in Area III near the former French post with the Caisquetebanna guides, two mounted Indians met De León and escorted him to the encampment where the children were held. Chapa's story indicates that neighboring tribes to the north occasionally visited the Karankawa and also confirms that the Karankawa had horses by 1690.

5. Cascosi (Caocose, Cauguese, Cauquesi, Caucosi, Clamcoeh, Karankawa). In 1690 De León recovered three French children at the head of San Antonio Bay in Area III from the Cascosi, a name used by the Spaniards to identify the Karankawa. Pierre Meunier refers to the coastal tribe as the "Cauquesi." In 1718 Martín de Alarcón met the "Caocose" in Area III on the northeastern shore of Matagorda Bay.

6. Cibola. According to testimony taken by the governor of Nueva Vizcaya in Parral in early 1689, a Cibola scouting party visited Area III earlier that year and found the ruins of Fort St. Louis. Although the Cibola encountered no local Indians in the immediate area on the trip, the report confirms that Karankawa country was known to and had been visited frequently by Native people living on the Big Bend and in present-day northern Chihuahua.

7. Coapite (Guapite). The Coapite were among the Karankawan bands resident at the Spanish mission on Matagorda Bay in the early 1720s. Sixteenth- and seventeenth-century expedition documents contain no record of a Texas coastal tribe by that specific name.

8. Copane. The Copane were first identified by this name in the middle eighteenth century when the tribal name appears on Spanish mission records and government reports. Campbell places the tribe as living primarily between the Copano and San Antonio Bays. Early Spanish expedition records do not mention the tribe.

9. Cujane (Cojame). The Cujane were among the Karankawan bands that first entered the Spanish mission on Garcitas Creek in the early 1720s. The tribe was not mentioned by that name in any seventeenth-century Spanish or French expedition documents, and Campbell doubts that the Cujane can be identified with Cabeza de Vaca's Quevene or Douay's Quinet or Kouan.

10. Doguene. In 1534 Doguene women from Area I guided Cabeza de Vaca into Area III along the coast east of Matagorda Bay. A short time before the trip, the Quevene (who lived in Area III) attacked the Doguene village in which Cabeza de Vaca was staying in Area I, and soon thereafter the Doguene raided a Quevene village.

11. Flatheads. Minet reported that in 1685, when La Salle asked a gathering of coastal Indians if they had ever herd of the Indians called Flatheads, one elderly man indicated by signs and the use of his bow that he had fought the Flatheads. La Salle considered the references to Flatheads made by the Palaquechare in Central Texas in 1687 to mean the Flatheads whom he had encountered on the lower Mississippi in 1682.

12. Karankawa (Cascosi). Some contemporary writers include within the Karankawan group all Texas coastal tribes who were residents of the coastal area from Galveston Bay to Corpus Christi Bay. However, Ricklis and other scholars narrow the Karankawa range based on archeological evidence to the coastal area between the Colorado River basin and Baffin Bay. The historical record analyzed herein supports the more narrow range employed by Ricklis. See also entry "Cascosi."

13. Pacpul. According to the accounts of De León's 1689 expedition to find La Salle's fort in Area III (by De León, Massanet, and Chapa), a Pacpul guide from Coahuila called Juanillo, retained by Massanet, guided the expedition party to Area III and the French post.

14. Quem. Chapa reported that a Quem Indian served as a principal guide on De León's 1689 expedition to La Salle's fort in Area III. The Quem guide several months earlier had visited Area III and the French at the settlement during his search for his wife, who had been abducted by enemy Indians. Chapa said that the Quem guide was very familiar with the land between the Rio Grande and the central Texas coast.

15. Quevene (Guevene). Cabeza de Vaca stayed for a short period with the Quevene in Area III in 1534. Campbell notes that the Quevene have been identified as the Karankawan tribe or band called the Cujane in seventeenth- and eighteenth-century Spanish documents be-

cause they occupied the same area and there is a phonetic similarity in the names. Cabeza de Vaca's account indicated that the Quevene were at war with the Doguene, their coastal neighbors to the east.

16. Quinet. Douay identified the Quinet as a nonsedentary Area III tribe who were neighbors at Fort St. Louis; he added that the French colony was at war with the tribe. Douay also noted that La Salle's 1687 expedition party encountered the Quinet soon after arriving at the Lavaca River.

    La Salle's men, riding horses, overtook the Quinet and peace was made. Douay's account matches very closely Joutel's 1687 account of the first several days' march from the bay, at which time La Salle's men, riding horses, captured an unidentified local Area III Indian whom La Salle treated kindly and offered peace. Campbell writes that it is likely that the French Quinet and the Spanish Cujane are the same tribe.

17. Quoaque (Coco?). Douay identified the Quoaque as a neighbor at Fort St. Louis. According to Douay, the tribe raised corn and sold horses at a low price. Campbell equates Douay's "Quoaque" with the Spanish Coco. Douay added that the tribe moved from one location to another without a permanent settlement and that La Salle was at war with the Quoaque. As no other French or Spanish chronicler reports that any Indians in Area III either raised corn or sold horses, this tribal identification (or at least the observation that the tribe raised corn and sold horses) might be regarded as suspect. However, if Campbell's assessment that the Quoaque were the Coco Indians, the description may be accurate.

18. Temerlouan. Pierre and Jean-Baptiste Talon reported that the Temerlouan lived near the bay and that La Salle's men took the tribe's canoes by force. This is the only reference to a bay-area tribe by this name. The report that the Temerlouan had canoes taken by La Salle's men suggests that the tribe resided in the immediate bay area or possibly on the lower Guadalupe River.

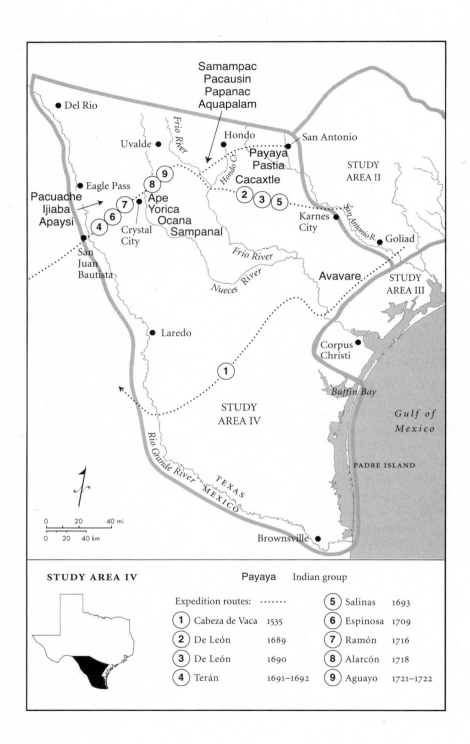

Samampac
Pacausin
Papanac
Aquapalam

● Del Rio

Frio River

Uvalde ●

Hondo

San Antonio ●

STUDY
AREA II

● Eagle Pass

9

8

Hondo Cr.

Payaya
Pastia
Cacaxtle

Pacuache
Ijiaba
Apaysi

7

6

Ape
Yorica
Ocana
Sampanal

2   3   5

Karnes
City

San Antonio R.

Goliad ●

4

Crystal
City

San
Juan
Bautista

Frio River

Nueces River

Avavare

STUDY
AREA III

● Laredo

Corpus
Christi ●

1

Baffin Bay

STUDY
AREA IV

*Gulf of
Mexico*

Rio Grande River

TEXAS
MEXICO

PADRE ISLAND

0   20   40 mi

0   20   40 km

Brownsville ●

STUDY AREA IV   Payaya   Indian group

Expedition routes: ·······

1 Cabeza de Vaca 1535
2 De León 1689
3 De León 1690
4 Terán 1691–1692

5 Salinas 1693
6 Espinosa 1709
7 Ramón 1716
8 Alarcón 1718
9 Aguayo 1721–1722

MAP 4.1

4 SOUTH TEXAS

STUDY AREA IV

Study Area IV includes the historic Native peoples of South Texas (see Map 4.1). The area boundary follows the lower Gulf Coast from Baffin Bay south to the Rio Grande, tracks the Rio Grande upstream to the river's intersection with the Pecos River west of Del Rio, follows the southern edge of the Balcones Escarpment eastward to the San Antonio River, and then turns southward downriver to the inland boundary of Study Area III. Area IV has also been identified as the Texas Gulf Coastal Plain and as a part of the Southern Plains during the study period. The northeastern part of the study area is drained by the San Antonio River, the northeastern boundary line of Area IV. The Nueces River system (which includes the Frio, Hondo, Leona, and Atascosa Rivers) drains the central part of the area. A large number of creeks that originate in South Texas flow southward into the Rio Grande or eastward into the Laguna Madre and the Gulf of Mexico. The area includes all or part of thirty-two counties.[1]

For the purposes of this study, the San Antonio River forms an ethno-geographic boundary, separating the tribes that lived east of the river (in Area II) from tribes living to the southwest (in Area IV).[2] The Balcones Escarpment from the Rio Grande to the San Antonio River served as a natural boundary during the historic period, separating the Plains Indians (principally the Apache) who occupied the Hill Country north of the Balcones from the Native peoples living to the south on the coastal plain. Unlike the San Antonio and Colorado Rivers, the Rio Grande did not serve as a Native cultural boundary.

Sixteenth- and seventeenth-century historic documents describe the topography of the region, the local flora and fauna, and the climatic conditions during the study period. The dramatic change from a 450-year warmer climatic period called the Medieval Warm period (ca. AD 900 to

107

1350) to a 500-year wetter and colder period called the Little Ice Age (ca. AD 1350 to 1850) accounts for expedition diary descriptions of weather conditions that were much colder and wetter than we know today. There are numerous reports of spring snowstorms and large bison herds on the lower Rio Grande in the 1600s and early 1700s and observations of full and flowing rivers that are today small streams. With the Little Ice Age came a significant increase in moisture to the coastal plain that attracted huge bison herds (reported to number 3,000 to 4,000 head) into the present study area and smaller herds that roamed south of the Rio Grande into present-day northern Coahuila.

According to Alonso de León (the elder) and Juan Bautista Chapa, Native tribes in the area immediately south of Area IV below the Rio Grande were numerous and diverse in the 1600s. Chapa writes that European diseases had a serious impact on the Native population in Nuevo León and Coahuila during the study period, and the historian names over 160 tribes or small bands in Nuevo León, Coahuila, and South Texas that had been depopulated or annihilated by European-introduced diseases and wars by the close of the seventeenth century.

Undoubtedly, numerous river crossings were available to Native peoples along the lower Rio Grande, but two significant and popular fording areas were referenced repeatedly in seventeenth-century Spanish accounts. One crossing, called Paso de Francia (near San Juan Bautista), was used by the Indians who guided De León across the river in 1688 to capture the Frenchman Jean Géry and was used subsequently on expeditions throughout the sixteenth and seventeenth centuries (see Map 4.1). There were several other associated fords nearby with favorable natural features such as a hard bottom and shallow water in the crossing area. A second natural crossing on the lower Rio Grande was north of Cerralvo; that ford served traffic moving between Nuevo León and the lower Texas coastal area.

In the late 1600s the most popular Indian crossing area on the middle Nueces River in Zavala County was located a few miles north of modern-day Crystal City, where the river widens into multiple shallow streams. On the Frio River in Frio County one crossing was called "Las Cruces," and a second crossing was in the flat terrain about twelve miles downriver, immediately below the junction of the Frio with the Hondo. A customary crossing on the middle San Antonio River was located in Karnes County; it is the natural hard-rock shallow ford designated the Conquista Crossing on many contemporary maps.

On movements through Area IV in the late seventeenth century, a Native trail ran out of Coahuila, through Paso de Francia and "Las

Cruces" northeast toward modern-day San Antonio and Austin; a second travel route ran from Coahuila northeast across the lower Frio crossing eastward toward the Texas coastal prairies and then northeastward to East Texas. As indicated on Map 4.1, Spanish and French documents permit a rather precise location of these old Native trails through Area IV.

A rich archival collection of sixteenth- and seventeenth-century Spanish documents is available that identify by name many of the Native tribes and bands found in Area IV. Ethnographic information is given in expedition accounts, official testimony, letters, associated reports, diaries, and journals. To summarize, our documentary story of the Native peoples in Area IV begins with Cabeza de Vaca and his party's trek across Area IV in 1535. Cabeza de Vaca crossed the lower Rio Grande near the present-day International Falcon Reservoir and then generally moved westward through Coahuila following the Río Sabinas upriver. Although a part of this journey is across northern Coahuila and thus outside Area IV, the full account of Cabeza de Vaca's journey through Coahuila is critical to understanding the relationship between the Native peoples in South Texas and their relatives and neighbors in northeastern Mexico. Near the close of the sixteenth century, Castaño de Sosa led a colonizing expedition from Monclova through northern Coahuila to the Rio Grande crossing and into Area IV near Eagle Pass. The ultimate destination of the Castaño party was New Mexico, and the expedition route through Areas V and VI is covered in the study of Area VI.

The most comprehensive relevant document from the first half of the seventeenth century that pertains to Native tribes in Area IV was prepared by Alonso de León (the elder), a very observant historian who describes the Native peoples in Nuevo León and on the lower Rio Grande. Juan Bautista Chapa gives an excellent account of Native people in northeastern Mexico and parts of South Texas covering the period 1650–1690. We also have accounts of the expeditions into Area IV by Fray Juan Larios and Fray Francisco Peñasco de Lozano in 1670 and 1674 and by Fernando del Bosque in 1675.

During the last two decades of the seventeenth century, La Salle's French chroniclers and diarists from Spanish overland expeditions from Monterrey and Monclova recorded accounts of Native life in Area IV. La Salle's soldiers explored from the lower San Antonio River across the 250-mile east-west stretch of Area IV to the mouth of the Pecos River. The record of French exploration in Area IV is found in notarized statements of French soldiers, in letters of Spanish officials, and in testimony of Area IV Indians.

Between 1686 and 1693 six Spanish expeditions crossed into or passed through Area IV. During the first two decades of the eighteenth century, Spanish authorities dispatched four more large expeditions through Area IV to explore and later colonize the San Antonio area and locations in East Texas. Multiple diary accounts and associated documents provide the core ethnographic information supporting this study of Area IV historic Native people.

Sixteenth- and Seventeenth-Century Spanish and French Expedition Documents

In the previous chapter, we left Cabeza de Vaca as he was entering Area IV on his journey southwest with the Mariame to visit the rich prickly pear fields west of modern-day Corpus Christi in Jim Wells, Nueces, and Duval Counties.[3] Cabeza de Vaca lists the name and location of sixteen tribes in Area IV living southwest of the lower San Antonio River and northeast of the lower Rio Grande crossing in Zapata County. Tribes identified by Cabeza de Vaca in northeastern Area IV include the Yguaze in the Refugio County area, Guaycone living closer to the coast, Atayo in Refugio County, and the Acubadao in Live Oak County. The Avavare, Como, Cuthalchuche, Maliacone, Susola and possibly the Coayo lived inland from the Quitole between present-day Corpus Christi and Copano Bay. The Camole and People of the Figs lived closer to the coast, south of Corpus Christi Bay. Closer to the Rio Grande in Zapata and Jim Hogg Counties lived the Arbadao and Cuchendado.

After escaping from the Mariame, Cabeza de Vaca and his party moved along a well-traveled route toward the Rio Grande crossing. On his escape from the prickly pear field near the lower Nueces River, Cabeza de Vaca and his party moved southward toward the present-day Falcon Reservoir. Oviedo gives a day-by-day diary account of the initial movement out of Texas, which began about August 1, 1535 (according to Oviedo), and ended about August 30 when the party crossed the Rio Grande.

The following is a condensation, using direct quotes from Oviedo's diary account, of Cabeza de Vaca's short, month-long trip from the location where his Indian captors held him near the Nueces to the Rio Grande. Oviedo writes as follows: "The month of August arriving, these three noblemen . . . fled from the place and the Indians mentioned before. And that same day that they departed [August 1, 1535], they walked seven leagues . . . and they remained there eight days. That day [August 9] they walked five or six leagues . . . and they stayed there with those Indians fifteen days. From there [on August 25], they went to other Indians two leagues ahead . . . and after they departed from there [on August 26], women followed the Christians . . . two or three leagues. And from then [August 27] they [the women] went with them, and they walked that day eight or nine long leagues [*leguas grandes*] without stopping all day long as they were able. Before the sun set [on August 27] they arrived at a river that appeared to them wider than the Guadalquivir at Sevilla [the Rio Grande]."[4]

Thus Cabeza de Vaca's party walked from the location of his captors to the Rio Grande about sixteen to eighteen Spanish leagues (ca. 2.6 miles per Spanish league) plus eight to nine "long" leagues (ca. 3.5 miles per Spanish long league), or approximately a total of seventy to seventy-eight miles.[5] If Cabeza de Vaca crossed the Rio Grande near the Falcon Reservoir, as suggested by Alonso de León (the elder) and Alex D. Krieger,[6] we can project that the Spanish party departed from their captors living near Freer in Duval County.

The projected Rio Grande crossing area is near the modern-day Falcon Reservoir into which the Río Salado flows from the west. Soon after crossing the big river, the Spaniards found an encampment of local Indians who celebrated their arrival with song and dance. Large dried gourds filled with small pebbles were used as musical instruments in the celebration. According to the Indians, the gourds were not locally grown but rather were found along the banks of the Rio Grande and originated from an unknown source far upriver. The Indians gave Estevan a special large gourd to carry on the remainder of his journey as a symbol of authority.[7]

About a week later, when Cabeza de Vaca's party was traveling along a pathway that ran beside a river (probably along the Río Salado or its tributary, the Río Sabinas),[8] they met two women who were walking in the opposite direction, downriver. To Cabeza de Vaca's amazement, the Indian women were carrying large bags of finely ground maize. Knowing that the local Indians did not cultivate maize, gourds, or any other cultigen, Cabeza de Vaca asked where the women got the maize. The women replied that they had received the maize from people whom the Spaniards would find farther upriver.

As the Indian women said, several days later Cabeza de Vaca met a large, friendly, foreign trading party that apparently had provided the maize to the women. The foreigners had been visiting farther east toward the Gulf, but now the long-distance trading party was traveling west, returning to their homeland. Cabeza de Vaca's description of the trading party encountered en route across Coahuila suggests that the Spaniards and the trading party may have been following an ancient east-west trade route connecting northeast and northwest Mexico.

The visiting traders gave Cabeza de Vaca two surprising gifts—cotton blankets and a cast copper bell or crotal (*cascabel*) with a human facial imprint on its side.[9] Cabeza de Vaca had not seen Indian cotton goods or Native cast copper bells elsewhere on his long journey across the continent and had not seen ground maize since he left Florida.

Local Natives in Coahuila who knew and apparently had traded on other occasions with the foreigners told Cabeza de Vaca that the traders resided far to the west at a highly populated permanent settlement where there were many large houses and that the foreign traders cultivated fields of maize, cotton, and other crops and mined copper.[10] Cabeza de Vaca was greatly impressed and added that the visiting traders must also have an understanding of metallurgy, a technology that was unknown to Mississippian people.

The closest and most obvious source of cast copper bells and cotton goods to the west of northern Coahuila was the Casas Grandes people residing about 500 miles away in northwest Chihuahua. For several hundred years before Cabeza de Vaca's journey, a large cultural center called Paquimé, located on the Río Casas Grandes, had produced and traded extensively in colorful cotton blankets, cast copper bells, and premature scarlet macaw parrots.

Cotton and copper were produced locally near Paquimé, but scarlet macaw had to be imported into Paquimé and other points in the American Southwest from the closest source, namely, the lowland rain forests of Tamaulipas and Nuevo León in northeast Mexico where Cabeza de Vaca encountered the trading party.[11] Premature scarlet macaw, hatched in the spring, were available for trade and travel by late summer, when the trading party was visiting northern Nuevo León and Coahuila. Macaw bird handlers at Paquimé fed the caged parrots a mush of ground maize and amaranth.[12] The traders brought ground maize with them; amaranth was available all along the route between Nuevo León and the Río Casas Grandes.[13]

As the city of Paquimé had been abandoned by ca. AD 1450 and residents had moved downriver perhaps only fifty miles,[14] it appears that Casas Grandes traders, as late as the 1530s, were still dispatching long-distance trading parties to northeast Mexico to procure premature scarlet macaws. Later, as we will note, Cabeza de Vaca's party visited the Casas Grandes river valley.

After finding ground maize and receiving the copper bell and cotton blankets in northern Coahuila, Cabeza de Vaca's party continued to move westward, following generally the Río Sabinas upstream. We will pick up Cabeza de Vaca in the following chapter where he reenters Texas near the junction of the Río Conchos and the Rio Grande in the Big Bend (Area V).

In the 1570s Spanish explorers moved inland and northwest from Pánuco and the Huasteca area on the Gulf of Mexico. In 1579 the Spanish Crown granted Luis Carvajal an area that extended from Pánuco over 500 miles north along the Gulf Coast of Mexico and northward inland into present-day Central Texas and over 500 miles westward. In executing his responsibilities under the grant, Carvajal explored parts of present-day Tamaulipas, Nuevo León, and Coahuila and in 1580 established León, a small silver mining community (near modern Cerralvo) thirty miles south of the lower Rio Grande.

In his history of Nuevo León, Alonso de León (the elder) describes the exploration of Carvajal and his second-in-command, Gaspar Castaño de Sosa, in the 1590s and provides information on Native tribes that lived at the time in northeastern Mexico and along the lower Rio Grande.[15] Both Alonso de León (the elder) and Juan Bautista Chapa give extensive firsthand accounts of Natives on the lower Rio Grande in the early and middle 1600s.[16]

Chapa writes that based on official government records of the former governor of Nuevo León, Don Martín de Zavala, 160 specifically named and recorded tribal groups or Indian bands in the area had been seriously depopulated or entirely extinguished by Spanish-introduced diseases. Chapa adds that the rapid Native depopulation forced Spanish officials and colonists to "gather" (to capture by force) another 88 named tribes or bands that resided within a range of 130 miles of Monterrey or Cerralvo or possibly well inside Area IV.[17]

As mentioned, De León wrote that Cabeza de Vaca had crossed the Rio Grande from Texas into Mexico about fifty miles north of Cerralvo, or near the present-day Falcon Reservoir.[18] The route projected in this study crosses the Rio Grande at the reservoir about thirty to forty miles above the reservoir dam itself. As mentioned by Krieger, a careful review of the sixteenth-century Spanish documentary record of Cabeza de Vaca's journey suggests that Spanish authorities, including the cartographers, had a very accurate picture of his route.[19]

As would be expected during the Little Ice Age, De León (the elder) describes the weather in the 1650s as being much colder and wetter than we know today. The historian lists both the wild and domesticated animals and plants in the region near the lower Rio Grande. For purposes of our study, it is significant that De León lists watermelons as one of the melons grown locally by Spaniards in the early 1600s on the lower Rio

Grande and says large parrots (perhaps the large macaws) were raised in northern Nuevo León for trade.

De León writes that in the general area along the lower Rio Grande there were hundreds of small independent tribes or bands, each with its own name and language. Their lifeways, however, were similar. They planted no crops, but they hunted deer and smaller game and gathered local plant products. De León describes how the Natives would harvest the heart and fleshy part of the lechuguilla and cook the product for two days and three nights before consuming the juicy parts and chewing and sucking the stringy leaves. This is one of the few historic accounts that describes how Indians cooked sotol, yucca, and lechuguilla on the lower Rio Grande.

De León was also clear that in addition to the large number of local tribes, the area at that time was visited by members of large foreign tribes that resided several hundred miles to the south and southwest. He describes skirmishes that occurred near Monterrey involving the Tepehuan, a large tribe from the Durango area, the Guachachile from southwestern Chihuahua, and the Chichimeca and Borrodo from the Tamaulipas Mountains. The friendly Otomi and Tlaxcala were brought by the Spaniards from central Mexico. This information is significant because it demonstrates that the Native peoples living along the lower Rio Grande in the middle 1600s included representatives of major tribes whose principal residence was over 300 miles to the west and to the east of Monterrey. In Chapa's account, Texas tribes living 100 miles north of the Rio Grande are also identified and described as raiders that periodically visited Monterrey 100 miles south of the Rio Grande to steal horses and capture slaves.

In addition to identifying Native tribes that customarily lived a substantial distance from the lower Rio Grande, De León identified the major trade routes that connected the Monterrey area with the Gulf of Mexico to the east and with Chihuahua to the west. The historian mentions specifically a military road that crossed northern Mexico from Chihuahua running eastward to the Monterrey area and on farther southeast to the Gulf Coast. This road may have followed in part the earlier Native route that Cabeza de Vaca used traveling westward from the lower Rio Grande to western Chihuahua.

Chapa picks up the history of Nuevo León and the Native people of the lower Rio Grande beginning in the 1630s. Chapa writes that the Indians from the north (north of the Rio Grande in Area IV) continued to raid Spanish communities near Cerralvo and Monterrey to acquire horses and slaves. It appears that during the middle 1600s, Texas tribes from Area IV may have captured large horse herds on raids of Spanish communities, missions, and military posts. In response to this threat from Texas Indian raiding parties from Area IV, Spanish authorities initiated from Monterrey and Saltillo two military expeditions in the 1660s to punish the Texas tribes.

On the first punitive expedition, initiated in October 1663, Mayor Juan de la Garza led a company of Spanish troops and a company of friendly Tlaxcala Indians from Saltillo along with Spanish colonists from Nuevo León to attack the Cacaxtle Indians in South Texas. The seriousness of the 1663 military effort is reflected in its duration (six months in the field) and its size—over 100 enlisted Spanish troops and 800 horses. In comparison, the 1663 expedition matched in size and duration Governor De León's 1689 and 1690 expeditions to locate and torch La Salle's fort on the central Texas coast.

The land of the Cacaxtle was reported to be more than 150 miles from Monterrey, but the account fails to mention whether the Spanish troops crossed the Rio Grande. However, most authorities suggest that Garza's troops in the 1663–1664 campaign engaged the Cacaxtle along the middle Rio Grande near Eagle Pass. During this engagement the Spaniards killed about 100 Area IV Indians and captured 125, counting all ages and both sexes. The historical record indicates that the captured Area IV Texas Indians were sent to Zacatecas to work in the local mines.

The year after Garza's troops returned, a second military expedition was organized, the objective of which was to enter the land of the Cacaxtle in South Texas and to eradicate the base of the Cacaxtle encampments. Don Fernando de Azcué formed a company of 103 soldiers from Saltillo, augmented by a company of 30 enlisted troops from Monterrey, to march northward across the Rio Grande into Area IV. To support the Spanish troops, a friendly Indian leader named Don Nicolas de Carretero assembled more than 300 local Indians, mostly Boboles. According to Chapa's account, Ambrosio de Cepeda was designated the captain of the Indian troops. Significantly, Chapa adds that Cepeda was fluent in many languages of the tribes in Area IV, which suggests that tribes within one hundred miles of the lower Rio Grande intermixed, although they spoke different languages.

After a six-day march that probably took the expedition over sixty miles north of the Rio Grande into Area IV, the Spanish troops surrounded the Cacaxtle, who were gathered in thick brush and woods within a barricade that the Spaniards could not penetrate. In the middle of the battle a Cacaxtle leader who had been given the name Juan and who spoke Spanish well asked for a truce. The Spaniards refused, considering his request a trick to give the Indians time to strengthen their fortification with more limbs, brush, and prickly pear. Toward the end of the battle, after the Natives' supply of arrows had long been exhausted, the Cacaxtle fought with clubs. During the battle, over one hundred Cacaxtles were killed, twenty-two Spaniards were wounded, and two Indians fighting with the Spaniards were killed.

Chapa writes that during the battle an elderly Indian woman who was being held captive by the Spaniards began playing a flute to give courage to her encircled Cacaxtle family and friends. In retribution for her action in support of the Cacaxtle, the Boboles wanted to cook and eat her that evening, but the Spaniards would not permit this. Nevertheless, the Boboles prevailed indirectly, as Chapa says, by secretly cooking and eating a young captive boy who was related to her. Chapa adds that after the battle Nuevo León was, for a time, relatively free of Indian raids from the Texas tribes in Area IV.

According to late seventeenth-century clerical reports, about five years after Azcué's expedition, a small Franciscan contingent arrived south of the Rio Grande in the area opposite Area IV.[20] Later this area in northern Mexico was formally organized as the province of Coahuila. Fray Juan Larios was one of the principal early leaders in the exploration of the area. In his reports from the early 1670s, Larios identifies by name a number of tribes that were encountered near the Rio Grande by the priests, including the "Catzales" (Cacaxtle), Toboso, Obayo, Bobole (who also lived near the Río Sabinas), and Gueiquesale. On one trip Larios spent three weeks in Area IV north and east of present-day Eagle Pass. The priest records crossing into Texas over a wide ford, in the middle of which was an island of sand. This description fits generally the Rio Grande crossing area that was used by De León in 1689 and that was subsequently named Paso de Francia.

The priest Francisco Peñasco de Lozano crossed the Rio Grande from Coahuila into Area IV in the summer of 1674.[21] He was in search of the Manosprieta Indians, who were at the time hunting bison north of the river. On his trip Peñasco also met the Giora Indians, who were holding a boy of the Quezale tribe. At their mission at Santa Rosa, near the Río Sabinas, the priests wrote of prickly pear growing in abundance and noted that the pear fruit, or tuna, would last until November. The fathers added that in the winter, if there was heavy snow and the weather was very cold (which apparently was expected), they would have only fish to eat. This comment on the weather tends to confirm other reports indicating that the climate in the region was much colder in the late 1600s than we know today.

In early May 1675, following the earlier steps of Larios and Peñasco, Fernando del Bosque commanded an expedition from the town of Guadalupe (Monclova) that proceeded northward into present-day

HISTORIC NATIVE PEOPLES OF TEXAS

Texas and Area IV.[22] Larios was at his side. Like other Spanish diarists in the late seventeenth century, Bosque maintained an expedition account that includes information on the direction and number of leagues traveled daily, the names of rivers and large creeks crossed, the names (and occasionally a brief description) of Indian tribes met and the flora and fauna recognized. For example, Bosque describes the fish taken from the Río de los Nadadores (the same name that is used for the small dry creek bed today) at a location a few leagues north of Monclova and identifies the fish as large river catfish, bream, *bobos,* and *mojarras.* The party also found mud turtles and eels.

A week later, at the Río Sabinas, Bosque describes tall grass growing on wide plains dotted with cottonwood, willows, mesquite, and huisache. About four leagues north of the Rio Grande (in Area IV), near present-day Eagle Pass, the expedition party found fifty-four adult Yorica and Jeapa Indians who said that their enemies were the nearby Ocane (Ocana), Pataguaque, and Yurbipane. After moving northward eight to ten leagues, Bosque met with several other nomadic tribes—the Bibit, Jume, Pinanaca, Xaeser, Tenimama, Cocoma, Xoman, Teroodan, Teaname, and Teimamar. He also recovered a twelve-year old Spanish boy who was held captive by the Cabeza. As the Spaniards moved farther north into Area IV, the Geniocane, Catujano, Tilijae, Ape, Pachaque, and Jeniocane were encountered; at the end of May Bosque returned southward to cross the Rio Grande and return to Monclova.

Bosque's account confirms the names of many tribes living in the Eagle Pass area of Area IV in the 1670s, the presence of rich grazing lands and bison herds hunted by the Natives, and the availability of substantial fishery and other aquatic resources. The account also suggests that the small tribes or bands lived in shared encampments, engaged in slave trading, and frequently were at war. It also supports the thesis that the climatic conditions in the middle Rio Grande area in the late 1600 were much wetter and colder than those we know today.

The French Arrive

In 1685 France, a rival European power to Spain, established a fort and colony on the central Texas coast and sent scouts from the post into Area IV.[23] The historical record is not clear as to whether La Salle, the leader of the French expedition, accompanied the French soldiers to the Rio Grande. But the record is clear that French troops visited Area IV, seeking information about Spanish silver mines at Parral in southern Chihuahua.[24]

We also know that one of La Salle's party, Jean Géry, was captured by Captain Alonso de León near the Rio Grande in Area IV in 1688.[25] Géry's story is one of the most astonishing tales associated with La Salle's expedition and deserves special attention because Géry identifies the names of more tribes in Area IV than any other French source.

For a European, Géry forged a unique relationship with the Native population in South Texas. Cabeza de Vaca and his companions lived in Area II often as mistreated servants or slaves who were trying to escape. On the other hand, the Frenchman Géry was at home with the Native people of Area IV, happily living a new life with his Indian wife and child and functioning as a respected leader over numerous tribes openly loyal to him.

Géry was obviously enjoying the comforts of Native life and able not only to communicate freely in the Native tongue of tribes with whom he lived in Area IV but also to speak the Native languages of distant tribes living in Area II over one hundred miles northeast of the Rio Grande. Alonso de León, who developed a respect and true fondness for Géry, wrote of his sadness and loss when Géry later slipped away from Spanish authorities and returned back across the Rio Grande to rejoin his Indian family and friends in Area IV. As Géry is the sole firsthand French source of information on Area IV, his capture and ethnographic contributions will be reviewed in more detail.

In 1688 a friendly Tlaxcala resident of the newly established frontier province of Coahuila informed the provincial governor, Alonso de León (the younger), that he had visited a large Indian encampment about eighty miles north of the Rio Grande on his last bison hunt and that he had seen a European who was said to be a Frenchman. This report startled De León, who had conducted two expeditions to the Gulf Coast to search for evidence of a French presence north of the Rio Grande. This Indian report, if true, meant that information about the French colony was attainable from a Frenchman living only about 175 miles north of Monclova, the provincial capital.

Based on the Native's information, De León in May 1688 found Jean Géry in a large enclosed lodge roofed with bison hides located about fifty miles north of the Rio Grande, probably in Dimmit County.[26] De León later wrote that Géry had gained the loyalty of local tribes in the area while waiting for the opportune moment to advise his fellow countrymen at the French colony to send troops to attack the Spanish frontier towns. De León adds that such an attack might have been successful because few Spanish forces were available to resist a French attack.

De León writes that within the large Indian shared encampment of five tribes, 300 warriors were gathered around Géry like bodyguards. Géry himself was tall, had light skin and gray hair, and appeared to be about fifty years of age. His face was painted with stripes as the Indians painted their faces. Géry was seated alone on a large pile of bison robes. He told De León that his motive in seeking the loyalty of the Natives in Area IV was to make them subjects of the king of France. He said he had been living among the tribes near the Rio Grande for about three years (since 1685), during which time he had married within the tribe and had a little girl. Significantly, Géry added that before coming to the Rio Grande he had "reduced" or pacified in a similar manner tribes that lived north of the French settlement. Also significant for purposes of this study, Géry said that about a year earlier (in the summer of 1687) he had been visited by sixteen French soldiers (not mentioning La Salle personally) who had come to see how his efforts were progressing.

De León returned to Monclova with Géry as his captive and later sent the Frenchman south to the viceroy in Mexico to be interrogated again. The viceroy learned little new from Géry, who was returned to De León with a directive that Géry serve as a guide to locate the French post on the central Texas coast. Géry had assured the viceroy that the journey between the Rio Grande and the French fort had taken him twelve days and that he knew and had marked the route well.

As directed by the viceroy, De León used Géry as a guide on his 1689 expedition to find the French post, and several events occurred on the expedition journey that indicated the accuracy of Géry's testimony and his credibility as a source of information.[27] First, his services as a guide on the expedition proved very valuable, as acknowledged by De León, and the time required to march from the Rio Grande to the French post was approximately the time estimated by Géry. Second, Géry's services as an interpreter among the Sanan-speaking tribes living in Area II and the open and joyous reception he received by Area II tribes confirmed that he in fact had been at work pacifying and recruiting tribes in Area II before he traveled west to the Rio Grande and Area IV. Finally, Géry skillfully led De León over fifty miles from the ravaged Fort St. Louis area to the entrance of Matagorda Bay, where he told De León that he had arrived with La Salle through the pass identified. These events substantiated Géry's earlier testimony and, along with other factors, suggest that reliance can be given to Géry's reports on the activities of Frenchmen on the Rio Grande and the names and locations of Texas tribes.

Another report of Frenchmen visiting the lower Rio Grande is found in a letter dated June 15, 1686, from the governor of Nuevo León, the Marqués de San Miguel de Aguayo, to the viceroy who had written in early May of that year ordering Governor Aguayo to solicit support to reconnoiter the Bay of Espiritu Santo and the French settlement on the bay. The letter was written by Aguayo about two weeks before General Alonso de León began his 1686 expedition down the Rio Grande to the coast.[28]

Aguayo wrote that the Blanco and Pajarito Indians (living near the Rio Grande) had reported that very friendly white people, who looked like the Spaniards, had visited the lower Rio Grande. The Indians added that these white men cared for and liked Indians, giving them clothes to dress themselves. They had seen an Indian servant of these white men dressed in trousers, a jacket, and a big hat. The Indian servant of the white men was staying with the Blancos while recovering from an injury. This report suggests that in the spring of 1686 Frenchmen with an Indian servant visited the lower Rio Grande and that the Frenchmen had contacted the Blanco and Pajarito Indians.

Although Géry provided his Spanish captors with a list of Indian tribes from Areas II and IV that were loyal to him, the Blanco and Pajarito were not included in his list.[29] Géry gave to Chapa the following list of names of Indian tribes he considered loyal to him and to France: Cuba, Emot, Sanatoo (Sana, Toho?), Poguan, Cosmojoo, Piyai, Piguen, Panaa, Pataoo, Tamireguan, Cagremoa, Agaaunimi, Chile, Cobapo, Huiapico, Etayax, Cuajin, Caomopac, and Saurum.

The Spanish Return

On his 1689 expedition De León records finding good pasture across northern Coahuila en route to the Rio Grande and meeting the Jumano, Mescale, Hape, and Xiabu (or Ijiaba) at the Rio Grande crossing in Maverick County in late March.[30] In addition to De León's own diary account of the 1689 expedition, Juan Bautista Chapa and the priest Damián Massanet wrote accounts of the trip.

According to Chapa, the four tribes on the Rio Grande prepared a celebration in honor of the return of their dear friend and leader the Frenchman Jean Géry. Géry's wide and deep popularity among Area IV Indians surprised the Spaniards. The tribes were gathered in a shared encampment that numbered 490 individuals, as recorded by Chapa based on a head count. Chapa adds that this number did not include members who were nearby on a bison hunt. This is just one of a number of reports of bison ranging near and south of the Rio Grande into Coahuila in the 1680s. But the report that the number of Indians at the encampment was determined by an actual head count is unusual; generally only estimates are given by the diarist.

In the Indian encampment De León noticed that the tribes had on display the skulls of their enemy atop tall poles around their lodges. This display was not intended as a sign to the Spaniards that the Natives were unfriendly. By 1689 the Spaniards had been in that general area of the Rio Grande with small and large forays for over twenty years. De León expected, and received, no opposition or trouble from the Indians. To confirm his friendship, De León contributed two steers for the Indians to barbecue that evening.

About a week after crossing the Rio Grande, the Coahuila Indian guides led the expedition across the Nueces River (which De León named) and farther northeast to the present-day Frio River, which De León named the Río Hondo because of the river's steep banks. At the location where the Indian guides suggested that he camp, De León observed a large white rock on which a cross had been carved and pecked many years earlier.

A site in the bed of the Frio where De León is projected to have camped has been recorded recently by archeologists associated with the Texas Archeological Research Laboratory. The crossing, which was later called Las Cruces, is located on a stretch of the Frio River in which numerous distinctive, three- to four-meter-wide turtle-back white rocks are located, and one white rock has a large cross, measuring three feet by two feet, carefully chipped and pecked deeply into it. After crossing the Frio, De León recorded no other Indians on the expedition until the party was east of the San Antonio River and outside Area IV.

In 1690 the same tribes (which De León calls "the Frenchman's Indians") were at the Rio Grande crossing when the De León expedition crossed the river moving northeastward.[31] But a short time before the 1690 trip was organized, Jean Géry had slipped away from Spanish control in Coahuila and returned to his Indian family and followers in Area IV. De León writes that he missed his loyal friend Géry, and when the expedition party reached the Frio and the camp location called Las Cruces, De León stopped for a day to search for Géry. Although about fifteen miles upriver from Las Cruces De León encountered a group of Indians that included members of tribes that Géry had been living with when he was captured, the Spaniards did not find Géry. But De León does note significantly that one of the Indians in the group had in his possession a French musket.

After leaving the Frio, De León continued across Area IV toward Matagorda Bay but again reported no engagements with any Indians en route through the area. However, he reports a curious event that suggests that Indians may have been aware of his party even if he failed to observe them. Near the same location that De León's large horse herd had been spooked and had broken away in 1689, part of his remuda of over 800 horses went on a rampage and ran loose again in 1690. We should note that on De León's return trip to Monclova that year, he engaged a band of Toho Indians at the same location. De León knew that Indians would intentionally spook Spanish horse herds at night to collect the stray horses the next day. De León's horses had also gone on a rampage near a Toho encampment in DeWitt County on his first expedition in 1689.

On Terán's 1691 expedition the governor reported meeting near the Rio Grande crossing the Mescal, Odoesmade, and Momon.[32] Massanet writes that the Mescal, Yorica, Jumano, Parchaca, Alachome, and Pamai Indians followed the expedition party after crossing the river. Several days later, near modern-day Comanche Creek in southwestern Zavala County, Massanet records encountering the Quem, Pacpul, Ocana, Chaquash, Pastaloca, and Paac Indians. Three days later, on the Frio River in northwestern Frio County, Massanet records meeting the Sampanal, Patchal, Papanac, Aguapalam, Samampac, Vauca, Payavan, Patavo, Pitanay, Apaysi, and Patsau. As Massanet's account of the 1691 expedition closes when he reached the Tejas in East Texas and Terán's account closes when he departed Texas from Matagorda Bay in 1692, these sources contain no further references to encounters with tribes in Area IV in 1691 and 1692.

Governor Salinas Varona in 1693 followed De León's route across Area IV on his march to East Texas.[33] Near the Rio Grande crossing he found the Cacaxtle, Ocana, and Piedras Blancas Indians on the south side of the river and the Agualoke on the north bank. The Pacuache were encountered between the Rio Grande and the Nueces in northeast Dimmit County, and the following day near Comanche Creek he found the Tepacuache and Sacuache. Near the Leona River he saw another gathering of friendly Pacuache.

On his return march, Governor Salinas visited the San Antonio area and met the Payaya Indians, as Massanet had in 1691. On the following day, along his route through Area IV, a Saquita Indian guide told the governor that the hills between the Hondo and San Miguel creeks were named for the Cacaxtle Indians. When he reached the Rio Grande, Salinas received the assistance of Mescale, Hape, and Cacase in the crossing. Soon after Salinas returned to Monclova, the Caddo drove Massanet and his clerical group out of East Texas and closed East Texas to the Spaniards.

1700S

In 1709 the mission at San Juan Bautista on the Rio Grande received word that the Caddo Indians in East Texas would be pleased to meet a Spanish delegation on the lower Colorado River. As a result of this promising news, Spanish authorities sent a small military and clerical expedition from the Rio Grande across Area IV to the Colorado.[34] Although the report turned out to be incorrect and the expedition unfruitful, valuable ethnographic and natural ecological information was obtained by the leaders Fray Isidro de Espinosa and Captain Pedro de Aguirre during the movement through Area IV.

Between the Rio Grande and the Frio River in northern Area IV, Espinosa's party met small groups and hunting parties of the Pacuasin and Xarame Indians. The diarists reported crossing several named rivers and creeks lined with oak, elm, mulberry, and pecan trees. Between the Frio River and the San Antonio area, the expedition hunted wild turkey and deer. Espinosa adds that the wildlife included bison, bear, cougar, and jaguar.

The Spaniards encountered the Payaya and Pampopa Indians near San Antonio. It is significant for the present study that when Espinosa reached San Antonio he also encountered over 500 Indians from three large tribes whose homeland was in northern Mexico.[35] Members of the three tribes—the Siupam, Xarame, and Sijame—served the Spaniards in their march farther east toward the Colorado River. The ethnographic information tends to confirm the cosmopolitan nature of Texas Indians because the homeland of the three tribes was over 250 miles southwest of the Colorado River destination.

When Espinosa and the Spanish troops returned to San Juan Bautista, they filed a negative report acknowledging that the Caddo would not meet with or receive a delegation from the church or the Spanish government. There was no thought of forcing the issue further at the time.

For reasons not fully understood, the position of the Caddo nation was reversed in 1716, and Caddo leaders agreed to accept the establishment of one or more missions and presidios in East Texas. In response to the Caddo invitation, a Spanish expedition led by Captain Domingo Ramón and the priest Isidro de Espinosa left San Juan Bautista in late April 1716.[36] The expedition party basically followed the route pioneered by De León in 1689 and by Espinosa in 1709 through Area IV. Espinosa repeatedly comments on the pecan, cottonwood, palmetto, mulberry, yucca, mesquite, prickly pear, grapevine, and mottes of live oak seen along the way. The Pacuache, Mesquite, and Pataguo were encountered when the Spaniards approached the San Antonio area and marched beyond Area IV. As the purpose of the expedition was to establish a permanent Spanish presence in East Texas, the diarists conclude the narrative with the arrival in Caddo country.

Two years after the Ramón-Espinosa expedition reached East Texas, Spanish authorities dispatched a second colonizing expedition through Area IV to expand the East Texas area served by the Spanish missions and presidios. In 1718 Governor Martín de Alarcón, the expedition leader, tracked Espinosa's 1709 route through Area IV from the Rio Grande to San Antonio.[37] Although no bison were reported en route, the party found many deer and wild turkey. Only the friendly Pacuache Indians were encountered near the Nueces River.

The last large expedition sent by the Spanish government through Area IV during the colonizing period was led in 1721 by Governor Marqués de San Miguel de Aguayo.[38] Unlike most previous expeditions, Aguayo's party crossed the Rio Grande in the winter rather than during the warmer spring months. Snow and ice storms delayed the crossing of the river for over a month. These weather reports on the crossing area in South Texas during January and February tend to confirm that the Little Ice Age that occurred across North America between ca. AD 1350 and 1850 was reflected in the much colder and more mesic period in Area IV at the same time.

Juan Antonio de la Peña, Aguayo's principal expedition diarist, noted the local fauna observed en route across Area IV. He recorded wild turkey, quail, prairie chicken, jackrabbits, cottontails, deer, and antelope. The diarist counted over 300 deer and antelope in one group. Whereas wild game was abundant, no Indian tribes were reported in Area IV.

The purpose of this section is to review several regional histories and archeological overviews covering Area IV that help interpret and supplement the ethnographic and environmental information found in the expedition records. First, we will note the historical studies and overviews.

The seventeenth-century Spanish historian and frontiersman Alonso de León (the elder) writes that in northern Nuevo León and Coahuila there were hundreds of small bands and that each had its own language or dialect.[39] In addition, distant tribes from West Texas and northwestern Mexico such as the Jumano, Toboso, and Tepehuan were frequent visitors to Area IV and the lower Rio Grande. De León notes that European-introduced diseases seriously depopulated local Area IV tribes and visiting tribes as well.

De León describes several forms of ritual cannibalism practiced on the lower Rio Grande and the use of peyote during ceremonial dances involving one hundred or more dancers and singers streaked with red ocher. The musical instruments played to accompany the dancers-singers included gourds filled with tiny pebbles gathered from ant beds, grooved ebony sticks, and tambourines.

De León provides a list of wild animals and colorful birds found on the lower Rio Grande in the early 1600s. The historian includes herds of up to fifty deer moving together, many large parrots (macaws?), antelope, cottontail rabbits, jackrabbits, prairie chickens, javelinas, armadillos, bobcats, and lynx.

A more recent study of South Texas that focuses on historic Indian groups was written by T. N. Campbell and T. J. Campbell.[40] The Campbell study helps locate the seventeen named tribes or bands identified by Cabeza de Vaca plus seventeen other Native groups in the area. This information is referenced in the chapter supplement, which lists alphabetically the historic Indians of Area IV. In 1990 Martin Salinas prepared a comprehensive study of the Indians of the Rio Grande delta.[41] Salinas's study covers the period from 1596 through and beyond our study period, which closes in the early 1700s.

The most recent overview of the prehistoric Native population in Area IV was published in 2004.[42] In this work, entitled *The Prehistory of Texas*, Thomas Hester focuses on the interior of South Texas, Robert Ricklis writes about the eastern Gulf shore area of Area IV, and Solveig Turpin reviews the lower Pecos River region of the present subject area.

Thomas Hester reviews with informative comment and the use of drawings the principal Paleo-Indian and Archaic period spear and dart points used by the Native hunters in South Texas.[43] The author also includes illustrations of the tubular stone pipes, Oliva shell tinklers, tubular bone beads, and precious stone pendants recovered at archeological sites in the area. As there are numerous cemetery sites, many of the listed artifacts were found in a mortuary context in the area.

Hester provides detailed close comparisons between the design elements in South Texas and Huastecan pottery from the northeast coast of Mexico. Hester also details other evidence of long-distance trade or interaction between South Texas and Mesoamerica. Black opaque obsidian found in Cameron County is tied to sources in the Mexican state of Hidalgo; green obsidian flakes have been linked possibly to the famous Cerro de las Navajas source. Artifacts have been recovered that are made of jadeite, a "green stone" closely associated with Mesoamerican cultures. The author finds that the connecting link between the lower Rio Grande delta people and Mesoamerica ran through the Huastecan frontier villages and campsites excavated within 300 miles south of Brownsville. Trade moving south was probably shell ornaments produced in the delta.

In his review of the prehistory of the lower Texas Gulf Coast in the eastern part of Area IV, Robert Ricklis notes that the Paleo-Indian material found included dart points in possible association with bones of mammoth and archaic bison (*Bison antiquus*).[44]

Ricklis expands on the comments made by Hester on the evidence of exchange between the Brownsville-area people and the Huastecans living south of the Rio Grande near the Mexican coast. The author also notes that ethnohistorical research indicates that the Rio Grande delta was a rich biotic area that supported a relatively dense and stable population.

The western corner of Area IV, which includes the lower Pecos River region, is covered in the recently published book *The Prehistory of Texas* by Solveig A. Turpin, who has studied and written extensively on early bison hunting and the rock art in the area.[45] Turpin reviews the evidence of Paleo-Indian dart points associated with the remains of now extinct bison driven over the cliff above Bonfire Shelter. The record suggests that on several occasions large bison herds numbering over one hundred animals were killed or disabled (by the fall over the cliff), butchered, and processed. According to Turpin, the location represents the oldest known example of Paleo-Indians killing herd animals such as bison employing the jump technique.

During the middle Archaic period (6000 to 3000 BP), there emerged in the same area the earliest of the Pecos River pictographic rock art styles. These monumental polychrome rock art paintings are, according to Turpin, among the oldest and also the most elaborate, presently known religious art forms in the Americas. The pictograph paintings on the walls of the shelter include religious leaders (called shamans), anthropomorphic figures, and images of lions, panthers, deer, and birds.[46]

Turpin reviews four prehistoric pictograph styles that emerged in the area prior to the present study period. One late style incorporated abstract geometric designs in petroglyphs as well as pictographs. Although some parallels may be seen between the abstract rock art in the American Southwest and northern Mexico and the rock art in Area IV, Turpin concludes that the similarities are unlikely to be from contact or diffusion.

Conclusions

The documentary record describing the physical ecology of Area IV makes abundantly clear that a mesic climatic interlude was occurring during the study period and probably had been present for several decades or centuries. The weather reports and descriptions of the flora and fauna given in the numerous diary accounts confirm that the much colder and wetter Little Ice Age that arrived in the Northern Hemisphere in ca. AD 1350 was reflected, as expected, in South Texas as well. During the period rich grasslands of the Southern Plains extended throughout Area IV and into northern Coahuila, Nuevo León, and Chihuahua. The presence of large bison herds in northern Mexico confirms the unusually favorable mesic climatic conditions in Area IV.

In addition to reports of good pasturage in northern Mexico and in

126

Area IV generally, there are also reports of thick mottes of oak trees as well as large mesquite, pecan, cypress, and willow trees in the area. Diarists write of Indians and Spanish soldiers hunting not only bison but also deer and wild turkey near the Frio and Hondo Rivers. Below the Rio Grande, Alonso de León reported javelinas, armadillos, large parrots, and lynx.

Spaniards described Area IV Natives generally as cultivating nothing but pursuing a hunter-gatherer lifestyle, moving frequently in small family-related bands of under one hundred. The customary dress was simple, and frequently the Indians were naked. Each small group had its own language or dialect. The hunters used the bow and arrow and had earlier employed the spear thrower or atlatl. For rabbit hunting, hunters had specially designed arched sticks to throw, and some hunters or fishermen had carefully crafted small stone objects called "sinkers" by archeologists.

The deep spiritual component in the world view of the Native peoples of Texas is found in numerous aspects of the daily lives of the Area IV population. As in other areas in the state, Area IV Natives buried their dead accompanied with grave goods, indicating a world view that included an active physical afterlife. The spectacular colorful rock art paintings of religious shamans on the broad canvaslike brown-gray-cream walls of rock shelters in Area IV illustrate graphically the strong spiritual impulse of the Native people living near the lower Pecos River.

Evidence of the spiritual foundation of the Indians' daily lives is seen also in the peyote-stimulated dance-song bonfire ceremonies celebrated in Area IV and other regions to the south and west. Cabeza de Vaca indicates that special occasions where cannibalism was practiced could be understood within their spiritual purposes.

The cosmopolitan lifestyle of the people reported in Area IV is perhaps best represented in the evidence of trade between the people of the lower Rio Grande and the Huastecan culture a few hundred miles to the south. But as Cabeza de Vaca indicates, there was a trade network running between the lower Rio Grande and the Río Casas Grandes people in northwest Chihuahua. It certainly appears that the turquoise and cotton blankets found by Moscoso among the East Texas Caddo in the 1540s arrived at their destination along a sixteenth-century or earlier trade route that ran from northern Coahuila through Area IV to East Texas.

Long-distance interaction is noted also in the presence in Area IV of many hunters and traders from distant lands. Jumano, Cibolo, and Toboso Indians—all from the Big Bend area and northern Mexico—were seen and reported in Area IV hunting or moving through the area. The

Tepehuan from the Durango, Mexico, area were also recorded. Although there is limited documentary evidence that the numerous small Native groups were of a cosmopolitan character, there is ample evidence that Area IV Indians participated fully in broader regional trade patterns.

SUPPLEMENT: STUDY AREA IV
SOUTH TEXAS

This supplement lists alphabetically the names of Indian tribes or bands reported in Study Area IV in sixteenth- and seventeenth-century French and Spanish expedition documents. It should be noted that the author of one documentary source, Juan Bautista Chapa, gives the names of 70 tribes or bands on the lower Rio Grande that had been extinguished during the seventeenth century and the names of another 80 tribes that had been relocated from distant lands to replace those that perished on the lower Rio Grande. The names of these 150 tribes given by Chapa are not included below.

In compiling this supplement, I consulted the following sources: Rolena Adorno and Patrick Charles Pautz, trans., *Álvar Núñez Cabeza de Vaca: His Account, His Life, and the Expedition of Pánfilo de Narváez*; Alex D. Krieger, *We Came Naked and Barefoot: The Journey of Cabeza de Vaca across North America*; Carl L. Duaine, *Caverns of Oblivion*; Juan Bautista Chapa, *Texas and Northeastern Mexico, 1630–1690*; Mariah F. Wade, *The Native Americans of the Texas Edwards Plateau, 1582–1799*; Herbert E. Bolton, ed., *Spanish Exploration in the Southwest, 1542–1706*; and William C. Foster, *Spanish Expeditions into Texas, 1689–1768*.

1. Acubadao. Cabeza de Vaca described the location of the Acubadao as inland from the Atayo.
2. Agaaunimi. Géry told Chapa that the Agaaunimi were loyal to him and to France.
3. Agualoke. In 1693 Salinas met the Agualoke near the customary crossing of the Rio Grande into Maverick County.
4. Aguapalam. Terán met the Aguapalam and twelve other tribes gathered on the Frio River in Frio County.
5. Alachome. In 1691 Massanet and Terán met the Alachome near the customary crossing of the Rio Grande in Maverick County.
6. Anagado (Enagado). In 1535 Castillo was living with the Anagado, who released him to join Cabeza de Vaca's party in their escape across Area IV.
7. Apaysi. In June 1691 Terán encountered the Apaysi encamped with twelve other tribes near the Frio River in Frio County.

8. Ape (Api, Hape). On May 23, 1763, Bosque wrote that the Ape were allied with the Catujano in South Texas. Massanet wrote that in 1688 Governor De León found Géry living with the Api and seven other tribes in Area IV about fifty miles north of the Rio Grande.

9. Arbadao. Cabeza de Vaca wrote that the Arbadao lived south of the Maliacone toward the Rio Grande.

10. Atayo. Cabeza de Vaca identified the location of the Atayo as near the coast southwest of the Guaycone and Yguase. The Atayo were at war with the Susola.

11. Avavare (Chavavare). Cabeza de Vaca describes the location of the Avavare as inland from the coastal Quitole.

12. Bacora. On June 1, 1675, Bosque met the Bacora near the Rio Grande in the Maverick County area.

13. Bibit. On May 14, 1675, Bosque wrote that the Bibit were encountered in Area IV about thirty-five miles north of the Rio Grande. About two weeks later, Bosque met them again in Maverick County.

14. Bobole. Chapa wrote that over a hundred Boboles joined the Fernando de Azcué expedition of 1663 against the Cacaxtle near the Rio Grande.

15. Borrodo. Chapa wrote that the Borrodo raided Spanish settlements in northern Nuevo León in the 1660s.

16. Cabeza. During Bosque's 1675 expedition to South Texas, the Spanish party was told that the Cabeza held Spanish children as slaves. The children apparently were captured by the Cabezas near Parral and subsequently traded.

17. Cacaxtle. Chapa recorded that the Cacaxtle in Area IV were attacked by Spanish forces in late 1663 and early 1664.

18. Cagremoa. Géry told Chapa that the Cagremoa were loyal to him and to France.

19. Camole. Cabeza de Vaca identified the Camole on the coast south of the Quitole.

20. Caomopac. Géry told Chapa that the Caomopac were loyal to him and to France.

21. Catujano. On May 23, 1675, Bosque wrote that he found the Catujano allied with the Tilijae, Ape, and Pachaque in Area IV.

22. Caurame. On his 1686 expedition to the mouth of the Rio Grande, General Alonso de León was accompanied by forty-four Caurame.

23. Chaguan. Massanet recorded meeting the Chaguan with Terán in Zavala County in 1691.

24. Chichimeca. Alonso de León (the elder) reported engaging the Chichimeca in Tamaulipas in the 1640s.

25. Chile. Géry told Chapa that the Chile were loyal to him and to France.

26. Chomene. Massanet wrote that in 1688 Governor De León located Géry living with the Chomene and seven other tribes in Area IV about fifty miles north of the Rio Grande.

27. Coayo. Cabeza de Vaca identified the location of the Coayo near the Cuthalchuche and Maliacone.

28. Cobapo. Géry told Chapa that the Cobapo were loyal to him and to France.

29. Cocoma. On May 14, 1675, Bosque wrote that his expedition party encountered the Cocoma in Area IV.

30. Como. Cabeza de Vaca identified the location of the Como as near the Avavare.

31. Contotore. On June 10, 1675, Bosque met the Contotore near the Río Sabinas.

32. Cosmojoo. Géry told Chapa that the Cosmojoo were loyal to him and to France.

33. Cuajin. Géry told Chapa that the Cuajin were loyal to him and to France.

34. Cuchendado. Cabeza de Vaca identified the Cuchendado as living near the crossing area on the Rio Grande.

35. Cuthalchuche. Cabeza de Vaca placed the Cuthalchuche in an area next to the Avavare.

36. Etayax. Géry told Chapa that the Etayax were loyal to him and France.

37. Geniocane. On May 20, 1675, Bosque wrote that his expedition party, marching into Area IV, encountered the Geniocane, numbering 178 individuals and including women, boys, and girls.

38. Guachachile (Hatachichile). Alonso de León (the elder) reported that the Guachachile raided Spanish settlements in northern Nuevo León in the 1620s.

39. Guaycone. Cabeza de Vaca described the location of the Guaycone as along the coast southwest of the Quevenes.

40. Huiapico. Géry told Chapa that the Huiapico were loyal to him and to France.

41. Ijiaba (Xiabu). On his 1689 expedition to Texas, Governor De León met the Xiabu at the Rio Grande crossing in Maverick County.

42. Jeapa. Bosque wrote that the Jeapa were encountered on May 13, 1675, about ten miles north of the Rio Grande in Area IV.

43. Jeniocane. On May 23, 1675, Bosque wrote that he instructed the Jeniocane to remain in South Texas to await conversion.

44. Jume (Jumene). On May 14, 1675, Bosque says that the Jume were

met in Area IV about thirty-five miles north of the Rio Grande. On his 1689 expedition to Texas, Governor De León encountered the Jumene at the Rio Grande crossing.

45. Machomenesa. Massanet wrote that in 1688 Governor De León located Géry living with the Machomenesa and seven other tribes in Area IV about fifty miles north of the Rio Grande.

46. Maliacone. Cabeza de Vaca identified the residential area of the Maliacone as next to the Avavare.

47. Manosprieta. On June 5, 1675, Bosque met the Manosprieta between the Rio Grande and the Río Sabinas.

48. Mescal. Massanet wrote that in 1688 Governor De León found Géry living with the Mescal and seven other tribes in Area IV about fifty miles north of the Rio Grande.

49. Momon. Governor Terán in 1691 wrote that the Momon lived in Maverick County near the Rio Grande crossing area.

50. Ocana (Ocane, Acani). Terán met the Ocana on Comanche Creek in Zavala County in 1691. Salinas found the tribe near the customary Rio Grande crossing in 1693.

51. Ocare. On Bosque's 1675 expedition into South Texas, the diarist recorded that the Ocare was one of three tribes that had attacked the Yorica and Jeapa.

52. Odoesmade. Governor Terán in 1691 wrote that the Odoesmade lived in Maverick County near the Rio Grande.

53. Otomi. Chapa reported that the Otomi were brought from central Mexico into Nuevo León by the Spaniards in the 1650s to serve as herders or workmen.

54. Paac. In June 1691 Terán met the Paac in Zavala County with the Quem, Pachal, Ocana, and other tribes.

55. Pacausin (Pacuachiam). In 1691 Terán encountered the Pacuachiam in Frio County. In 1709 Espinosa met the tribe in Zavala County.

56. Pachaque. On May 23, 1675, Bosque wrote that Pachaque were allied with the Catujano in South Texas.

57. Pacpul. Massanet wrote that a Pacpul served as a guide on Governor De León's 1689 expedition to locate the French settlement on Matagorda Bay.

58. Pacuache (Pacoche). In 1693 Salinas met the Pacuache near the customary crossing of the Rio Grande into Maverick County.

59. Pacuasim (Paquasin). Massanet and Terán encountered the Pacuasim in Frio County in Area IV. Espinosa, in 1709, met the tribe in Zavala County and the following day near the Leona River.

60. Pajarito. On July 23, 1686, Governor De León met the Pajarito on the San Juan River near the Rio Grande in Nuevo León.

61. Pamaya (Pamai). In 1691 Massanet and Terán encountered the Pamaya near the customary crossing area of the Rio Grande in Maverick County.

62. Panaa. Géry told Chapa that the Panaa were loyal to him and to France.

63. Papanac (Panac). According to Massanet, Terán's expedition party found the Papanac in Frio County in June 1691.

64. Paquachiam. Massanet wrote that in 1688 Governor De León found Géry living with the Sampanal and seven other tribes in Area IV about fifty miles north of the Rio Grande.

65. Parchaca (Parchaque). In 1691 Massanet recorded meeting the Parchaca near the Rio Grande crossing in Maverick County and in Frio County.

66. Pastaloca. Terán met the Pastaloca in Zavala County in 1691 according to Massanet's account of the expedition.

67. Pastia (Paxti). Espinosa encountered the Paxti in the San Antonio area in April 1709.

68. Pataguaque. On May 13, 1675, Bosque wrote that his party was informed that the Pataguaque had attacked the Yorica and Jeapa in Area IV.

69. Pataguo (Patavo). Terán met the Patavo in 1691 near the Frio River in Frio County. Later the tribe was seen near the present-day Zavala-Frio county line.

70. Pataoo. Géry told Chapa that the Pataoo were loyal to him and to France.

71. Patchal (Pachal). In June 1691 Terán met the Patchal near the customary crossing of the Rio Grande in Maverick County.

72. Patsau (Patzau). In June 1691 Terán met the Patsau in Frio County.

73. Payaguan (Payavan). In 1691 Terán met the Payaguan in Frio County. Later the tribe was reported in Coahuila.

74. Payaya (Peyaye). In 1691 Terán met the Payaya near present-day San Antonio. In 1693 Salinas met the tribe at the Medina River near San Antonio.

75. Pelon. Chapa reports that in the 1660s the Pelon lived about thirty miles south of the Rio Grande in Nuevo León.

76. People of the Figs. Cabeza de Vaca placed the People of the Figs at a coastal area south of Camoles. The name of the tribe may indicate that the tribe had a special connection to the cactus fruit called tuna (or figs) by Spanish writers.

77. Piedras Blancas. In 1693 Salinas encountered the Piedras Blancas near the Rio Grande crossing in Maverick County.

78. Piguen. Géry told Chapa that the Piguen were loyal to him and to France.
79. Pinanaca. On May 14, 1675, Bosque recorded that the Pinanaca were encountered in Area IV about thirty-five miles north of the Rio Grande.
80. Pitahay (Pitanay). Terán met the Pitahay and twelve other tribes near the Frio River in Frio County in 1691.
81. Piyai. Géry told Chapa that the Piyai were loyal to him and to France.
82. Poguan. Géry told Chapa that the Poguan were loyal to him and to France.
83. Pujai. Géry told Chapa that the Pujai were loyal to him and to France.
84. Quem. Massanet wrote that a member of the Quem tribe told him that he had visited the French post on Matagorda Bay. The Quem served as a guide on De León's 1689 expedition to the French post.
85. Quitole. Cabeza de Vaca identified the Quitole as residing on the coast south of the Atayo.
86. Sacuache (Saquache). Salinas encountered the Sacuache in May 1693 on Comanche Creek and near the Leona River.
87. Samampac. In June 1691 Terán met the Samampac in Frio County.
88. Sampanal. Massanet wrote that in 1688 Governor De León found Géry living with the Sampanal and seven other tribes in Area IV about fifty miles north of the Rio Grande.
89. Sanatoo (Sana? Toho?). Géry told Chapa that the Sanatoo were loyal to him and to France. As the Sana and Toho were often found camped together, Géry may have considered them one tribe.
90. Saquita. In 1693 a Saquita served as a guide for Salinas through Area IV near the junction of the Hondo and Frio Rivers.
91. Saurum. Géry told Chapa that the Saurum were loyal to him and to France.
92. Susola. Cabeza de Vaca described the residential area of the Susola as next to the Avavare. The Susola were at war with the Atayo.
93. Tamireguan. Géry told Chapa that the Tamireguan were loyal to him and to France.
94. Teaname. In 1675 Bosque encountered the Teaname with the Xoman in South Texas.
95. Teimamar. On the 1675 Bosque expedition to South Texas, the party found the Teimamar with the Xoman.
96. Tenimama. On May 14, 1675, Bosque says that his expedition party met the Tenimama in Area IV.

97. Tepacuache (Tepaquache). In 1693 Salinas found the Tepaquache in Zavala County.
98. Tepehuan. Alonso de León (the elder) reported that the Tepehuan raided Spanish communities in northern Nuevo León near the lower Rio Grande during the 1630s and 1640s. In 1616 the Tepehuan revolted in Nueva Vizcaya, which was their permanent residence. The tribe was also reported in Area V.
99. Teroodan. Bosque wrote that on his 1675 expedition to South Texas, he found the Teroodan with the Xoman.
100. Tetecore. On June 12, 1675, Bosque met the Tetecores near the Rio Grande crossing area in Maverick County.
101. Tilijae. On May 23, 1673, Bosque says that the Tilijae were allied with the Catujano in South Texas.
102. Tilpayay. Massanet wrote that in 1688 Governor De León found Géry living with the Tilpayay and seven other tribes in Area IV about fifty miles north of the Rio Grande.
103. Tlaxcala. Chapa wrote that a company of Tlaxcala accompanied Spanish soldiers during the 1663–1664 expedition to fight the Cacaxtle near the Rio Grande. Their original homeland was in central Mexico, but Spanish authorities brought willing Tlaxcala families as settlers into northern Mexico.
104. Toboso. In May 1693 Salinas was warned by the Pacuache in Area IV that the Toboso and Jumano were planning an attack on his convoy. The Toboso were permanent residents of Nueva Vizcaya.
105. Toho (Thooe, Tohau). On General De León's 1689 expedition to Texas, the party met the Thooe in Area IV between the Nueces and San Antonio Rivers. The traditional residence of the tribe was in Area II.
106. Vanca (Vauca). Massanet wrote that Terán's party encountered the Vanca and twelve other tribes on the Frio River in Frio County in 1691.
107. Xaeser. On May 14, 1675, Bosque wrote that his party encountered the Xaeser in Area IV.
108. Xoman. Bosque wrote that on his 1675 expedition to South Texas, his party found a Xoman Indian who had met Spaniards before and who spoke "Mexican," meaning the Aztec language.
109. Yguaze. Cabeza de Vaca wrote that the Yguaze lived in northeastern Area IV.
110. Yorica (Yorca). In 1675 Bosque wrote that he met the Yorica on May 13 about ten miles north of the Rio Grande in Area IV. Massanet wrote that Governor De León in 1688 found Jean Géry living

in a shared encampment of eight tribes, including the Yorica, about fifty miles north of the Rio Grande.

111. Yurbipane. On May 13, 1675, Bosque wrote that the Yurbipane had attacked the Yorica and Jeapa in Area IV.

112. Zacatil. A friendly leader of the Zacatil accompanied General Alonso de León on his 1686 expedition to the Rio Grande.

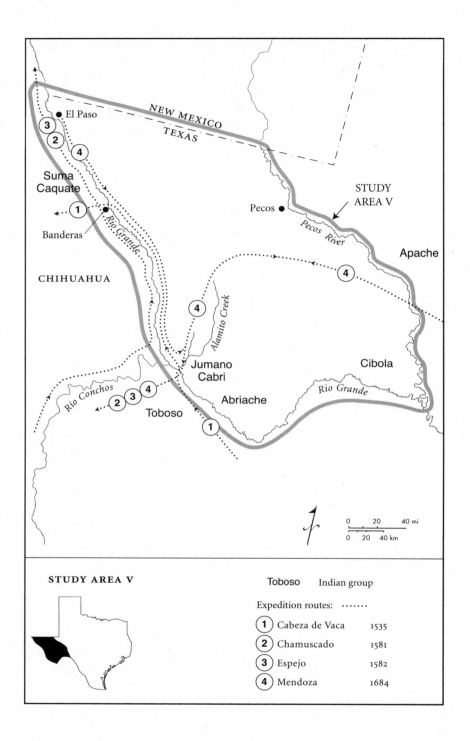

NEW MEXICO
TEXAS

● El Paso

③
②
④

Suma
Caquate

① Banderas

CHIHUAHUA

Rio Grande

Pecos ●

Pecos River

STUDY
AREA V

Apache

④

④

Alamito Creek

Jumano
Cabri

Cibola

Rio Grande

Rio Conchos

② ③ ④

Toboso

Abriache

①

0   20   40 mi
0   20   40 km

STUDY AREA V

Toboso   Indian group

Expedition routes: ·······

① Cabeza de Vaca   1535
② Chamuscado   1581
③ Espejo   1582
④ Mendoza   1684

MAP 5.1

5 THE TEXAS TRANS-PECOS

STUDY AREA V

The boundary of the Indian country included in Study Area V, or the Trans-Pecos, extends from the junction of the Rio Grande and the Pecos River up the Rio Grande to El Paso and then turns east following the state boundary line between Texas and New Mexico to the Pecos River. The boundary then runs southeast down the Pecos and back to its junction with the Rio Grande (see Map 5.1). In volume 9 of the Smithsonian Institution's *Handbook of North American Indians,* the editor depicts Study Area V in ca. 1700 on a map of the American Southwest showing the Jumano Indians occupying the eastern part of the Trans-Pecos, the Conchos Indians located in the south (including Big Bend), the Suma residing along the Rio Grande from the junction of the Mexican Río Conchos upstream to a location near modern El Paso, and the Mescalero Apache living in the northern part of the Trans-Pecos and into New Mexico.[1]

Topographically, the area is dominated by two river systems, the Rio Grande and the Pecos, and a mountain range that crosses the western section of the area. Area V is generally dryer than other study areas to the east, with precipitation averaging frequently only one-fifth or less of the rain recorded in more eastern areas. The study area includes the western part of Val Verde County and all of Terrell, Brewster, Presidio, Jeff Davis, Pecos, Reeves, Culberson, Hudspeth, and El Paso Counties. During the study period Native peoples in the more eastern counties were related culturally more closely to their allies in Central Texas and north-central Mexico; the Indians in the western counties were by culture related closely to the people of the Southwest, particularly southern New Mexico.[2]

To summarize, no fewer than seven major Spanish and French expeditions crossed or reached the Trans-Pecos and western Chihuahua during the study period. In the early fall of 1535 Cabeza de Vaca and his three companions returned to the Rio Grande in the Trans-Pecos from north-central Mexico and visited Indian villages near La Junta de los Ríos. About a month later, after moving up the Rio Grande about 170 miles, Cabeza de Vaca's party crossed the large river for the last time to march westward another 170 miles across two broad river valleys in western Chihuahua to visit the Río Casas Grandes people, who were closely related by culture and trade with the Rio Grande folk in Area V.

In 1565, about twenty-nine years after Cabeza de Vaca visited the Casas Grandes area, the Spanish explorer Francisco de Ibarra camped near the ruins of Casas Grandes, which his diarist Baltasar de Obregón calls Paquimé. Obregón writes that only thirty years earlier, Cabeza de Vaca had visited the same Casas Grandes area, and according to the local Indians, many of the former residents of Paquimé (which had a population of perhaps 20,000 or more) had simply moved about sixty miles north upriver after the city had been defeated by an enemy from the west. Obregón adds that large bison herds and bison hunters, whom he calls Querecho, were found nearby.

In 1581, about fifteen years after Ibarra's party visited Paquimé, a small Spanish expeditionary force led by Captain Francisco Sánchez Chamuscado left Parral in southern Chihuahua near the present-day state line with Durango to visit La Junta de los Ríos in Area V and to explore New Mexico along the upper Rio Grande. Soon after the 1581 expedition group had completed their tour and had returned, a second expedition from Parral was dispatched to New Mexico. The 1581 and 1582 expedition accounts provide descriptions of the fauna and flora and detailed ethnographic information on the Native people living along the Río Conchos in Mexico and along the Rio Grande from La Junta to central New Mexico.

In 1590 Gaspar Castaño de Sosa led a large colonizing expedition from Monclova, Coahuila, to the Rio Grande crossing and up the Pecos River to New Mexico. The route took the caravan along the border separating Areas V and VI; as the route was frequently north of the Pecos in Area VI, Castaño's journey will be covered in the following chapter.

A second colonizing expedition to New Mexico, led by Juan de Oñate, was commenced in 1598 near Parral. As the journey passed through only the westernmost tip of Area V, limited ethnographic information on Area V Indians is found in the records of Oñate's journey. However, one of Oñate's officers, Vicente de Zaldívar, led a hunting expedition onto the bison plains in 1598 that does provide important information on the Plains Indians and the plants and animals identified. This information will be reviewed in detail in Chapter Six.

During the early and middle seventeenth century, Spanish colonial efforts continued to concentrate on New Mexico rather than West Texas. The next large Spanish expedition to travel through Area V was led by Juan Domínguez de Mendoza in 1684. The general and his troops, with Jumano Indian guides, marched from El Paso down the Rio Grande to La Junta and then probably up Alamito Creek to the northeast to cross the Pecos River and leave Area V.

When Robert Cavelier, Sieur de La Salle, landed on the central Texas coast in 1685 (a year after the commencement of Domínguez de Mendoza's expedition), his primary attention was focused eastward toward the Mississippi River, his assigned destination. But, under orders from his king, La Salle was also to obtain information about the rich and highly prized silver mines in the Parral area. La Salle's journeys westward to Area V and ethnographic information found in documents associated with these journeys will also be reviewed in this chapter. In closing, we will cover the 1715 expedition from Parral to La Junta to reestablish a clerical presence among the La Junta tribes in Area V.

Sixteenth- and Seventeenth-Century Spanish and French Expeditions

Cabeza de Vaca was the first European to leave a documentary record of encounters with the Native peoples in the Texas Trans-Pecos. As mentioned earlier, Cabeza de Vaca's party landed on the central Texas coast in November 1528, and he remained principally in the coastal area until 1533, when he moved down the coast into South Texas to live with the Mariame Indians and some of his companions from the Narváez expedition. In 1535 Cabeza de Vaca and three companions escaped their local Indian hosts and initially headed southward toward Pánuco, a port city on the Gulf of Mexico. The party of four crossed the Rio Grande into northeastern Mexico near the present-day International Falcon Reservoir in Zapata County.[3]

During the next several months, Cabeza's party moved westward through northeastern Mexico, at times along the Río Sabinas, and returned to the Rio Grande near its junction with the Río Conchos. I have concluded that, in general, the Cabeza de Vaca routes through Texas and northern Mexico as projected by Alex D. Krieger and more recently in a study by Rolena Adorno and Patrick Pautz are the most accurate route projections to date, and they are followed (with minor modifications) in this study.[4]

Cabeza de Vaca describes the Indian village near La Junta de los Ríos in 1535 as having permanent houses that were located near a river that flowed between mountains. Although the men were naked and the women wore only deerskins, the La Junta Indians cultivated corn, beans, squash, and gourds. Without specifically noting it, Cabeza de Vaca likely identified the source of the distinctive gourd that Estevan had been given by local Natives earlier downriver in Nuevo León. Cabeza de Vaca writes that they were the liveliest, most capable, and best physically structured people he had encountered on his journey.

When asked by the Spaniards to explain why they were not growing maize at the time, the Natives replied that during the previous two years there had been a drought and that they would plant maize only after it had rained very hard. The drought conditions in West Texas tend to confirm Cabeza de Vaca's earlier report of temporary dry conditions in Area IV. When asked where they had originally obtained their seed corn, the Natives replied that the seed had come from the west (probably from the Río Casas Grandes area) and that it was plentiful there. The village people also had a supply of bison hides, and Cabeza de Vaca called the residents the "People of the Cows (or Bison)." It appears that the Cow People were closely aligned with their neighbors and allies living both upriver and downstream on the Rio Grande. Some researchers, including Alex Krieger, equate the Cow People with the Jumano Indians and their associated tribes recorded in seventeenth-century documents.

Cabeza de Vaca also describes how the Cow People cooked beans and squash without using pottery. The author writes that the Indians filled a medium-size gourd with water and dropped hot rocks into the water, causing the water to heat. The hot water was used to cook beans or other food, and the Natives kept the water boiling by using wooden tongs to pick up and replace cooler rocks in the water with hotter rocks from the fire. The Cow People said that bison was available to the north.

Cabeza de Vaca's party remained with the Cow People for only a day and then moved up the Rio Grande with local Native escorts, visiting similar villages with permanent houses and an abundant supply of bison skins. The fact that Cabeza de Vaca does not include cotton as one of the local crops suggests that the cotton blankets and other cotton goods found among residents of the Rio Grande villages were likely imports from the Casas Grandes region, where cotton was grown. He added that all the people met along the Rio Grande route upriver from La Junta spoke the same language as the Cow People but that sign language was also used.

At the end of a seventeen-day march upriver, Cabeza de Vaca's party crossed the Rio Grande moving toward the west, leaving Texas and Area V. Krieger places Cabeza de Vaca's turn west across the Rio Grande at a ford near the small modern town of Banderas in Chihuahua, about seventy-five miles downriver from present-day El Paso. The projected location of this crossing assumes that the party moved, on average, about ten miles a day during the seventeen-day march, a reasonable assumption as the pace conforms generally to that of Spanish expedition parties through the same area later.

As mentioned earlier, Cabeza de Vaca's account is supplemented by a report prepared by the Spanish historian Gonzalo Fernández de Oviedo y Valdez, who was not a member of Cabeza de Vaca's party.[5] Oviedo's account is based primarily on a joint report prepared by the three Spaniards on the journey. Oviedo writes that while in Area V Cabeza de Vaca visited four Indian villages located on the large river (Rio Grande), that the area along the river was heavily populated, and that each village had permanent houses. The historian reports that the Natives had bows and arrows and had bison-hide robes and served corn, beans, and squash. Oviedo adds that the stones used in heating water for cooking were small and clean and that the beans were ground into a powder before being placed into the boiling water to make soup. Oviedo also confirms that bison were to be found to the north of the villages (probably referring to the Southern Plains) and that the seed corn and cotton goods originated in the area to the west, toward Casas Grandes and the Pacific.

According to Oviedo, Cabeza's party marched up the Rio Grande for fifteen days, although Cabeza de Vaca says the trip took seventeen days. After leaving the Rio Grande, Cabeza de Vaca's party moved west and crossed the basin and range and two large river valleys in northwestern Chihuahua. Local Natives encountered en route provided the Spaniards with rabbits and some form of "powdered herbs," most likely domesticated amaranth.[6]

After traveling westward for seventeen days (according to Cabeza de Vaca) or twenty days (according to Oviedo), the party arrived at a large permanent community located on a plain between very high mountains. These people had flat-roofed adobe houses and an abundant supply of corn, squashes, beans, cotton goods, and turquoise, as the Rio Grande Indians had told Cabeza's party earlier. These people were called the "Maize People" by Cabeza de Vaca.

Based on the direction and distance traveled from the Rio Grande crossing near Banderas, it appears that Cabeza de Vaca's party with accompanying Rio Grande guides arrived near or perhaps 40 to 50 miles north of the well-known ancient Indian cultural center known as Paquimé or Casas Grandes (ca. 107° 52' West and 30° 22' North), which is about 160 miles west-southwest of modern Banderas. In their projections of Cabeza de Vaca's route west from the Rio Grande, Krieger and Adorno and Pautz write that the "Maize People" met by Cabeza de Vaca were likely either the O'patas in Sonora or people living in or near the Río Casas Grandes.[7] I believe the people were the latter and not the O'patas, who lived west of the Sierra Madre in Sonora, over 100 miles beyond the Casas Grandes area. I also believe the Maize People may have included remnants of the Paquimé population who had moved about 60 miles to the north downriver, as reported in 1665 by the historian Obregón.

Casas Grandes, or Paquimé, was one of the most influential metropolitan cities in northwest Mexico and the American Southwest during the period ca. AD 1200 to 1500. The Casas Grandes exchange network extended from their homeland at Paquimé eastward to Nuevo León and the Gulf of Mexico and westward to the Gulf of California and the Pacific. Scarlet macaws and macaw feathers, Gulf of California marine shells, and locally cast copper bells and distinctive cotton blankets were prestige items of exchange from Casas Grandes, and subsequent Spanish expedition parties reported these same trade goods among Texas Indians on the Rio Grande in Area V.

The Maize People generously gave goods and food supplies to the Rio Grande guides who had accompanied the Spaniards, and Cabeza de Vaca adds that the guides returned home to the Rio Grande very happy with the food and goods given them.

The Maize People showed the Spaniards coral beads that they had secured from the west (the Gulf of California) and turquoise from people living to the north (New Mexico), who in exchange were given by the Casas Grandes traders parrot plumes from scarlet macaws held and bred in large, especially constructed adobe macaw parrot cages by Casas Grandes people.

Cabeza de Vaca adds that the Indian women wore knee-length cotton skirts and open deerskin blouses tied with strings and that all wore shoes. From these people living in northwest Chihuahua, Cabeza de Vaca's party moved farther westward toward the Pacific Coast, where they were found by Spanish soldiers and were escorted to Mexico.

Reports of Cabeza de Vaca's travels sparked further Spanish exploration during the 1540s by Francisco de Coronado and Hernando de Soto, who explored the American Southwest and Southeast, but neither of these large expedition parties entered Area V. Perhaps because neither Coronado nor De Soto discovered attractive mineral prospects north of Cabeza de Vaca's route, the Spanish crown and Spanish explorers lost interest in Texas for about two decades, until the 1560s.

In 1565, when General Francisco de Ibarra and his chronicler, Baltasar de Obregón, visited Paquimé, Obregón writes that the large vacated city with buildings up to seven stories high seemed to have been constructed by highly skilled builders such as the ancient Romans.[8] Obregón comments that the walls of the houses were whitewashed and painted many colors and shades with pictures. This style of mural paining was found during the same period in Mexico and throughout the Southwest, including La Junta.[9] According to Obregón, walls were adobe mixed with stone and wood for strength, and "there were great and wide canals used to carry water from the river to their houses." William Doolittle, who has written the definitive work on canals and irrigation in Mexico, writes that the water control system at Paquimé was the most sophisticated in the Southwest and in Mesoamerica at the time.[10]

Ibarra's men also found copper slag and two copper plates cast from molds by skillful Paquimé artisans. Obregón reports that clusters of houses were spread northward from Paquimé over a distance of twenty miles downriver.

The Native people living near Paquimé in 1565 did not live in the big houses and buildings of Paquimé but rather lived in straw huts in areas nearby. The Spaniards communicated with the local Indians by signs, and by signs the local Natives explained that the former residents of Paquimé had moved only six days' journey downriver to the north.[11] The best available documentary evidence of the migration of the people of Paquimé after the fall of the city in ca. 1450 to 1500 is found in Obregón's account, given in 1565.

During Ibarra's stay near Paquimé, a Plains Indian bison hunting band (called Querechos by Obregón) visited the Spaniards. The large group included 300 men with their "attractive" women and children, who arrived singing and dancing around the camp. The Querechos told Ibarra that large bison herds were nearby, four days' journey to the north. Obregón believed the reports because Ibarra's troop found in situ bison bones, hides, and manure near their campground.

The report of large bison herds grazing across northwestern Chihuahua near Paquimé is consistent with other information regarding the southern extent of rangelands for bison during the Little Ice Age. In a recent study of the impact of climate change on North American Native populations and cultures, Richardson B. Gill argues that the excellent grazing lands and vegetation available in the northern Chihuahuan Desert were established under and adapted to the Little Ice Age and are not supported under the existing warmer period.[12]

Obregón's description of the ruins of Paquimé was basically repeated in several subsequent Spanish military reports from visits to the Casas Grandes area. In February 1727 Don Pedro de Rivera visited the small town and mission of Antonio de Casas Grandes, located near the ruins of Paquimé. At that time the mission and town were populated with only six Conchos and Suma Indian families. Rivera declares that he marched through the ruins of a "palace" that was built (he thought) by the "Emperor Montezuma" before he left with his Aztec followers and their culture to settle Mexico City. Rivera says that the buildings were constructed in the form of a parallelogram that measured about 540 meters on each side.[13] Rivera's comments regarding the origin of the Aztec people and Montezuma are not considered accurate, but his measurements of the parameters of the city come remarkably close to the mark.

In October 1766, about forty years after Rivera's visit, the Marqués de Rubí visited the same Casas Grandes area. Rubí writes that following the Río Casas Grandes upstream (moving southward), his party found the ruins of the old settlement of "Moctezuma," which appeared as a very large city. Rubí says that the vacated ruins called Casas Grandes "were among the most opulent in Nueva Vizcaya."[14]

Rubí's engineer, Nicolás de Lafora, also maintained a detailed diary account of the 1766–1767 expedition, and Lafora describes Casas Grandes in more detail.[15] The engineer writes of discovering the remains of a very old city, which Lafora calls "Casas Grandes de Moctezuma." Lafora also reports finding walls several meters high constructed of blocks of earth three to five feet thick, plastered and whitewashed.

Lafora, like Rivera, apparently associated Paquimé with the Aztec people and their leader, Montezuma. The engineer writes that on one side of the rectangle formed by two plazas were small pens or enclosures in rows that he thought were intended "for wild animal cages." Charles Di Peso identifies the rows of "animal cages" described and carefully measured by Lafora as holding pens for scarlet macaw that were bred and raised at Paquimé after being imported over 600 miles from northeast Mexico.[16]

Apparently Spanish authorities had difficulty in the eighteenth century understanding the significance of the Casas Grandes phenomena and the cultural center's role in the history of Mexico. Many of these questions and others regarding Casas Grandes remain unresolved, but the critical significance of Casas Grandes to the La Junta people with respect to trade and alliances in the sixteenth century is clear.

Between 1560 and 1580 two developments—one in Spain and the second in northern Mexico—altered the pattern of Spanish exploration in the Southwest. Stung by criticisms from vocal clerics, the Spanish crown in 1573 adopted new Colonization Laws that prohibited private excursions by Spaniards into unexplored lands in northern Mexico without specific approval of the viceroy. The second development was the rapid expansion of mining ventures in north-central Mexico, particularly into

HISTORIC NATIVE PEOPLES OF TEXAS

the Parral–Santa Bárbara area near the headwaters of the Río Conchos, which flows northward to La Junta on the middle Rio Grande in Area V.

About forty-five years after Cabeza de Vaca visited Area V and approximately fifteen years after Obregón visited Casas Grandes, the viceroy authorized a small expedition party to explore the Río Conchos north of Parral and the Rio Grande pueblo communities in Texas and New Mexico. The 1581 expedition was led by Captain Francisco Sánchez Chamuscado; it was composed of only nine soldiers, three priests, and nineteen Indians. The Natives served as guides and interpreters along the route down the Río Conchos to the junction with the Rio Grande. Captain Chamuscado also took with him ninety horses and 600 head of stock.

The soldiers included Hernán Gallegos, Hernando Barrado, and Felipe de Escalante each of whom either prepared a written account of the journey or testified about the expedition in Mexico after their return. No account of the journey was prepared by the captain or the clerical contingent because they did not return to Santa Bárbara. The priests were killed by Indians in New Mexico; Chamuscado became ill and died on the return trip.

The most comprehensive and detailed account of the Chamuscado expedition was written by the soldier Hernán Gallegos in July 1582, rendered in the form of a journal or *relación*. Earlier in May, Gallegos had given a testimonial summarizing the trip.[17] In the introduction to his journal, Gallegos states that his intention is not only to give an account of the exploration route but also to describe "the various customs and rituals that we learned about from the natives." This type of statement, disclosing a specific interest in recording ethnographic information on the lifeways of the Native population, is seldom found explicitly expressed in sixteenth-century expedition diaries prepared by Spanish soldiers in the Southwest.

According to Hernán Gallegos, the expedition party set out on June 6, 1581, from the valley of San Gregorio, which was within the jurisdiction of Santa Bárbara, Chihuahua. The party, following local guides, marched about thirty miles from Santa Bárbara down the Río San Gregorio toward its junction with the Río Conchos, and then the party continued downstream along the Conchos. Several of the names of rivers in Chihuahua given in the 1582 account are the same as those found on contemporary maps.

Gallegos reports that the party met first the Conchos Indians along the upper route and later the Raya, who inhabited the same country and spoke the same language as the Conchos. At this point Gallegos reports a latitude reading of 29° north, which appears to be reasonably accurate, according to contemporary maps of Mexico. The 29° north latitude line intersects the Río Conchos a few miles north of the large lake now formed at the junction of the Conchos and Las Víboras rivers. The chronicler reports that the Conchos and Raya Indians were unattractive and wore no clothing; the Natives survived on ground mesquite beans, mescal, prickly pear, fish from the river, and a species of squash that they cultivated. Gallegos indicates that the Indians on the upper Conchos were at least part-time farmers.

About thirteen miles farther down the Conchos, the party met members of the Cabri nation who spoke a language different from the one spoken by the Conchos. The Cabri were described as very handsome, spirited, intelligent, and well built. They too were horticulturists who grew both squash and beans. When asked about the Native people farther north, the Cabri apparently knew of the New Mexico Pueblo people, who they said lived very far from there. The local Natives on the Río Conchos said that the pueblo Natives in New Mexico lived in many large houses, had stocks of corn and beans, and wore white clothing. We should note that these semisedentary people in northern Mexico were aware of the lifeways of pueblo people living 400 miles up the Rio Grande in New Mexico.

After leaving the Cabri at a point near the junction of the Río Conchos and the Rio Grande, a large delegation of unidentified Indians greeted the Spanish party. As reported by Cabeza de Vaca earlier, the Natives near La Junta were cheerful and handsome, and the women beautiful. A tribal leader claimed that their people occupied an area that extended over 260 miles and that he knew of the pueblo people to the northwest in New Mexico. The locals spoke a language that the Indians called "Amoto-manco," which was different from the language of the Cabri, although the two could understand each other.

Like the Cabri and Conchos Indians, La Junta people wore no clothes, but they were very accomplished horticulturists, cultivating corn, beans, and squash. For weapons they had very fine large bows and shields of bison hide. While the bow and arrow with comparatively smaller arrowheads replaced the atlatl and the larger dart points in most areas of Texas in ca. AD 500 to 700, the Trans-Pecos archeologist Bob Mallouf projects that the spear-thrower continued to be used in West Texas until about AD 1100.[18]

Gallegos describes the permanent houses at La Junta as square with heavy forked corner posts upon which were placed rounded logs the thickness of a man's thigh. La Junta craftsmen filled in the open wall area between the corner posts with staked poles plastered with mud. Gallegos thought that the houses looked like many of the Indian houses he had seen near Mexico City. Again, in the fashion of Mexican (Aztec) Indians, according to Gallegos, the La Junta people had separate storehouses built of willow branches near their fields to hold provisions and the harvest. The local Indians greeted the Spaniards from crowded standing positions on the flat housetops. The first village or pueblo visited by the party near La Junta had eight large square houses, each accommodating thirty-five to forty occupants.

Gallegos reports that Natives wore pieces of copper strung on necklaces made of cotton thread and carried small copper bells. The Indians also wore white and red coral beads and had exotic feathers and turquoise. Gallegos writes that the local Indians said that they had obtained all of these foreign items by trade from tribes living to the west, probably referring to trading centers on the Río Casas Grandes. But the La Junta people apparently did not actively engage in direct trade with Pueblo Indians to the north up the Rio Grande in New Mexico.

When the Chamuscado party left the La Junta area, many local Natives accompanied the Spaniards marching up the Rio Grande. During the eighteen-day trip toward present-day El Paso, the Natives entertained the Spanish troops nightly with song-dances. Gallegos observed that the Rio Grande Natives had a natural rhythm in their dances and that the cadence was maintained by drumbeat. The drum was tightly covered with an animal skin "in the fashion of a tambourine." Gallegos writes that the song-dance was performed with such unity and harmony, that although there were 300 in the dance, it seemed as if it were being sung and danced by only one person.[19]

Two days beyond the point where the La Junta Natives turned back to return home, the Spanish party met members of another friendly Indian tribe. This tribe (unnamed by Gallegos) offered the Spaniards assistance and gifts, including some exotic headdresses made of macaw parrot feathers. Scarlet macaw parrots and feathers (like small copper bells, colorful marine shells, and coral) were hallmark trade items exported from the Casas Grandes region, which was located only about 170 miles west of where the Chamuscado party was then visiting.

Zooarcheologists write that scarlet macaw parrots reported in the American Southwest were not local to the area but rather originated from the lowlands of northeastern Mexico in Tamaulipas and Nuevo León.[20] These writers indicate that in the mid-fifteenth century the trade network from Casas Grandes extended eastward down the middle Rio Grande to La Junta and on farther eastward across northeastern Mexico to the Gulf of Mexico.[21]

As the Spaniards had no interpreter available to communicate with the Natives encountered on the Rio Grande south of present-day El Paso, the Spaniards and Natives communicated by the use of signs. The Indians indicated that the Spaniards would find no other settlements in the next week or so as they marched up the river, but that soon thereafter they would see the first large pueblo communities. The Chamuscado party continued upstream for another three days and encountered no Indians but found a marshy, uninhabited valley. The party was probably near the swampy area of the Rio Grande that extends south of El Paso.

After the expedition party passed present-day El Paso, the Spaniards traveled for another fifteen days, continuing upriver and outside Area V before reaching on August 21 the first New Mexico pueblo, located near modern-day San Marcial. It appears that the route west from the Rio Grande below El Paso to the Río Casas Grandes people was shorter than the route north up the desolate Rio Grande to the first pueblos in New Mexico and was a much easier way with rest stops where two river valleys crossed northwest Chihuahua.

After leaving the crossing of the Rio Grande near Banderas along the route projected, Cabeza de Vaca traveled about sixty-five miles west through a pass in modest Sierra San José del Prisco to a point near Laguna de Patos on the Río del Carmen and then another fifty-five miles to the Río Santa María and finally about another fifty miles to the Río Casas Grandes near Janos.[22]

The first Rio Grande pueblo visited by Chamuscado was uninhabited, but it was sizable with many three-story houses. In the surrounding area there were large fields of maize, beans, squash, and cotton. The houses were constructed in blocks, with mud walls whitewashed inside. The houses had many ceramic pots, large earthen jars, and flat pans that Gallegos claims "surpass the quality of pottery made in Portugal." The Pueblo people made corn tortillas "similar to those in New Spain" and a corn-flour gruel (atole), and they had bison meat. They had corrals to hold flocks of domestic turkeys that numbered up to one hundred birds in each corral. The local Natives also raised small shaggy dogs that they held in underground pens.

According to Gallegos, the Pueblo people frequently traded with the Plains Indians, exchanging their cotton blankets and corn for bison hides and meat. Gallegos added that this exchange pattern had encouraged each party to learn the other's language.

Gallegos was obviously fascinated by the lifeways of the Pueblo Natives and seemed to understand the importance of carefully observing and recording the dress, economic activity, trade patterns, language, and religion of the Pueblo Indians. The diarist frequently compares elements of the Pueblo culture with those "of the Mexicans," referring to the Aztec in Mexico. Gallegos observes that "the manner of carrying loads, sleeping, eating, and sitting is the same as that of the Mexicans. . . . It is all very interesting." The careful detail given to Indian lifeways is reminiscent of the detail found in the expedition narrative prepared by Cabeza de Vaca, a copy of which Gallegos apparently had at hand.

Chamuscado's party remained in New Mexico visiting one pueblo after another, and the party ventured farther eastward toward the Southern Plains to hunt bison between the Pecos and the Canadian Rivers. At the close of the five-month exploration in New Mexico, Chamuscado's party visited the salt marshes and the pueblos east of the present-day Manzano Mountains (called the Sierra Morena by Gallegos), closer to the Texas border but not within Area VI.

On April 15, 1582, the soldiers in the Chamuscado party, having retraced their route down the Rio Grande, returned to Santa Bárbara. Gallegos gives only a cursory three-paragraph statement summarizing the return trip. As mentioned earlier, Gallegos and Pedro de Bustamante gave testimonials on the expedition journey in Mexico City in May 1582, but these statements add nothing significant regarding Texas Indians beyond that found in Gallegos's *Relación*.

Reports from the Chamuscado expedition describing the Pueblo people and the plight of the three Franciscan priests who remained in New Mexico encouraged the viceroy to authorize a second expedition in late 1582 to investigate the possible deaths of the priests who remained in New Mexico and to continue explorations. Antonio de Espejo was the leader of the second expedition from the Santa Bárbara area to the Texas Rio Grande in Area V and upstream to the New Mexico pueblos. Two firsthand accounts of the trip were prepared; the first and more definitive account was recorded by Diego Pérez de Luxán.[23]

Luxán writes that the 1582 expedition was launched from the Valle de San Gregorio on November 10. This also was a small expedition party with only two friars and thirteen men (one with his wife and three children). After marching about forty-five miles down the Río San Gregorio, as Chamuscado had marched the year before, the party arrived at the junction of the San Gregorio and Conchos rivers. Near the junction, the Spaniards found a large settlement of friendly Conchos Indians. Luxán writes that the Conchos hunted deer and rabbit, fished the rivers, raised squash, and made mescal from maguey. The party continued down the Río Conchos, engaging friendly groups of Conchos Indians each day and receiving items of food, including rabbit meat and fish.

On December 5 the expedition arrived at the northern boundary of the Conchos Indians and entered the domain of the "striped" Indians at a place that the Spanish named "El Puerto de la Raya de los Conchos."

Luxán identified the tribe as the "warlike Passaquates" (Passaguates) who were friends of the Conchos living upstream and friends of the people living downstream closer to La Junta de los Ríos. Male members of the tribes were naked, but women wore rabbit or deerskin skirts. Two young boys, one a Passaguate named Juan and the second an Otomoaco called Pedro, followed the party willingly to serve as guides and interpreters on the trip to New Mexico. On December 6, about ten miles farther down-river on the Conchos, Espejo came upon Indians that he identified as "Jumano and Otomoaco."

The Otomoaco were different in several respects from the tribes met earlier. Unlike the Conchos, the Otomoaco were bison hunters. Their bows were exceptionally strong and reinforced; their bowstrings were made of bison sinews. Luxán reports that bison ranged to within about eighty miles of the junction of the rivers (later called La Junta), which places the closest herds in western Pecos County. Some women wore tanned deerskin bodices and bison-skin cloaks. They fastened feathers of geese, cranes, and hawks to a tassel of their hair. The Otomoaco farmed together large fields of corn, beans, squash, and gourds (but no cotton) along the Río Conchos and Rio Grande. Luxán refers to the communities as pueblos and says that in each there were numerous flat-roofed houses built half below the ground.

When the Otomoaco first heard that the Spanish party was advancing in their direction, the Indians dispersed in fear into the mountains, but when the young Otomoaco boy-guide, Pedro, assured them that the Spaniards' visit was to make peace, the Natives (up to 600 counted) re-turned. Many were whistling or, as Luxán describes, "making musical sounds with their mouths similar to those of the flute." As will be noted, Indians of the Pueblo de Los Jumanos in eastern New Mexico had small mouth whistles.

The pueblo situated on the Texas side of the Rio Grande near the junction was on a high ridge and contained numerous flat-roofed houses. Below the high ridges, there were many other houses. The "cacique" in this pueblo was named Casica Mayo.

The Spanish party remained in the area for over a week visiting three pueblos upstream and downstream from La Junta. About six miles down-river from La Junta at a place called La Paz, Espejo found the Abriache, who spoke a language different from that of the Otomoaco. They were, however, interrelated and friends. Luxán adds that all the Indians near La Junta had the same style of houses, clothes, and arrows.

Luxán writes that the broad area near the river junction was an ideal location for agriculture with its damp sandy islands and broad areas to cultivate near the river bottom. The people received the Spaniard graciously in each pueblo, celebrating and making music by whistling. The Otomoaco told the Spaniards that three men who looked like them and a black man had visited their people long ago. This is the second expedition account that records Cabeza de Vaca's party visiting the La Junta area, and Luxán writes that "in this pueblo, as well as in all of the three, they told us of how Cabeza de Vaca and his two companions and a Negro had been there."

On December 17 the Spanish party moved "up the river named Del Norte [the Rio Grande]" through areas in which the streambed at its widest part was about eight miles across and the banks were covered with cottonwood, willows, screwbean, and mesquite. Luxán also called the Indians along the upper river Otomoaco. The Spaniards were well received by over 200 Indians celebrating at night with music, accompanied by clapping hands and singing and dancing with strict rhythm and in unison. The Natives may have been the same singing and dancing group that entertained the Chamuscado party the year before along the same stretch of the Rio Grande. Also, as they did the year before, these Natives presented the Spaniards with gifts, including cotton shawls and colorful feather headdresses that they had obtained from Indian traders living to the west (not farther upriver to the north). Again we have documentary evidence of an important trade route linking the middle Rio Grande tribes living upstream from La Junta with the Casas Grandes culture in the 1580s.

On January 2, 1583, the Espejo expedition passed out of Jumano country and encountered the Caguate Indians in what was later known as the territory of the Suma Indians. According to Luxán, the Caguate had intermarried with the Otomoaco and spoke a similar language. The leader of the Caguate, whom Luxán records as being the grandfather of the young Jumano guide Pedro, greeted the Spanish party. There were over 300 men and women in the Caguate settlement. In the evenings the Caguate performed impressive dances for their Spanish guests. Here the Espejo party was apparently south of El Paso in a region described as swampy, with large flocks of ducks, geese, and cranes.

As the Espejo party continued to travel upstream, they encountered the Tanpachoa Indians, who were also related to the Otomoaco and had the same manner of dress. The Tanpachoa had corn, mesquite beans, and fish that they caught using small dragnets in the numerous small pools along the river. For fighting, the Tanpachoa used two-foot-long bludgeons made of tornillo (screwbean) wood as well as the bow and arrow.

By January 23, Espejo had traveled beyond El Paso, out of Area V, and into New Mexico. The weather turned extremely cold, freezing hard the ponds of water near the river. The thick ice had to be broken with picks to obtain drinking water. According to Luxán, five days later the party reached an impressive large black rocky butte (perhaps Elephant Butte). Continuing upriver to the north, Espejo marched another forty miles to the pueblo that had been named San Felipe by Chamuscado in August 1581.

During the spring and early summer, Espejo's party visited many of the pueblos up the Rio Grande. Luxán writes that in early July the party visited a large pueblo that had four-story, flat-roofed houses with drainage troughs and movable ladders. The Natives gave the Spaniards turkeys, pinole, and other things they requested.

On the return trip Espejo's party captured two Indians to guide them to the bison hunting grounds along the Pecos River to the east. Luxán reports that there were numerous vines, cottonwoods, mesquite, and rosebushes along the Río de las Vacas (the name given the Pecos River), which the party followed downstream in early July. During the first four days of travel (which covered about fifty miles) the party found bison trails, skulls, and bones, but saw no bison. By July 19 the party had reached the area near the modern-day city of Roswell, New Mexico, and probably entered Texas and Area V on or about August 1. Still no bison were reported.

On August 7 the party met three Indian hunters whom Luxán identifies as Jumano. The Spaniards communicated easily with the Jumano using the young boy Pedro as an interpreter. The Jumano agreed to guide the expedition party southward back to La Junta. Many other Jumano were engaged in hunting in the area, which was probably near modern Pecos, Texas. The men and women at the Jumano hunting camp celebrated the arrival of the Spaniards with a dance held in an area that was in the middle of their temporary huts. It appears that the Indian encampment may have been near present-day Toyah Lake because Luxán tells that they caught large catfish and *mojarra* over fifteen inches in length. Luxán explains that the Jumano were similar to (or perhaps the same as) the Otomoaco in their clothing, appearance, and customs.

After passing through several different Jumano camps as they moved southward, the party reached a valley with a large stream (perhaps Toyah Creek) and many wild grapes and live oaks. Luxán notes that this was the first grove of oaks that the party had seen in the country. When the party reached the Rio Grande, the local Natives celebrated with a reception and feast that included ears of green corn, squash, beans, catfish, and another fish called *matalote*.

On the return trip up the Río Conchos, Espejo encountered some Toboso Indians who appeared friendly, but during the night the Toboso wounded two mules and a valuable horse. The friendly Conchos Indians were met a week before the party arrived in the Parral area on September 10, 1583.

In October 1583, soon after the expedition party returned to Parral, Espejo gave his account of the trip.[24] This was about twenty years before Luxán recorded his more complete account. Although there are few conflicts between the two accounts, we will now review the second journal account because Espejo's observations about Native horticulture and lifeways add substantially to Luxán's story.

According to Espejo's version of the 1582 expedition to New Mexico, the expedition party departed from the valley of San Bartolomé, located about twenty-five miles from Santa Bárbara. During the two-day march of about twenty-six miles, the party encountered a gathering of over 1,000 friendly Conchos Indians. Espejo says that the Conchos hunted cottontail, jackrabbit, and deer (which he said were plentiful) and cultivated corn, squash, "Castile melons," and "watermelons [sandía]."

The reference to Conchos Indians cultivating their own domesticated corn and squash is not surprising, but their cultivation of Old World watermelons and Castile melons is very significant because both melons were of European rather than North American origin and both were being cultivated at the time in Spanish communities and missions in the Parral area. This report indicates that by the 1580s Indian farmers in southern Chihuahua had secured Old World seeds and plants and were cultivating Old World melons and perhaps Old World fruit trees in their own fields.

About one hundred years after Espejo's expedition, the French chronicler Henri Joutel and several other French chroniclers wrote of finding watermelons on Hasinai farms in East Texas and seeing watermelon and Old World fruit trees among the crops grown by the Acansa and Taensa Indians on the west side of the lower Mississippi in 1673, 1682, and 1687.[25] It is recognized that the Jumano from La Junta supplied Spanish horses to their allies the Hasinai. Therefore, the Jumano (friends and trading neighbors of the Conchos) are a likely source of the watermelons grown by the Hasinai and cultivated by the lower Mississippi River tribes that were close allies of the Caddo.

After traveling with Conchos guides an additional six days and about sixty miles north down the Río Conchos, Espejo writes that his party arrived at the land of the "Pazaguante" (Passaguate), who were allies of the Conchos. This distance places the Pazaguante near the junction of the Conchos and Las Víboras rivers. The Pazaguante traveled with Espejo's party another four days, covering about thirty-six miles north before meeting the more troublesome Toboso. It took the party three days to march the twenty-eight miles through Toboso country and on to the land of the people that the chronicler calls the "Jumano." Espejo explains that the Jumano were called "Patarabuey" by the Spaniards.

Espejo reports visiting five Jumano "pueblos" and notes that the Jumano painted their faces in stripes. In other respects as well, Espejo's description of the Jumano is similar to that given by both Luxán and Gallegos for the tribes called the Otomoaco and Abriache.

Espejo also recounts the story that the Jumano told about "three Christians and a Negro" passing through their land, and the author surmises that the Jumano referred to "Álvar Núñez Cabeza de Vaca, Dorantes, Castillo Maldonado, and a Negro, all survivors from the fleet with which Pánfilo de Narváez came to Florida." Thus we have a third report from a Spanish chronicler that Cabeza de Vaca visited the Jumano near La Junta—first from Gallegos, second from Luxán's account, and now from Espejo.

It should be noted that in 1650 Alonso de León wrote that Cabeza de Vaca initially crossed the lower Rio Grande into Mexico at a ford located north of Cerralvo (near the present-day Falcon Reservoir) and that in 1565 Obregón wrote that Cabeza de Vaca visited the Río Casas Grandes people.[26] It appears that Spanish authorities in the sixteenth and seventeenth centuries had a remarkably clear picture of the route that Cabeza de Vaca had traveled, a route that I believe is projected accurately by Alex Krieger and most current researchers.

From the La Junta area, Espejo reports that the party moved up the Rio Grande through numerous friendly Jumano settlements with flat-roofed houses and cane or straw huts. The Jumano gave the Spaniards finely dressed deerskins, hides of bison, articles made of feathers of different colors, and blue and white striped cotton shawls. The Jumano explained that the feather articles and cotton goods were obtained by trade with Indian neighbors living to the west. When the Spaniards pointed to the metal objects that they were carrying, the Jumano indicated that they could guide the Spaniards on a five-day trip west to a community (presumably in western Chihuahua) where there was a large amount of copper and that their own people were there at the time.

After traveling another four days, the Spaniards arrived at a large Indian community near several lagoons associated with the Rio Grande. Among these people Espejo met a visiting Conchos Indian who invited Espejo to leave the river and travel with him for fifteen days westward rather than to continue northward upstream. The Conchos said that he would guide the Spaniards to numerous settlements that included large houses many stories high located on the shore of a very large lake.

The most obvious cultural center located about fifteen days' travel

154

west of the expedition party's camp on the Rio Grande is the Casas Grandes area, which is associated with a large lake (Laguna Guzmán) in the western Chihuahuan basin and range. The estimated fifteen-day march distance to the west matches the distance west that Cabeza de Vaca traveled from the Rio Grande to the "Maize People" living near the Río Casas Grandes.

The Conchos Indian also said that the people living to the west wore clothes and had large stores of corn, turkeys, and other goods. The local Indians and the Conchos Indian said that their own people, the Conchos, were at this large trading center to the west. If in the 1580s there had been a large trading center near present-day Laguna Guzmán or nearby Lago Santa María, no historic or archeological record of a trading center at the location has been published to the author's knowledge.

Continuing upriver for another nineteen days, Espejo reports meeting few Natives but passing through many mesquite groves, cactus fields, and forests of piñon pine, juniper, cottonwood, white poplar, and walnut draped with grapevines. Like Luxán, Espejo emphasizes that the Pueblo people appear to be very heavily influenced by the "Mexican culture," but there was limited contact between the Pueblo people in New Mexico and the Rio Grande Natives in Texas. Espejo finds the Mexican cultural influence in the way the New Mexico Indians wear blankets over their shoulders and paint their houses, in their dances and music, and in their use of irrigation ditches to cultivate their fields of corn, beans, squash, and tobacco. Espejo's description of the return trip down the Pecos River adds nothing significant to that written by Luxán.

Based on the reports from the Chamuscado and Espejo expeditions, the viceroy began preparing for a larger and more formal *entrada* to the pueblo communities in New Mexico. The first legally authorized colonizing expedition from northern New Spain was led by Gaspar Castaño de Sosa in the summer of 1590.[27] The Castaño expedition began near present-day Monclova in Coahuila and proceeded across northern Coahuila to the Rio Grande. From the Rio Grande the expedition route continued generally along the northeastern side of the Pecos River in Area VI and thus will be reviewed in the following chapter.

Three years after Castaño's expedition to New Mexico, Francisco Leyva de Bonilla led an unauthorized expedition from his post in Chihuahua, initially to punish a group of Toboso Indians. However, Bonilla decided to continue his venture beyond Chihuahua and into New Mexico pueblo country.[28] We have no diary account of this unauthorized expedition covering the period when Bonilla crossed Area V and moved farther northward, but a "Mexican" (Aztec?) Indian named Josephe, who apparently was the sole survivor of the expedition party, later testified about the party's excursion into the Texas Panhandle (in Area VI) to hunt bison and visit Quivira. We will therefore also pick up Josephe's account in the following chapter.

In 1598 the viceroy selected Juan de Oñate to lead a second authorized expedition to occupy and settle New Mexico.[29] Oñate's party forged a new Spanish route to the pueblo communities on the upper Rio Grande that avoided the Big Bend region of Texas and forded the Rio Grande at the crossing located a few miles downstream from present-day El Paso. As this was the only part of Area V crossed by Oñate, limited information on local Texas Indians is found in Oñate's account or in associated expedition documents. As Oñate later ventured eastward into the bison hunting grounds in Area VI, the Oñate expedition into the Southern Plains in Texas will also be covered in the next chapter.

We have no diary account of any important military expedition crossing Area V during the middle of the seventeenth century. However, in 1684 Spanish officials authorized Juan Domínguez de Mendoza to lead a large military expedition from the El Paso area across Area V to meet with tribes from Central and East Texas.[30]

Official authorization for the expedition was given by Governor Antonio de Otermín, who earlier in El Paso had received a delegation of Trans-Pecos tribal leaders requesting that the expedition be undertaken. After granting the Native leaders' request, Governor Otermín presented gifts to the visiting tribal captains. To the Native leaders as a group, the governor gave twelve small machetes, twelve pairs of earrings for women, one cow, and a supply of tobacco and corn. To the principal leader, Juan Sabeata, Otermín gave the most prestigious gift—"two red feathers." These red feathers were most likely long tail feathers of the scarlet macaw, recognized as highly prestigious gifts by Native Americans in Area V and throughout the American Southwest. The governor was apparently familiar with the symbolism associated with the scarlet macaw parrot and with their long red tail feathers (over two feet in length) and indicated to Sabeata that he was familiar with and respected the Native customs and traditions.

At the meeting Sabeata informed the governor that two Hasinai Caddo (called "Tejas") were at that time in La Junta awaiting the governor's word that they could take back home in East Texas and to their allies. Thus, we have documentary evidence of both a Jumano physical presence in East Texas visiting the Hasinai and a Hasinai delegation visiting the Jumano at La Junta in West Texas.

The diary account of Mendoza's expedition gives information on the names and location of a number of tribes in Area V. On December 15, 1683, Mendoza, commanding only a small detachment of soldiers, left the

Real de San Lorenzo thirty miles downstream on the Rio Grande from Paso del Rio Grande and marched downriver toward La Junta de los Ríos. The Jumano, including their chieftain Sabeata, and several other tribes apparently from Area V were a part of the expedition. The diarist identifies the names of the tribes that were with Mendoza as follows: Jumano, Ororoso, Beitonijure, Achubale, Cujalo, Toreme, Gediondo (Jediondo), Siacucha, Suajo, Isucho, Cujaco, Caula, Hinchi, Ylame, Cunquebaco, Quitaca, Quicuchabe, Los Que Hacen Arcos, and Hanacine.

The second day out, the party passed an encampment of Suma Indians who requested that the Spaniards help them against their common enemy, the Apache. The diarist also reports that the Rio Grande was lined with cottonwood, mesquite, and lechuguilla. On December 29 Mendoza's party reached the Julime Indians, who raised corn and hunted bison. After continuing downstream about eighteen miles from the first Julime village, the party turned northward and traveled upstream along a large creek that was probably present-day Alamito Creek. The route northward likely took the party near modern Alpine.

By January 13, 1684, Mendoza was out of the mountains and into the open West Texas plains. The diarist reports large grapevines, ash trees, "white and yellow mesquites," oaks, and cedars. By February 5, Mendoza had reached southwestern Pecos County. The following day the diarist records finding unspecified nut trees, and hunters in the party killed deer. Two days later the party reached the Pecos River (called the Río Salado), which the diarist correctly says originated in New Mexico. Moving downstream along the right bank of the Pecos River, Mendoza's party found an encampment of friendly Jediondo; some of the Indians were mounted, but most were traveling by foot. He also reported a large burned area of grassland.

The Mendoza party continued eastward from the Pecos River into Area VI, and the remainder of his expedition will be covered in the following chapter. It should be noted that a description of Mendoza's return trip from the Pecos to the Rio Grande is only summarized by the diarist and that on the return to the Rio Grande, Mendoza followed the same route he described marching northeast. On his return to El Paso from La Junta, Mendoza marched up the Río Conchos into northern Mexico rather than up the Rio Grande because, the diarist writes, the Suma were in revolt. About one hundred miles upriver on the Conchos, Mendoza's party turned first west and then northwest to return to El Paso.

After the Mendoza expedition, no large Spanish expedition crossed into Area V until early November 1688, when General Juan Fernández de Retana crossed the Rio Grande into Area V at La Junta de los Ríos. The general was investigating reports that foreigners thought to be Frenchmen had visited the middle Rio Grande. General Retana was also responding to complaints of Spanish settlers living north of Parral that the Toboso, Salinero, Cabeza, Chisos, Chichitame, and Cholome Indians had raided their settlements. But Retana was acting principally on reports indicating French forces had located a settlement on Matagorda Bay that Spanish troops had been unable to locate.

After crossing the Rio Grande and traveling four days east of the river into Area V, Retana met Juan Sabeata and his party returning from the bison hunting grounds and trade fairs near the Colorado River in Area II. Sabeata told Retana that the Indians living close to the French colony had killed the Frenchmen at the post near the bay. Sabeata had French documents and a parchment with a ship painted on it to prove his French connection. Accompanied by Sabeata and several of his fellow Indian leaders, Retana returned to Parral to inform the governor.

The oral statements made by Retana and the Indian leaders in Parral in April 1689 were given under oath in a proceeding in which Spanish officials questioned General Retana and the Indian witnesses.[31] The depositions were taken from four Indian leaders who had participated in the visit to Matagorda Bay in Area III and the nearby Indian villages in Area II. The first witness, Juan Sabeata, stated that he was the principal leader of the Cibolo and Jumano tribes that lived near La Junta. Sabeata said that it was well known among his people that some foreigners had visited the Rio Grande, traveling by canoe and by foot, and that a Cibolo Indian called Miguel had told him that men wearing coats of steel and accompanied by an Indian interpreter had visited his village. The armed visitors had inquired about Spanish silver mines in Nueva Vizcaya.

Apparently Sabeata had traveled seven days from his Jumano village near La Junta to the Cibolo encampment where he had received word of the Frenchmen's visit. The interpreter estimated the distance traveled by Sabeata to be about 160 to 180 miles. This projection would place the Cibolo camp visited by the Frenchmen in the area near the junction of the Pecos River and the Rio Grande.

Sabeata continued his testimony by saying he had taken Miguel and other Indians with him to a location near the Gulf Coast where annual trade fairs were held by the local Indian tribes. Sabeata's party had visited a camp in Area II where the local Indians were celebrating the destruction of the French settlement. The Indians in this encampment told Sabeata that they had killed all the Frenchmen except those who had left earlier to visit the Caddo in East Texas. At the camp Sabeata saw booty taken from the French fort, including dresses, men's clothing, and other French objects.

The next day Sabeata visited a nearby second encampment in Area

II that was also celebrating their success in helping destroy the French colony. Here Sabeata found not only French civilian clothing and dresses but also, significantly, a black clerical cloak. As Sabeata was a Catholic convert familiar with the dress of Franciscan priests living near La Junta, he identified the robe as similar to the one worn by priests of the Order of St. Francis. It will be remembered from our review of Area II that on April 16 of the same year, when the Franciscan priest Damián Massanet, a member of Governor De León's 1689 expedition, arrived at two Indian encampments near the lower Guadalupe in DeWitt County, a few months after Sabeata had visited the area, Massanet and De León also saw an Indian wearing a black Franciscan robe. Sabeata said that he then traveled on to visit the Hasinai Caddo villages.

The second witness was Miguel, a leader of the Cibolo Indians. He testified, through an interpreter called Nicolás (chieftain of the Julime), that the Cibolo lived on the north side of the Rio Grande where there were many bison. He said his people told him that some foreigners on the lower Rio Grande had visited their encampment, had run and danced with them, had given them hatchets and glass beads, and had promised to return. When the foreigners (Frenchmen?) returned as promised in about three months, six men came by canoe and later another four men arrived by foot. The strangers gave the Cibolo copper utensils, ribbons, and knives. The witness testified that the visitors were dressed in coats of steel and had their own Indian interpreter, who inquired about the Spanish mining operations near Parral.

This record of direct testimony given by several Area V Natives covering the same meetings with La Salle's men and the same long-distance scouting trip from Area V to Areas II and III is of special interest because most ethnographic information found in historical documents consists of observations made by European chroniclers. The testimony of the Jumano and Cibolo confirms the cosmopolitan character of Area V tribes residing near La Junta.

A detailed identification and description of Native residents living near La Junta in the early 1700s is found in the diary account Don Juan Antonio Trasviña y Retis, who led a clerical group to reestablish missions in the La Junta area in 1715.[32] The Catholic Church and Spanish troops had been forced earlier to retreat out of La Junta southward into Mexico during the last two decades of the 1600s just as Spaniards were forced out of New Mexico and East Texas during the same period. Now the restoration was underway in West Texas as well as in East Texas and New Mexico.

Retis writes that, with thirty soldiers, twenty local Indians, and four priests, his party departed from the upper Río Conchos in southern Nueva Vizcaya to march down to the mouth of the Conchos at La Junta. Major Retis notes that en route the party expected trouble from several hostile Indian groups, including the Sinsible, Chisos, Chinarra, Cocoyame, and Acolame.

On the trip down the Conchos, the Retis party visited a village of Auchane Indians and later a large horticultural village of Jumano Indians (called "Cholome") who were cultivating (with irrigation) fields of maize, wheat, watermelons, and pumpkins. The Jumano also had gardens with string beans.

Near La Junta the priest established eight small missions—for the Cocoyame, Mesquite, Cacalote, Opoxme, Conejo, Polacme, Pulique, Conchos, and Poxsalme (Poxalma). During the major's visits among the several tribes along the Rio Grande, the Spaniards encountered the Suma, Chinarra, and Totame. These specific tribes are mentioned to demonstrate that the Native groups collectively referred to as the La Junta people in fact included at times up to a dozen or more tribes, several of which were not only bison hunters but also successful farmers.

Review of Area V Indian Tribes

Approximately sixty-five Indian tribes or bands were identified by name and by geographical location in the Texas Trans-Pecos in expedition documentary accounts during the ca. 200-year study period. Most of the recorded tribes resided along the Rio Grande from near modern Del Rio, through the Big Bend, to near El Paso. A large number of tribes listed in the chapter supplement for Study Area V lived along or near the Río Conchos in Chihuahua but frequently visited allies in Texas. Several others reported tribes were nonresident visitors to Area V.

Spanish expedition chroniclers name several tribes that lived near La Junta de Los Ríos. The Abriache lived about six to eight miles downstream from the junction of the river. The Cabri lived (primarily as horticulturists) near La Junta in the 1590s, and the Mesquite resided there in 1715. During most of this ca. 100-year history (and probably earlier and later), the Jumano (also called Chouman by the French and Otomoaco and Patarabuey by the Spaniards) also lived nearby and operated as long-distance hunters and traders out of La Junta.

Upriver on the Rio Grande, the Tanpachoa and the Caguate Indians (who apparently were related to the Jumano) lived near the swampy region closer to El Paso in the late sixteenth century. In the 1680s Spanish expedition diarists refer to the same area as Suma country.

A large number of tribes living near the Río Conchos in Chihuahua frequently visited Area V. These included the Chisos, Cocoyame, Conchos, Julime, Passaguate, and Raya. The Toboso occupied a large area to the east of the Río Conchos, and the Salineros and Tepeguan were in regions farther south toward Durango.

The Cibolo Indians lived in the southeastern part of Area V closer to modern Del Rio. During the study period, the Apache were encroaching into Area V and were the enemy of many of the local tribes, including the Jumano. As an ally of the Jumano, the Hasinai Caddo, whose homeland was in East Texas, visited the Jumano homeland.

Conclusions

The documentary history indicates that the historic Native population of the Trans-Pecos was cosmopolitan, not provincial. The "capital" of the eastern part of Area V was the pueblo community area near La Junta de los Ríos, the homeland of the shifting population of perhaps a dozen or more tribes or small bands over several centuries during the historic period. Some La Junta residents were accomplished horticulturists who cultivated maize, beans, squash, pumpkin, and watermelon along the Río Conchos and Rio Grande floodplains. Other residents were seasonal or terminal long-distance bison hunters and traders who principally wintered at La Junta.

The cosmopolitan character of the La Junta people and their neighbors is reflected in evidence of their interaction with the Native populations in southern and western Chihuahua, on the Southern Plains, in the Edwards Plateau, in East Texas, and near the Gulf of Mexico. Several prominent tribes from southern Chihuahua and the Durango area were reported visiting Area V. The Tepeguan, Toboso, and Salinero traveled several hundreds miles to visit and hunt bison in Area V. Western Chihuahua pottery from Casas Grandes and Ahumada has been found in West Texas and, on the other hand, El Paso Plain pottery and polychrome ceramics have been recovered at numerous sites in northwestern Chihuahua.

Bands of Jumano and allied tribes moved out of La Junta in the spring each year to hunt bison on the Southern Plains, on the Edwards Plateau, and in south-central Texas. Trans-Pecos Indians visited the East Texas Hasinai and, at times, the Hasinai visited La Junta. Caddoan ceramics have been recovered near the mouth of the Pecos River, at La Junta, and at sites farther west in New Mexico. Shells from the Gulf of California have been recovered near La Junta. In sum, historic and late prehistoric Trans-Pecos Indians had a very broad interaction sphere that stretched east-west over 800 miles from northeast Texas to northwest Chihuahua.

This supplement is an alphabetical list of the Native tribes and bands mentioned in Spanish and French expedition documents cited in the review of Area V. As noted in the supplement, some Indians identified by name in Area V are considered local tribes that resided in the Trans-Pecos during the study period, but several tribes were visitors, primarily from north-central Mexico. Each entry includes information regarding the name of the tribe most frequently used in the documentary record, variants of the customary name, the name of the diarist who recorded the encounter, and the date and location of the meeting. If the encounter involved more than a single tribe, the names of the other tribes identified in the shared encampment are included.

The following documentary sources are among those consulted in preparing the listing: Alex D. Krieger, *We Came Naked and Barefoot: The Journey of Cabeza de Vaca across North America*; William C. Foster, ed., *Spanish Expeditions into Texas, 1689–1768*; Mariah F. Wade, *The Native Americans of the Texas Edwards Plateau, 1582–1799*; Andrés Pérez de Ribas, *My Life among the Savage Nations of New Spain*; and George P. Hammond and Agapito Rey, *The Rediscovery of New Mexico, 1580–1594*.

1. Abriache. In his diary account of the 1582 Espejo expedition, Diego Pérez de Luxán wrote that the Abriache lived a short distance (about six to eight miles) downstream on the Rio Grande from La Junta de los Ríos, the home of their friends, the Otomoaco.
2. Achubale. Juan Domínguez de Mendoza reported that the Achubale accompanied his party on the 1684 expedition across Area V.
3. Acolame. In 1715 Major Antonio de Trasviña y Retis identified the Acolame as a hostile Indian tribe that lived along the Río Conchos.
4. Amotomanco. Hernán Gallegos, the notary on the 1581 Chamuscado expedition, wrote that Amotomanco was the language spoken by Natives near La Junta.
5. Apache. Along Mendoza's 1684 route, several tribes, including the Suma, asked the general for help in fighting their enemy, the Apache.
6. Auchane. In 1715 Retis wrote that the Auchane were living at the pueblo called San Antonio de Julimes on the lower Río Conchos.
7. Beitonijure. Mendoza identified the Beitonijure as a tribe that accompanied his party on the expedition from El Paso to the Edwards Plateau.

8. Cabeza. The Cabeza, along with the Chisos, Toboso, Cholome, and other tribes, engaged in an uprising in Chihuahua in 1688.
9. Cabri. In his account of the 1581 Chamuscado expedition, Gallegos wrote that the Cabri were living near the Rio Grande at La Junta. He also wrote that the Cabri were horticulturists.
10. Cacalote. In 1715 Retis encountered the Cacalote about ten miles up-river on the Río Conchos near La Junta.
11. Cacuytattom. The Cacuytattom joined the Cholome, Chisos, and other tribes residing along the Rio Grande and Río Conchos in an uprising in 1684.
12. Caguate. In Luxán's account of the 1582 Espejo expedition, the diarist recorded that the Caguate, who were related to the Otomoaco, lived about eighteen miles downriver on the Rio Grande from the swampy marshes and shallow ponds immediately below present-day El Paso.
13. Casas Grandes People. The Spaniards did not identify and probably did not know the name of the Native people who resided along the Río Casas Grandes in northwestern Chihuahua in the tenth to the sixteenth centuries. The earlier cultural center that emerged on the Río Casas Grandes is usually referred to as Paquimé, a name used by the sixteenth-century Spanish historian Baltasar de Obregón, but no tribal name is known for the residents.
14. Caula. According to Mendoza, the Caula accompanied him on his 1684 expedition to the Edwards Plateau.
15. Chichitame. In the fall of 1688 the Chichitame, along with the Toboso, Salinero, Cabeza, Chisos, and Cholome, were in rebellion along the Río Conchos.
16. Chinarra. In 1715 Retis described the Chinarra as a hostile tribe that threatened Spanish convoys moving between Parral and La Junta.
17. Chisos. The Chisos joined the Cholome, Mamitte, Cibolo, and Julime in the revolt against the Spaniards near Parral in 1684. In 1688 the Chisos, along with the Cholome, Toboso, Salinero, and other tribes of Chihuahua, were again in revolt.
18. Cholome. In his November 15, 1688, order directing General Juan Fernández de Retana to attack the local Indians in rebellion, the governor of Chihuahua, Don Juan Isidro de Pardiñas Villar de Francos, said that the Cholome were among the tribes in rebellion.
19. Cibola (Cibolo, Sibolo, Sibula). The Cibola leader testified in Parral in April 1689 that he had joined the Jumano in a scouting expedition to the sacked French fort on Matagorda Bay and that annually the Cibola visited the same area near the bay and the Hasinai Caddo to trade and hunt.

20. Cocoione. Retana considered the Cocoione an extremely vicious and destructive enemy in Chihuahua. The general found the Cocoione near the Río Conchos in 1688 and defeated them.
21. Cocoyame. Retis identified the Cocoyame as a hostile Indian tribe that often resided along the Río Conchos between Parral and La Junta.
22. Conchos (Conchas). During the 1581 Chamuscado expedition, Gallegos recorded that proceeding from the junction of the Río Conchos and the Río Florida down the Río Conchos for about 130 miles, the expedition party encountered friendly Conchos Indian villages that had maize and other cultigens under cultivation.
23. Conejo. In 1715 Retis wrote that the Conejo lived in the pueblo Nuestra Señora de Begoña del Cuchillo Parado and that Nuestra Señora de Aranzazu was established later for the Conejo.
24. Cujalo. Mendoza recorded that the Cujalo accompanied his party on the 1684 expedition to the Edwards Plateau.
25. Cunquebaco. Mendoza wrote that the Cunquebaco accompanied his 1684 expedition party across Area V to the Edwards Plateau.
26. Gavilan. Retana defeated the Gavilan and punished the tribe on his expedition from Parral to La Junta in 1688.
27. Hanasine. According to Mendoza, the Hanasine accompanied his 1684 expedition party across Area V to the Edwards Plateau.
28. Hijos de las Piedras. Retana defeated the Hijos de las Piedras near the Río Conchos in 1688. He wrote that the tribe had invaded Chihuahua and had been very destructive.
29. Hinchi. Mendoza recorded that the Hinchi accompanied his 1684 expedition across Area V to the Edwards Plateau.
30. Isucho. The Isucho accompanied Mendoza on his 1684 expedition to the Edwards Plateau.
31. Jediondo (Gediondo). Mendoza met the Jediondo near the Horsehead Crossing on the Pecos River on his 1684 expedition.
32. Julime. According to civil archival records in Parral, the Julime, along with the Cholome, Mamitte, Chisos, and Cibolo, participated in an uprising against Parral and neighboring communities in 1684.
33. Jumano (Chouman). In the account of his 1582 expedition, Antonio de Espejo wrote that he found the Jumano at the junction of the Río Conchos and Rio Grande living in five permanent pueblos of low, flat-roofed houses. On his return trip in July 1583, Espejo recorded meeting a large, friendly Jumano bison hunting party near the Pecos River north of present-day Marfa.
34. Los Que Asen Arcos. According to Mendoza, the Los Que Asen

Arcos accompanied his 1684 expedition party across Area V to the Edwards Plateau.

35. Mamitte (Mamite). According to municipal archival records in Parral, the Mamitte contributed to the extensive civil unrest near Parral in 1684, along with the Cholome, Chisos, Cibolo, and other tribes.

36. Mesquite. In 1715 Retis stated that the Mesquite were living near La Junta at the pueblo Nuestra Señora de Loreto. .

37. Opoxme (Oposme). On his 1715 expedition Retis observed that the Opoxme resided at the pueblo San Francisco at La Junta.

38. Ororoso. The Ororoso accompanied Mendoza in 1684 from El Paso across Area V eastward to the Concho River.

39. Osatayolida (Osatayogligla). The Osatayolida joined the Julime, Chichitame, Chisos, Mamitte, Conchos, and other local tribes in the uprising near Parral in 1684.

40. Otomoaco. In Luxán's account of the 1582 Espejo expedition, the diarist wrote that the Otomoaco were also called the Patarabuey and that the tribe lived near the junction of the Río Conchos and Rio Grande. The Otomoaco also had villages upriver on the Rio Grande as far north as the Caguates, to whom they were related.

41. Passaguate (Pazaguante). In Luxán's account of the 1582 Espejo expedition, the diarist wrote that his party encountered the Passaguate living downstream from the Conchos Indians and upstream from the Patarabuey.

42. Patarabuey. Luxán wrote that on the 1582 Espejo expedition, they found the Patarabuey living downstream from the Passaguate on the Río Conchos. The diarist added that they were also called the Otomoaco. Espejo wrote that the tribe is the same as the Jumano. Obregón also considered the Patarabuey to be the same as the Jumano.

43. People of the Cows. Cabeza de Vaca refers to the natives who lived in permanent houses near the junction of the Rio Grande and Río Conchos as "the people of the cows [bison]."

44. Polacme. In 1715 Retis reported that the Polacme were residing with the Cibolo at a pueblo near La Junta.

45. Poxalma (Poxsalme, Posalme). In 1715 Retis recorded that the Poxalma resided at La Junta and, at the time, numbered 180.

46. Pulique. In 1715 Retis recorded that the Pulique lived on the banks of the Rio Grande near La Junta where there were three pueblos close together. The Pulique numbered ninety-two persons.

47. Querecho. Obregón recorded that in 1565 the Spanish explorer Francisco de Ibarra encountered friendly bison hunters that Obregón re-

ferred to as Querecho near Paquimé on the Río Casas Grandes. The Querecho said that bison were four days' travel to the north.

48. Quicuchabe. Mendoza recorded that the Quicuchabe accompanied his 1684 expedition party across Area V to the Edwards Plateau.

49. Quitaca. According to Mendoza, the Quitaca accompanied his 1684 expedition party across Area V to the Edwards Plateau.

50. Raya. Gallegos wrote that on the 1581 Chamuscado expedition the Raya were found along the Río Conchos downstream from the Conchos Indians.

51. Salinero. The Salinero from southern Chihuahua near a large terminal lake or lagoon called "San Padre" attacked Mendoza's expedition party in 1684 at a location near San Angelo. The Spanish priest Ribas referred to the Indians living near the same lagoon as the "Laguna" Indians.

52. Siacucha. Mendoza recorded that the Siacucha accompanied his party on his 1684 expedition from near El Paso to the Edwards Plateau.

53. Sinsible. Retis wrote in 1715 that the Sinsible, along with the Chisos, Chinarra, Cocoyame, and Accolame, were very hostile to Spaniards and frequently attacked Spanish forces moving between Parral and La Junta.

54. Sonora. According to seventeenth-century municipal archival documents from Parral, the Sonora and the Taraumara did not join forces with the Julime, Chisos, and other Native tribes living near Parral in the uprising in 1684.

55. Suajo. According to Mendoza, the Suajo accompanied his expedition party through Area V in 1684.

56. Suma. On his 1684 expedition from the present-day El Paso area, Mendoza encountered the Suma about sixty miles downriver from "Paso del Río del Norte."

57. Tanpachoa. Luxán, the diarist on the 1582 Espejo expedition, recorded that the Tanpachoa, who were of the same blood as the Otomoaco, lived near the marshes and shallow pools close to the Caguate on the Rio Grande.

58. Taraumara. According to 1684 civil records in the Parral archives, about one hundred Taraumara Indians served with Spanish forces stationed on the upper Río Conchos to engage enemy tribes.

59. Tejas (Hasinai Caddo). Two "Tejas" Indians from East Texas were visiting the Jumano at La Junta in October 1683, according to the Jumano leader Sabeata. The Jumano and Cibolo scouts from the Trans-Pecos visited the Hasinai Caddo in early 1689 after their visit to the site of the destroyed French fort on Matagorda Bay.

60. Tepeguan (Tepehuan, Depesguan). On Gaspar Castaño de Sosa's 1590 expedition across Areas V and VI to New Mexico, the party met a large tribe called the Tepeguan from near Durango at the present-day ruins of Fort Lancaster in Crockett County.
61. Toboso (Joboso). In his account of his 1582 expedition, Espejo wrote that the Toboso were encountered immediately before reaching the Jumano near the junction of the Río Conchos and Rio Grande.
62. Toposme. In 1684 the Toposme joined the Cibolo, Julime, and other tribes living along the Río Conchos and Rio Grande in an uprising.
63. Toreme. Mendoza reported that the Toreme accompanied his party on the 1684 expedition to the Edwards Plateau.
64. Totame. In 1715 Retis identified the Totame along with the Suma, Cholome, and Chinarra as heathen and apostate Indians who raided near El Paso del Río and farms in Chihuahua.
65. Ylame. According to Mendoza, the Ylame accompanied his party across Area V to the Edwards Plateau in 1684.

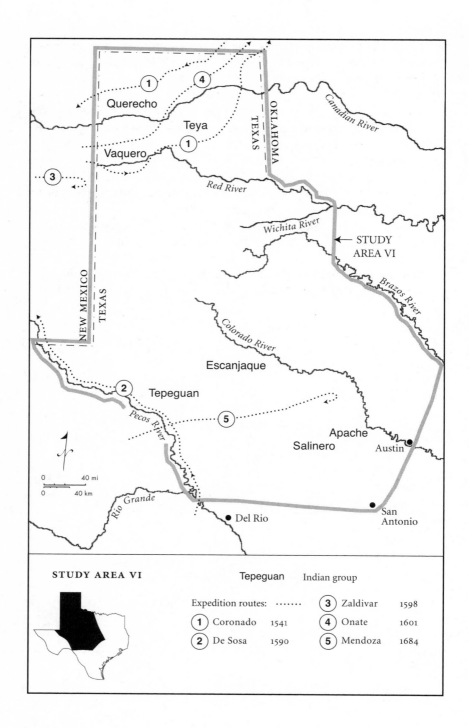

STUDY AREA VI
←— STUDY
AREA VI

NEW MEXICO
TEXAS

OKLAHOMA
TEXAS

Canadian River

Querecho

Teya

Vaquero

Red River

Wichita River

Brazos River

Colorado River

Escanjaque

Tepeguan

Pecos River

Apache
Salinero

Austin

Rio Grande

● Del Rio

San
Antonio

N

0   40 mi

0   40 km

STUDY AREA VI

Tepeguan   Indian group

Expedition routes: ·······

① Coronado   1541

② De Sosa   1590

③ Zaldivar   1598

④ Onate   1601

⑤ Mendoza   1684

MAP 6.1

6

THE TEXAS SOUTHERN PLAINS

STUDY AREA VI

Mobile bison hunters, principally the Apache in the seventeenth century, occupied or otherwise controlled most of Study Area VI during the study period. The area includes the country north and northeast of the Pecos River to the Texas state boundary line with New Mexico and western Oklahoma. The southern boundary of the area runs along a line drawn from the mouth of the Pecos River northeast, following the southern border of the Edwards Plateau through Austin and farther east to a point a few miles above the junction of the Little Brazos and Brazos Rivers. The study area extends from there northward along the Brazos River valley to the junction of the Red and Wichita Rivers (see Map 6.1).

The Canadian River cuts across the Texas Panhandle in Area VI, flowing from west to northeast. The Canadian, which drains water from the Rocky Mountains of New Mexico, merges with the Arkansas River in south-central Oklahoma. Area VI is also drained by the upper Brazos, Red, and Colorado Rivers, all flowing with the tilt of the state toward the southeast.

Sedentary Pueblo Indians living in large permanent agricultural communities along the Rio Grande and Pecos River in New Mexico occupied the country to the west of the Texas Panhandle and Area VI. Pueblo farmers were not bison hunters but were traders with contacts into northwest Mexico and in Area VI.

To the northeast of Area VI, in western Oklahoma and Kansas, Caddoan-speaking Wichita Indians and their allies cultivated maize, beans, and squash and also hunted bison on the Plains. Eastward, beyond the Blackland Prairies and the Brazos River, lived the East Texas Caddo.

The Jumano, Cibola, and associated tribes that were both farmers and long-distance hunters of bison (and other big game) lived to the

169

southwest of Area VI in the Texas Trans-Pecos. To the south of the area lived the numerous small hunter-gatherer bands that planted no crops, hunted both bison and deer, and were allied with the Caddo and Trans-Pecos tribes against the advancing Apache in Area VI.

To summarize the earliest exploration of Area VI: the Spanish explorer Francisco Vázquez de Coronado was the first European to visit the Texas Plains. Coronado crossed Area VI during his expedition from New Mexico to Quivira in central Kansas in 1541, only six years after Cabeza de Vaca had visited Area V to the south along the Rio Grande.

In the late sixteenth century, two Spanish expeditions followed the Pecos River along the southern border of Area VI. The first was the Antonio de Espejo expedition that, on the return route from New Mexico to Parral, followed the Pecos River downstream to a location near Pecos, Texas, and then marched south to La Junta de Los Ríos in Area V. That expedition was covered in part in the previous chapter. The second was the 1590 Gaspar Castaño de Sosa expedition that followed the Pecos River in the opposite direction, upstream, from the junction of the Rio Grande and the Pecos to New Mexico. This chapter covers Castaño's colonizing expedition as well as Juan de Oñate's 1598 expedition, which crossed the tip of West Texas, and Vicente de Zaldívar's 1598 bison-hunting trip onto the Southern Plains.

During the early years of the seventeenth century, Juan Pérez de Oñate and his troops, with cannon and guided by a survivor of the 1593 unauthorized expedition of Captain Francisco Leyva de Bonilla, crossed Area VI on an expedition to Quivira in Kansas. We close our review of major Spanish expeditions into Area VI with the 1684 Spanish expedition to the Edwards Plateau led by Juan Domínguez de Mendoza from El Paso, which traveled through the Big Bend into Area VI northeast of the Pecos River and into the Hill Country.

Documents relating to these Spanish expeditions contain the first recorded information regarding the regional ecology and the lifeways and long-distance interaction network of Indians of Area VI. The chapter ends with several general observations and conclusions regarding the cultures of Native peoples in Area VI during the Medieval Warm period (ca. AD 900–1350) and the subsequent Little Ice Age (ca. AD 1350–1850).

Sixteenth- and Seventeenth-Century Spanish Expeditions

Within four years after Cabeza de Vaca completed his journey across the North American continent in 1536, Spanish authorities dispatched two new major expeditions into the large area that was north of the route that Cabeza de Vaca traveled from Florida to northwest Mexico. The first expedition, led by Hernando de Soto, landed in western Florida in June

1539. The second was led by Francisco Vázquez de Coronado, who assembled his expedition party on Mexico's west coast in February of the following year. Coronado marched across northwest Mexico and into New Mexico in late 1540.[1]

Coronado spent the cold winter of 1540–1541 near present-day Albuquerque, New Mexico, while De Soto remained frozen in place for two cold months at Chicaca east of the Mississippi. Weather reports of the ice conditions and deep snow that forced the two winter camps to remain fixed for several months reflect the severe winter weather pattern that prevailed across the American Southwest and throughout North America during the Little Ice Age.[2]

In the spring of 1541 Coronado and his troops marched northeastward from the Albuquerque area across eastern New Mexico and into Texas (in Area VI). Coronado's destination was an Indian province in present-day south-central Kansas called Quivira, which was reported to have gold and silver. To guide him to Quivira, Coronado had secured two Indian guides familiar with the route between the upper Pecos River in New Mexico and Quivira. The two guides were Wichita Caddoans and former residents of the area to be visited in Kansas, but at the time of Coronado's expedition, the Natives were either visitors or slaves held in New Mexico.

The first Area VI Indians encountered en route were the Querecho. These people hunted bison along the Canadian River and elsewhere in Area VI. Most writers consider the Querecho to be Plains Indians closely related or ancestral to the Apache, but the specifics of this association are unclear. Pedro de Castañeda de Nájera, Coronado's diarist, describes the Querecho as people who lived following the large bison herds while the animals drifted across the plains. The Querecho were not only hunters but also gatherers, as Area VI had rich flora resources as well as bison. Domesticated shaggy dogs, strung out in pack trains, carried loads on their backs, pulling long tent or teepee poles across the flat plains and hauling bison hides and other camp goods and supplies for the Querecho. Castañeda writes that the Querecho were so skillful in the use of Native hand signs that it seemed that they were speaking and an interpreter was not needed. We recall that the Natives in coastal and South Texas and in northern Mexico also used hand signs.

The second tribe met by Coronado was the Teya, some of whom lived in a village called Cona and other smaller villages and camps located near Blanco Canyon in Area VI. The Teyas were enemies of the Querechos. We know that sedentary horticulturists (called Antelope Creek People) had lived in the same area a hundred years or so earlier. It is also clear that the Teyas knew their way around the Southern Plains. For Coronado, they proved to be his most loyal and knowledgeable guides on his trek northward to the Wichita villages in Kansas. Some writers have associated the Teya with the Wichita, who were Plains Caddoan people living to the north in western Oklahoma; other writers consider the Teyas to be indigenous folk influenced by the Pueblo Indians to the southwest.

On Coronado's march from the Teya settlements in the Texas Panhandle northward toward Quivira, the two Wichita guides disagreed strongly on the direction that Coronado's party should take. As the story was eventually told, the Indian guide called the Turk was held in chains and finally executed for deceiving Coronado; the second guide, Isopete, proved to be very helpful and was rewarded. But it appears that the Teya guides picked up by Coronado in Texas were primarily responsible for directing the expedition to the Quivira villages and, significantly, for guiding Coronado's party using a more direct route back to New Mexico.

When Coronado met the Wichita Indian leader at Quivira, the chieftain was wearing a copper pendant that the diarist Castañeda describes as being highly prized. The chronicler adds that copper was the only precious metal found among the Wichita at Quivira and that the pendant was not of local origin. The failure to find gold and silver at Quivira was an immense disappointment to Coronado and to his men, who had anticipated finding and sharing rich treasures. In central Kansas Coronado and his troops turned around to return to New Mexico and eventually to Mexico City.

For the purposes of our study, however, the discovery of copper was very significant because Coronado himself wrote the king that the Wichita leader had given him not only a copper pendant but also "some small copper bells."[3] The presence of small copper bells, or crotals (called "*caxcabeles*" by Coronado and "*cascabel*" by Cabeza de Vaca), is very significant because it suggests some form of direct or indirect interaction by the Wichita not only with the Pueblo people in New Mexico but possibly with Casas Grandes people and other exporters of copper crotals from western Mexico.[4]

Indian artisans working with copper on the Mississippi and in the eastern Woodlands were familiar only with a copper technology in which the metal was cold-hammered flat and rolled into copper tinklers in the shape of a cone, but they had no knowledge of copper metallurgy or of casting small copper crotals, as was known in Casas Grandes and on the west coast of Mexico and in Peru.[5]

Skillfully crafted and decorated cast copper crotals and copper pendants were hallmark trade items exported from Casas Grandes into West Texas and New Mexico during the prehistoric period. We recall the cast copper bell that Cabeza de Vaca was given in northern Coahuila by the foreign trading party apparently from the Río Casas Grandes area. And we remember the cast copper bells worn by the La Junta people. Here we discover that the trade network in cast copper bells from Casas Grandes apparently extended across the Plains to the Wichita Caddo in Kansas in the early sixteenth century.

The discovery of cast copper bells at the Wichita villages is also significant because in the seventeenth century La Salle's French chroniclers on the middle Mississippi report that two captured Wichita slaves from the Great Plains were held by the local Tamaroa Indians on the Mississippi near the mouth of the Missouri River.[6] The Wichita villages that were visited by Coronado along the bend of the Arkansas River in central Kansas were about 500 miles east-northeast of the Pueblo people on the Rio Grande in New Mexico and about 500 miles west of the Mississippi River. These were not exceptional distances for interaction that was routinely conducted between the prehistoric Pueblo people and the Wichita or between the Wichita and the Mississippian people.

Mississippian raiding parties may have traveled west to capture Wichita slaves and brought the slaves to the junction of the Missouri and Mississippi Rivers where La Salle reported finding them. This evidence supports the thesis that there was a well-used northern historic and possibly prehistoric route of interaction between New Mexico and the Mississippi that followed, in part, the Missouri River watercourse.

With respect to historic routes of interaction between the Mississippian and the Pueblo peoples in the American Southwest, it appears that the movements may not have laterally crossed the Texas Panhandle along the east-west course of the Red River or the Canadian-Arkansas river system. After noting the presence of extensive Southwestern ceramics and obsidian at Antelope Creek sites, Robert Brooks writes: "Trade items from the Southeast and the Plains are extremely limited in the assemblages of Antelope Creek settlements. There are virtually no Caddoan wares from the Red River region nor are there any Spiroan materials from the Arkansas River valley."[7]

Castañeda's account of Coronado's expedition is the narrative most frequently cited, but another member of the 1541 expedition, Juan Jaramillo, also prepared an account of the exploration across Area VI, including the visit to Quivira.[8] Jaramillo describes the pueblos on the Rio Grande as having flat-roofed houses built of earth (not stone), with some houses having two stories. The pueblo farmers cultivated maize, beans, and squash and made robes by twisting together feathers and strands of cotton.

When Coronado's party reached the land of the bison in Area VI, Jaramillo explains that because the New Mexico Pueblo people referred to the bison hunters as "Querechos," the Spaniards used the same name for the highly mobile group.

Near the Arkansas River in Kansas, Jaramillo describes the land as superior to any that he had seen in Spain, Italy, or France. The author writes that the party found a type of Castilian plum, flax, sumac, and wild grapes.

At the close of his narrative, Jaramillo mentions that the Catholic friar and lay brother who were left in Quivira retained with them several slaves and a black family with children. This note is significant because some Spanish diarists fail to mention that slaves and blacks played a role in the early exploration of the New World.

After the accounts of Coronado's journey, the next documentary report we have on the Querecho is from General Francisco de Ibarra's 1565 expedition, which visited the ruins of Casas Grandes (called Paquimé) in northwestern Chihuahua, located about 600 miles south-southwest of where Coronado encountered a band of the same tribe in Area VI.[9] The Spanish chronicler and historian Baltasar de Obregón writes that when General Ibarra's expedition party visited the ruins of Paquimé, the large prehistoric urban city on the Río Casas Grandes, a large band of about 300 Querechos (counting women and children) visited the general's camp. Obregón, who was a member of the expedition party, describes the Querecho as lively, of noble disposition, friendly, and brave. The Querecho sang and danced around Ibarra's camp and seemed happy to find the Spaniards in their bison-hunting territory. Using sign language, the Indians said that bison herds at that time were only about a four-day journey (perhaps sixty to eighty miles) to the north.

Obregón notes that the Querecho followed bison herds and used dogs as pack animals. The picture of large herds of bison in northwest Chihuahua, which today is a part of the dry Chihuahuan Desert, reminds us again that in the 1560s North America was in the middle of the mesic Little Ice Age. During the maximum period of the Little Ice Age (in the late 1600s), the glaciers in the Rocky Mountains were larger than they had been in the previous 10,000 years.[10] The southmost Southern Plains were lush with deep grass that attracted large bison herds and long-distance bison hunters like the Querecho much farther south than many contemporary writers acknowledge.

About fifteen years after General Ibarra visited the ruins of Paquimé, Spanish officials in Parral (in southern Chihuahua) authorized a small expedition party led by Captain Francisco Sánchez Chamuscado to investigate the region north of Parral along the Rio Grande and to visit the pueblo country in New Mexico.[11] Chamuscado's party followed the Río Conchos downriver to the junction with the Rio Grande and up the Rio

Grande into New Mexico (as reviewed in the previous chapter). However, the party did not enter Area VI.

Several members of Chamuscado's party describe in some detail the Pueblo people who lived in New Mexico to the west of Area VI. The diarists wrote that the Natives resided in flat-topped two- to six-story apartment complexes that surrounded open public squares. The residents lived in large permanent settlements and cultivated tropical maize, beans, squash, tobacco, pumpkins, and cotton. The Pueblo people also raised domestic turkeys and kept shaggy dogs in underground cages. Turkeys were eaten; their feathers were woven into cotton blankets to add warmth; and the large birds contributed to the horticultural operation by eating grasshoppers (a threat to the crops) and depositing their droppings, which fertilized the soil. The dogs were also eaten on special occasions and were available for trade.

We have no record of domestic turkeys being raised in Area VI. The zooarcheologist Charmion R. McKusick writes that the Pueblo people raised at least two species of Indian domestic turkeys, one larger than the wild breed found in Area VI and the other considerably smaller.[12] McKusick speculates that the small breed reported in the prehistoric period in the Tompiro area in eastern New Mexico may have been imported into the Southwest across Texas from Huasteca on the northeast coast of Mexico. This may have been the same trade route used to import scarlet macaws from the lowlands and rain forests of Tamaulipas and Nuevo León into the Southwest during the same period.[13]

Within a few months after the Chamuscado party returned to Parral in 1582, a second small expedition party was dispatched to rescue or at least try to determine the fate of two priests who remained in New Mexico when Chamuscado's main expedition party returned to Parral. The second expedition was led by Antonio de Espejo, who prepared a full diary account of the trip.[14] Espejo followed the Chamuscado route down the Río Conchos and then turned northwestward up the Rio Grande to New Mexico. The only time Espejo entered Area VI was during his return down the Pecos River, which serves as a study area boundary line separating Area V and Area VI. The return was reviewed in the study of Area V, so it will not be repeated here.

When Spanish operators opened silver mines near Santa Bárbara in the 1570s, Spanish colonists were also mining silver to the east in Nuevo León, about fifty miles below the lower Rio Grande, across the river from Area IV. Spanish miners and colonists had arrived in northeast Mexico via the Gulf Coast port city of Pánuco rather than overland through central Mexico and Durango. Captain Don Luis Carvajal y de la Cueva and his lieutenant, Gaspar Castaño de Sosa, led the first large colony of some 200 men northwest beyond the Tamaulipas Mountains near Pánuco into present-day Nuevo León to a location near the modest modern city of Cerralvo. The colonizers selected this area to search for silver perhaps because Cabeza de Vaca recorded a few decades earlier that he had been given bags of silver by the local Natives in the area soon after crossing the Rio Grande. We might add that seventeenth-century Spanish historians, such as Alonso de León (the elder), indicate that Spanish officials understood with some precision where Cabeza de Vaca had crossed the Rio Grande into present-day Mexico and thus where he had been given silver.[15]

In the late 1580s Carvajal moved his colony from near Cerralvo farther west to an area near the present-day city of Monclova, Coahuila. During this time Spanish authorities in Mexico recalled Carvajal, a Portuguese of Jewish decent, to face charges brought against him by the Catholic Church. In the absence of Carvajal, Castaño assumed command of the colony, and in 1590 he sought and apparently received permission from Spanish authorities to abandon the search for silver in northeast Mexico and to move the colony to New Mexico. By July 1590, Castaño's colony was on the move northwest to become the first to colonize New Mexico.[16]

From the account of Castaño's journey through northern Mexico and West Texas, we receive an early glimpse of the Native people and the country along the Pecos River from its junction with the Rio Grande to interior New Mexico. Comparisons can be made between Castaño's account and information received from Espejo's chroniclers regarding the stretch of the middle Pecos reported seven years earlier.

We should first note the impressive size of Castaño's Spanish colony moving across Texas. Over 170 men, women, and children traveled over 600 miles across Coahuila and the Southern Plains into central New Mexico along the uncharted river trail by horse, on foot, and by two-wheeled ox carts. The colonists carried their belongings and herded the livestock, which included the oxen, cattle, goats, and a young fawn.

Castaño began the journey from Monclova on July 27, 1590, and six weeks later, after traveling northwest about 200 miles, the colony reached the Rio Grande near Del Rio, Texas. The party continued northwest following along the southwestern boundary of Area VI and the Pecos River. During the first three weeks of the trip across Texas, the colony worked their way through the deep canyons of the Devils River and found the Pecos River (called the Río Salado), which they somehow knew originated in New Mexico.

Soon after finding the Pecos in late October, Castaño's scouts encoun-

tered the Tepeguan Indians, the first large encampment of Indians identified by Castaño in Area VI. The Tepeguan appeared to be visiting the
area to hunt bison and trade. The scouts and Native interpreters whom
Castaño had brought along from Coahuila reported that they could con-
verse with the Tepeguan because they were their neighbors from southern Chihuahua and Durango, an area over 350 miles to the south.[17]

About thirty years after Castaño met the Tepeguan in West Texas,
members of the same large, cosmopolitan tribe from the Durango area
were reported repeatedly raiding Spanish outposts and settlements in
Nuevo León.[18] Therefore, the local Coahuilan Natives had probably encountered the Tepeguan in their homeland on numerous previous occasions. But on this occasion the Tepeguan received the Spaniards very cor-
dially and gave Castaño's men bison and antelope skins, bison meat, and
shoes that the Natives had fashioned from leather. The Tepeguan even
offered to escort Castaño to a large permanent Native village to the south
where the Spaniards could find a supply of maize. Castaño declined. The
closest location (unknown to Castaño) that meets this description would
have been La Junta de los Ríos, which was about 150 miles southwest of
Castaño's camp and was undoubtedly well known to the Tepeguan.

After leaving the Tepeguan, Castaño continued to find small abandoned Indian camps. In early November, near present-day Fort Stock-
ton, the party encountered for the first time a band of unidentified Plains
Indians traveling with dogs loaded with packs. Members of Castaño's
colony were delighted because neither they nor their Indian escorts from
Coahuila had ever seen Plains Indians with dog trains on the move. Apparently the Tepeguan from the south around Durango did not use dogs
as pack animals as the Plains Indians from the north did.

As the Coahuila Native interpreters did not know the language of the
Plains Indians, they used signs to tell the Indians that they should not be
fearful. Thus, as Coronado's people used signs to communicate with the
Querecho in the Texas Panhandle and Obregón's men used signs with
the Querecho at Casas Grandes, Castaño's Indian guides used signs in
communicating with the Plains Indians on the lower Pecos. Castaño gave
the Natives some meat and maize, and then the Plains Indians departed.
Their dogs were heavily loaded, tied to one another with ropes secured
to the harnesses. Their colorful departure was made to the delight and
entertainment of everyone in Castaño's party, says the chronicler.

On the following day, the colony was attacked by an aggressive unidentified Indian band, and in the skirmish several Indians were killed.
One was captured and later hanged. Along the route the Indians from
Coahuila found thick groves of mesquite and ripe mesquite beans to
supplement the usual Spanish diet of bison meat and maize. It was not

until mid-November, when the party was near Horsehead Crossing on the Pecos River, that any sign of bison was found. Here the diarist records finding only bison tracks, no animals. This report is consistent with accounts written earlier by Espejo and later by Mendoza, who also reported no large bison herds along the Pecos. Wolves and deer, however, had been observed frequently, and one wolf pack killed several stray goats.

About a week later, as the party was approaching the present New Mexico state line, Castaño's scouts discovered a very large abandoned Indian enclosure or trap that the diarist thought had been constructed to hold some unspecified large herd animals, perhaps antelope.

From the New Mexico state line Castaño's colonists marched another 200 miles northward up the Pecos River to the Pecos Pueblo, where they first met strong organized resistance from the local Native population. After a bloody battle Castaño's forces occupied Pecos and then moved ahead to explore the upper Pecos River and Rio Grande pueblos.

Castaño's exploration came to an abrupt halt with the arrival in New Mexico of Captain Juan Morlete, who arrested Castaño and returned him to Mexico City.[19] Castaño was charged with invading New Mexico and enslaving Indians without proper government authorization. A criminal court in the royal audiencia in Mexico City found Castaño guilty as charged and condemned him to six years' exile from Mexico. Acting in 1593, the court ordered that during the six-year period Captain Castaño should serve the king with full pay in the Philippine Islands.

In 1602, about nine years after the court action in Mexico City, the Spanish priest Juan de Montoya published his account of the discovery of New Mexico in which the historian describes Castaño's 1590 expedition to New Mexico.[20] Montoya concludes that Castaño's expedition was properly authorized by the Spanish government. Montoya writes: "Captain Castaño . . . had received information of this land [New Mexico], [and he] determined to go and conquer it, since he had the permission of the governor of New Spain."[21]

While Montoya was preparing his account, the Council of the Indies reversed the earlier ruling of the lower criminal court in Mexico City and upheld Castaño's actions as authorized and proper. The council declared Castaño's expedition lawful and directed that Castaño be returned to New Mexico to assume his duties. While Castaño's case was being considered and acted upon in Spain, Castaño lost his life in the Philippines serving the king.[22]

About fifty years after Castaño was killed, the highly regarded Spanish historian Alonso de León (the elder) wrote a history of Coahuila and Nuevo León that included an account of Castaño's activities in the province and of Castaño's trial.[23] De León writes that Spanish officials in Mexico City were misled about Castaño's service to the king and his actions in New Mexico. He reports that at the Mexico City trial, passion overwhelmed the court and error was made in the decision finding Castaño guilty. De León confirms that while Castaño was serving the king in the Philippines, Castaño was killed in battle. De León adds that the court decision in Mexico City was appealed to the Council of the Indies, which was the final legal authority regarding such matters. According to De León, the council revoked the sentence against Castaño that had been imposed in Mexico City and ordered that Castaño be returned to New Mexico and to his prior government position.[24]

Citing De León's account, the historian George P. Hammond agrees that the Council of the Indies declared Castaño innocent as charged and revoked the prior sentence. Hammond writes that Castaño's name "had been cleared."[25] But contemporary historians frequently overlook the fact that Castaño's actions and his expedition were determined to have been authorized. Writers today frequently give the honor of being the leader of the first expedition to colonize New Mexico to Juan de Oñate, whose colonists arrived in New Mexico from southern Chihuahua about eight years after Castaño and his colonists had arrived from Nuevo León. Many contemporary historians still insist that Castaño's expedition was unauthorized.[26]

Like the expeditions of Chamuscado and Espejo, the 1598 expedition led by Juan de Oñate to colonize New Mexico commenced from the Parral area in southern Chihuahua.[27] But unlike the earlier expeditions from Parral that followed the Río Conchos downriver to La Junta de los Ríos, Oñate's expedition sought a new, more direct route northward from Parral to the El Paso crossing of the Rio Grande. Moreover, Oñate had received reports that both the Conchos and Tepeguan Indians were in revolt and might cause problems if the Río Conchos route were taken.

The large Oñate expedition party of about 500 members moved north from Parral in March 1598. Only after completion of a very difficult 350-mile journey through uncharted dry desert regions and around high and deep sand hills did the colonists reach Paso del Río Grande in early May. The friendly local Manso Indians helped the Spaniards ford the Rio Grande across the westernmost corner of Area V.

The second leg of the march upriver from El Paso was no easier than the initial two-month trip to El Paso. The barren area north of El Paso was later called the "*Jornada del Muerto*," or Dead Man's March. The description of the difficulties that travelers faced upriver north of El Paso is very similar to that given by the chroniclers of the earlier Chamuscado and Espejo expeditions. The long, difficult, and desolate journey north of El Paso may help explain why, at least during the historic period, Indians living downstream below El Paso customarily traded with Indians living to the west on the Río Casas Grandes in western Chihuahua rather than farther up the Rio Grande north of El Paso in New Mexico.

The first large pueblo reached by Oñate's colony was located about 180 miles up the Rio Grande from El Paso and was appropriately named Socorro, meaning "assistance." But here the natural and human ecological scene changed drastically. The numerous pueblos north of Socorro were stocked with surplus maize and had abundant supplies of beans, squash, and other food as well. Taos, the northernmost large pueblo, was reached in July. Oñate was then faced with consolidating his control over the local Pueblo people and preparing for the bitter cold winter months that he knew were ahead.

Fortunately, as Oñate was preparing to send his nephew Vicente Zaldívar east to hunt bison, a displaced Aztec Indian called Jusepe arrived at camp headquarters. Jusepe Gutiérrez was an ideal guide and interpreter for Zaldívar because he had been living for several years with the Apache and other tribes on the Southern Plains and knew the Plains people and the bison territory well. With Jusepe as his guide, Zaldívar and sixty soldiers rode east from the Pecos River on September 15, 1598, to secure a supply of bison meat for the winter.[28]

About twenty-five miles east of the Pecos River, Zaldívar encountered the "Vaquero" Indians, who supplied the Spaniards with one of their own to guide the party farther east. The diarist notes that the Vaquero Indians traded meat, hides, fat, and tallow for the Pueblo people's blankets, cotton, pottery, maize, and turquoise. The Vaquero had medium-size shaggy dogs that the chroniclers said "served as their mules." The dogs were harnessed at the chest and haunches, carried 100-pound loads, and trotted in a line with the ends of the long tent poles dragging behind. The description of the dog train and the lifeways of the Vaquero given by Zaldívar parallels that given earlier by Castaño's diarist of the dog train witnessed on the middle Pecos in Area V and by Coronado's diarist of the Querechos' dog train in the Panhandle and given by Obregón near Casas Grandes.

Apparently the bison hunt concentrated in an area about one hundred miles east of the Pecos River, which places the bison herds along the western shoulder of Area VI. The account says that the Indians, lying hidden in skillfully made blinds, hunted bison at watering holes. The report adds that there were countless springs in the ravines with large groves of juniper, cottonwood, and wild plum trees. We are reminded by the chronicler's description of the weather, vegetation, and availability of water that the hunting trip was taken during the Little Ice Age, a period vastly different from the warming period that we have known for the last 150 years.

Zaldívar writes that most Indian hunters carried flint-tipped arrows and long leather-wrapped bows that he called "Turkish bows." We recall that earlier Espejo described the bows that the La Junta bison hunters carried as "Turkish" bows because of the special wrap used to strengthen the bows.[29] Zaldívar added that the Indians ate bison meat almost raw, using the fat and tallow as bread. Zaldívar noticed that several Vaquero bison hunters had arrows with long bone tips rather than the customary flint arrow points. Although sharpened split-base bone points were made and employed widely by Upper Paleolithic hunters in western Eurasia ca. 30,000 years ago,[30] there are few documentary reports of bone spear or bone arrow points recorded in historic expedition documents.[31] By early November Zaldívar had accomplished his mission and returned to the base camp on the Rio Grande with a supply of bison meat for the winter.

1600s

About two and one-half years after Vicente's expedition westward toward Area VI, Oñate himself led an expedition across Area VI to Quivira along the same general route that Coronado had taken about sixty years earlier.[32] Unlike Coronado's expedition party, Oñate's troops were supported by six mule and ox carts carrying cannon. Vicente de Zaldívar, Jusepe, and two Franciscan friars accompanied seventy soldiers. Governor Oñate reached the Pecos River in five days from the Rio Grande; with an additional three-day march the party reached the Canadian River. Here a group of Indians that the chroniclers called Apache welcomed the Spaniards in a peaceful manner. From the location of the Apache, it appears that the Natives may have been related to Southern Plains people who earlier had been called either the Querecho or the Vaquero by Spanish diarists.

For the next 300 miles of the journey, Oñate's troops followed the flow and direction of the Canadian River commenting frequently on the lifeways of the numerous Apache bands encountered and on the flora and wild animals found in the northern part of Area VI. Apaches were described as the masters of the Plains, people who had no permanent settlements and cultivated no crops, just as reported during Vicente's 1598 journey to the Plains. The Teyas, who proved so helpful to Coronado in the same area, were not mentioned.

Oñate located the first bison soon after entering the Texas Panhandle in Area VI, and thereafter the party was never far from large herds.

Oñate's chroniclers write that often bison would not even run as the Spaniards approached and that the animals were far too numerous to count. In addition to bison, the Spanish scouts also saw large herds of 200 to 300 antelope which "in their deformed shape" made the soldiers uncertain if they were a special species of deer or some other animal. They also reported seeing deer, jackrabbits, wild turkey, and quail.

Soon after entering Area VI, the chroniclers reported finding plums and other unrecognized wild fruit. The Apaches' first gifts to the Spanish troops included small black and yellow fruit the size of small tomatoes, which might have been wild plums or persimmons or both. The soldiers found a variety of plums that grew on small trees and picked sweet and tasty grapes on vines all along the route through Area VI. In the wooded ravines spring water was also often found, as was reported on Coronado's earlier expedition through the area.

After marching eastward along the Canadian River for about 200 miles, Oñate turned northeast and then moved more northward toward Quivira. Before reaching Quivira and the Wichita Indians on the Arkansas River in central Kansas, Oñate encountered a second tribe who, like the Apache, were nomadic and followed the bison herds. Oñate decided to call the Indians the Escanjaque because it sounded like a word that the tribal members often repeated.[33] These Plains Indians were at war with the sedentary Wichita farmers, who had numerous permanent villages located as close as twenty-five miles northeast of where the Escanjaque were found.

Along the route northeast from the Apache to the Escanjaque, Oñate's chroniclers found no other Indians but did identify hardwood trees, including oak and tall trees with nuts "as good as those in Spain." Again huge bison herds were seen each day as well as deer, turkey, and other game.

The mobile Escanjaque (like the Apache) constructed their huts or dwellings with tree branches or brush rather than with long poles covered with hides (used by other Plains Indians) or with straw and grass (used by the Caddo). The branches were stacked about ten feet high, placed in a circle, and covered with tanned skins.

Like the Apache, the nomadic Escanjaque did not plant crops but depended primarily on bison for meat. Escanjaque scouts guided Oñate's party over twenty miles to a river and the settlements of the Escanjaques' enemy, the Wichita Indians. At Quivira, Oñate found maize, the first he had seen growing since leaving New Mexico.

The diarists describe the Wichita villages and people in some detail. Like other Caddoan tribes, the Wichita constructed permanent round straw- or grass-covered lodges designed to accommodate eight or ten individuals. Beds with mats as bedding were built along the sides of the interior walls. The Wichita also had smaller flat-roofed structures with portable wooden ladders, which were used to ascend to the top of the unit. The villages were surrounded by fields of maize, gardens with beans and squash, and plum trees between the fields. Unlike the maize fields in drier New Mexico, these crops were not irrigated. We are reminded that about sixty years earlier, Pedro de Castañeda reported finding *frijoles,* or beans (mesquite beans?), growing in the land of the Teya in the Panhandle and that the Teya and Wichita Quivira were friends and trading partners, looked alike, and perhaps were ethnically related.

Like the Hasinai Caddo, the Wichita Caddo were located in an area with an easy access to bison hunting grounds. So these sedentary horticulturists in Kansas were also terminal hunters who seasonally sent bison-hunting parties from the Wichita villages to bison grounds on the Plains to supplement the cultigen grown locally. We recall that this same lifeway was found also among the La Junta people, who planted the same cultigen as the Wichita and Hasinai and who also sent hunting parties out to secure bison on the Southern Plains.

Oñate's chroniclers observed that some Wichita carried on their foreheads shells that were thought to have been brought to the Plains from the Atlantic Coast. This assumption by the Spaniards might have been accurate because subsequent historic records suggest that the Wichita interacted with Mississippian tribes that possessed shells, reported to have originated in New England. At this point Oñate's expedition record closes, noting only that the party had traveled about 570 miles from their base camp in New Mexico. The distance estimate appears to be reasonably accurate.

When he returned from his trek to visit the Wichita at Quivira, Oñate directed his attention to the numerous local problems of his colonists (some of whom wanted to return to Mexico) and to the security needs of his troops stationed at several pueblos that continued in revolt. Oñate had earlier suppressed uprisings in Acoma located west of the Rio Grande and in several pueblos in the Salines district east of the river. By early 1609 the situation appeared beyond his control, and the viceroy ordered Oñate to return to Mexico City to stand trial and face charges that stemmed from his alleged excessive use of force and his brutality against the pueblo villages.[34]

Oñate was convicted by the court in Mexico City of abuses to Indians and of other criminal charges. As punishment, Oñate was banished from New Mexico permanently. His banishment was more severe than that assessed against Castaño, who was given only a six-year term. And unlike Castaño's conviction, Oñate's was never reversed by the king. At the time of his death, Oñate was still banished from New Mexico for his excesses against the Native people of the territory.

After Oñate, no large formal Spanish expedition crossed into Area VI from New Mexico during the seventeenth century. Although several visitations were made by Spanish clergy with escort into the southern part of Area VI, none resulted in the establishment of a permanent mission.[35] In 1632 and again twice in the 1650s, Spanish priests accompanied by a small unit of military guards visited the Concho River in Area VI. Limited ethnographic information is contained in records of these visits, but it appears that in the 1650s the Spaniards encountered and fought the Cuita, the Escanjaque, and the Ahijado.[36] The Escanjaque were probably the same nomadic bison hunters that Oñate had encountered in central Kansas about fifty years earlier.

The next large Spanish expedition from New Mexico that entered Area VI was led by Juan Domínguez Mendoza in 1683.[37] As the trip originated near El Paso and proceeded down the Rio Grande to near La Junta and then moved northward, probably along Alamito Creek toward the Pecos River, the first part of the journey was covered in the study of Area V. We pick up Mendoza's expedition in early January 1684 when it crossed the Pecos River marching northeastward into Area VI.

As mentioned earlier, the principal purpose of the expedition was for Mendoza and the church fathers from El Paso to meet formally at an agreed location on the Edwards Plateau with representatives of the Hasinai Caddo and their numerous allies, who lived principally in Areas I and II. The two had never met formally before.

On January 17 Mendoza's party encountered the first large local Indian tribe at an encampment near the crossing of the Pecos River. The Indians were called the Jediondo and were closely allied with the Jumano. The captains of the Jediondo plus some unidentified visiting tribal leaders welcomed Mendoza warmly. Although the Indian leaders were mounted, numerous other tribal members moved on foot. This report is consistent with similar documentary accounts describing large tribal groups in Central Texas at the time in which only the leaders were mounted. Near the Jediondo encampment Mendoza's men found the first bison reported on the trip.

The Jediondo carried an old but well-made, heavy, seven-foot wooden cross painted red and yellow (cardinal colors for Indians of the Southwest). The Jediondo also carried on high an even more surprising Old World cultural symbol: a white four-foot-long flag in the middle of which two parallel blue taffeta crosses had been carefully stitched. The original source of the old red and yellow painted cross and the large blue and white flag is unknown, as is the meaning of the cross and flag to the Jediondo. We do know that on Spanish expeditions the Spanish flag and a Christian banner were carried at the head of the expeditionary formation.

This was not the only occasion in which Spanish chroniclers report finding large Texas Indian groups carrying banners and crosses as if they were on parade. For example, in 1691, Governor Domingo Terán de los Ríos encountered a large gathering of 2,000 to 3,000 Indians from West Texas and north-central Mexico in northern Area II near modern-day San Marcos. One column of Indians carried a large, well-preserved wooden cross; two other parade groups from West Texas (the Catqueza and the Cibola) carried banners with an image of Our Lady of Guadalupe. Moreover, in 1709, Fray Isidro Espinosa met an encampment of about 2,000 Indians in northwest Area I near the upper Colorado River crossing at Onion Creek. These tribes also carried in file a carefully made cane cross and painted images of Our Lady of Guadalupe.

On January 25 members of another well-known Indian tribe called the Arcos Tuertos (Twisted Bows) or Arcos Fuertes (Strong Bows; probably from the Big Bend area of the Rio Grande) joined the Mendoza party.[38] A tribe had been identified by the same name near La Junta by diarists with Chamuscado and Espeda about 100 years earlier. Mendoza's diarist comments that the Arcos Fuertes resembled in all respects, including their dress, the Suma, who resided at the time along the Rio Grande between La Junta and El Paso.

As Mendoza's party moved northeast toward the middle Colorado River, the diarist notes the local wild animals and plants seen each day. The diarist reports the turkeys were seen almost every day, and bear, deer, and antelope were frequently spotted also. The account indicates that nut trees (possibly pecan) along with wild grape, mulberry, and plum trees were plentiful.

After moving farther northeast into Area VI, Mendoza's party reportedly killed several thousand bison, far more than required to supply meat for the expedition party. Mendoza's diarist describes the bison herds as follows: "The buffalo were so many that only God could attempt to count them. The Spaniards and Native Americans killed 4,030 buffalo."[39] However, this number includes only the adult bison killed and brought into camp to butcher for meat. The number does not include the numerous calves killed or the number of adult bison killed for only their hide and left in the field.

This firsthand report suggests the enormous size of bison herds in Area VI and Central Texas during the study period. But according to the archeologist Tom Dillehay, this was not always the case. In his frequently cited 1974 study of the fluctuation of the bison population on the Central and Southern Plains, Dillehay writes that bison were not prominently present in large numbers on the Southern Plains in Texas between ca. AD 500 and 1300.[40] The author assumes, and I think correctly, that during the warm and relatively dry climatic periods leading up to AD 1350, the lack of sufficient moisture for grassland resulted over time in the deterioration of the grasslands as a food source for bison and in a shrinkage of the geographic boundary of the Plains. By inference, bison were not present in large numbers on the Southern Plains during the Medieval Warm period (ca. AD 900–1350).

But Dillehay writes that he knows of no postulated warm climatic period between AD 500 and 1300 to explain the absence of bison on the Southern Plains during the years immediately preceding the fourteenth century.[41] That observation was made over thirty years ago. Recently climatologists have confirmed a warm and occasionally dry Medieval Warm period in Europe, North America, and the Plains between ca. AD 900 and 1300.[42] I believe that this is the warm-dry climatic period for which Dillehay was searching in order to explain the relative absence of bison on the Southern Plains during the period AD 500–1300.

Although Dillehay did not identify the cooler and wetter Little Ice Age (ca. AD 1350–1850) by name, the author notes in his 1974 study that the increase in the number and range of bison on the plains after ca. AD 1300 could be attributed to a climatic change that increased rainfall and expanded the grassland. A 2005 study of climate change and directly associated changes in sea level in the Gulf of Mexico confirms that the climatic fluctuation recorded in studies of climatic change in the Northern Hemisphere by climatologists in fact occurred in Texas and on the Gulf Coast during the Medieval Warm period and the Little Ice Age.[43] The historic record generally confirms that large bison herds were on the Southern Plains and on the prairies of Central and South Texas in the sixteenth, seventeenth, and eighteenth centuries, at the height of the Little Ice Age.

On May 1, the day Mendoza commenced his return trip to the Pecos, the leader writes that he was forced to leave the Hill Country because of continued raids by the Apache and the Salinero Indians. The diarist specifically identifies the Salinero as a "pirate tribe" from Chihuahua. The night before Mendoza decided to leave, the Salinero attacked Mendoza's camp three times. The Salinero were a well-known large and aggressive tribe whose primary residence was in southeastern Chihuahua and southern Coahuila, over 400 miles to the south. Apparently the Spanish gave the tribe the name "Salinero" because they lived near salt flats and lagoons northwest of Parras.[44] The presence of Salinero in West Texas and the Edwards Plateau suggests that the tribe, and most likely many other tribes from northern Mexico, frequently traveled over 400 miles north to hunt bison on the Southern Plains of Texas during the study period.

Another justification for Mendoza's sudden decision to return to El Paso was the failure of the Hasinai Caddo and their allies to show up at the agreed meeting ground to confer with the Spaniards. In commenting on their failure and his disappointment, Mendoza lists thirty-six tribes whom he was waiting to meet. The leader first names the Hasinai, whom he refers to as "the people of the Río de los Tejas" (the Trinity River or possibly the Angelina River). The remaining thirty-five tribes include several recognized groups reported in Areas II and VII, including possibly the Bidai (Bobida), the Cava (Saba), and the Iscani (Isconi).

On the return march, the killing (or slaughter) of bison continued, but the number of bison killed was substantially reduced as the party approached the drier and lower elevation near the Pecos River crossing used in mid-January. En route to the Pecos crossing, the Spaniards killed 120 bison on May 4; 255 on May 5, 6, and 7; 150 on May 8. However, only one or two bison were killed each day thereafter as Mendoza's party reached the open prairies below the Balcones Escarpment leading to the Pecos crossing and into Area V.

About eighty years after the Mendoza expedition returned to El Paso, the Marqués de Rubí marched into Area VI to inspect the presidio for the mission Santa Cruz de San Sabá in Menard County. Rubí's report deals primarily with military affairs and measures to be taken to defend the post from the Comanche—a recently arrived foe to Area VI that was unmentioned in Mendoza's day.

Conclusions

As indicated in the study of Area VI, the Indian country covered is comparatively large, including parts of the Llano Escarpment, the Caprock Canyonland, the Southern Plains, the Rolling Plains, the Panhandle, the Blackland Prairies, and the Edwards Plateau. But during the later part of the historic period, the area represented a unified Native cultural area and homeland for nomadic bison hunters, principally the southerly advancing Apache.

During the prehistoric period from ca. AD 1200 to 1350, the Antelope Creek people constructed slab rock and earth structures with contiguous rooms at locations along the Canadian River in the Panhandle. According to Christopher Lintz and Robert Brooks, these horticulturists grew tropical domesticates of corn, beans, and squash.[45] This culture dramatically changed in ca. 1350, which was the end of the Medieval

Warm period and the beginning of the colder and wetter Little Ice Age. According to Lintz and Brooks, the Antelope Creek people after 1350 may have switched from a dependence primarily on cultigen to a lifestyle dependent primarily on hunting bison as a result of a dramatic change in climate.[46] This same change in climatic conditions and patterns of subsistence or abandonment has been documented at sites in western Oklahoma and in New Mexico.

In his 1999 study of the sudden emergence of warfare among the Anasazi in the 1300s, Steven LeBlanc concludes that the principal factor contributing to warfare was the abrupt climatic change that occurred during the period. LeBlanc summarizes the climatic change in the Southwest as follows: "From the period AD 900 to around AD 1200 or so, the climate was warmer than the long-term average. This interval has been termed 'the Medieval Warm Period.' The subsequent time period, from around AD 1300 to the early 1800s, was colder than average. The last period is sometimes called the 'the Little Ice Age.'"[47]

LeBlanc explains that the Medieval Warm period was very favorable for horticulture in the Southwest. But the Little Ice Age created a disaster for farming in marginal areas and brought stress, warfare, and eventually abandonment to parts of the Anasazi country. LeBlanc's assessment may well apply to the Texas Panhandle and the gradual abandonment of the horticultural ways of the Antelope Creek people in the 1300s.

I concur with LeBlanc's interpretation of the impact of the Medieval Warm period and the Little Ice Age on horticultural development and later warfare and abandonment in the Southwest. Further, I believe that the Little Ice Age had other significant ramifications. It appears to me that the Little Ice Age contributed to the extension of the range of bison and Plains Indians farther and farther south to the central Texas coast and into northern Coahuila and Chihuahua during the study period.

The large bison population in the southern part of Area VI attracted long-distance terminal or seasonal hunters from West Texas and north-central Mexico. Castaño met Tepeguan bison hunters (from near Durango) on the Pecos River in Area VI during his 1590 expedition from Coahuila to New Mexico. In 1684 Mendoza fought with the Salinero Indians from southern Coahuila on the bison hunting grounds of the Edwards Plateau in Area VI. Jumano and other West Texas tribes had regularly hunted bison in the southern part of Area VI during the early years of the study period. Throughout the study period, visiting long-distance terminal or seasonal hunting bands were reported along the southern skirts of Area VI and farther southeast into Areas II and IV and into northern Mexico.

This transition in hunting patterns and long-distance interaction is reflected in the chapter supplement for Study Area VI. Seventeen named Native tribes or bands were identified in the Spanish documents reviewed in this chapter. Ten of the seventeen tribes are considered residents of the area, and the remainder are either long-distance visitors or neighbors.

SUPPLEMENT: STUDY AREA VI
THE TEXAS SOUTHERN PLAINS

This supplement contains an alphabetical list of the Native tribes and bands referenced in Spanish expedition documents cited in the review of Study Area VI. Entries note that some groups are considered local to Area VI during the study period while other tribes were visitors from West Texas, northern Mexico, and East Texas. Each entry includes the name and variants of the name of the tribe used by chroniclers, the name of the diarist who recorded the encounter, and the date and location of the meeting.

Below are the names of the thirty-six tribes that Juan Domínguez de Mendoza was scheduled to meet in Area VI. For purposes of the list, these tribes are considered as invited visitors to Area VI who failed to show up or came late; they are therefore not included. Mendoza gives the following list of the invited tribes: People of the Río de los Tejas (Hasinai), Huicasique, Aieli (Ais?), Aguida, Flechas Chiquitas, Echancote, Anchimo, Bobida (Bidai?), Injame (Inhame), Diju, Colabrote, Unofita, Juama, Yoyehi, Acani (Ocana), Hume, Bibi (Bibit, Bidai?), Conchamucha, Teanda, Hinsa, Pojue, Quisaba, Paiabuna, Papane, Pucha, Puguahiane, Isconi (Iscani?), Tojuma, Pagaiame, Saba (Cava?), Bajunero, Novrach, Pulcha, Detobiti, Pucham, and Orancho.

The following documentary sources were among those consulted in preparing the list: Richard Flint and Shirley Cushing Flint, eds., *Documents of the Coronado Expedition, 1539–1542*; George P. Hammond and Agapito Rey, eds. and trans., *Obregón's History of 16th Century Exploration in Western America*; Hammond and Rey, *The Rediscovery of New Mexico, 1580–1594*; Jerry R. Craddock, ed., *Zaldívar and the Cattle of Cibola: Vicente de Zaldívar's Expedition to the Buffalo Plains in 1598*; Mariah F. Wade, *The Native Americans of the Edwards Plateau, 1582–1799*; and Brian Imhoff, ed., *The Diary of Juan Domínguez de Mendoza's Expedition into Texas (1683–1684)*.

1. Ahijado. In 1654 Major Diego de Guadalajara reportedly encountered the Ahijado (along with the Cuitoa and Escanjaque) near the Concho River in Area VI. According to W. W. Newcomb and T. N. Campbell, it is most likely that the tribal name is fictitious.

2. Antelope Creek People. Texas archeologists refer to the prehistoric horticulturists who lived in villages and farmed along the Canadian River in the Texas Panhandle between ca. AD 1250 to 1450 as the Antelope Creek people. The Panhandle farmers in Texas are seen by some archeologists as a connecting link between the agricultural Pueblo people in New Mexico and the eastern or Woodland horticulturists as represented by the Caddoan Wichita Indians in western Oklahoma and Kansas.

3. Apache. In his testimony before Governor Oñate in early 1599, Jusepe Gutiérrez, a former servant of Captain Antonio Gutiérrez de Humaña, said that he had traveled east from New Mexico with Captain Humaña to visit the Vaquero Indians and traveled on to the bison plains. After Humaña killed Captain Francisco Leyva de Bonilla, Jusepe escaped to live for a year with the "Apache and Vaquero Indians." Apparently Jusepe considered the Apache and Vaquero as separate tribes. Later Jusepe escaped again to return to New Mexico. Jusepe's account is one of the earliest in which the term Apache is used. On the 1683–1684 Mendoza expedition, the diarist wrote that Apaches attacked Mendoza's troops on several occasions near the Concho River in the Edwards Plateau. In 1714 Apaches attacked the Derbanne's French commercial convoy from Indian camps near the Colorado River in Travis County.

4. Arcos Tuertos (Arcos Fuertes). The Mendoza expedition found the Arcos Tuertos or Twisted Bows (perhaps also called Arcos Fuertes or Strong Bows) in January 1684 a few miles east of the crossing of the Pecos River. The tribe had been identified on the Rio Grande by chroniclers of the Chamuscado and Espejo expeditions. Mendoza's diarist wrote that the tribe was similar in all respects to the Suma, who lived along the Rio Grande near and below present-day El Paso.

5. Comanche. The Comanche were not a significant factor in Area VI during the study period, which closes ca. 1720. But by the 1760s, when the Marqués de Rubí visited the southern part of Area VI, Comanches were one of the principal forces opposing both the Spaniards and the Apaches.

6. Cuita (Cuitoa, Cuytoa). On the 1650 visit to the Concho River in Area VI, Spanish troops engaged the Cuita in battle and captured several hundred tribal members. In a study of the Cuytoa by W. W. Newcomb and T. N. Campbell, the authors cite a 1686 report of the Spanish writer Alonso de Posada on the expeditions of Hernán Martín and Diego del Castillo (in 1650) and the Spaniard Diego de Guadalajara (1654) to the present Concho River, where the Cuytoa,

Escanjaque, and Ahijado were met. Although Newcomb and Camp-bell found no other reference to the Cuytoas in the historic record, they conclude that "it is not now possible to prove that Cuitoas is the name of an authentic ethnic unit."

7. Escanjaque (Aquacane). On Oñate's 1601 trip to Quivira, the Escan-jaque were met a few miles south of the Arkansas River in Kansas. The warlike tribe was nomadic and an enemy of the Quivirans, who had large villages on the Arkansas River in central Kansas. In 1650 and again in 1654, Spanish troops fought the Escanjaque (along with the Cuitoa and Ahijado) near the Concho River in Area VI.

8. Jediondo (Gediondo). In 1684 the Mendoza expedition encountered the Jediondo on the Pecos River soon after crossing the river moving northeast. The tribe was friendly with the Jumano and Spaniards at the time and were enemies of the Apache.

9. Jumano. The Jumano accompanied Mendoza's expedition party in 1683 and 1684 into Area VI northeast of the Pecos River. Although the tribe was often friendly with the Spaniards, a disagreement arose on the Mendoza expedition, and the Jumano and some of their allies left the expedition early.

10. Pueblo Indians. Coronado was the first Spaniard to visit the Pueblo Indians on the Rio Grande in New Mexico in 1541. The Natives lived in separate pueblos located along the Rio Grande and the Pecos River in large permanent adobe dwellings several stories high. The Indians were horticulturists who grew cotton, beans, maize, squash, and tobacco, and they had domesticated dogs and turkeys.

11. Querecho. Coronado's diarist, Pedro de Castañeda, wrote that the Coronado expedition party first encountered the Querecho after traveling ten days east of the Pecos River marching toward Area VI. Castañeda reported that the Indians conversed by the use of signs so well that no interpreter was needed. The Querecho were nomadic people who followed the bison herds and used pack dogs. Castañeda added that the Querecho had very fine flint tools that they sharpened with their teeth.

12. Quivira Indians. The residents of Quivira, located in central Kansas along the Arkansas River, were Wichita Caddoan Indians who lived in permanent settlements, grew maize, beans, and squash, and hunted bison. Coronado visited the tribe and was given a copper piece and some small copper bells by the chieftain. Coronado's dia-rist, Castañeda, wrote that the Wichita dressed and acted like the Teya.

13. Salinero. On the 1683–1684 Mendoza expedition to the Edwards Plateau, Mendoza reported that the "pirate" Natives of Nueva Viz-

caya, whom they called Salineros, attacked their camp three times one night. The Salinero also killed two friendly Gediondo (Jediondo) who had gone out to hunt. The Salinero were a large, well-known tribe that lived in southern Chihuahua (as correctly noted by Mendoza's diarist), over 300 miles to the southwest of Mendoza's camp. The Salinero, along with their western neighbor the Tepeguan, apparently traveled several hundred miles to hunt bison in the southern part of Area VI.

14. Tepeguan (Tepehuan). Gaspar Castaño de Sosa met the Tepeguan in late October 1590 along the Pecos River near Pecos, Texas. The friendly Indians gave Castaño's party bison skins and meat and offered to lead the Spaniards to an Indian settlement that had maize. As the homeland of the Tepeguan was in the Durango area, it appears that they, like the Salinero, traveled several hundred miles to hunt bison in Area V and in the southern part of Area VI. In the 1640s Juan Bautista Chapa reported that the Tepeguan repeatedly raided the Spanish outpost in Nuevo León.

15. Teya. Coronado met the Teya near the Canadian River in Area VI. A principle Teya village was called Cona. They were enemies of the Querecho. The Teyas furnished Coronado with guides who led his party to Quivira and guided Coronado on his return trip to New Mexico. Although Castañeda writes that the Teya did not cultivate maize, the diarist adds that the country produced abundant beans, plums, and wild grapes. Wild plums and grapes are known to grow in the Texas Panhandle; the only wild bean known to grow there is the bean of the mesquite tree. But domesticated beans were cultivated by the Wichita, who were allies of and perhaps related to Teya.

16. Vaquero. In his account of the 1565 Ibarra expedition, Obregón uses the term "Querechos" to identify the bison hunters he met near the Río Casas Grandes. Later Obregón uses the terms "Vaquero" and "Querecho" to describe nomadic tribes that followed the bison herds with dog trains.

17. Wichita. In 1541 Coronado visited the Wichita Caddoans on the Arkansas River in central Kansas. The tribe was described as sedentary horticulturists who lived in round grass houses like the Hasinai Caddo in East Texas. They were also terminal bison hunters. The Wichita chieftain had small copper bells, which suggest direct or more likely indirect trade with Casas Grandes. Wichita slaves were given to La Salle on the Mississippi in 1682.

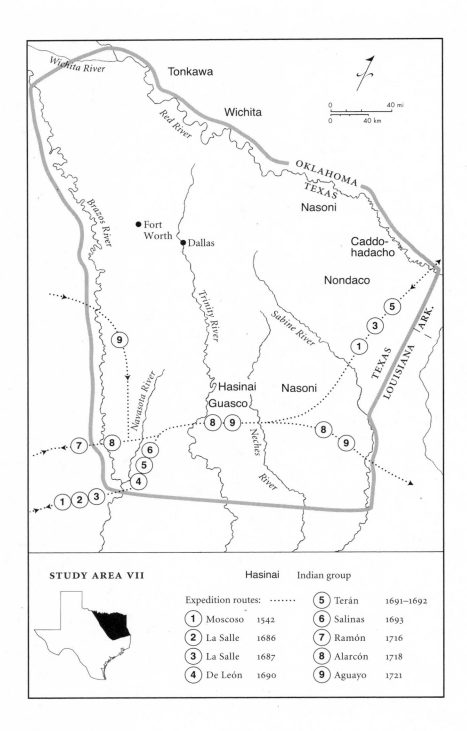

STUDY AREA VII

Hasinai   Indian group

Expedition routes: ·······

1 Moscoso 1542
2 La Salle 1686
3 La Salle 1687
4 De León 1690
5 Terán 1691–1692
6 Salinas 1693
7 Ramón 1716
8 Alarcón 1718
9 Aguayo 1721

MAP 7.1

7   NORTHEAST TEXAS

STUDY AREA VII

Study Area VII is only a part of the area occupied by Caddoan people and the larger region in which the Caddoan language was spoken during the study period. The Caddoan people occupied the Pineywoods of northeast Texas and also the area farther to the north and east in eastern Oklahoma, southwestern Arkansas, and northwestern Louisiana.[1] For purposes of this study, the Red River is the northern boundary of Area VII (see Map 7.1); the eastern boundary follows the Texas state line from the Texarkana corner south to a point near the small community of Burkeville in Newton County. The boundary line then runs generally southwest to the Brazos River to a point a few miles south of the modern city of Navasota and then upstream along the Brazos River valley and the eastern boundary of Area VI back to a point near the junction of the Wichita and Red Rivers.

The study area includes all or parts of sixty-six counties.[2] The area east of the Trinity River is referred to in this chapter as the Texas Caddoan homeland. During the study period the area between the Trinity and the middle Brazos (referred to herein as the Post Oak Savanna or Post Oak Belt) was shared by the Caddo with local tribes and with visiting or intruding groups, principally from the north and the Southwest.

During the study period the Apache (who were enemies of the Caddo) occupied or exercised dominant control over the more open bison hunting grounds on the Blackland Prairies west of the Brazos (into Area VI). Numerous local tribes residing southwest of the Caddo in Areas I and II were allies and trading partners of the Hasinai Caddo. The Bidai Road connected the Hasinai to the Bidai and other more coastal tribes in Area VIII.

Several large rivers running generally southeast drain Area VII, but the Red River flows from west to east, forming the northern boundary

195

of Area VII. During the early historic period a major channel of the Red River flowed into the Mississippi at a point opposite the Mississippi-Louisiana border on the east side of the big river. The Brazos, Trinity, and Sabine Rivers flow to the southeast directly into the Gulf of Mexico. The Wichita River drains the area to the west and flows into the Red River near the northwest corner of the area. Piney woods similar to the wooded areas farther east into Arkansas, Louisiana, and the American Southeast cover much of Area VII.

The tall pine woodlands and the heavier precipitation found in Area VII are in contrast to the more open, often treeless xeric plains to the west in parts of Area VI. The more mesic environment in the Caddo area was favorable for horticulture, and the densely wooded and swampy areas provided a degree of natural protection from mounted Plains enemy tribes.

Luis de Moscoso de Alvarado, Hernando de Soto's successor, led the first European expedition into Area VII. Between July and October 1542 Moscoso marched his troops across the Red River near present-day Texarkana and then southward into East Texas. After visiting the Hasinai in modern Houston County, Moscoso turned around and took his expedition party out of Texas along the earlier route back to the Mississippi River. After Moscoso departed Texas, no European explorers visited Area VII for over 140 years.

The second European visitors to Area VII were members of a French expedition party led by Robert Cavelier, Sieur de La Salle, who had landed on the Texas coast in early 1685. La Salle established a colony and fort on Matagorda Bay; in early 1686 the French explorer, using local guides, led a small expedition party to visit the Hasinai in La Salle's search for the Mississippi River. Although illness forced him to remain for several months with the Hasinai, La Salle recovered and returned to the bay in late 1686. On the trip the French leader established an important ally with the Hasinai. The following year, La Salle was killed by his own men soon after crossing the Brazos en route to visit the Hasinai a second time. After La Salle's death, several of his men, including La Salle's brother, Jean Cavelier, the priest Anastase Douay, and the chronicler Henri Joutel marched on to the Hasinai. After spending several months with the Hasinai and Nasoni, the French party continued farther northeast to the Mississippi and eventually on to Canada and France.

The French presence at Matagorda Bay stimulated Spanish authorities in Mexico to dispatch a series of maritime and overland expeditions into Texas. The first overland effort from Monclova to reach Area VII was led by Governor Alonso de León in 1690. Other Spanish expeditions followed to East Texas in 1691–1692 and in 1693. After a twenty-three year suspension, Spanish expeditions to colonize the Hasinai country began in 1716 and occurred again in 1718 and in 1721 when the new Spanish capital of the province of Texas was established at the eastern Caddoan settlement called Los Adaes. Accounts from each of these expeditions will be reviewed for ethnographic information on the Native peoples of northeast Texas.

Sixteenth- and Seventeenth-Century Spanish and French Expeditions

The first Europeans to visit the Caddo people in Area VII were Spanish soldiers led by Luis de Moscoso de Alvarado in 1542. As mentioned earlier, Cabeza de Vaca's maximum market and inland travel extended about 130 miles from the coast, a distance that might have permitted him to encounter visiting Caddoan hunters in perhaps the Navasota-Brenham area but that would not have allowed him to visit the Caddoan homeland.

The Spanish expedition force originally commanded by Hernando de Soto first landed on the Gulf Coast of Florida in the spring of 1539, about a year before Coronado left the Pacific coast of Mexico for New Mexico and only three years after Cabeza de Vaca had left West Texas on his journey to the Pacific coast of Mexico and Mexico City. For the next two years, from June 1539 to June 1541, De Soto's large entrada marched across the Southeast, slowly exploring westward from one Mississippian chiefdom to the next in search of gold and silver.[3]

Several chroniclers on the De Soto expedition describe the Native population in the Mississippian-style communities in the Southeast as mound builders and successful sedentary farmers.[4] The horticultural chiefdoms spread across the Southeast were usually located near the floodplain of a large river or creek, and the local farmers cultivated varieties of the same tropical food crops that had been cultivated earlier in Mexico: maize, squash, and beans. They also cultivated locally domesticated plants such as sunflowers. Reflecting the same Mississippian cultural heritage, the sedentary chiefdoms from Georgia to the Mississippi River all had large earthen mounds and ceremonial temples built around open public plazas.[5] Native residents worshiped the sun but recognized other ceremonial objects as well, and the community elite engaged extensively in long-distance interaction that extended over hundreds of miles south to the Gulf Coast, north to the Great Lakes, and westward as far as eastern Oklahoma.

In the early summer of 1541 De Soto crossed the Mississippi at a location thought to be near present-day Memphis, Tennessee, and traveled farther westward along a route that generally followed the Arkansas

River upstream. De Soto found a continuation of the same Mississippian regional chiefdoms in central Arkansas as he had encountered east of the Mississippi. Although he explored as far west as perhaps near the Arkansas-Oklahoma state line, no gold, silver, or bison were observed.[6] We should note that in summer of 1541 Coronado and De Soto both were exploring stretches of the Arkansas River. Unknown to De Soto, Coronado was visiting the Wichita Caddoan villages on the middle Arkansas River in central Kansas while De Soto was on the lower Arkansas visiting Mississippian chiefdoms. Only about 300 miles separated the two Spanish expedition routes.

De Soto and his Spanish troops left western Arkansas and returned eastward to spend the very cold Little Ice Age winter of 1541–1542 near the Mississippi River. De Soto's chroniclers write that at the winter camp the troops were unable to move for over one month because of heavy snow and extreme icy conditions.[7]

In the spring of 1542 De Soto died, and his body was slipped into the Mississippi River. With the concurrence of the troops, Luis de Moscoso assumed command and in July marched the expedition party to the southwest. Moscoso's intention was to travel overland across Texas to Mexico. At a large Indian village called Naguatex, apparently located on the Red River near present-day Texarkana,[8] the Spaniards met strong resistance from the local Indians, but Moscoso's soldiers prevailed and continued their journey and battles southward into East Texas.

By October, the Spanish force had pushed about 200 miles into Texas, encountering numerous settlements but moving generally south-southwest to modern Houston County where they met the Hasinai Caddo in what was called by the Spaniards the province of Guasco.[9] Here one of Moscoso's most credible chroniclers, the Gentleman from Elvas, records that the Hasinai showed the Spaniards cotton blankets and turquoise, which were hallmark trade goods of the American Southwest. We recall that when traveling six years earlier through northern Coahuila (only about 400 miles southwest of Guasco), Cabeza de Vaca had received cotton blankets and a cast copper bell from a large Indian trading party that was returning from northeastern Mexico to their homeland in western Chihuahua.

The Gentleman from Elvas writes that the Hasinai confirmed that the cotton blankets and turquoise were obtained originally from Native people who lived toward the southwest. As mentioned in the chapters on Areas V and VI, the source of cotton blankets, turquoise beads, and cast copper bells reported by Spanish chroniclers was likely northwestern Chihuahua, perhaps, more specifically, the Río Casas Grandes region.

By the 1540s, the Spanish had sufficient hard evidence of the broad interregional Native trade network across the Southwest. Moscoso had found turquoise and cotton goods from the Southwest while he was visiting the Caddo in East Texas, Coronado was given cast copper bells from the Southwest on his visit to central Kansas, and Cabeza de Vaca was given a cast copper bell and cotton blankets from the American Southwest while traveling through Nuevo León in northeast Mexico. According to Timothy Perttula, interaction by the Hasinai and non-Caddoan peoples residing in the Edwards Plateau during the protohistoric period is supported by the archeological record.[10]

Moscoso dispatched from Guasco a small scouting party to determine whether the Indians living farther to the southwest had stores of maize and other food supplies required to support the Spanish troops, horses, and hogs. The Hasinai of Guasco told Moscoso's scouts that after marching ten days west, the troops would reach a large river that the Caddo called "Daycao," where they hunted deer. However, the Caddo insisted that they were unfamiliar with the Indians on the other (west) side of the river.

From late seventeenth-century Spanish expedition accounts, we learn that the Hasinai customarily hunted up to the east bank of the Colorado River, but that they did not hunt on the west side because the Hasinai, Central Texas tribes, and Trans-Pecos Indians all considered the lower Colorado River to be a border river not to be crossed to hunt. It therefore seems likely that the Daycao was the Colorado River.[11] In addition, seventeenth-century expedition accounts indicate that it took about ten days to travel from the Hasinai in East Texas along the customary lower route to the lower Colorado a few miles upriver from La Grange in Fayette County.[12]

Spanish scouts dispatched by Moscoso located and crossed the Daycao but found only small temporary Indian encampments with no stores of grain on the west side of the river in Area II. Two Indians who were captured west of the Daycao and were returned to Moscoso for interrogation spoke a language that could not be understood by any of Moscoso's interpreters or by the Hasinai people of Guasco.

Disappointed but realistic, Moscoso and his men turned around to return again to spend the winter on the Mississippi River. The large Spanish expedition, still numbering over 300 men, had been supported and supplied with surplus and stored maize and other cultigen taken by force from Mississippian-style chiefdoms from Florida to East Texas during the previous three years, but the southwestern boundary of the successful Mississippian and Caddoan horticultural tradition was reached at the Hasinai villages in Area VII. West of Area VII the lifeways of the Native peoples in Texas changed quickly from highly complex chiefdom cultures to that of a simpler hunter-gatherer lifestyle, which was generally practiced throughout most of Areas I, II, III, and IV. Moscoso and his men recognized this drastic cultural, economic, and geographical change and retreated along the route they had taken in the spring when they marched to Texas from the Mississippi.

The winter of 1542–1543 on the Mississippi was as severe and as crippling as the previous winter.[13] The intense cold and deep snow permitted very limited activity in Moscoso's camp until April, when work began on constructing seven large seaworthy vessels to sail and row down the Mississippi and westward along the Gulf Coast to Mexico. In the summer of 1543 Moscoso and his men sailed down the big river and into the coastal waters of the Gulf of Mexico. Moscoso's soldiers, turned sailors, stopped along the coast of Texas in Area VIII as they sailed westward toward the Spanish port of Pánuco, located several miles inland from the present-day Mexican city of Tampico. Moscoso's encounter with the Native population on the coast of Area VIII near Galveston Bay is covered in the following chapter.

For over 140 years after Moscoso's visit to Texas, no European entered Area VII. During that period the Spanish government concentrated on exploring and colonizing parts of northern Mexico and the Southwest, the French expanded operations in Canada and the Great Lakes region, and the English continued colonizing along the Atlantic coast and moved farther inland. But in the 1670s and 1680s French explorers from Canada moved south into the Mississippi Valley. First came Louis Jolliet and Jacques Marquette in 1673, and nine years later Robert Cavelier, Sieur de La Salle, explored the Mississippi from Canada. La Salle's 1682 exploration was the first to reach the Gulf of Mexico and resulted in a French claim to the Mississippi, which drastically changed the relationships among the major European powers on the North American continent.[14]

La Salle followed his 1682 claim over western lands drained by the Mississippi River with his 1684–1685 maritime voyage from France to establish a French colony and fort near the mouth of the Mississippi. Having missed the Mississippi, La Salle settled temporarily for a military post on the central Texas coast in Area III.[15] In 1686, on his search for the Mississippi to the northeast of his Texas coastal colony, La Salle visited the East Texas Hasinai Caddo in Area VII. Apparently these were the same people whom Moscoso had visited 144 years earlier.

On his 1686 expedition to visit to the Hasinai, La Salle took with him his brother, the Abbé Jean Cavelier, as well as the priest Anastase Douay, but he left Henri Joutel at the fort as post commander. Both Douay and Abbé Cavelier prepared accounts of the trip, but Douay's chronicle is more comprehensive and reliable.[16] Douay writes that the French party of about twenty men departed the French fort on Garcitas Creek in late April and arrived in Area VII in early summer.

According to Douay, the Hasinai possessed numerous Spanish items that had been brought to the Caddo by West Texas tribes who had obtained the goods initially from Spanish outposts, mining centers, and missions in Chihuahua and New Mexico. We recall that many Spanish mission and military posts had been abandoned in the Southwest during the Pueblo revolt of 1680.[17] The items observed by Douay included Spanish lace, clothing, official documents, silver spoons, and coins. Douay says that the large horse herd held by the Hasinai had been acquired directly from the Chouman Indians (Jumano) and other tribes from northern Mexico and West Texas and, of course, indirectly from Spanish sources in northern Mexico.

The Hasinai told La Salle that their range of interaction and trade network extended westward across Texas to New Mexico and that they had fought in New Mexico as allies of the Jumano.[18] The Caddo added that they also traded with allies who lived eastward to the Mississippi River. This assertion was supported by a Hasinai captain who sketched on tree bark for La Salle their customary route from East Texas to the Mississippi.[19]

This account helps confirm that the cotton blankets and turquoise seen by Moscoso with the Hasinai in 1542 were likely objects brought to the Caddo via the Jumano or their allies from the Southwest. The suggested pattern of trade in turquoise and cotton goods between the Hasinai and the Native people in northern Chihuahua and the American Southwest that Moscoso discovered had apparently not diminished during the intervening years. If anything, the trade and other forms of interaction between the two distant regions across Texas may have increased.

Douay writes in detail about the Trans-Pecos Jumano, whom he called "ambassadors," suggesting perhaps that their presence represented more than a short-term visit. He writes that the Jumanos kissed his hand, folded their hands as in prayer, and said that there were priests like him where they lived (near La Junta de los Ríos). We know that Mendoza left several priests at La Junta when he visited the area two years earlier at the close of his 1684 campaign.

During his stay with the Caddo, La Salle became very ill and was required to remain at the Hasinai village for about three months to recover his strength. During this period three of La Salle's men deserted, deciding that they preferred the more open lifestyle of the Hasinai to the disciplined service with La Salle. The diminished French party with a fully recovered La Salle returned to the colony on Garcitas Creek late that fall. Although he returned to Fort St. Louis without the three deserters, La

Salle brought back to the post a much-needed supply of dried maize and beans and five pack horses that he had acquired from the Hasinai.

On the return trip from the Hasinai to the fort, La Salle left a cache of maize hidden near the customary crossings at the two largest rivers—the Brazos and the Colorado. La Salle intended this cache to be available if he was required to return to visit the Hasinai at some future time. As anticipated, La Salle did attempt to return to the Hasinai in early 1687 after discovering that his small ship, *La Belle,* had been lost in Matagorda Bay during his 1686 trip to East Texas. It is significant that the loss of *La Belle* cut off La Salle's marine resupply route to Hispaniola.

In January 1687 La Salle, Joutel, and about twenty men departed Fort St. Louis to march again to East Texas in their search for the Mississippi River.[20] A few miles east of the Brazos River crossing in Area VII, several of La Salle's men ambushed and killed their leader and two members of La Salle's party. After the incident the remaining Frenchmen, with Hasinai hunters serving as guides, proceeded northeast about sixty miles to the Trinity River crossing (probably near the present-day crossing of the Trinity on Texas State Highway 21) and on to the Hasinai homeland about thirty to forty miles east of the Trinity River in Houston County.

Henri Joutel prepared the most detailed and reliable account of the Area VII people encountered by La Salle's party in 1687. Joutel reports that when the Frenchmen arrived, the Hasinai elders were dressed in special costumes that included colored feathered headdresses. They had Spanish sword blades at their sides; they carried several unspecified large bells; and they wore pieces of blue material. The diarist writes that the Hasinai had obtained the foreign objects by trade with allies living to the west. However, the tobacco smoked by the Hasinai and shared with their French guests was grown locally. We cannot be certain of the source of these foreign items included in the Hasinai ceremonial dress, but we do know that, as suspected by Joutel, substantial trade flowed between the Hasinai and the Indians of West Texas and, indirectly, of the American Southwest. We also know that brightly colored feather headdresses, copper bells, and blue cotton material had earlier been traditional export items from the Casas Grandes area to La Junta and farther east.

After spending about two months with the Hasinai and Nasoni, Joutel and his party marched northward to the Caddohadacho, who occupied several village sites along the Red River near modern-day Texarkana. The trip through the Pineywoods of deep East Texas was accomplished with Nasoni guides and took about a month. But in contrast to accounts of French and Spanish journeys of a comparable distance through Areas I and II, where numerous tribes were encountered, Joutel records no encounters with any Caddoans or any other groups along the 120-mile trail.[21] At the Red River Joutel records more evidence of the long-range interaction between the Caddohadacho and their trading partners on the Mississippi and their distant allies in West Texas. The Caddohadacho chieftain named for Joutel over forty tribes that he considered to be either allies or enemies.

The list of allies copied by Joutel includes the Cappa, who occupied an Acansa village on the Mississippi River, and the Jumano, who lived on the Rio Grande near La Junta in the Trans-Pecos country. The straight-line distance between these two important allies, one on the Mississippi and the second on the Rio Grande, is over 800 miles. A comparable report from the East Coast would be one in which an Indian tribal leader in Virginia identified by tribal names his close allies in New York and Florida. The story and report illustrates clearly the pivotal role that the Texas Caddo played in the interaction between the Native peoples in the American Southwest and the chiefdom cultures of the Southeast during the study period.

While visiting the Caddohadacho, Joutel was introduced to a young Caddoan who had escaped from his Chickasaw captors living east of the Mississippi. This report tends to confirm other accounts suggesting that Texas tribes in Areas I, VII, and VIII were at times at war with the Chickasaw or other "Flatheads" on the Mississippi.[22] In a 2002 study of the late seventeenth- and early eighteenth-century Indian slave trade instigated by the British in the Southeast, Alan Gallay estimates that up to 2,000 Indian slaves were captured in raids on tribes friendly to the French living west of Mississippi. Chickasaw raiders associated with British merchants in the Carolinas preyed on the Acansa, Taensa, Tunica (Tanico), and Caddoans in the late 1600s. Gallay confirms that many Indian slaves brought to Carolina were exported to New England and the West Indies.[23]

Two Cahinno Indians, who were visiting the Caddohadacho and whose village was located about eighty miles to the east, agreed to guide Joutel's party to their homeland. The Cahinno were visiting the Caddo to obtain highly regarded bois d'arc bows.[24] When Joutel's party neared the Cahinno village on the Ouachita River in southwest Arkansas, a local Indian representative of the tribe arrived to greet the Frenchmen. The emissary (or elder) carried at his side a Spanish-style sword blade, colorful feathers, and two small bells. This ceremonial attire is strikingly similar to that worn by the Hasinai when Joutel arrived in East Texas.

Joutel writes that the Cahinno possessed two highly prized and very attractive horses. This account is significant because it represents one of the earliest firsthand European reports of Indians holding horses in eastern Arkansas, within about one hundred miles of the Mississippi River. Joutel writes later that his party left their horses with the Acansa Indians on the Mississippi and that at the time the Mississippi tribes had none.

On his march farther east toward the Mississippi, Joutel writes that the Cahinno guides stopped one day to visit their allies, the "Tonico," who were salt traders along the Saline River in eastern Arkansas. The Tonico were most likely the same as the Tunica (Tanico), whom La Salle's chroniclers identified near the Yazoo River basin on his 1682 discovery expedition on the Mississippi.[25]

When Joutel's party reached the Mississippi River and the Cappa Indians (also called the Acansa), the full transcontinental range of an interconnecting North American Native trade network became apparent. Here the French diarists report finding European apple, peach, pear, plum, pomegranate, and watermelon, which apparently originated from Spanish communities and missions in north-central Mexico; they also found a Native necklace made of marine shells that had reportedly originated in New England.[26]

It appears that Indian horticulturists and traders in southern Chihuahua exchanged the Old World fruit and melons, taken from Spanish missions and outposts, with other Native horticulturists living downstream on the Conchos River and with Native farmers at La Junta. As mentioned, during the historic period and perhaps earlier, Jumanos and other horticultural tribes from La Junta were in regular contact with the East Texas Caddo horticulturists, who in turn interacted with their cultural and trading partners, the Acansa, on the Mississippi. Local Acansas told Joutel that their marine shells had been acquired via a Native trade network that reached up the Ohio River to New England and the Atlantic.

An Illinois Indian who was identified as a "hermaphrodite," or homosexual, guided Joutel's party up the Mississippi from Arkansas to the Great Lakes in August 1687. We should note that both French and Spanish chroniclers referred to Indian homosexuals and cross-dressers as "hermaphrodites" in seventeen-century documents. However, in the eighteenth century, French writers used the term "berdaches." After reaching Canada, Joutel, La Salle's brother (the Abbé), and other members of the party returned to France to write their accounts of La Salle's expedition to Texas.

In the spring of 1690, about two and one-half years after Joutel left Texas, the Hasinai in Area VII received as guests representatives of both France and Spain, the two opposing European powers in Texas. The French party arrived first and was unexpected; the Spanish delegation that arrived a short time later had been invited. We will review the history of this close international encounter in Area VII, beginning chronologically with the first visitor to arrive, the Frenchman Henri de Tonty (or Tonti).

In January 1690 La Salle's lieutenant, Tonty, left Canada and canoed down the Mississippi on a journey that was designed to take him to visit the Hasinai in East Texas and on to Fort St. Louis on the Texas coast.[27] He was unaware at the time that about a year earlier the local Indians had killed most of the colonists and had destroyed the French post. Tonty reached his friends the Acansa near the mouth of the Arkansas River on January 16.

The Acansa greeted Tonty as an old friend; he had first met the Acansa eight years earlier on La Salle's 1682 discovery expedition on the Mississippi. Upon hearing of Tonty's plan to visit the Caddohadacho and the Hasinai, the Acansa asked Tonty to take with him two Caddohadacho women who at the time were visiting the Acansa but needed an escort to return home to northeast Texas.

With the two Caddoan travelers, Tonty left the Acansa and continued down the Mississippi for about a week to visit a second friendly tribe, the Taensa. Tonty writes that the impressive cabins of the Taensa were forty feet square, made of dried mud brick walls that were ten feet high and a foot thick. The roofs were covered with cane mats. The Taensa gave Tonty twelve guides to travel west with him about eighty miles to the Natchitoche Indians (also a Caddoan tribe) on the lower Red River.

From the Natchitoche, Tonty moved up the Red River to the Caddohadacho (called Cadodaquis by the French), where he met their leader, the widow of the former chieftain who had recently been killed by the Osage. Tonty observed that the Caddohadacho made fine bows that they traded to distant tribes living up to one hundred miles away. We are reminded of Joutel's comments about the excellent bois d'arc bows made and traded by the Caddohadacho.

Tonty reports that the Caddohadacho held over thirty Spanish horses in their sizable herd. He describes the Caddohadacho men and women as tattooed all over the body. This report also confirms earlier observations by Joutel.

On April 6 Tonty moved on southward toward the Hasinai, whom he called the "Naocadiché." But the meeting with Hasinai leaders turned ugly. Although Tonty expected to find seven Frenchmen living with the Hasinai, there were none. Moreover, the Hasinai gave conflicting reports to Tonty on whether the Frenchmen who had earlier lived with them were alive or were in the hands of Spanish authorities. The Hasinai might have been reluctant to admit that the year before they had turned over their last two young Frenchmen (Pierre Talon and Pierre Meunier) to the Spanish governor, Alonso de León.

In frustration, Tonty refused to accept the calumet ceremony offered. Although this action seriously offended the Hasinai, they did provide him with four horses in exchange for seven hatchets and a string of large glass beads for his return trip to the Mississippi. He arrived back with the Acansa in late June.

In late May of 1690, about a month after Tonty's visit, Governor Alonso de León visited the Hasinai.[28] De León and the Spanish troops and missionaries were well received by the Caddo chieftain who had agreed to welcome them to the Hasinai homeland when they had parted after their first encounter the year before at the Governor's Crossing on the Guadalupe River in Area II.

De León and the priest Damián Massanet both write in their separate accounts of the 1690 trip that the Hasinai cultivated maize, beans, squash, and watermelons.[29] Like the Aztec in Old Mexico and the Pueblo Indians in New Mexico, the Hasinai prepared a special dish called tamales.[30]

In his study of prehistoric Native cultivation in North America, William E. Doolittle describes the horticultural practices of the Hasinai. Doolittle writes that Caddoan fields were generally no larger than 60 by 180 yards and that Caddoan farmers practiced the intercropping of maize and beans. Two kinds of maize were planted; the second planting matured in about three months. Specially designed hoes were used to mound and clean the area around the immature corn stalks.[31]

De León and Massanet also report that Hasinai lifeways were much more sophisticated and complex than those of Native tribes in South Texas and Coahuila. Massanet writes that the Hasinai lived in large permanent houses covered with grass or straw, sat on wooden benches, slept on raised wooden beds, and ate from ceramic bowls.[32] Much of the information from Spanish diarists concerning the cosmopolitan character of the Caddo confirms the ethnographic information found in earlier French accounts, including reports of meeting Hasinai hunting parties in the northern part of Area I.

When De León and Massanet left East Texas in the summer of 1690, several close members of the family of the Hasinai chieftain, including his brother, joined them on their return to Mexico. The Spaniards' special attention to the family of Native leaders in Texas was unusual, although Spanish authorities earlier took Timucua Indians from Florida to Spain in the 1560s.[33]

The following year, in August 1691, another Spanish expedition, this one led by Governor Domingo Terán de los Ríos, visited the Hasinai Caddo.[34] Later the same year, the Governor returned for a second visit to the Hasinai on his journey farther north to see the Caddohadacho on the Red River. Terán found the Caddohadacho villages near the crossing area on the Red River that had been used by Joutel's party in 1687 and probably earlier by Moscoso. The accounts of Terán's visits to the Caddo provide no new significant documentary information on the lifeways of the Caddo, but a map prepared during Terán's visit to the Caddohadacho illustrates the spatial organization of the Caddoan village.

After Terán departed Area VII in 1691, Massanet with other clerics remained behind to minister to the Hasinai and their close neighbors. But troubles mounted for the Spanish priest because the Hasinai refused to accept the Catholic faith over their own traditional beliefs and even blamed (and perhaps properly so) the priests for an epidemic that struck the Hasinai that year.

By the time Governor Gregorio de Salinas Varona initiated a resupply effort for Massanet from Monclova in 1693,[35] Massanet's situation in East Texas had deteriorated further. In his diary account Salinas does not comment on the troubles facing the mission or give any new ethnographic information on the Area VII Indians. However, near the customary Colorado River crossing in Fayette County, the same used earlier by both La Salle and Spanish expedition leaders, Salinas encountered Hasinais meeting on the west side of the Colorado in Area II with West Texas Jumanos and local Cantonas.[36] The following day, June 24, Salinas found other Hasinais in a shared encampment about ten miles west of the Colorado crossing with the Simaoma, a tribe from Coahuila.[37]

The following day, and several miles farther west, Salinas met another well-known tribe from below the Rio Grande, the Saquita.[38] The evidence suggests that the visitors from below the Rio Grande and the Hasinai visitors were engaged in trade at this general location, which was apparently recognized as a customary Indian trading ground. These reports of Caddoan trade delegations on the west side of the lower Colorado trading with distant tribes from northern Mexico and West Texas tend to confirm the geographic scope of the Caddoan trading area during the study period.

Hasinai hunters operated as far west as the lower Colorado, but apparently no tribe living west of the Colorado crossed the lower Colorado to hunt bison east of the river. Trade grounds were on the west side of the river, and on these special grounds local tribes hosted annually large trade delegations, including the Hasinai and numerous tribes from the west. It appears clear that the Caddo people maintained during the historic period a much broader range of interaction with the Native people of Chihuahua and Coahuila than most writers acknowledge.

The Spanish expedition led by Espinosa in 1709 did not reach Area VII; however, the three Spanish expeditions initiated in 1716, 1718, and 1721 visited the East Texas Hasinai and other Caddoan settlements farther east into Louisiana. In addition, a French military reconnaissance journey was conducted by Bénard de La Harpe from the lower Mississippi westward to Caddoan villages on the Red River and into south-central Oklahoma in 1718–1719.

On the 1716 Spanish expedition led by Captain Domingo Ramón and Fray Isidro de Espinosa, the expedition party first met Hasinai Indians a few miles west of the Brazos crossing in Burleson County near the western edge of Area VII.[39] Being very familiar with the area, the Hasinai were well qualified to serve as guides to the Brazos River crossing area. Other Hasinais served as guides for Espinosa and Ramón as the Spanish party moved east-northeast into country new to them along the modern Robertson-Brazos county line. Between the Brazos and the Navasota (about eight miles east of the Brazos River crossing), Espinosa's party met a Hasinai bison-hunting party of four men and two women.[40] The Hasinai hunters turned guides to lead the Spanish expedition party farther northeast to the customary Navasota River crossing. These encounters with the Hasinai on the middle Brazos support the placement of the western boundary of Area VII along the middle and upper Brazos River valley.

About ten miles east of the Navasota crossing, Ramón and Espinosa stopped in modern Leon County to visit a Hasinai farming village with over twenty Caddoan residents.[41] The Hasinai fed the Spanish visitors new corn and fresh melon, both of which had been grown in their local fields. It appears from the historic record that the territorial boundary of the Hasinai during the historic period (and perhaps for several centuries earlier) extended well west of the middle Trinity River.[42]

When Ramón and Espinosa reached the Hasinai homeland east of the Trinity, the local authorities greeted them with a formal pipe-smoking ceremony. Espinosa notes that even the women smoked and passed the pipe around. Espinosa's comments about how the Hasinai respected women reminds us of Tonty's 1690 report of meeting with the chieftain of the Caddohadacho, who was the former chieftain's widow, and of Fray Gaspar de Solis's 1768 report of meeting a Hasinai leader and her five husbands.[43] The Spaniards were fed locally produced maize, beans, sunflower seed cakes, and melon, all served on earthenware.

The western expanse of Hasinai influence is documented further in the diary accounts of the 1718 expedition led by Governor Martín de Alarcón and the expedition of Governor Marqués de San Miguel de Aguayo in 1720–1721. When Alarcón departed San Antonio to visit Matagorda Bay and later East Texas and Louisiana, his principal guide and interpreter for the entire trip was a Hasinai.[44] The Hasinai guide skillfully led the Spanish party from San Antonio to the Guadalupe River and then downstream past Cuero and on eastward to the lower Colorado River. The guide took Alarcón to the eastern part of Matagorda Bay, back again to the Colorado, north to the customary crossing of the Brazos, and eastward across the Trinity to the Hasinai homeland. The diary account records the line of march followed by Alarcón and how familiar the Hasinai guide was of Areas I, II, and III in addition to his own area.

On Aguayo's expedition in 1720 to visit the East Texas Hasinai and to establish the first capital of the province of Texas near the Red River at Los Adaes, the governor visited a Hasinai farming village between the Navasota and Trinity Rivers.[45] This report represents further evidence of permanent Hasinai farming villages established ten to twenty miles west of the Trinity. Near the same area, Aguayo met two Caddo-allied tribes from the south, the Deadose and the Bidai, who are mentioned in the study of Area VIII. Diarists on the three expeditions confirm again that the boundaries of Caddo intense interaction, although not permanent exclusive occupation, extended westward to the central Brazos.

During the period 1718–1722, when the Spanish sent expeditions into East Texas and western Louisiana, the French in Louisiana sent envoys westward to forge new alliances with the Caddo and their northern allies. In 1718 the Frenchman Bénard de La Harpe commanded a small unit to visit the Caddo on the Red River.

La Harpe maintained a diary account of his trip that located major Caddoan villages and Caddoan allies to the north. In addition, La Harpe provided information on the relationships between the Caddo and their northern neighbors, the Norteños.[46]

During his journey La Harpe met with the Natchitoches, Adayes, and Yatasi on the lower Red River in central Louisiana and later with the "Cadodaquious" (Cadodaquis), Nasoni, and Nanatsoho near modern-day Texarkana. La Harpe writes that the Caddo were at war with the Osage, Lipan Apache, and the Chickasaw from east of the Mississippi.

Traveling farther northwest to the South Canadian River in south-central Oklahoma, La Harpe encountered a large gathering of about 6,000 friendly Taovaya, Tawakoni, Tonkawa, Wichita, Comanche, Yscani, and Waco Indians. At the large gathering of Norteños and their allies, the tribes celebrated the calumet for La Harpe.

At the close of the calumet ceremony, the chief of the Taovayas apologized to La Harpe because he had only one small eight-year-old Apache slave to give to La Harpe as a present. The chief explained that he would have given La Harpe seventeen Apache slaves had they not been eaten at a public feast about a month earlier. These alliances among the northern tribes evolved further as the northern groups moved farther south into Central Texas during the following decades.

As an observant diarist, La Harpe also comments on the fauna and flora observed on the journey. The animals recorded include bison, antelope, bear, deer, and wild turkey.

Conclusions

During the pre-Columbian period, and likely for centuries earlier, the East Texas Caddoan Indians represented the most complex, sophisticated, and cosmopolitan Native culture in the state. Caddoan horticultural settlements during the Medieval Warm period (ca. AD 900–1350), when Mississippian-style agricultural chiefdoms emerged across the Southeast, numerous sedentary horticultural centers matured in the Texas Panhandle, on the Rio Grande in West Texas, and in the American Southwest. Caddoan people, like their neighbors in the Southeast and Southwest, depended primarily on the bountiful production and storage of surplus maize, beans, sunflowers, and tobacco while continuing to hunt game, fish, and gather food from wild plants. The Caddo were sedentary horticulturists and mound builders. In his 2004 overview of the prehistory of the Caddo people in Texas, Timothy Perttula notes that mound building in the general area occupied by the Caddo has been traced back in northern Louisiana to over 5,000 years ago,[47] a thousand years before the Egyptian pyramids, the English Stonehenge, or the monumental Mayan mounds and temples.

These large-scale mound builders of the Middle Archaic period included in their group craftsmen who fashioned small, delicate, microdrilled tubular beads of red jasper. These semisedentary or seasonally sedentary tribes or bands subsisted on the rich aquatic resources along the ancient course of the Arkansas River rather than on a horticultural subsistence.[48]

Beyond the efforts of their neighbors to the east and west, Caddo Indians engaged in extensive interregional trade, diplomacy, and other forms of long-distance interaction. Caddoan traders, hunters, and warriors visited the Trans-Pecos, South Texas, northern Mexico, the Gulf of Mexico, and the Mississippi. The Caddo in Texas were in a pivotal position because they traded directly with the Jumano people and other Native communities in the Southwest, and they interacted with their cultural neighbors and trading partners farther to the east on the Mississippi.

SUPPLEMENT: STUDY AREA VII
NORTHEAST TEXAS

This supplement lists alphabetically the names of Indian tribes and bands reported in diary accounts and other expedition records referenced in the Area VII study. The objectives of the supplement are to locate geographically as precisely as possible where the tribe or band was encountered and the relationship of the tribe to other Native groups. Where appropriate, the entries include the name of the expedition leader or the chronicler reporting the encounter and the date of the report.

On La Salle's 1687 expedition through Area VII, Henri Joutel prepared a list of the names of the tribes that a local Caddohadacho leader said were allies or enemies of the Caddo. As the report by Joutel does not indicate the homeland of the tribe and is the only reference made to many of the named tribes, the entries below include only a brief comment noting that the tribe was one listed by Joutel as either a friend or foe.

The following documentary sources were among those consulted in preparing the supplement: Timothy K. Perttula, "The Prehistoric and Caddoan Archeology of the Northeastern Texas Pineywoods," in Perttula, ed., *The Prehistory of Texas*; Lawrence A. Clayton, Vernon James Knight Jr., and Edward C. Moore, eds., *The De Soto Chronicles: The Expedition of Hernando De Soto to North America in 1539–1543*; William C. Foster, ed., *The La Salle Expedition on the Mississippi River*; Isaac J. Cox, ed., *The Journeys of René Robert Cavelier, Sieur de La Salle*; Herbert E. Bolton, *The Hasinais*; and William C. Foster, *Spanish Expeditions into Texas, 1689–1768*.

1. Acansa (Quapaw). In 1687 Henri Joutel visited the Acansa near the junction of the Arkansas and Mississippi Rivers. They were allies of the Caddo.
2. Annaho. Joutel identified the Annaho as allies of the Cadodaquis (called Caddohadacho by the Spaniards).
3. Apache (Cancy). The Frenchman Bénard de La Harpe in 1719 described the Apache observed on his journey about one hundred miles north of the Red River and Area VII on the Southern Canadian River in Oklahoma. La Harpe wrote that the Apache were so hostile to tribes such as the Tonkawa that the victors ate the vanquished. He

added: "The advantage that the Cancy have over their enemies is that they have good horses." La Harpe wrote that the Apache used dogs to "carry their houses on their backs."

4. Aqui. Joutel identified the Aqui as enemies of the Cadodaquis.
5. Bidai. In 1721 Governor Marqués de San Miguel de Aguayo met the Bidai with the Deadose near the Trinity River crossing.
6. Cadaquis. Joutel identified the Cadaquis as enemies of the Cadodaquis.
7. Cadodaquis (Caddohadacho). Joutel and the French priest Anastase Douay wrote that the 1687 French party visited the Cadodaquis, who told the names of their enemies and friends.
8. Cahinno (Cahinio, Cahaynihoua). Joutel identified the Cahinno as allies of the Cadodaquis. They were residents of south-central Arkansas and are generally considered a Caddoan tribe.
9. Caiasban. Joutel identified the Caiasban as enemies of the Cadodaquis.
10. Caitsodammo. Joutel identified the Caitsodammo as enemies of the Cadodaquis.
11. Cannaha. Joutel identified the Cannaha as enemies of the Cadodaquis.
12. Cannahio. Joutel identified the Cannahio as enemies of the Cadodaquis.
13. Canoatinno (Cannohatinno, Canotino, Cannoatinno, Kanoutioa, Kanotinno). Joutel identified the Canoatinno as enemies of the Cadodaquis. Douay and Joutel wrote that the Cenis went to fight the Kanoatinno while the Frenchmen visited the area in 1687.
14. Cantey. Joutel identified the Cantey as enemies of the Cadodaquis.
15. Cappa (Acansa). Joutel identified the Cappa as allies of the Cadodaquis.
16. Cassia. Joutel identified the Cassia as allies of the Cadodaquis.
17. Catcho. Joutel identified the Catcho as allies of the Cadodaquis.
18. Catouinayo. Joutel identified the Catouinayo as enemies of the Cadodaquis.
19. Chaye. Joutel identified the Chaye as enemies of the Cadodaquis.
20. Chicksaw (Chepoussa). Joutel wrote that the Chepoussa were enemies of the Cadodaquis. The Chickasaw, who lived east of the Mississippi, had captured a young Cadodaquis and had cut off his nose and ears. The young man escaped and returned home. In 1682 La Salle met the Chickasaw south of the junction of the Ohio and Mississippi Rivers. They were enemies of the Acansa and Caddo.
21. Chouman (Choumay, Jumano). The French priest Anastase Douay wrote that the Cenis (Hasinai) and the Jumano were allies and that

during the 1686 trip to East Texas La Salle met Jumano "ambassadors" who were staying with the Hasinai.

22. Comanche (Caumuche). La Harpe identified the Comanche as one of the several tribes he met in 1719 on the Lower Canadian River in Oklahoma about one hundred miles north of Area VII.

23. Coroa. In 1682 La Salle met the Coroa, who were with the Natchez on the lower Mississippi. The designated chronicler on La Salle's 1682 expedition on the Mississippi, Nicolas de La Salle (no relation), wrote that the Coroa all had flat heads.

24. Daquinatinno (Daquinatino). Joutel identified the Daquinatinno as allies of the Cadodaquis.

25. Daquio. Joutel identified the Daquio as allies of the Cadodaquis. The Hasinai referred to the present-day Colorado River as the Daycao, according to Moscoso's chroniclers.

26. Datcho. Joutel identified the Datcho as enemies of the Cadodaquis.

27. Deadose. In 1721 Aguayo met the Deadose with some Bidais near the Trinity River crossing.

28. Dotchetonne. Joutel identified the Dotchetonne as allies of the Cadodaquis.

29. Douesdonqua. Joutel identified the Douesdonqua as allies of the Cadodaquis.

30. Enoqua. Joutel identified the Enoqua as allies of the Cadodaquis.

31. Guasco. According to De Soto's chroniclers, Moscoso reached the people and province called Guasco after marching about six weeks south from the Red River and crossing into East Texas. Most writers associate the Guasco with the Hasinai Caddo in Houston County. The Spaniards found turquoise and cotton blankets with the Hasinai (Guasco), which suggests some form of interaction with Native people in the Southwest.

32. Haqui. Douay wrote that the 1687 French party encountered the Haqui during their march north from the Cenis to the Red River in northeast Texas. The Haqui were enemies of the Cenis.

33. Hasinai (Cenis). Douay wrote that in the spring of 1686 La Salle first visited the Cenis in East Texas. Joutel and Douay wrote that the Cenis were visited again in 1687 after La Salle's death. Between 1690 and the close of the study period, Spanish expeditions visited the Hasinai in 1691, 1693, 1716, 1718, and 1721.

34. Haychis. Joutel identified the Haychis as allies of the Cadodaquis.

35. Hianagouy. Joutel identified the Hianagouy as enemies of the Cadodaquis.

36. Hiantatsi. Joutel identified the Hiantatsi as enemies of the Cadodaquis.

37. Houaneiha. Joutel identified the Houaneiha as enemies of the Cadodaquis.

38. Karankawa. In 1690 the two Talon brothers testified that the Karankawa raided the Caddo in East Texas and captured a number of tribal members and horses.

39. Kiowa (Quataquois). La Harpe identified the Kiowa as one of the several tribes he met in 1719 on the Lower Canadian River in Oklahoma about one hundred miles north of Area VII.

40. Maye. Moscoso's chroniclers wrote that the chieftain of the Maye met Moscoso near the Red River in the summer of 1543.

41. Naansi. Douay wrote that the Naansi lived in East Texas between the Nasoni and the Caddohadacho and were enemies of the Cenis.

42. Nabedache. Bolton writes that the Nabedache were the westernmost Caddoan tribe in Area VII, located about six miles west of the Neches River.

43. Nabiri. According to Douay, the Nabiri, who were enemies of the Cenis, lived in East Texas north of the Nasoni and south of the Caddohadacho.

44. Nacacahoz. According to Moscoso's chroniclers, the Nacacahoz lived in a village of the same name, located about two travel days east of Guasco in East Texas.

45. Nacao (Nacau). Bolton writes that the Nacao were among the most important Caddoan tribes in the early eighteenth century.

46. Nacassa. Joutel identified the Nacassa as enemies of the Cadodaquis.

47. Nacodissy. Joutel identified the Nacodissy as allies of the Cadodaquis.

48. Nacodoche. Herbert Bolton identifies the Nacodache as living near the mission of Nuestra Señora de Guadalupe in 1716 when Captain Domingo Ramón and Fray Isidro Espinosa visited the area.

49. Nacoho. Joutel identified the Nacoho as enemies of the Cadodaquis.

50. Nacono. According to Ramón in 1716, the Nacono lived near the mission of Nuestro Padre San Francisco de los Tejas.

51. Nadaco. Joutel identified the Nadaco as allies of the Cadodaquis.

52. Nadaho. Joutel identified the Nadaho as enemies of the Cadodaquis. Bolton includes the Nadaco as a tribe affiliated with the Hasinai.

53. Nadamin. Joutel identified the Nadamin as allies of the Cadodaquis.

54. Nadatcho. Joutel identified the Nadatcho as enemies of the Cadodaquis.

55. Nadeicha. Joutel identified the Nadeicha as enemies of the Cadodaquis.
56. Naguatex. Moscoso's chroniclers reported that Moscoso engaged the Naguatex near their very large village in northeast Texas along the Red River in the summer of 1542.
57. Nahacassi. Joutel identified the Nahacassi as enemies of the Cadodaquis.
58. Nanatsoho. The Nanatsoho were one of the tribes associated with the Caddohadacho and living on the Red River. This location is identified by Perttula.
59. Nardichia. Joutel identified the Nardichia as enemies of the Cadodaquis.
60. Nasayaya. Alonso de León wrote that the Nasayaya formed one of nine Caddoan settlements associated with the core tribe called the Nabedache.
61. Nasitti. Joutel identified the Nasitti as enemies of the Cadodaquis.
62. Nasoni (Assoni, Nassoni). On La Salle's 1686 trip to the East Texas Caddo, Douay said that his French party visited the Nasoni, who lived on the east side of a large river (the Angelina River) between the Cenis and the Nasoni. Joutel described his visits with the Nasoni in 1687.
63. Nastchez (Natsoho). Joutel wrote that the Nastchez were a Caddoan tribe or band that lived near the Caddohadacho on the Red River.
64. Natachitoche. The Natachitoche lived on the Red River in close association with the Caddohadacho. The village location is identified by Perttula.
65. Natschita (Natchitta, Natchitoche, Natschito). Joutel wrote that the Natschita were one of three Caddoan tribes or bands that lived near the Cadodaquis on the Red River in East Texas.
66. Natsshostanno. Joutel identified the Natsshostanno as enemies of the Cadodaquis.
67. Nechaui. Ramón wrote that the Nechaui and the Nacono resided southeast of the main Nabedache village.
68. Neche. Espinosa wrote that the Neche village was about two miles east of the Neches River crossing.
69. Neihahat. Joutel identified the Neihahat as allies of the Cadodaquis.
70. Nisohone. Moscoso's chroniclers wrote that Moscoso visited a small village in the Nisohone province in East Texas after traveling three days south of the Red River.
71. Nondaco (Nondacao). According to the chroniclers of Moscoso, Nondacao was a large, well-populated area with a surplus of maize.

Moscoso reached the area in East Texas after traveling about one week south of the Red River. Joutel identified the Nondaco as allies of the Cadodaquis.

72. Nouista. Joutel identified the Nouista as allies of the Cadodaquis.

73. Osage (Anahons). La Harpe described the Osage, whom he encountered on his 1719 journey to visit the Cadodaquious (Caddohadacho). He wrote that his Caddohadacho guide was very fearful that they would encounter some enemy party, particularly the Osage.

74. Quiouaha. Joutel identified the Quiouaha as enemies of the Cadodaquis.

75. Sacahaye. Joutel identified the Sacahaye as allies of the Cadodaquis.

76. Soacatino. Moscoso was engaged in a serious fight at Soacatino; according to Moscoso's chroniclers, the Spaniards prevailed. There was very little maize at Soacatino. The location and people were reached after Moscoso had traveled about two weeks southward from the Red River in East Texas.

77. Souanetto. Joutel identified the Souanetto as enemies of the Cadodaquis.

78. Taensa. In 1682 La Salle visited the Taensa, who lived several miles upriver and on the west bank of the Mississippi opposite their enemy, the Natchez Indians. Taensa guides led Tonty in 1690 from the Mississippi to the Caddoan villages on the lower Red River.

79. Tahiannihouq. Joutel identified the Tahiannihouq as enemies of the Cadodaquis.

80. Taneaho. Joutel identified the Taneaho as enemies of the Cadodaquis.

81. Tanico (Tonica). Joutel identified the Tanico as allies of the Cadodaquis.

82. Tanquinno. Joutel identified the Tanquinno as allies of the Cadodaquis.

83. Taovaya (Toayas, Tawehash). La Harpe wrote that his party met the "Taovayes" in 1719 with several other tribes near the South Canadian River about one hundred miles north of Area VII.

84. Tawakoni (Toucara). La Harpe wrote that his party met the Tawakoni in 1719 with several other tribes near the South Canadian River about one hundred miles north of Area VII.

85. Tchanhe. Joutel identified the Tchanhe as enemies of the Cadodaquis.

86. Tonkawa (Tancaouse). La Harpe wrote that he encountered the Tonkawa on his journey along the Red River in 1719. The author says that the Tonkawa and Apache were so hostile toward each other that

they ate each other, "not sparing even the women nor the children." Still, La Harpe adds, the Tonkawa are "renowned above the others."

87. Waco (Honecha). La Harpe wrote that the Waco were one of the several tribes that he met in 1719 on the lower Canadian River about one hundred miles north of Area VII.

88. Wichita (Quicasquiri). In 1719 La Harpe met with several tribes, including the Wichita, near the lower Canadian River about one hundred miles north of the Red River and Area VII.

89. Yatisi (Yatasi). La Harpe met the Yatisi with the Natchitoches on the Red River in Louisiana in 1719.

90. Yojuane (Joyvan). La Harpe's account of his 1719 trip to visit the Caddohadacho places the Yojuane with the Waco and the Tonkawa at a location about 200 miles west-northwest of the Caddohadacho village.

91. Yscani (Ascanis). La Harpe met with the Yscani and several other tribes near the South Canadian River about 100 mile north of Area VII in 1719.

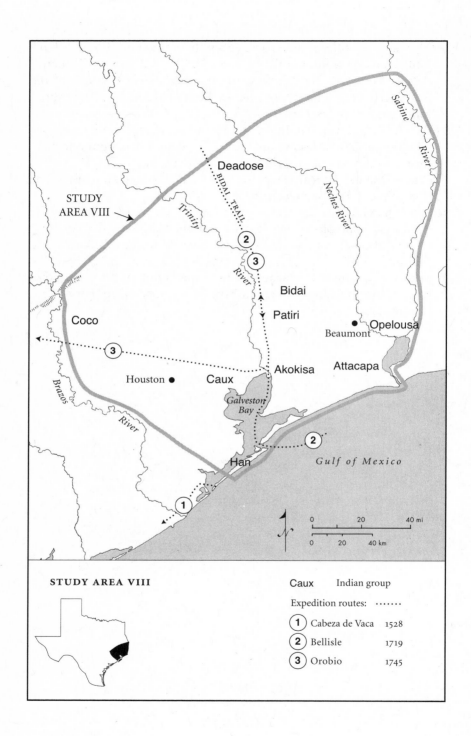

STUDY AREA VIII

Deadose

BIDAI TRAIL

②

③

Trinity

STUDY
AREA VIII →

Bidai

River

Patiri

Coco

③

Neches River

Opelousa ●

Beaumont

Sabine
River

Akokisa

Attacapa

Houston ●

Caux

Brazos

*Galveston
Bay*

River

②

Han

Gulf of Mexico

①

N

0   20   40 mi

0   20   40 km

STUDY AREA VIII

Caux   Indian group

Expedition routes: ········

① Cabeza de Vaca   1528

② Bellisle   1719

③ Orobio   1745

MAP 8.1

8 THE UPPER TEXAS COAST

STUDY AREA VIII

The Indian country of the upper Texas coast included in Study Area VIII extends from northeastern Galveston Island eastward along the Gulf Coast to Sabine Pass and follows the Sabine River upriver to a point near the present community of Burkeville (ca. 31° north latitude). The northern boundary runs westward from Burkeville following generally the 31° north latitude line and the southern boundary of Area VII to a point on the Brazos River valley a few miles below the junction of the Brazos and Navasota Rivers. The western boundary of the area follows the Brazos River valley downstream to a point near the city of Rosenberg and from there the boundary turns southeastward back to Galveston Island (see Map 8.1).

In his study of the Indian tribes of the lower Mississippi and adjacent Gulf Coast (including Area VIII), the ethnologist John R. Swanton prepared an area map that indicated Area VIII was occupied by Attakapa Indians.[1] Swanton identifies by name only two Attakapa tribes in Area VIII: the Arcoquisa (Orcoquiza), who resided north of Galveston Bay, and the principal Attakapa tribe who lived inland and eastward between Galveston Bay and Sabine Lake. The Attakapa also occupied the Gulf coastal area farther east into Louisiana to Vermilion Bay. The boundaries of Area VIII follow generally the homeland of the Attakapa in southeast Texas as identified by Swanton plus that of the more northern Bidai Indians. Study Area VIII includes all or parts of seventeen counties.[2]

What follows is a summary of the expeditions that crossed Area VIII. Cabeza de Vaca sailed along the coastal boundary of Area VIII in 1528 before landing on the southern tip of Galveston Island in Area I. Cabeza de Vaca writes that during his travels as an itinerant trader on the central Texas coast, he traveled along the coast and thus presumably visited

219

Area VIII. On his 1543 coastal voyage from the mouth of the Mississippi River along the Texas coast to Pánuco, Mexico, Moscoso landed on the coast of Area VIII and apparently traded with local residents.

In the latter part of December 1684, La Salle sailed along the coast of Area VIII; he never landed but saw bison and deer near the coast. La Salle did not cross Area VIII on his excursions in 1686 and 1687 from Fort St. Louis (in Area III) to the Hasinai Caddo (in Area VII). Spanish explorers in the 1690s followed La Salle's overland route from Matagorda Bay to the Caddo, thus skirting above the northwest corner of Area VIII.

Moscoso's 1543 visit was the last recorded European expedition or journey to Area VIII until the early eighteenth century. Reports from several important eighteenth-century French and Spanish expeditions into Area VIII provide the most significant firsthand ethnographic information on the local tribes. These expedition accounts include reports from Simars de Bellisle in 1719, Bénard de La Harpe in 1721, Captain Joachín de Orobio y Basterra in 1745, and Marqués de Rubí in 1767.

According to Cabeza de Vaca's account of his 1528 voyage from the coast of Florida westward, his boat with sails stopped for several days near the mouth of a very large river (thought to be the Mississippi) before being forced out to sea and sailing on westward along the Louisiana coast.[3] Cabeza de Vaca's boat was near the shore and in about twenty feet of water when the currents and wind off the Louisiana coast again forced his party farther out to sea. Although the Spaniards saw smoke from the mainland near the Texas-Louisiana state line, they did not report seeing any Native people. About a week later, having reached the coast of Area VIII in Texas, Cabeza de Vaca's float was tossed up on the beach at a location that is projected to be near San Luis Pass at the south end of Galveston Island (in Area I).

Cabeza de Vaca first encountered and later lived about a year with a local Indian band that he refers to as the Capoque on the southwest end of the island. The Spaniard says that all members of the band were of the same family linage. Cabeza de Vaca does not give the total population of the Capoques, but he writes that the group included over 100 warriors.[4]

Cabeza de Vaca notes that on the upper or eastern end of the island lived another Indian band called the Han, who had their own family linage and their own language. Although W. W. Newcomb considers the Han a Karankawan band,[5] this identification is considered incorrect. For purposes of the present study, the Han are considered as an Area VIII band associated with the Akokisa near Trinity Bay.

In commenting on the weather during the winter of 1528 on lower

Galveston Bay, Oviedo writes that the Spaniards experienced both snow and hail and that fish froze in the bay waters.[6]

Cabeza de Vaca writes that during the next five years he moved to the mainland to live with the Charruco (Chorruco). While staying with the Charruco, Cabeza de Vaca lived principally as an itinerant trader, and being highly mobile, he visited Native people living within an area that extended more than 130 miles along the central Texas coast and about the same distance into the interior. Herbert E. Bolton suggests that Cabeza de Vaca's marketing area probably included direct contacts with the Trinity Bay Indians and the inland Bidai in Area VIII.[7] However, the marketing range of ca. 130 miles inland would not include the homeland of the Caddo in Area VII.

About fifteen years after Cabeza de Vaca sailed westward along the coast of Area VIII, survivors of a second Spanish expedition passed along the Texas coast, also sailing westward in an attempt to reach the Spanish Gulf port of Pánuco on Mexico's northeast coast.[8] These men were a part of Hernando de Soto's 1539 expedition, which crossed the Southeast and the Mississippi River and in 1542 visited East Texas. The following year Luis de Moscoso, who had succeeded De Soto as the expedition leader, sailed with his men downriver to the mouth of the Mississippi. According to Moscoso's chroniclers, large and fearsome tribes battled the departing Spaniards from the banks of the river and from fleets of large canoes. In one encounter a Spaniard was fatally wounded by a dart or short spear (*bohordo*) thrown by the use of a weapon called a spear thrower, or atlatl.

The De Soto chronicler called the Inca, Garcilaso de la Vega, who recorded the incident, mentions that the spear or dart thrower called an atlatl was widely used by Indians in "El Peru" in South America. The Inca writes that the Indians in El Peru used it a great deal and that the Spaniards there feared the weapon more than any other the Indians had. The heads or points for the atlatl were fashioned of deer horn and could pass through a man armed in a coat of mail.[9]

The Inca concludes with an assertion that this was the only time the weapon had been seen by Spaniards on De Soto's expedition.[10] As noted in the Introduction, the spear thrower was a weapon devised apparently by Upper Paleolithic people in Europe and western Asia over 20,000 years ago and was probably brought to the Americas by the earliest settlers. Archeologists conclude that the atlatl was replaced by the bow and arrow across most of Texas during the period ca. AD 700 to 800.[11]

According to Moscoso's chroniclers, the Spanish party sailed through Sabine Pass and into Area VIII on July 29, 1543.[12] The seven boats had been scattered earlier along the upper Texas coast by a summer storm. Although the men ventured ashore, no Indians were reported. After the ships reassembled in the coastal waters, Moscoso and his men sailed farther westward along the coastline and apparently into Galveston Bay and Area VIII on the fifteenth day after leaving the mouth of the Mississippi River.[13]

The Inca writes that the bay area included four or five islets not far from the mainland. Innumerable waterfowl nested on the ground. While on the beach gathering shellfish, the Spaniards found washed ashore numerous large slabs of black bitumen or tar (called "copee" by the Inca). Recognizing that the bitumen could be used to repair leaks in the seven caravels, the men beached the watercraft and spent the next eight days working on them.

The Inca says that during the time spent repairing the ships on the beach, a peaceful group of eight local Indians visited the Spaniards' temporary camp to exchange a large quantity of "ears of Indian corn" for Spanish trade items.[14] The exchange of fresh ears of corn occurred on three subsequent occasions during the eight-day stay. If the projection that the bay area in which the Spaniards repaired the caravels was in fact Galveston Bay, the 1543 report is the earliest account that Natives in southwestern Area VIII cultivated or otherwise had access to maize.

The projection of the location of the bay is based in part on a note on the "De Soto Map" that locates the point where "copee" was used to repair the Spanish vessels. Charles Hudson, who studied the routes of De Soto and Moscoso, writes that the bay where the Spaniards repaired their ships was Galveston Bay.[15] After repairing the caravels, Moscoso and his men sailed out into the Gulf and continued westward along the coastal waters of Areas I, III, and IV.

By mid-September 1543, Moscoso's men had arrived at Río de Pánuco. The viceroy in Mexico City was pleased to receive the news of the arrival of De Soto's troops and sent special foods, including sugar, raisins, and pomegranates, thought by the Spaniards to be beneficial to the survivors who were sick.[16]

The news from the Moscoso expedition survivors that no gold was found in the Southeast and Texas discouraged the Spanish government from dispatching any major expeditions back to Texas for about 160 years. However, in the second half of the seventeenth century, French authorities authorized Robert Cavelier, Sieur de La Salle, to explore the Mississippi River from Canada. In 1682 La Salle completed his journey down the Mississippi to the Gulf of Mexico and claimed the big river and its western drainage areas for France.[17] To confirm the international claim, the king of France, Louis XIV, sent La Salle back to the New World in 1684 to establish a French fort and colony near the mouth of the Mississippi River. However, La Salle was unable to locate his assigned destination and sailed too far west.

According to the French chronicler Henri Joutel, La Salle's three ships first landed on the mainland of the North American continent on January 1, 1685, in Louisiana about fifty miles east of the Sabine River, which serves as the eastern boundary of Area VIII.[18] This visit by La Salle and several of his men on the coast of Louisiana lasted only a few hours because soon after they landed an unfavorable wind arose, forcing the Frenchmen to return to their vessels.

Between January 3 and January 10, the three French vessels coasted the shallow waters off Area VIII. No Indians or animals were observed. But on January 10, a reading indicated the ships were about 29° 23' north latitude, near the entrance to Galveston Bay. Convinced that he was to the east of the Mississippi River, and perhaps at Mobile Bay, La Salle directed that the ships continue westward beyond the coastal waters of Area VIII.

In early February La Salle's party had landed near the mouth of Matagorda Bay and then proceeded inland to establish a fort and colony on Garcitas Creek in Victoria County. During the remaining months of 1685, La Salle led several limited excursions into the area near the fort and west to the Rio Grande, but there was no exploration eastward into Area VIII. On La Salle's 1686 and 1687 expeditions to East Texas, La Salle crossed the Brazos River below its junction with the Navasota River, so the route did not take the Frenchmen into Area VIII.[19]

The four large Spanish expeditions that originated in Coahuila to visit the Hasinai in East Texas in the late seventeenth century also crossed the Brazos at the customary ford near the junction of the Brazos and Navasota Rivers, northwest of Area VIII. As all European expeditions and journeys into Texas in the sixteenth and seventeenth centuries missed Area VIII, except that short visit by Cabeza de Vaca, our review begins with European recorded explorations and visits of the area that commenced in 1719.

The first report of an extended European visit to Area VIII is found in the 1719–1721 account of the odyssey of the young French officer Simars de Bellisle.[20] In the fall of 1719 Bellisle's French ship grounded near the entrance to Galveston Bay. Bellisle and four other officers received permission from the captain to take the ship's small shallop ashore to secure fresh water and to explore. Bellisle's fifteen-month odyssey began the morning after Bellisle landed in Area VIII, when the five French officers realized that their ship had sailed away and they were stranded without provisions.

Bellisle tells that the five French officers decided first to follow the Gulf shoreline eastward toward Louisiana in search of their ship or other help. Four days later their coastal route was cut off by a very large and boggy river (perhaps the Sabine River), so they retraced their route back to Galveston Bay. During the return trip, they killed several deer and found a rowboat, but no Indians were reported.

The French officers searched Galveston Bay and the lower Trinity River area using the recently secured rowboat. After continuing upstream on an unidentified nearby creek for eight or nine days, the stranded officers found the headwaters of the creek near a small pond. The frustrated Frenchmen then returned downstream to Galveston Bay.

After searching fruitlessly for another month, the officers with Bellisle became exhausted and several began to expire. About two weeks after the last of his comrades died, Bellisle saw his first Indians. They were hunting along the beach and had accumulated over 500 eggs. This is thought to be the same area in which Moscoso's men found a rich nesting area for wildfowl, gathered eggs, and repaired their caravels in 1543. The local Indians at first greeted Bellisle with compassion and accepted him into their company, but Bellisle's situation deteriorated rapidly.

Bellisle remained with the same small band of Indians, numbering about twenty adults, for about a year. During much of this time, he was treated more like a slave than a guest. Nevertheless, the author gives very valuable firsthand information about Native life near Galveston Bay in Area VIII in the early 1720s.

Bellisle writes that the small band at first gave him only some boiled wild potatoes (roots) to eat. The Indian band, called Caux, had five or six large canoes, but they had no permanent residence and planted no crops. The women searched for wild potatoes and other plants; the men brought deer and sometimes bison meat back to camp. For a time Bellisle lived with an Indian matron who gave him protection from the beatings he received from other tribal members.

During the first winter Bellisle wrote a letter that he addressed to the "whites" whom the Caux said lived inland, apparently referring to the Spaniards or French living near or with the Hasinai in northeast Texas. The Caux agreed to pass Bellisle's letter along to other tribes farther inland, but Bellisle was unsure that his message requesting help would ever be delivered.

Bellisle tells of joining the Caux on a bison hunt that turned into a raid on an enemy's hunting camp. The Frenchman says that the Caux had good horses and used deerskins for saddles on the hunt, but they made him walk and at times run to keep up.

After traveling forty or fifty miles inland to the northwest, the hunters arrived at a very extensive and open prairie with numerous small herds of a hundred or more bison. By noon, the hunters had killed at least fifteen head by skillfully shooting arrows from their horses, running at full gallop.

The following day the Caux saw smoke at a distance from their hunting camp and decided the distant campfire revealed the presence of their enemy, the Tojal. In their attack the Caux hunters were able to capture and kill one of the enemy. Bellisle writes as follows: "When the man [the Tojal] was dead, they loaded him on their horses and brought him to the place where we had stayed to wait for them. When they returned, they threw this Indian on the prairie. One of them cut his head off and another one cut the arms off, while they skinned him at the same time. Several of them ate the yellow fat, which was still raw, and they devoured him completely."[21] When the hunting party returned to their families and displayed the bones of the Tojal, the Caux women danced in celebration.

This account is one of many documentary reports of cannibalism by the Indians of Texas and their neighbors during the study period. Cabeza de Vaca reported in nearby Area I that the Natives drank a liquid mixture that included the crushed bones of their cremated shaman. In Area III Eustache Bréman and Jean-Baptiste Talon observed firsthand Karankawa devouring bodies of their Caddo enemy captured in a raid into East Texas from the bay.

In Area VII Joutel writes that Hasinai women fed the flesh of their enemy to their slaves. In Area IV Juan Bautista Chapa writes that after a battle the Bobole Indians from Nuevo León ate one of their enemy, a young Cacaxtle boy.

On the lower Mississippi in 1682, the Wolf Indians, who were originally from New England, asked the explorer La Salle for permission to eat an enemy whom they had killed in battle. Earlier, La Salle's party had found a smoked child's hand, a man's foot, and human top ribs in an Indian fishing canoe. There is also substantial documentary and archeological evidence of cannibalism in the Southwest, northwest Mexico, and among other earlier groups as well.[22]

These reports of cannibalism conflict directly with some assertions made by contemporary anthropologists like Richard G. Klein, who states: "Cannibalism was very rare among historic Native people."[23] This observation is unsupported by the historic record. However, the historic record indicates that most, if not all, acts of cannibalism were performed in a ceremonial or ritual context.

After the Caux hunting party returned home, Bellisle's letter reached the Hasinai, who were friends of the French authorities in Louisiana. As requested by the French, a small rescue party composed of only two mounted Hasinai scouts was dispatched to bring Bellisle to the principal Hasinai village in present-day Houston County. During the rescue of the Frenchman, a fight almost broke out between the Caux and the two Caddo scouts. The Hasinai, who apparently were well known and respected by the Caux, won the day and took Bellisle with them on the return trip to northeast Texas.

Bellisle says that after traveling northward for about four days (perhaps forty to sixty miles on horseback) along the path through the thick swampy woodlands of East Texas, the party visited the Bidai Indians and then proceeded up the Bidai Trail for another two weeks before arriving at the Hasinai villages in the fall of 1720. The report of the distance between the Bidai and the coast places the Bidai in the northern part of Area VIII. Bellisle was sustained principally by the Hasinai woman called Angelica for several months before leaving for the French fort at Natchitoches in February 1721.[24]

French interest in exploring and occupying the central and upper Texas coast did not wane with the return of Bellisle in early 1721. In August of the same year, Jean Baptiste Le Moyne, Sieur de Bienville, commandant of Louisiana for the French king, ordered Bénard de La Harpe, Bellisle, and Captain Jean Béranger with twenty soldiers to build a fort at "St. Bernard's Bay," apparently referring to present Matagorda Bay.[25] Bienville added in his written directive to La Harpe that the French claim to St. Bernard's Bay was based on La Salle's possession of the bay in 1685. Apparently the French were still confused over the locations of Matagorda and Galveston Bays.

The French ship sailed into Galveston Bay rather than Matagorda Bay that fall, but the local Caux, who were immediately encountered, were very displeased to see Bellisle again. After extended discussions, the Caux refused to allow the French to occupy the Galveston Bay area. The effort by Bienville to build a fort at Galveston Bay was apparently abandoned in late 1721.[26]

However, French interest in securing trade with the Indians living near Galveston Bay in Area VIII continued. Rumors of the French interest in establishing trade and possibly a coastal trading post near Galveston Bay were the basis of the first Spanish overland survey trip to the Galveston Bay area. The reconnaissance was conducted in 1745 by Joachín de Orobio y Basterra, the captain of the Spanish presidio of La Bahía, then located on the left bank of the Guadalupe River near the present-day community of Mission Valley in western Victoria County.

Captain Orobio writes that the viceroy requested information regarding the Indian tribes residing along the coast near Galveston and Trinity

Bays and tribes living farther inland. Orobio commenced his journey in late December 1745.[27] Following the nearby customary route to Los Adaes that he calls the Camino Real, the captain reached the Caddoan village called San Pedro de Nabedachos near the Neches River in East Texas on January 12, 1746.

Orobio consulted with the local Caddoan leader, called Tama, who gave the captain very valuable information about the Indian population in Areas VII and VIII, including the Native population living immediately to the south toward the coast. Tama said that the Hasinai often raided Apache and other enemy camps to the west to secure horses that were later traded to the French in Louisiana for rifles, powder, bullets, and cloth. Tama added that a neighboring Caddo tribe, the Caudacho, facilitated the French trade. Although Tama had never been to the coast (located about 150 miles to the south), he said that he had heard that French traders were there and that Frenchmen had built houses and married Indian women. But, Tama said, Orobio would have to go to Nacogdoches to take the old Bidai Trail south to travel to the coast.

Following Tama's advice, Orobio marched to the Spanish mission at Nacogdoches and then farther eastward to Los Adaes in Louisiana, which was then the capital of the province of Texas, to meet with the Spanish governor of the province, Francisco García Larios. Governor García Larios advised Orobio to return to Nacogdoches and proceed southward on the Bidai Trail to the coast using local Indian guides. He also asked to be kept advised as to what Orobio discovered.

On February 7 Orobio departed Nacogdoches with Indian guides along the Bidai Trail south to visit the Galveston Bay area, but it took the mounted party about a month to reach the principal villages of the Bidai. This march represents the first visit by Spanish authorities to the northern part of Area VIII. The travel time between the villages of the Hasinai and the Bidai taken by Orobio is about the same as the time taken on a similar trip by the mounted Caddoan two-man party that rescued Bellisle about twenty years earlier.

Captain Orobio named the seven-village area of the Bidai Santa Rosa de Viterbo. Orobio met with a friendly local chieftain who admitted that the captain was the first Spaniard who had visited the area, although the French frequently came to trade. The Bidai leader explained that French traders arrived with goods each year, some coming by canoe along the coast from the east and others arriving by foot overland.

The Bidai leader identified by name for Orobio the several Indian bands or tribes that resided in Area VIII and indicated the respective territorial range of each group. First, the leader said, the Pachina lived on the Sabine River and eastward into Louisiana. He added that a large Pachina village was located about fifteen miles west of the French fort on the Red River. The leader said that several Frenchmen lived with the Pachina at the village and traded regularly with the Bidai.

The Bidai leader explained that the Orcoquiza (Akokisa) Indians lived along the lower Neches River and westward to a point between the Trinity and Brazos Rivers. As the chieftain said that the western boundary of the Orcoquiza was a river that ran into the Gulf, the Orcoquiza may have extended westward to Oyster Creek, which is east of the Brazos and empties directly into Gulf waters. The chieftain explained that farther west, inland from the coast, the Coco, Cujane, and Karankawa lived.

After leaving the Bidai villages, Orobio traveled about seventy miles west-southwest to visit two of the Orcoquiza villages identified by the Bidai chieftain. Although no Frenchmen were living at or near the Orcoquiza villages at the time of Orobio's visit, the local Indians said that Frenchmen planned to build houses the next summer on a river about thirty-five miles southwest of the Orcoquiza villages.

Once Orobio had determined that there were no Frenchmen or French settlements near Galveston Bay at that time, the captain returned to his post at La Bahía and gave his report to the viceroy and the governor. French trade apparently continued after Orobio's inspection, eventually requiring Spanish authorities to establish a presidio and mission near Trinity Bay in 1756.

The Spanish fort and mission on Trinity Bay was unsuccessful, and their tumultuous history was concluded at the recommendation of the Marqués de Rubí.[28] As indicated in the Introduction, most accounts of European expeditions conducted in the late eighteenth century provide limited information on the lifeways of the Native population in Texas. However, Rubí's 1767 expedition through Area VIII represents the only major Spanish expedition that crossed the area.

On September 28, 1767, Rubí completed his formal inspection of the Los Adaes presidio and his visit to the Los Adaes mission where, Rubí notes, "there is not one single Indian in the mission." Rubí's next destination was to the "Presidio Orcoquizá" near Trinity bay in Area VIII. Rubí's party returned to Nacogdoches and headed southward along the Bidai Trail. About twenty-five miles south of Nacogdoches, the French party found a large but deserted Bidai village. Rubí continued southward through dense forest of tall pine and marshes. It appears that the party passed the small farm called El Atascoso about four to six leagues north of the presidio and about three leagues east of the Trinity River.[29] In the same general area Rubí's engineer, Nicolás de Lafora, reported a number of flat-topped mounds that were twelve to eighteen feet in diameter and three to six feet above the water table. These dry mounds served Rubí's caravan as resting places, which made the crossing of the swamp possible.[30]

Rubí inspected the Presidio Orcoquizá and found the conditions similar to those observed at Los Adaes. There was a small cavalry company of thirty-one men, and there were no Orcoquiza converts at the mission. Although deer and bear were available, the local Indians did not hunt the game. However, they harpooned fish in the bay waters and captured alligators.

After inspecting the presidio, Rubí proceeded on October 16 to march to the lower Brazos River (the western boundary of Area VIII) and into Area I. Near the Brazos Lafora comments that the Aranama Indians were a threat to the expedition party and attempted to steal horses.

Conclusions

Study Area VIII is a special corner of Texas that was comparatively isolated from sixteenth- and seventeenth-century routes of European exploration and from any documented early French or Spanish colonization. In 1543 Moscoso's fleet of seven boats probably visited the Galveston Bay area and met local Natives in Area VIII on several occasions during their visit of a week or so, but French and Spanish explorers skirted the northwest boundary of Area VIII below the modern city of Navasota in the late seventeenth century.

Several eighteenth-century French and Spanish accounts provide some of the earliest documentary evidence of the Native populations of Area VIII. The archival record and documentary sources reviewed suggest that at least maize and other crops were cultivated in parts of Area VIII during the early historic period, and perhaps in late Prehistoric times. It also appears that the Bidai and associated tribes in the northern part of Area VIII were sedentary or semisedentary.

The earliest documentary record of Indians in the Galveston Bay area having maize is from Moscoso's 1543 journey account along the Texas coast. Moscoso's chroniclers write that fresh ears of corn were traded to the Spaniards while they repaired their small fleet and took shelter from a Gulf storm. About 180 years later, the French officer Bellisle was held captive by the Caux Indians in the Galveston Bay area and later wrote that the local Natives planted no crops. But about twenty-five years later, Spanish reports from Orobio and others indicate that maize was grown near Galveston and Trinity Bays and farther inland and that maize grown in Area VIII was traded for French weapons.

With respect to long-distance interaction, we know that the Bidai Road connected Area VII residents to the Caddo people. By 1720 the Indians near the coast in Area VIII had Spanish horses, and by 1750 the Akokisa were trading horses for French weapons from Louisiana. With regard to the range of bison during the 1720s, it appears from the historic record that bison herds of several hundred head were found within forty to sixty miles northeast of the Galveston Bay area and a few miles east of the Brazos in northwest Area VIII.

SUPPLEMENT: STUDY AREA VIII
THE UPPER TEXAS COAST

This supplement lists alphabetically the names of Indian tribes and bands reported in diary accounts and associated documents referenced in the Area VIII study. Where appropriate, entries include the name of the diarist who recorded the encounter and the date of the event.

The following documentary sources were among those consulted in preparing the supplement: Alex D. Krieger, *We Came Naked and Barefoot: The Journey of Cabeza de Vaca across North America;* John R. Swanton, *Indian Tribes of the Lower Mississippi Valley* (Washington, D.C.: U.S. Government Printing Office, 1911); William C. Foster, *Spanish Expeditions into Texas, 1689–1768;* Thomas N. Campbell, "Caux Indians," in Tyler et al., *The New Handbook of Texas;* and Henri Folmer, "De Bellisle on the Texas Coast," *Southwestern Historical Quarterly* 44, no. 2 (Oct. 1940): 204–231.

1. Akokisa (Orcoquiza). The Spanish captain Joachín de Orobio reported finding four Orcoquiza villages near Trinity Bay in 1745. Each village had its own chieftain. Thomas N. Campbell writes that the tribe spoke Atakapan and were likely closely associated with the Coaque (Cabeza de Vaca) and the Caux (Simars de Bellisle).
2. Attacapa (Atakapa, Attakapa). The Attacapa homeland includes parts of southeast Texas and extends farther east into Louisiana, according to the ethnologist John R. Swanton. Some Attacapa were mound builders who lived in fixed or semipermanent locations with seasonal winter movements farther inland. Rubí's diarist, Nicolás de Lafora, wrote that in 1767 the Atakapa were residents of the Province of Texas.
3. Bidai (Biday, Vidai). T. N. Campbell writes that the Bidai cultivated crops, including maize, only in small gardens rather than on large farms. The Bidai maintained a trail that ran north-south between the

Nacogdoches area and Trinity Bay. Orobio visited seven villages of the Bidai that were located the distance of about four travel days north of Trinity Bay. The Spanish governor Marqués de San Miguel de Aguayo found the tribe between the Navasota and Trinity Rivers in 1721.

4. Caux. Simars de Bellisle wrote that the Caux were the tribe or small band with which he lived for about a year near Galveston Bay. T. N. Campbell writes that the band has been identified as the Coco, but they may have been the Akokisa.

5. Coco. The Coco lived between the lower Brazos and lower Colorado Rivers, according to Orobio in 1745. Based on several Spanish expedition reports of encountering the Coco a hundred miles or more inland from the coast and associated with tribes that were not Karankawan, it appears that the Coco are not one of the traditional Karankawa bands.

6. Cujane (Cujano). According to Orobio and an Akokisa chieftain, the Cujane were associated with the coastal Karankawa west of the Colorado River. T. N. Campbell writes that the tribe occupied the coastal areas between the Colorado and Guadalupe Rivers.

7. Deadose (Ygodsa). The Spanish expedition diarist with Aguayo and later the priest Fray Gaspar José de Solís reported meeting the Deadose together with the Bidai between the Navasota and Trinity Rivers in the eighteenth century. T. N. Campbell writes that the tribe was closely related to the Bidai and spoke an Atakapan language.

8. Han. Cabeza de Vaca wrote that the Han lived on the eastern end of the island on which he landed.

9. Hasinai (Tejas). The coastal Indians in Area VIII knew and had great respect for and perhaps fear of the Hasinai. Only two Hasinai warriors were dispatched to rescue the Frenchman Bellisle from the Caux band in Area VIII.

10. Karankawa. An Akokisa chieftain told Orobio that he had advised a French search party not to pursue their search for a lost Frenchman farther west down the Texas coast toward Matagorda Bay because it was likely that the Karankawa would capture and eat them.

11. Opelousa. Swanton writes that the Opelousa lived along and to the east of the lower Sabine River, which forms the state line between Texas and Louisiana.

12. Pachina. Orobio wrote that the Pachina lived along the Sabine River and eastward into Louisiana.

13. Patiri. T. N. Campbell erroneously places the Patiri Indians in southeast Texas between the Bidai and the Akokisa. The copy of Henri

Joutel's journal published by Pierre Margry and cited by Campbell mistakenly includes the tribal name in a list of tribes living east of the Colorado.

14. Tojal (Toyal). Bellisle wrote that the Tojal were enemies of the Caux. The Caux hunting party killed and devoured a Tojal while Bellisle was with them on a bison hunt.

9 ♠ CONCLUSIONS

Information from over forty chroniclers who accompanied twenty-seven major Spanish and French expeditions into Texas indicates that during the study period (ca. AD 1528–1722) and undoubtedly for millennia earlier, the Native peoples of Texas displayed a broad range of cultures and followed a wide diversity of lifestyles. The diversity was reflected in Native subsistence and settlement patterns and in their networks of long-distance interaction. Some Texas Natives were primarily agriculturists who constructed permanent dwellings in established villages or farmsteads located near the floodplains of major rivers. These people followed a sedentary horticultural lifestyle that greatly intensified and spread widely throughout the American Southwest and Southeast during the Medieval Warm period (ca. AD 900–1350).

Other relatively small dispersed Native groups, living primarily in the southeastern part of the state, were semisedentary folk who, according to the historic record, cultivated small gardens but lived primarily by fishing, hunting small woodland game, and gathering local plants and plant products. These semisedentary people were apparently in an intermediate phase from the hunter-gatherer lifestyle to the more complex lifeways of sedentary farmers.

Throughout most of Central, South, and West Texas, small mobile hunter-gatherer groups that cultivated no crops lived in family bands of 100 to 200. These seminomadic people followed a subsistence tradition that was similar to that pursued by modern *Homo sapiens* throughout the Old World 30,000 or more years ago and was the same or similar subsistence and settlement pattern as that followed throughout the Americas at the time of first settlement. For subsistence, these small clanlike groups moved periodically, perhaps weekly or monthly, to favorite former campsite locations or stations, as required by the season and the local environment, to hunt, fish, and forage for berries, nuts, roots, and other carefully selected plant resources.

Bison hunters who moved across the Southern Plains and prairies of Texas followed a more nomadic lifestyle, continuously following large bison herds. For food, shelter, and clothing, these big game hunters depended primarily on the numerous, drifting, large bison herds that numbered up to 4,000 or 5,000 head in each herd. The Plains Indians in Texas were not only bison hunters but also major traders who exchanged their dried bison meat, hides, and tallow to sedentary horticultural Indians for maize, beans, and cotton goods and who traded with local hunter-gatherer groups for their trade goods and perhaps for permission to share the hunting grounds of the local Indians. During the latter part of the study period, the Plains Apache moved into hunting grounds farther south and into parts of Central and South Texas, which frequently occasioned direct conflict and warfare with resident Native tribes.

Long-distance seasonal hunting parties whose homeland was several hundred miles south of the Rio Grande in southern Coahuila and Chihuahua, Mexico, competed with both the nomadic bison hunters on the Southern Plains and local hunter-gatherers, particularly in south-central Texas. The historic record confirms that during the Little Ice Age (ca. AD 1350–1850) there was an expansion of the rich grazing grasslands in Texas that supported large bison herds and attracted distant hunting parties. This constant interaction among different Native groups, facilitated by the use of a common sign language, contributed to the rich cultural heritage of the Native peoples of Texas during the study period.

Diversity of Texas Indian Cultures

To be more specific, by ca. 1350, and certainly well before the beginning of the study period, highly concentrated and heavily populated permanent agricultural villages were well established in at least three areas of the state—in northeast Texas, at La Junta de los Ríos in the Trans-Pecos, and along the Canadian River in the Texas Panhandle. Although located in three distant corners of the state (separated by over 500 miles from each other), the three horticultural areas emerged or greatly expanded almost simultaneously at the beginning of the warmer climatic episode called the Medieval Warm period.[1]

During the early years of the Medieval Warm period, numerous large permanent Native horticultural villages appeared or greatly expanded in the Temperate Zone across North America from Arizona to Florida. Dominate regional cultural centers like Cahokia on the middle Mississippi, Moundville in Alabama, Etowah in Georgia, Apalache in Florida, the Caddo homeland in East Texas, Spiro in Oklahoma, Chaco Canyon in New Mexico, Casas Grandes in northwest Chihuahua, and dozens of smaller horticultural communities arose almost in unison, and all flourished across the American Southwest and Southeast between ca. AD 1000 and 1450.

These larger cultural communities increased in population, constructed monumental earthworks in the Southeast and monumental stoneworks and large adobe buildings in the Southwest, developed highly social-tiered cultural centers, extended patterns of long-distance interaction, and created imaginative new forms of artistic expression. These enumerated mature cultural traits are the traditional hallmarks of a classic period. The span of about five centuries, from ca. AD 950 to 1450, is considered the Classic period of North American Native culture.

THE CADDO

In northeast Texas (Study Area VII), Caddo Indians lived in permanent villages and farmsteads, constructed mounds, and successfully cultivated domesticated maize, beans, squash, sunflowers, and tobacco. These crops were the same or similar to those that Mississippian farmers at Cahokia and elsewhere in the Southeast had been growing since ca. AD 1100. Beginning much earlier, part-time gardeners in the Eastern Woodlands had first collected and later cultivated a wide range of local domesticates, including sunflower, knotweed, marsh elder, chenopodium, small herbs, and seeds of grass. We are reminded that by ca. 3500 BC, semisedentary mound builders in northern Louisiana were gathering and collecting chenopodium, knotweed, and possibly marsh elder.

Evidence that the Caddo people shared numerous traditions with the Mississippian folk is found in their close cultural parallels. Both the people of Cahokia and the Caddo were mound builders; both worshipped the sun as a central deity and kept a sacred fire burning perpetually. Both were organized as highly ranked societies that followed similar traditions of cranial modeling and human retainer sacrifice at burial ceremonies for prominent members. Both constructed complex facilities for astronomical readings and for use in marking seasonal rotations. Archeological studies indicate that Caddoans living in East Texas, northwest Louisiana, eastern Oklahoma, and western Arkansas traded extensively with Mississippian people.

According to French and Spanish expedition diarists, the Hasinai Caddo as well as the Acansa and Taensa on the Mississippi had acquired

Old World domesticated peach, plum, apple, pear, and pomegranate trees and watermelons from Spanish sources. These European domesticated fruit trees and melons probably originated in sixteenth-century Spanish mission orchards and government outposts in north-central Mexico and are thought to have been carried by Jumano and other La Junta long-distance traders across South and Central Texas along Native trade networks that extended to the Hasinai and on to tribes on the west side of the lower Mississippi. As indicated earlier, the ethnohistorian John R. Swanton concludes that the Old World fruit trees and melons reported in Native orchards on the Mississippi originated from Mexico and had been transported across Texas.

Although Old World fruit trees and melons were brought from Europe to early English settlements on the Atlantic coast and to Spanish colonies on the eastern Gulf of Mexico, there were in the 1660s and 1670s no frequently used and established trade networks across the Southeast that reached tribes living west of the Mississippi. Henri Joutel clearly details the frequently used trade network connecting tribes on the west bank of the Mississippi to South Texas and on farther to the southwest. There was, in fact, bitter conflict and warfare between tribes living east of the Mississippi and those living to the west, such as the Acansa and their allies the Taensa, where the European fruit trees and melons were first reported by the French in the 1670s and the 1680s. During this period no European fruit trees or melons were reported growing in the Indian villages on the east side of the Mississippi.

Although they were sedentary horticulturists, the Caddo did not give up their hunting ways. Hasinai leaders dispatched long-distance big game hunting parties as far west as the deer and bison hunting grounds east of the lower Colorado River and to the middle Brazos, which the Hasinai shared with numerous closely allied local tribes.

The present study cites documentary evidence of Hasinai tribal members interacting with the Palaquechare and Teao between the lower Brazos and Colorado Rivers; with the Toho, Sana, Cantona, and Emet between the Colorado and San Antonio Rivers; the Karankawa in Area III; the Simaoma from South Texas and northern Mexico; the Jumano and Cibolo in the Trans-Pecos; the Caux and Bidai on the upper Texas coast; the Acansa on the Mississippi River; and the Pueblo Indians in New Mexico.

LA JUNTA DE LOS RÍOS

In the Trans-Pecos during the study period, many Native groups near La Junta de los Ríos and upriver (and perhaps downriver) on the Rio

Grande lived in permanent pueblos and cultivated many of the same basic tropical crops raised by the Caddoan and Mississippian farmers—maize, beans, and squash or gourds. These Trans-Pecos sedentary farmers were culturally and economically affiliated most directly with the Pueblo people living in the Casas Grandes river valley, about 170 miles to the west. They were aware of, but not allies of, the Pueblo people in central New Mexico. In contrast to the Pueblo agriculturist, Texas horticulturists cultivated no cotton.

According to Cabeza de Vaca, the La Junta seed stock of maize and beans originated from the area to the west, presumably the Casas Grandes river valley, not from the upper Rio Grande to the north. Espejo and other Spanish diarists write that traditional Casas Grandes trade goods, including scarlet macaw headdresses, blue and white cotton goods, small cast copper bells (crotals), copper pendants, turquoise beads, and Pacific coast red coral and shell beads were found among the Indians living on the Rio Grande between La Junta and modern-day El Paso. Detailed reports from late sixteenth-century Spanish chroniclers indicate that communal farming was practiced at several locations along the floodplain of the Rio Grande from La Junta upriver to the swampy area about ten to fifteen miles below El Paso, but farming communities were not found at any location along the desolate 170-mile stretch of the Rio Grande immediately north of El Paso in New Mexico.

Researchers generally agree that tropical maize and possibly domesticated amaranth were cultivated in the American Southwest by ca. 1200 BC. These recent projections predate reports of farming tropical cultigens by Caddoan and Mississippian horticulturists and in the American Southeast. There is, however, disagreement among zooarcheologists as to whether the large and small species of Native domestic turkeys that were bred and raised at Casas Grandes and other pueblos in the American Southwest originated in the Southwest, Huasteca, or central Mexico. It appears that during the study period no macaw parrots or domestic turkeys were bred and raised in the Trans-Pecos or any other part of Texas or in the Southeast.

The La Junta people (like the Caddo) had a mixed economy in which long-distance hunters stationed at or near La Junta seasonally supplied bison meat, hides, and tallow to residents of the La Junta farming community. The Jumano were only one of many large hunting and trading tribes that were living or temporarily stationed near La Junta during the study period. As mentioned, Jumano acquired and later traded Spanish ponies to several hunter-gatherer tribes in Study Areas I and II as well as to the Hasinai in East Texas.

The third group of Native horticulturists in Texas in ca. 1200–1500 lived in permanent slab-stone villages located along the Canadian River in the Texas Panhandle. Archeologists refer to these Texas farmers as the Antelope Creek people and report that their culture emerged rather suddenly in ca. AD 1200 or about the same time (during the Medieval Warm period) that the other agricultural centers greatly intensified or emerged in Texas, the American Southwest, and the Southeast.

The Antelope Creek people constructed stone-slab, flat-top structures using stone masonry in both the foundation and walls. Many of the rooms were contiguous in an architectural style similar to that found in Pueblo villages in northern New Mexico. Like the Caddo and La Junta farmers in the fifteenth century, the Antelope Creek people raised maize, squash, beans, and sunflowers and gathered wild plum, persimmon, and mesquite beans.

Evidence of trade with the Southwest is found at Antelope Creek sites in the form of turquoise, shell beads, and Southwestern-style pottery. On the other hand, there is scant evidence of trade with the East Texas Caddo. Although Antelope Creek people maintained close trade relationships with Pueblo people living in northern New Mexico, Robert Mallouf writes that there is no evidence to suggest that Antelope Creek farmers were transplanted immigrants from the Southwest.

Panhandle farmers also had a close affiliation with the Plains Caddoan-speaking horticulturists in western Oklahoma and Kansas. Archeologists suggest that when the Antelope Creek people abandoned their horticultural lifestyle in the early sixteenth century, the farming folk may have dispersed to the north or may have reverted to a nomadic lifestyle as bison hunters.

The latter suggestion is consistent with significant climatic changes that occurred at the end of the Medieval Warm period and at the beginning of the more mesic-hydric Little Ice Age in ca. 1350. The emerging Little Ice Age greatly expanded the rich grasslands on the prairies that attracted larger herds of bison south to the Southern Plains in Texas. By 1500, the changing climatic conditions had encouraged the Plains Athapascan people to follow the bison into the expanded Southern Plains.

The Southwestern archeologist Steven A. LeBlanc suggests that the Medieval Warm period sparked the agricultural revolution among the people of the Southwest and that later the Little Ice Age ended the favorable climatic conditions and brought conflict, war, and abandonment to the area. In describing agricultural developments in the Southwest, Le Blanc writes that there was "a greatly improved carrying capacity as a result of the Medieval Warm Period. There was not only an increase in population but also decline in warfare—and the most extravagantly large architectural construction ever created in the Southwest were built . . . The optimal time period ceased when the climatic changes leading up to the Little Ice Age began."[2]

LeBlanc also argues (and I think correctly so) that the cooler Little Ice Age had a negative impact on Native horticulturists not only in New Mexico but across all North America.[3] The documentary record is replete with weather and other environmental reports that confirm that the climate during the study period was significantly colder and more hydric than the climatic conditions recorded during the Medieval Warm period or the past century. It also seems clear that the Little Ice Age, which is so fully documented in Europe and more recently by geologists and climatologists in the United States, had a defining impact on the lifeways of the Native population in Texas and in the Southwest during the study period.

In addition to reports of intensive horticultural production in parts of the Trans-Pecos, along the Canadian River in the Panhandle, and in most of northeast Texas, there is substantial documentary evidence (but little archeological evidence) that part-time gardeners cultivated crops in the area to the south of the Hasinai Caddo during the study period. It appears from French sources that not only the Bidai but perhaps the Deadose and Orcoquiza (Akokisa) Indians occasionally cultivated maize and other crops. Both Henri Joutel and Anastase Douay write that tribal groups living between the crossings on the lower Colorado and Brazos Rivers planted maize and beans when the tribes could protect the crops from their enemies and could remain in the same location for a sufficient period to harvest the cultigen. But the majority of Texas Native residents outside the northeast lived principally as hunter-gatherers during the study period, just as their ancestors did who first arrived in North America.

Cabeza de Vaca, Luis de Moscoso's scouts, the French Talon brothers, and Damián Massanet all confirm that the Native peoples living in Central and South Texas cultivated no crops but had the bow and arrow and used pottery. In this large region small independent foraging bands and tribes, speaking many different languages and dialects but with no written language, moved periodically from one campsite to another within a customary territorial range of perhaps thirty to fifty miles. Natives whose homeland was in one study area were only occasionally reported by diarists in another area, usually when they were encountered on a mission to hunt, trade, or raid.

According to several French and Spanish accounts, the hunter-gatherer bands often numbered several hundred and were frequently reported in encampments shared by two or more tribes or bands. For example, when Jean Géry was captured in 1688 about fifty miles north of the Rio Grande in South Texas, the Frenchman was at an encampment that included the Hape (Ape), Jumano, Mescal, and Xiabu (Ijiaba). When Alonso de León's 1689 entrada reached the Guadalupe River crossing in DeWitt County near present-day Cuero, De León visited a joint encampment of Emet and Cava Indians, and the following day about twenty miles to the north near modern Yoakum, he found a camp that included about 250 Toho and Tohaha. This pattern of encountering several rather small local tribes or bands sharing a common campground prevails throughout the historic period, particularly in Areas II and IV. But we should note that by the close of the study period, these smaller bands may have been gathered in shared encampments as a means of defense against the Spanish encroachment from the south or the fast-approaching mounted Apache Indians from the northwest.

These bands of hunter-gatherers often had a religious leader or shaman, as described by Cabeza de Vaca, but the small family groups were basically egalitarian. Cabeza de Vaca adds that they either cremated or buried their dead and used red ocher to decorate their bodies and hair. As noted in the Introduction, modern *H. sapiens* and perhaps Neanderthal buried their dead covered with red ocher over 40,000 years earlier in Europe and western Asia.

Hunter-gatherers frequently constructed huts using long flexible poles as a frame secured into the ground at the base and bent and tied together at the top with strips of bison or deer hide. The roof and sides were often covered with bison, deer, or bear hides. Perhaps copying the Plains Indians (who annually visited the lower Colorado River area), some local tribes (the Emet and Cava) used domesticated dogs as pack animals to carry on their backs the hut coverings and other loads.

During most of the study period, the mesic climatic conditions encouraged large bison herds and Plains Indians to visit South and Central Texas. According to linguists and expedition diarists, these highly mobile bison hunters from the Plains communicated by the use of signs with the numerous Texas tribes that spoke a multitude of languages and dialects.

Writing for the Smithsonian Institution in 1996, the linguist and language historian Allan R. Taylor says: "Trade may have been an important stimulus in the development of the sign language, and it was certainly an important factor in its diffusion after the rise of Plains horse nomadism. There is some reason to believe that the sign language originated in the extreme southern fringe of the Plains or on the Texas Gulf Coast."[4] It is significant that the authority who gives attribution for the origin of Indian sign language to Texas Gulf coastal tribes is Ives Goddard, the editor of the 1996 volume entitled "Languages" in the Smithsonian Institution series *The Handbook of North American Indians*.

The extensive use of signs by Texas Native peoples is confirmed most eloquently by Cabeza de Vaca. In explaining the diversity of languages and thus the importance of using signs in communicating with Texas Indians in the 1530s, the Spanish explorer wrote that tribes living on the bend of the central Texas coast spoke a multitude of different languages. After visiting the numerous tribes along the Rio Grande in Texas and the maize people in northwestern Chihuahua, Cabeza de Vaca records the significance of sign language in Texas and the Southwest as follows: "We passed through a great number and diversity of languages. With all of them God our Lord favored us, because they always understood us and we understood them. And thus we asked and they responded by signs as if they spoke our language and we theirs, because although we knew six languages, we could not make use of them in all areas because we found more than a thousand differences."[5]

Writing about the importance of sign language to Texas Indians, the priest Gaspar José de Solís says the following: "All the nations have one thing in common, that is the sign language with which they talk, not only for hours but entire days. The Religious who are newly come to these lands, immediately take up the signs in order to understand, and make themselves understood by all the Indians of the many and diverse nations."[6]

The Native peoples of Texas (like the Celtic people who were sophisticated enough to conquer Rome) had no written language, but this does not imply that their culture was not sophisticated and complex or that they were not cosmopolitan. As mentioned, however, Texas Indians on the Gulf Coast apparently originated and spread an ingenious means of communicating with intricate and uniform hand signs. The form of signs found in the current official American Sign Language and the sign forms recorded in the history of Indian sign language reveal many common or parallel sign forms. Figure 2.1 identifies twelve of the numerous signs that are the same or similar in both the earlier Indian sign language and contemporary American Sign Language.[7]

As mentioned, Plains bison hunters followed and depended primarily on bison herds. But they traded bison meat, hides, and tallow for maize, beans, and other food products, and they followed the bison herds using dog trains across the open prairies, perhaps as their ancestors had used dog trains across the open Arctic expanse. The precise relationship between the pre-Columbian bison hunters in Texas, the Apache, and the Athapascan Indians from Alaska is unclear. However, we do know that their linguistic roots run north across the Great Plains into Alaska. During the study period these long-distance bison hunters represented a special brand of Texas Indian and left their own distinct and colorful pattern on the tapestry of Texas Native cultures.

To add to the complex mix of in-state Texas Native cultures, we should note that a large number of out-of-state tribes from north-central Mexico were also attracted to the large bison herds roaming across the Central and South Texas prairies during the study period. From the country of the Tepehuan around Durango, Mexico (located about 500 miles north of Mexico City and about the same distance southwest of the Pecos River in West Texas), hunting parties traveled to the bison plains near the lower Pecos River. Specifically, Castaño de Sosa encountered a band of friendly Tepehuan bison hunters on the lower Pecos in 1590. Indicating their knowledge of the geography of the country to the south toward Mexico, the Tepehuan offered to lead Castaño and his party to permanent, heavily populated Indian settlements where the Tepehuan said there was an abundance of corn. Most likely the reference by the Tepehuan was to the horticultural pueblos near La Junta, which were en route between the lower Pecos and the Tepehuan homeland. It should be added that Alonso de León and Juan Bautista Chapa reported that Tepehuan were encountered frequently along the lower Rio Grande in Nuevo León during this same period.

During Juan Domínguez de Mendoza's expedition to Central Texas and the Hill Country in 1684, the chronicler writes that the Salinero Indians attacked the Spaniards' camp west of the Colorado River. The diarist identifies the Salineros as an unusually aggressive tribe from Nueva Vizcaya, Mexico. The Salineros were a well-known tribe whose homeland was in southern Coahuila and Chihuahua (Nueva Vizcaya) about 400 miles south of the Mendoza camp in the Edwards Plateau of Central Texas. In other words, Indians with Mendoza who were from El Paso (located about 400 miles to the west of the Spanish encampment) were scheduled to meet Hasinai Indians from East Texas (about 400 miles to the east) but instead were attacked by Salinero Indians from southern Chihuahua (about 400 miles to the south) and their allies, the Apache from the Plains.

In the seventeenth century dozens of other tribes from northern Mexico were recorded hunting and trading in South and Central Texas. On Governor Terán's 1691 expedition to Texas, chroniclers recorded a large gathering of five tribes (perhaps numbering 3,000) from northern Mexico and West Texas encamped near present-day San Marcos. The tribes included the Jumano, Cibolo, Catqueza, Chalome, and Chaymaya. These and other tribes from West Texas and northern Mexico traveled annually to the lower Colorado River to traditional trade grounds to hunt and exchange with the local population and with Caddoan allies from East Texas.

In 1693 Governor Salinas Varona encountered four tribes from northern Mexico—the Toboso, Simaoma, Mescal, and Cacaxtle in the trade grounds near modern La Grange, about forty miles south of the San Marcos area in Area II. These references are cited to indicate that a large number of tribes from below the Rio Grande were major players and a dominate cultural force in South and Central Texas during the study period. The Native peoples of northern Mexico added significantly to the kaleidoscope of Texas Indian cultures and to the wide diversity of Native cultural influences in the state.

Common Traditions in Texas Indian Cultures

The preceding chapters note wide cultural variations in the Texas Native population and also identify several cultural traditions that extended across all Native peoples in the state. One common cultural trait was an exceptionally strong propensity for long-distance movement, trade, and interaction with other tribal groups. This cosmopolitan disposition was expressed in various forms of exchange, warfare, and other means of direct and indirect interaction. Long-distance contacts by Texas tribes extended over 500 miles to the Mississippi River, central Kansas, northern New Mexico, western Chihuahua, southern Coahuila, and northern Nuevo León. This network of interaction was in place and operative in the early 1500s and 1600s, long before the horse became broadly available to expand long-distance contacts even farther in the late 1600s and 1700s. Although Apaches were often mounted by the late 1600s, the large visiting Native groups numbering several thousand and found visiting near the lower Colorado River in the late 1600s were not all mounted. The reports make clear that only the leaders of these large groups rode horseback.

The Native population in all eight study areas shared this strong propensity to interact over long distances. Although the population in some areas were more cosmopolitan than in others, the Native peoples in all areas seem much less provincial than most writers portray. As noted in the Introduction, this disposition to maintain interaction with Native people across a wide geographical space and to personally travel long distances was an integral part of the new culture of modern *H. sapiens,* who 40,000 years ago spread out of Europe and western Asia and ventured across the open ocean to reach Australia and colonize the Americas.

For example, French diarists, including Henri Joutel, wrote that the local hunter-gatherers living between the lower Brazos and Colorado Rivers were at war with maize-growing "Flatheads" who lived east of the Mississippi. Recent studies by Alan Gallay document that the "Flathead" Chickasaw, whose homeland was east of the Mississippi, raided and fought with tribes west of the Mississippi to capture Indian slaves for British interests on the East Coast. These same hunter-gatherer tribes in Area I were allies of the Trans-Pecos Jumano and the Hasinai to the north. French diarists say that they encountered local hunter-gatherer groups near the junction of the Navasota and Brazos Rivers that included members who spoke Caddoan and had visited West Texas. Although the Karankawa were relatively isolated along the central Texas coast, the French Talon brothers testified that the Karankawa raided Hasinai communities over 200 miles to their north. A Karankawa elder told La Salle that that they fought "Flatheads" living eastward toward the Mississippi.

Native hunter-gatherers in South Texas annually met with Native groups who came south from the Guadalupe to gather and feast on prickly pear tuna along the lower Nueces, and the same Guadalupe groups traded with bison-hunting groups from northern Mexico. The Trans-Pecos people were connected directly to both the Caddo residing 500 miles to their east and the Casas Grandes people in northwest Chihuahua over 200 miles to their west.

Nomadic bison hunters in the Texas Panhandle occupied the widest geographic range with close contacts into Kansas, New Mexico, South Texas, and northwest Chihuahua. Coronado's chroniclers encountered the bison people, called the Querecho, in the Texas Panhandle in 1541, and fifteen years later the historian Obregón recorded the Querecho hunting bison near Casas Grandes, 500 miles south of the earlier sighting of the tribe.

The Caddo traded with and visited tribes (including the Acansa) on the west side of Mississippi River, fought with the Chickasaw living on the east side of the big river, and, according to their own statements to the priest Douay, fought in New Mexico along with their allies, the Trans-Pecos Jumano. Even the more isolated tribes in the upper Gulf Coast area knew the Caddo 300 miles to their north, hunted bison in Area I, and traded with Louisiana tribes to their east. Texas tribes traveled long distances to trade, hunt, gather with allies, and fight enemies. The study record indicates that conflict with neighbors and enemies hundreds of miles away was a constant threat or opportunity for the Native peoples of Texas.

The historic record seems clear: the Indians of Texas had a broad regional and even interregional perspective that generally encompassed up to 300 to 400 miles in all directions surrounding their homeland. Texas Indians and their North American neighbors were in many respects similar to their well-traveled modern *H. sapiens* ancestors, who first ventured across the open ocean and circled the globe. In summary, Texas Native peoples were much more cosmopolitan than many historians, anthropologists, archeologists, and researchers generally acknowledge.

We should note also that, unfortunately, the cosmopolitan lifeways of the Native people contributed to the rapid spread of highly contagious European-introduced diseases, such as smallpox and measles, among the Native population in the state. Members of numerous infected tribes in northern Mexico (such as the Tepehuan) became carriers who spread the previously unknown diseases northward into Texas. As noted earlier, Chapa identifies by specific name over 160 tribes or bands in Nuevo León that were exterminated or decimated by deadly European diseases by the 1650s. Therefore, any study of the historic Indians of Texas must recognize that the health, vitality, and lifeways of the Native people were under severe physical and spiritual stress from highly contagious diseases that seriously depopulated the Native people during the study period.

A second common cultural feature or parallel that extended throughout all Native groups in the state was the firm and deep belief in a spiritual realm, a world that was so intimately intertwined with the natural physical realm that the two merged into one. For Native people, the two aspects of reality were indistinguishable.

Humans had spirits that continued in human form and with human needs and desires after death. Wildlife also had spiritual forms and powers as well. So did the sun, the clouds, caves, and other distinct landforms. In their daily lives, Texas Native peoples found spiritual influences constantly in play, directly intervening and affecting natural forces. We are reminded of Alonso de León's story of Nuevo León Indians throwing stones and shooting arrows at the swiftly moving clouds of thunder and lightning. In their spiritual afterlife Native peoples continued to require sustenance, weapons, and even the presence of sacrificed members of their own families and servants, who were buried with them.

The Native Americans' deep belief in an afterlife was described by one of De Soto's chroniclers. Immediately after De Soto died, an Indian chieftain in Arkansas approached De Soto's successor, Moscoso, and offered to sacrifice two of his own servants or slaves so they could serve De Soto on the next stage of his journey in the life beyond, as was their custom when a leader died. Moscoso refused the offer and spared the two volunteers by accepting them into his own service. Moscoso's chroniclers wrote that the custom of retainer sacrifice was widely spread among the chiefdoms encountered across the Southeast.[8]

Evidence of the Native American belief in an active spiritual world beyond death is found often in the documentary accounts of European expeditions. The French diarist Henri Joutel beautifully describes a compassionate story of a Caddoan chieftain's wife after the accidental drowning of a young visiting Frenchman named Marle. Joutel writes: "We must bear witness to these good people [the Caddo] whose humanity seemed remarkable in this sad accident, by the sensitive gestures they made, by their actions in all they could do to take part in our grief. The like of this we would not have found in many places in Europe. During our short stay, we witnessed a ceremony that the chief's wife conducted: every morning she carried a small basket of roasted ears of corn to the grave of the late Marle. We could not fathom the reason for this."[9] In the tragic death by drowning and the burial of the young Frenchman Marle, we see the same basic human belief in a life hereafter and the same sensitivity and mourning expressed by Marle's close French companions and the Caddoans to whom Marle was a total stranger.

The spiritual aspect of Native mortuary ceremonies conducted near the Gulf Coast in Area I is described by Cabeza de Vaca, who writes that most Indians in Area I were buried but that the spiritual leader, whom he called the shaman, was cremated. After cremation the shaman's bones were crushed and mixed with water, and the solution was drunk in a ceremony conducted by the senior tribal members. In this ceremony with shared cannibalistic and spiritual overtones, the shaman's supernatural powers were perhaps thought to be passed on to the living.

A joyful expression of the spiritual life of Texas Indians is recorded in accounts of ceremonial song-dances along the lower Texas Rio Grande, in the Big Bend, and in southern Coahuila. In describing the song-dances performed by Indians on the lower Rio Grande near Laredo in the 1620s, Alonso de León (the elder) writes that after the Indians made a bonfire, the males and females, numbering 100 or more, formed a ring around the fire. The Indians danced and sang the words in close harmony so uniformly that all seemed as one voice. The musical instruments used included the flute, rasp, and a dried gourd containing small pebbles. The celebrants drank ground peyote mixed with water.

In 1582, 500 miles farther up the Rio Grande in the Big Bend, the Spanish chronicler Hernán Gallegos describes the same type of song-dance performed by the Indians near La Junta as follows: "These people performed dances for us. The dancers rise and execute their movements, revolving to the rhythm of the music with much unity and harmony, in such a way that though there are three hundred in a dance, it seems as if it were being sung and danced by one man only."[10]

In 1594, 300 miles south of the Big Bend near Parras in southern Coahuila, Fray Andrés Pérez de Ribas describes a similar ritual. Ribas writes: "These people often celebrated with great numbers of people, all forming a circle, attired in gaudy head dress and trappings, moving and swaying in perfect rhythm and unison with each other. Such dances were held while circling about a great bonfire."[11] Ribas adds that "the herb called peyote" was a key ingredient in the celebration. The three isolated but similar documentary reports of stylized song-dance-peyote ceremonies, performed in unison by Indian groups of several hundred around the evening bonfires in northern Nuevo León, West Texas, and southern Coahuila, suggest a broad geographic consensus extending over 500 miles of common spiritual expressions.

The significance of the spiritual realm in the lives of the Indians of Texas is reflected in all aspects of their lives, not only on special ceremonial occasions. Manifestations of the spiritual can be found in their art— the dramatic and colorful rock art of the lower Pecos. Tall, imposing, and forceful images of shamans painted in white, black, and red on the high walls of rock shelters suggest a spiritual being. Compositions that include both figurative and nonfigurative painted objects from animals and hand prints to series of dots and stars cover stretches of the walls of rock overhangs and caves in the Southwest. Images of the rain god (Tlaloc) with his distinctive goggled eyes are found pecked into the hard surfaces of many open rock outcrops in West Texas and New Mexico.

Solveig Turpin notes that red ocher had magical connotations for Native peoples in Texas and on the Great Plains. Turpin writes that the discovery of a lightning bolt painted with red ocher on the bleached skull of a bison signals the spiritual component of the belief system of these hunting people.[12] These expressions are signs of a people with a deeply spiritual world view, one that may be traced back, archeologically, to the modern *H. sapiens* in Eurasia 40,000 years ago and earlier to the Neanderthal.

As mentioned in the Introduction, several larger mammals in North America became extinct or sharply downsized during the warming period after ca. 10,000 BC. Elephantlike mammoth and mastodon disappeared from the archeological record relatively early in the warming period, followed by the extinction of the saber-toothed tiger and the large dire wolf. After the ancient oversized long-horned bison became extinct, the large mammal's territory was occupied by the smaller, leaner bison hunted by the Native population in Texas during the study period. During the early warming years, the giant bighorn sheep, the huge armadillo, and the oversized javelina were all replaced by the smaller versions or subspecies encountered by Spanish and French explorers.

Although the drastic change in climate during the early Holocene had an adverse affect on the megafauna in North America, the archeological record, according to Tim Flannery, reflects no similar mass extinction or anatomical reduction in size of many smaller mammals such as deer, antelope, and rabbits, which were important to the diet of Native hunters during the study period. In addition, numerous species of cats (*Felidae*)—the cougar, jaguar, lynx, bobcat, ocelot, and jaguarundi—sighted by early Spanish and French explorers in Texas, the Southwest, and northern Mexico were all present in North America in essentially their present from at the beginnings of the early Holocene period.

Indian Cultural Continuity

Thomas Dillehay (as well as other American archeologists) concludes that modern *Homo sapiens,* who first settled the Americas, brought with them the cultural traits that first emerged in Europe and western Asia ca. 40,000 years ago. Dillehay writes as follows: "Anatomically modern people advance slowly across Europe and Asia until they reached China, Japan, and Australia around 40,000 BC. These people explored new continents and brought with them the basic cultural foundations of early American culture."[13] As indicated in the Introduction and the subsequent chapters, these ancient cultural traits formulated long ago began a cultural continuity that included a strong propensity for long-distance interaction, a deeply spiritual world view, advanced and complex hunting and lithic technologies, including the spear thrower (atlatl), the domestic animal (the dog), an artistic and musical temperament, and a flare for personal adornment. Many of these same cultural traits seem to be reflected in the lifeways of historic Texas Native peoples. However, we should note that the appearance of parallels between the cultural innovations introduced by modern *H. sapiens* in the Old World and cultural patterns found among historic Indians of Texas does not preclude the possibility that some of these apparent parallel manifestations may have originated in the New World independent of any diffusion of Old World culture. We also know that the Native population in the New World continued to devise and refine many cultural patterns into the Archaic and Prehistoric periods. These new patterns include the sedentary lifeways of horticulturists, the irrigation of crops, the use of sign language and the bow and arrow, sophisticated stone architecture, and the development of ceramics.

Modern *H. sapiens* painted red, black, and white images of local prehistoric mammals and birds (woolly mammoth and owls) and also non-figurative objects (series of white dots) on the walls of limestone rock caves in northern Spain and southern France 30,000 years ago.[14] Texas

Indians painted red, black, and white images of shamans, local mammals and birds (bison and parrots), and nonfigurative compositions (series of white dots) on the grayish white limestone walls of rock shelters and caves on the lower Pecos River 4,000 years ago.

Modern *H. sapiens* in 30,000 BP had musical instruments such as the flute, but Texas Indians on the lower Rio Grande also had the flute plus other musical instruments, including the tambourine, rasp, and gourd rattlers.

In Europe 30,000 years ago modern man used a sophisticated core and blade technology to produce knives and other tools. Ian Tattersall and Jeffrey Schwartz describe this lithic technology as follows: "Stone tools [were] made from long, narrow blades struck successively from carefully shaped cylindrical 'prismatic' stone cones."[15] According to Kenneth B. Tankersley and the Texas archeologist Michael B. Collins, lithic technologies known to modern *H. sapiens* in Eurasia were used by Clovis people.[16]

Hunting technologies were improved by modern *H. sapiens* who domesticated the dog and devised the spear thrower. Modern *H. sapiens* in Europe also fashioned sharp bone-tipped spear points and small, carefully grooved "sinkers" or plummets that Richard G. Klein writes was likely used as a fishing net weight or possibly as a type of bola hunting weapon.[17] Texas Indians also used domesticated dogs to hunt and carry loads, used a dart thrower called an atlatl, fashioned bone-tipped spear points, and had a similar sized and shaped "sinker" or hunting stone that archeologists also call a plummet or bola.[18]

Before 40,000 BP pre-modern *H. sapiens* wore or dressed with few or no personal items of adornment, but this changed with the arrival in Europe of modern *H. sapiens,* who dressed up. They painted their body with red ocher and tattooed themselves; they wore precious-stone pendants and small, tubular, microdrilled ivory beads and anthropomorphic stone pendants.[19]

Diarist on European expeditions into Texas during the study period witnessed the same or similar items of personal adornment worn by Texas Indians. The Native population in Texas and adjacent areas tattooed their bodies and painted their body and hair with red ocher. But the Native Texans added some extra flair to early European fancy dress by platting colorful tropical parrot feathers into their hair and by wearing red, blue, and yellow scarlet macaw feather headdresses. Beads worn by North American Native peoples were often made of the harder and more colorful shell, red jasper, or blue-green turquoise rather than the softer and whitish mammoth ivory and bone worked by modern *H. sapiens* 30,000 years ago. Craftsmen both in Europe 35,000 years ago and on the lower Mississippi about 5,000 years ago fashioned small, tubular, micro-drilled stone or ivory beads, some of which were shaped and polished into zoomorphic or anthropomorphic figures.

In his comments on the early settlement of the Americas, Dillehay explains that the human occupation of the New World may best be understood as a part of the modern *H. sapiens* "explosion" that occurred in Europe ca. 40,000 years ago. The present study suggests that the historic Native peoples of Texas may best be understood the same way.

And perhaps, so may we.

Like our ancient ancestors, we (at least in Texas) are still hunters and gatherers. Today we hunt white-tailed deer, wild turkey, ducks, and geese; we gather and pick pecans, mustang grapes, wild plums, and dewberries to put up.

And in the wild today we still see jackrabbits, cottontails, armadillos, coyotes, sandhill cranes, and buzzards, all Texas residents 10,000 years ago.

And when we dress up today, we still sport tattoos and wear brightly colored beads, earrings, fur coats, and feathered hats.

And when it's all over, like our ancient tribal ancestors, we still cremate or bury our dead with flowers and a faith in a life hereafter.

APPENDIX 1

SELECTED ANIMALS REPORTED ON
SPANISH AND FRENCH EXPEDITIONS
INTO TEXAS, 1528–1722

This appendix lists alphabetically selected wild and domesticated animals identified in diaries and other documents relating to Spanish and French expeditions into Texas and the American Southwest and Southeast undertaken between 1528 and 1722. Entries include the name of the diarist or historian who recorded the sighting and the approximate date and location of the report. Entries may also include information from expedition documents and regional histories from northern Mexico. Information on late Pleistocene and early Holocene species is added where available. The French and Spanish names for the animals are given where relevant.

Contemporary studies of prehistoric animals in Texas and North America most frequently consulted and cited include Tim Flannery, *The Eternal Frontier: An Ecological History of North America and Its People*; Robert C. West, ed., *Natural Environment and Early Cultures*; and Christine M. Janis et al., eds., *Evolution of Tertiary Mammals of North America*, vol. 1, *Terrestrial Carnivores, Ungulates, and Ungulatelike Mammals* (Cambridge: Cambridge University Press, 1998). The short references cited in the text give only the names of the expedition leader, diarist, or diary editor and the appropriate pages. Full citations are found in the bibliography.

List of Animals

1. Alligator	8. Bobcat	15. Javelina
2. Antelope	9. Cougar	16. Opossum
3. Armadillo	10. Deer	17. Parrot
4. Bear	11. Dog	18. Rabbit
5. Bighorn Sheep	12. Fish	19. Turkey
6. Birds	13. Horse	20. Wolf
7. Bison	14. Jaguar	

1. Alligator (*crocodile, caiman, cayman, cocodrilo*)
  Spanish and French expedition diarists reported a wide distribution of alli-

gator ranging from Cuba and the coastal areas of the Gulf of Mexico to the Gulf of California and northwest Mexico. Alligators were also reported in the rivers and coastal area of Central Texas and the lower Mississippi.

The Spanish priest Andrés Pérez de Ribas wrote that numerous alligators were found in the province of Sinaloa in western Mexico near the mouth of rivers emptying into the Gulf of California (Pérez de Ribas, 4). On his journey from France to Texas in 1684, La Salle shot a caiman or crocodile on a small island on the southwest coast of Cuba (Foster 1998, 61). Studies of the distribution of reptiles in Mexico indicate that alligator or caiman are found along the coast of Tamaulipas (West, 330).

On La Salle's 1682 exploration of the Mississippi River, he killed numerous alligators for food on the river south of the Arkansas River junction. French chroniclers in 1685–1687 reported the reptiles on Matagorda Bay, on the lower Colorado River in Texas, and on the lower Arkansas River (Foster 1998, 47, 141, 169; Foster 2003, 106, 114, 116, 141, 146). On late seventeenth-century and eighteenth-century Spanish expeditions, diarists recorded alligators on the San Antonio, Colorado, Brazos, and Trinity Rivers (Foster 1995, 233–234).

2. Antelope (*berrendo*)

Spanish chroniclers, including Pedro de Castañeda, Alonso de León (the elder), and Fray Isidro de Espinosa, wrote that antelope (*berrendo*) were found in northeastern Mexico and the Texas Panhandle in the 1500s, 1600s, and early 1700s (Foster 1995, 242, 243). Studies of fauna of Mexico indicate that antelope are found across the American Southwest, in Sonora, and on Baja California (West, 369).

La Salle's diarist, Henri Joutel, described large herds of deer and antelope north of Fort St. Louis near Matagorda Bay (Foster 1998, 74). Mendoza's troops killed antelope on his 1684 expedition to the Edwards Plateau (Wade, 113). For sighting of antelope on late seventeenth- and eighteenth-century Spanish expeditions into Texas from Coahuila, see Foster, *Spanish Expeditions into Texas,* 242–243.

According to studies of antelope in the Pleistocene, the pronghorn antelope ranged from Canada to Mexico and from the West Coast to the Great Plains (Harris, 124). During the early Holocene, the pronghorn occupied extensive areas in North America (Flannery, 158). At the Richard Beene site (41 BX 831) near San Antonio, archeologists have recovered the remains of antelope dated to the Early Archaic (7000 BP).

In 1719 the Frenchman Bénard de La Harpe reported antelope (called unicorns) near the South Canadian River in Oklahoma, about one hundred miles north of the Red River (R. Smith, 534).

3. Armadillo (*armadillo*)

Alonso de León (the elder) and Fray Espinosa wrote that armadillos were in northeast Mexico in the 1600s and 1700s, but there is no evidence of armadillo in the historic period in Texas until ca. 1850 (Foster 1995, 234, 235). The prehistoric-looking animals have since spread through many areas of Texas and across the Mississippi into the Southeast (Smith and Doughty, 11). In Mexico and Central America armadillos are still an important source of food (West, 318, 375).

During prehistoric period, ca. 14,000 years ago, much of North America was inhabited by a giant armadillo three times the size of the present-day version. The giant species moved out of the United States and into Central America during the early Holocene. Today the smaller version has returned toward its northernmost former range (Flannery, 348).

4. Bear (*oso*)

Bear had a range that extended across the North American continent in the sixteenth and seventeenth centuries. Bear were present in South America, Mexico, and many areas of the United States and Canada (West, 319). Fray Ribas reported that in 1610 bear were in the mountains of Topia, south of the Tarahumara country in western Mexico (Pérez de Ribas, 156). Obregón saw bear in 1565 near Casas Grandes in northwest Chihuahua (Hammond and Rey 1928, 197).

Coronado and Alonso de Benavides reported bear in New Mexico in the 1540s and 1620s (Castañeda et al., 52; Ayer, 37). La Salle's chroniclers wrote that in 1682 bear were along the Mississippi River from about fifty miles north of the mouth of the Arkansas downriver to Neches (Foster 2003, 99, 119, 124). Juan Domínguez de Mendoza and the Marqués de Rubí reported bear in the Edwards Plateau (Wade, 113, 202).

Spanish expedition diarists reported bear in Nuevo León and Coahuila and also across a wide area of Texas. In the eighteenth century bear were reported from near San Antonio eastward to northeast Texas, southeast to the lower Trinity, and along the lower San Antonio River. For specific sightings on Spanish expeditions of bear in Texas, see Foster 1995, 235.

In 1719 the Frenchman Bénard de La Harpe reported killing two bears along a stream that was "full of them" near the Red River in northwest Louisiana (R. Smith, 374).

During the late Pleistocene and early Holocene, spectacled bear (like large armadillo and turkey) moved southward out of Texas and into Mexico, but a different species later appeared north of the Rio Grande. The grizzly bear first appeared in North America after ca. 13,000 BP (Flannery, 212, 213).

5. Bighorn Sheep (*carnero*)

In 1540, while traveling through Sonora en route to New Mexico, Coronado's diarist, Pedro de Castañeda, wrote that Spanish troops found a herd of large, woolly mountain sheep with thick horns and that the sheep threw back their horns when they ran (Castañeda et al., 20). Alonso de Benavides wrote that bighorn sheep in New Mexico were as large as a pony and had heavy horns and short tails. The size of their horns, he said, was the most impressive (Ayer, 37, 38).

In 1581 in the Big Bend area of Texas, Hernán Gallegos, a notary on the Chamuscado expedition, discovered an abandoned Indian camp near the Rio Grande about fifty miles upriver from La Junta where he found a pile of large rams' horns weighing about thirty pounds each (Hammond and Rey 1966, 78).

Native Southwest artists' attraction to bighorn sheep is reflected in the numerous images of the animal in pre-Columbian murals, rock art, and pottery in New Mexico and West Texas (Brody, 71).

6. Birds

Expedition diarists occasionally provide a list of birds that they identified in the area of their exploration. Henri Joutel, La Salle's diarist on his 1685–1687 expedition to Texas, identified a number of shorebirds that were on the Texas coast near Fort St. Louis. Joutel reported finding cranes, Canada geese, ducks, swans, teal, coots, plover, jacksnipe, sandpipers, white and brown curlews, pheasant, prairie chickens, wild turkeys, pelicans, roseate spoonbill, hummingbirds, black and turkey vultures, caracaras, starlings, crows, doves, oyster catchers, cormorants, and herons (Foster 1998, 126, 127).

Fray Espinosa in the early eighteenth century listed the mockingbird, cardinal, sparrow, thrush, pelican, and osprey in Nuevo León (Tous, 1930, 36). In his essay on the birds along the lower Rio Grande, Espinosa listed the mockingbird, cardinal, sparrow, hummingbird, dove, white crane (whooping crane?), brown heavy-set crane (sandhill crane?), blackbird, raven, turkey buzzard, vulture, osprey, hawk, owl, duck, goose, and pelican. On the 1768 Solís inspection tour of Spanish missions in Texas, the priest reported seeing numerous species of birds in northern Nuevo León near the Rio Grande, including hawks, screech owls, crows, quail, scarlet macaws, small parrots, sparrows, pheasant, blackbirds, larks, thrushes, and blue ducks (Foster 1995, 235–240).

De Soto's diarist reported seeing cranes on his expedition across the Southeast (Clayton, Knight, and Moore, 1:170). In 1600 Fray Ribas recorded sandhill crane in Sonora (Pérez de Ribas, 3). In 1582 Luxán mentioned finding cranes near the ponds on the Rio Grande about twenty miles downriver from El Paso (Hammond and Rey 1966, 169). In 1682 La Salle's diarist recorded finding the tricolored heron near the mouth of the Mississippi (Foster 2003, 115). Spanish expedition diarists and historians in the eighteenth century identified both the white whooping crane and the gray-brown sandhill crane (Foster 1995, 237, 238).

French and Spanish diarists recorded finding ducks and geese in the Southeast, on the Mississippi, across Texas, and into the Southwest and northern Mexico. De Soto's chroniclers recorded ducks throughout the Southeast (Clayton, Knight, and Moore, 1:170). In the Southwest Coronado found the birds in New Mexico (Castañeda et al., 54), and Espejo saw large flocks of ducks and geese on the ponds and lagoons on the Rio Grande a few miles southeast of present-day El Paso (Hammond and Rey 1966, 169). On La Salle's 1682 exploration of the Mississippi, his chroniclers recorded seeing ducks and geese from the Great Lakes region to the Gulf of Mexico (Foster 2003, 96, 124, 128). In Texas Joutel identified teal and other ducks as well as Canada geese along the central Texas coast (Foster 1998, 76, 79, 126).

At the Middle Archaic Watson Brake site in northern Louisiana, Joe Saunders notes that duck remains were uncovered (Saunders, 1798).

7. Bison or American Buffalo (*cibolo*)

Information provided by chroniclers on the Spanish expeditions of Cabeza de Vaca, Coronado, and De Soto between 1528 and 1543 provides the basis for a preliminary projection of the range of bison in the American Southeast, Southwest, and northern Mexico at the time of first European contact. Cabeza de Vaca wrote that he had seen bison on three occasions near the central Texas coast and had eaten bison meat, which he considered better than beef in Spain. He described bison as having small horns and long, dark brown, woolly hair. He said that bison came to the coastal area of Texas from the north. Cabeza de Vaca added, significantly, that the Native hunters from far away followed the bison herds, lived off the bison, and brought with them many bison hides to trade (Krieger, 196).

When Cabeza de Vaca reached the Rio Grande near La Junta on his cross-country journey, he found many bison hides and bison hunters who traveled north to hunt on the Southern Plains (ibid., 223). However, the author did not indicate that he saw bison on his western swing up the Rio Grande and across northwestern Chihuahua.

Coronado likewise gave no indication of seeing bison on his trek across Sonora, Arizona, and western New Mexico. But Coronado's diarist described huge herds of bison on the Southern Plains a few days' travel east of the Pecos River, and the diarist recorded even more bison between the Texas Panhandle and the Arkansas River in central Kansas (Castañeda et al., 38).

Coming from the Southeast, De Soto's forces reported no bison east of the Mississippi, and De Soto's diarists recorded finding bison hides and other evidence of bison only at their farthest western travels near the Oklahoma-Arkansas border. The word received from local Indians near the state line was that large bison herds were to be found after another week's travel farther west (Clayton, Knight, and Moore, 1:241).

Information from subsequent European explorers generally supports and gives some refinement to the broad outline of the range of bison found in the documentary accounts of the three early Spanish expeditions. In 1565 Obregón described the bison hunters who met Ibarra's troops while they were camped near Casas Grandes in northwest Chihuahua. The Indian hunters (called Querecho) told Ibarra that bison herds were within three travel days of the Spaniards' camp. Obregón believed the report because Ibarra's men found bison bones and manure near the Casas Grandes river camp (Hammond and Rey 1928, 202, 208).

In 1684, on his journey from El Paso down the Rio Grande to La Junta and eastward to the middle Pecos River in West Texas, Mendoza saw no bison. He found bison only after he crossed to the northeast side of the Pecos, but there were herds of thousands of bison in the Edwards Plateau area (Wade, 115).

On La Salle's 1682 trip down the Mississippi, his men killed bison on his journey from the Great Lakes region to an area south of the junction of the Missouri and the Mississippi Rivers (Foster 2003, 64–65, 76–77). On his 1685–1687 expedition to Texas, La Salle found large bison herds all during the year on the Texas coast, and his diarist, Henri Joutel, wrote that he killed bison in eastern Arkansas within a four-day march of the Mississippi River (Foster 1998, 259–260). For an account of bison reported on Spanish expeditions into Texas during the period 1689–1768, see Foster, *Spanish Expeditions into Texas*, 236–237.

In 1719 the Frenchman Bénard de La Harpe reported seeing bison herds near the South Canadian River in Oklahoma about one hundred miles north of the Red River (R. Smith, 383, 535).

During the late Pleistocene period, there were two species of bison in North America—the larger, long-horned variety (*Bison antiqus*) and the more modern smaller version (*Bison bison*). The larger bison became extinct in the early Holocene period, and the smaller bison was hunted by the historic Indians of Texas (Flannery, 212, 319). At the Richard Beene site near San Antonio, archeologists have recovered bison or bison-size mammal remains dating to the late Pleistocene (Thoms and Mandel, 232.)

8. Bobcat (wildcat, *gatos montes,* lynx)

When reporting *gatos montes,* Spanish diarists may have observed a lynx, bobcat, or a number of other cats smaller than cougars and jaguars, including the dark, solid-colored, long-tailed jaguarundi or the ocelot, which has the appearance and is the size of a small bobcat. In the early seventeenth century Fray Benavides reported "wild cats" in New Mexico (Ayer, 37); Ribas observed them in Sonora (Pérez de Ribas, 3), and De León (the elder) wrote that they were numerous in Nuevo León (Duaine, 67).

Spanish chroniclers in the eighteenth century recorded *gatos montes* in South Texas and along the San Antonio River between Goliad and San Antonio (Foster 1995, 245).

At the close of the last glacial Ice Age (ca. 10,000 BC), there was a full array of the cat species in North America, including the puma, lynx, ocelot, bobcat, jaguarundi, and margay (Flannery, 161).

9. Cougar (mountain lion, puma, panther, *león*)

Sixteenth- and seventeenth-century Spanish expedition diarists recorded finding cougar or mountain lion in the Southeast, the Southwest, and northern Mexico. Coronado listed the mountain lion as one of the large cats found in New Mexico (Coronado, 94). Ribas said that the large cat was in Sonora as well (Pérez de Ribas, 3). In his summary of wild animals found on De Soto's expedition, the Gentleman from Elvas included the mountain lion (Clayton, Knight, and Moore, 1:170).

On seventeenth- and early eighteenth-century Spanish expeditions from northern Mexico to Texas, diarists (or their translators) referred to the mountain lion as cougar, panther, and puma. In 1689 General Alonso de León found a dead mountain lion near the San Antonio River and named the river Río León (Bolton 1916, 394). The friars Espinosa and Solís reported panthers in Texas and Nuevo León in the 1700s (Kress, 49; I. Espinosa, 764). In the late Pleistocene in North America, the giant lion was twice the size of the modern African lion (Flannery, 160).

10. Deer (*venado, ciervo, cerf*)

Coronado wrote the viceroy in 1543 that in New Mexico there were deer of two sizes—referring possibly to black-tailed deer and elk (Castañeda et al., 95). Deer are included in a summary of animals seen by De Soto's chroniclers in the Southeast (Clayton, Knight, and Moore, 1:170).

Obregón wrote that in 1665 many deer and stags were found in the mountains near Casas Grandes (Hammond and Rey 1928, 198). On Castaño's 1690 trip across West Texas, a tame pet fawn was taken along by a young Spanish girl. When Castaño's party reached the area near the present-day Texas–New Mexico state line, a large herd of deer was reported that the diarist said was too numerous to count. The size of the herd may suggest it was a large herd of antelope rather than deer (Hammond and Rey 1966, 261).

Fray Ribas confirmed that large numbers of deer were in Sonora in the early 1600s (Pérez de Ribas, 3). De León (the elder) wrote that deer in groups of up to fifty were in Nuevo León in the 1620s (Duaine, 67). Mendoza's soldiers killed a large number of deer in the Edwards Plateau area in 1684 (Wade, 115).

On La Salle's trip down the Mississippi in 1682, his men killed deer all along the way from the Great Lakes region to the Gulf of Mexico (Foster 2003, 96, 98, 99). In 1685 Joutel wrote that French troops and colonist killed deer for food near Fort St. Louis on Matagorda Bay and saw deer throughout the 1687 journey to the Mississippi River (Foster 1998, 126, 280).

In pre-Columbian times white-tailed deer were found throughout northern Mexico and into the central Valley of Mexico where they, along with rabbits, were apparently among the most hunted animals in the early Aztec period (West, 369, 372). From the Richard Beene site near San Antonio archeologists have recovered the remains of deer dated to the Early Archaic period. At a Middle Archaic (ca. 3400 BC) location in northern Louisiana, deer remains have been recovered from the Watson Brake site (Saunders, 1798).

11. Dog (*perro, chien*)

Spanish and French expedition diarists offer a widely divergent picture of how Native people in the Southeast and the Southwest related to their most significant and usually only domestic animal, the dog. Reports from the Southeast frequently indicated that domestic dogs were eaten on significant ceremonial occasions (Foster 2003, 123). In the Southwest dogs were often reported as highly valued beasts of burden (Bolton 1916, 395). Reports from Texas suggest that dogs may have been used also to hunt and as camp guards (Foster 1998, 160, 274).

Coronado's chroniclers described how Plains Indians (called Querecho and Teya) used dogs to carry packs on their backs tied with girths and a breast harness and to drag packs with sticks or house poles tied to their saddle packs (Castañeda et al., 38).

Castaño's 1590 expedition party of Spanish colonists from northeast Mexico were delighted at seeing Plains Indians with dog trains along the Pecos River in West Texas (Hammond and Rey 1966, 257, 258). In 1598 Zaldívar described the dog train used by Plains Indians as follows: "Indians use medium-sized shaggy dogs that serve as mules, and these move in a long string, harnessed at the chest and haunches; and even carrying at least a hundred pounds they lope along as fast as their masters . . . , one after the other, the tips of their poles dragging behind them. And to load them the women hold their heads between their legs and then load them or adjust the load" (Craddock, 59).

In 1689 General De León described seeing "eight or ten dogs loaded with bison hides," running into the woods following their frightened Indian masters near the Guadalupe River in DeWitt County (Bolton 1916, 395). In 1685 a few miles east of the Colorado River, Joutel and La Salle saw dogs used for hunting and guard duty at an Indian (probably Caddoan) hunting camp. The Frenchmen also saw dogs at the Nasoni villages that they visited in East Texas (Foster 1998, 236).

On his 1682 exploration of the Mississippi, La Salle's chroniclers wrote that the Loup Indians from New England, whom La Salle brought with him downriver from the Great Lakes region, ate the dogs of the Quinapisa Indians, who were killed in their attack on La Salle's camp (Foster 2003, 119). But La Salle refused to allow the northeastern Loup to eat the striped bodies of the lower Mississippi Quinapisa warriors, whom they had killed. When La Salle returned up the Mississippi to the Acansa Indians at the junction of the Arkansas River, the local chieftain treated the French party with a feast of dogs (ibid., 123).

Dogs were sometimes raised for food in Mesoamerica and were eaten at Cahokia on the middle Mississippi (Schwartz, 79). It is thought that the first settlers of the Americas (modern *H. sapiens*) brought the domesticated dog with them from Asia (Schwartz, 16). The remains of a dog have been recovered from the Watson Brake site in northern Louisiana, dated ca. 3400 BC (Saunders, 1798).

12. Fish (*pescado, poisson*)

De Soto's chroniclers identify large river catfish (called "*bagre*") on a channel of the Arkansas River that the Spaniards visited about a week after crossing the Mississippi moving westward. *Bagre* weighing up to 100 pounds were caught by De Soto's soldiers with hooks and by seine nets used by local residents of Pacaha, an Indian town with an estimated population of several thousand residents. The *bagre* are described by De Soto's chroniclers as being about one-third head with no scales but sharp spines protruding from either side of the throat (Clayton, Knight, and Moore, 1:118).

Spanish diarists also reported catching catfish in rivers across the Southwest. In 1590 Castaño's colonists caught *bagre* in the Pecos River in West Texas (Hammond and Rey 1966, 261); Fray Benavides reported that the fish was caught on the Rio Grande in New Mexico in the 1620s (Hammond and Rey 1928, 261); De León recorded in 1650 that *bagre* were in Nuevo León (Duaine, 30); Fernando del Bosque caught catfish on the Río de los Nadadores in Coahuila (Wade, 28); and Mendoza's troops fished for catfish on the Texas Concho River in 1684 (ibid., 105, 109). In some instances, the diarists listed other fish that were taken at the same time.

La Salle's journalist, Joutel, provided a list of bay fish caught by the colonists at Fort St. Louis on the central Texas coast. Joutel's description of catfish is similar to that given in De Soto's journals 140 years earlier. Joutel wrote that the local species found near the Texas coast was like the French catfish in that they have no scales but have "two quills on the sides of their gills and beards beneath their snouts" (Foster 1998, 127).

During their 1682 discovery trip down the Mississippi, La Salle's men observed Natives fishing from dugout canoes on several occasions on the lower part of the river. On one occasion, a Native fisherman left several smoked fish plus a smoked human hand and foot in his canoe (Foster 2003, 112).

In his report on Watson Brake, a Middle Archaic site in northern Louisiana, Joe Saunders, the lead archeologist, reports that aquatic species such as freshwater drum, catfish, suckers, and mussels predominated among the remains, dated to ca. 3400 BC (Saunders, 1798).

13. Horse (*caballo*)

Although there were several species of horses in North America during the late Pleistocene, the horse became extinct on this continent ca. 13,000 years ago (Flannery, 293). The animal survived in the Middle East and was reintroduced to the Americas principally by Spanish explorers. Relatively small Spanish horses or ponies that escaped Spanish control multiplied quickly and roamed the western frontier after the close of our study period.

Large horse herds were brought north into the American Southwest and Southeast by Coronado and De Soto. Some horses were left in the Southwest when the explorers returned to Mexico (Clayton, Knight, and Moore, 1:418), but all of De Soto–Moscoso's horses were killed before Moscoso's troops reached the Gulf of Mexico. There are no reports of the Indians in Texas having horses in the sixteenth century, but beginning in the middle seventeenth century Spanish chroniclers and historians wrote about Indian raids from South Texas on Spanish outposts in Nuevo León to obtain horses (Chapa, 53–56).

La Salle's chroniclers on his 1682 canoe trip down the Mississippi did not record finding any horses among the tribes encountered, but during his 1685–1687 expedition to Texas horses were not numerous but were widespread among the Texas Native tribes—both horticultural and hunter-gatherer groups (Foster 1998, 167, 212–213). Two horses were reported by Joutel as far east as the Ouachita River in Arkansas, about eighty miles west of the Mississippi (ibid., 257).

In West Texas in the 1680s the Jumano and many other tribes possessed and traded horses. But in the late seventeenth century horses were still in limited supply, used primarily as pack animals for hunts and ridden only by tribal leaders (Wade, 98).

By the close of the study period, the Plains Apache were very proficient horsemen, and Spanish officials in San Antonio were forced by the mounted Apache to switch the route of the Camino Real to East Texas southward along a corridor below the thick and near impenetrable Post Oak Belt (Foster 1995, 183–186). Aggressive Apaches on horses forced the change from the upper to the lower, more protected southern route of the Camino Real in the 1730s.

14. Jaguar (*tigre*)

Coronado wrote the viceroy in 1541 that the spotted jaguar (*tigre*) was found in New Mexico (Castañeda et al., 94). A report by the Spanish priest Ribas confirmed that the big cat was in the Southwest, including Sonora, in the early 1600s (Pérez de Ribas, 3). In 1709 Espinosa wrote that the jaguar was seen in north-central Texas and later reported the large cat in Nuevo León and Coahuila (I. Espinosa, 836). It appears that, except for a few isolated sightings in the 1800s, the jaguar's present range extends from South America to the lowlands of northern Mexico (West, 320).

The smaller but similarly marked ocelot is still found near Brownsville and in other areas of South Texas, New Mexico, and northern Mexico (Davis and Schmidly, 257).

In the late Pleistocene jaguars were well established in North America (Flannery, 161; Harris, 160).

15. Javelina (collared peccary, *jabalí*)

Eighteenth-century Spanish historians and expedition diarists filed numerous reports of javelina in northeast Mexico. De León wrote that they were in Nuevo León in the early 1600s (Clayton, Knight, and Moore, 82). Ribas reported that in 1600 javelina (*jabalí*) were in Sonora in northwest Mexico (Pérez de Ribas, 3). The range of collared peccary extends southward to Central America (West, 320).

A few expedition accounts recorded javelina in Texas before 1800. Solís in 1768 reported finding "*javalis*" along his route northward from the Rio Grande into Area IV. He recorded seeing them again when crossing the Nueces River, near Goliad, and between Goliad and San Antonio (Kress, 37, 43, 49).

During the late Pleistocene the peccary was over twice the size of the present javelina and had a wide range across North America (Flannery, 158). It moved out of Texas into Mexico with the large armadillo during the early Holocene, and a smaller version returned in the last several centuries.

16. Opossum (*churcha*)

The nocturnal opossum was an unrecognized or at least a seldom-reported animal by most Spanish and French chroniclers. La Salle's diarist, Henri Joutel, was an exception. La Salle's men apparently saw one that Joutel identified during La Salle's stopover on the west coast of Cuba (Foster 1998, 61). This sighting of an opossum is consistent with a similar report made by the early sixteenth-century Spanish historian Gonzalo Fernández de Oviedo y Valdez, who wrote that the opossum (*churcha*) was found in the West Indies (Oviedo, Natural History, 76).

Joutel later described in more detail the opossum that his party found near the customary crossing on the Colorado River in Fayette County. He wrote that the animal looked like a large rat with a larger snout, adding, "beneath one side of its abdomen is a sort of sack in which it carries its young" (Foster 1998, 170).

The opossum was a Pleistocene creature in North America and found its special ecological place then as today. Opossums eat almost anything and breed quickly (Flannery, 145). Opossum and raccoon remains were recovered at Watson Brake in northern Louisiana, dated ca. 3400 BC (Saunders, 1796). The late Pleistocene remains of the ringtail (*Bassariscus astutus*), which is closely related to the raccoon, were found at the Richard Beene site near San Antonio (Thoms and Mandel).

17. Parrots (scarlet macaw, military macaw, *papagayo, perico, guacamaya*)

Cabeza de Vaca was the first European diarist to write that Native Americans in northwest Chihuahua near the Casas Grandes river valley regularly traded parrot feathers and feather products to their trading neighbors to the north in New Mexico for turquoise (Krieger, 225). In the early 1580s both Chamuscado and Espejo wrote that while marching upstream from La Junta, the local Natives along the Rio Grande in Texas gave them parrot-feather headdresses and macaw parrot feathers (Hammond and Rey 1966, 79, 167).

The friar Ribas wrote in the early 1600s of finding the macaw, probably the green military macaw, high in the mountains of Sonora and farther south on the Pacific coast in the Sierra Madre near Topia (Pérez de Ribas, 4, 156). In contrast to the military macaw, the scarlet macaw is a tropical rain-forest parrot found in the lowlands of Nuevo León, Tamaulipas, and Oaxaca. It is therefore assumed that Ribas, who was traveling through the high Sierras, observed the military macaw.

Alonso de León (the elder) says that large parrots (macaws?) as well as small ones were raised in Nuevo León in the 1620s to 1650s (Duaine, 67). Although the northern range of the scarlet macaw has moved farther south since the end of the Little Ice Age in ca. 1850, Fray Solís identified the macaw, probably the scarlet macaw, along the lower Sabinas in Nuevo León in 1768 when the Little

Ice Age climate created a more favorable mesic-hydric environment along the lower Rio Grande than today (Foster 1995, 200).

When La Salle stopped briefly in Hispanola and Cuba in 1684, his men saw and killed small parrots (Foster 1998, 60, 61). In Mesoamerica the *amateca* made colorful feather mosaics using the blue, green, red, and yellow macaw feathers in their famous artistic creations (West, 383).

18. Rabbit (cottontail, jackrabbit, *conejo, liebre*)

The cottontail and jackrabbit may have been some of the most ubiquitous small game animals in North America during the study period. Cabeza de Vaca described the dense rabbit population in north-central Mexico and how the local Natives used specially designed two-foot-long curved rabbit sticks to kill them (Adorno, 1:211).

Coronado's diarist wrote that in the 1540s there were numerous rabbits all across the plains leading to Quivira in Kansas. The diarist commented that Coronado's soldiers on horseback could easily kill many rabbits with the tip of their lance, but when dismounted the men were unable to catch them. The report suggests that mounted hunters were not understood to be a threat by rabbits (Castañeda et al., 60). Fray Benavides confirms that in the 1620s there was a large population of both cottontails and jackrabbits in New Mexico (Ayer, 37).

De Soto's chroniclers wrote that both cottontails and jackrabbits were plentiful and were frequently hunted by Natives in the Southeast. In northern Mexico Ibarra's men reported seeing rabbits near the Casas Grandes river valley, and in the 1580s Espejo wrote that the Conchos Indians gave his party many rabbits on their trip down the Río Conchos. Today jackrabbits are found in Mexico and Central America but no farther south; cottontails are found in Mexico and throughout South America.

During the late Pleistocene both the snowshoe hare and the jackrabbit were widely dispersed across North America (Harris, 141). Archeologists at the Richard Beene site near San Antonio recovered rabbit remains dated to the late Pleistocene (Thoms and Mandel). At the Middle Archaic Watson Brake site in northern Louisiana, Joe Saunders reports that both rabbit and squirrel remains were recovered (Saunders, 1798).

19. Turkey (*guajolote, pavo de Indias*)

Wild and, perhaps on occasion, domestic turkey were donated as gifts to De Soto in Florida and elsewhere in the American Southeast (Clayton, Knight, and Moore, 1:309). Coronado and his chroniclers first described turkeys in New Mexico as native fowl with hanging chins, and the Spaniards noted the important role played by domestic turkey in New Mexico (Castañeda et al., 54). Coronado's observations regarding the importance of domestic turkeys are reinforced in the accounts of Captain Chamuscado and Fray Benavides (Ayer, 250, 271; Hammond and Rey 1966, 129). In his description of Topia on the Pacific side of Mexico, Fray Ribas wrote there were large flocks of wild turkeys (Pérez de Ribas, 156).

On La Salle's 1682 trip down the Mississippi, Indian hunters with La Salle killed turkeys all along the route from the junction of the Illinois River with the Mississippi to the lower stretch of the river in Louisiana (Foster 2003, 96, 119). On La Salle's 1687 trip to East Texas, Joutel wrote that wild turkeys were found en route (Foster 1998, 203).

In 1719 the Frenchman Bénard de La Harpe reported killing turkeys near the Red River in northwestern Louisiana (R. Smith, 83).

Wild turkeys are found across northern Mexico, but the smaller ocellated turkey with its coppery, greenish blue tail feathers is restricted to Mexico's eastern Gulf Coast and farther south (West, 322, 342). The turkey is recognized as one of the few animals domesticated in Mesoamerica (ibid., 448).

During the Pleistocene period, the ocellated turkey moved south out of the area north of the Rio Grande into Mexico, where it survives today (Flannery, 164). Turkey remains dated to ca. 3400 BC were recovered at the Watson Brake site in northern Louisiana (Saunders, 1796).

20. Wolf (*lobo*)

Wolf packs followed the large herds of bison on the Southern Plains, according to Coronado's diarist (Castañeda et al., 60). De Soto's chroniclers wrote that wolves were seen across the Southeast (Clayton, Knight, and Moore, 1:170). On two occasions during Castaño's trip across West Texas, wolves killed goats that the colonists had taken along (Hammond and Rey 1966, 259).

Fray Ribas wrote that there were many wolves in the mountains in Topia on Mexico's west coast (Pérez de Ribas, 156). In Texas and northeast Mexico, Spanish diarist reported many wolves. Espinosa said wolves were in Coahuila and Nuevo León (I. Espinosa, 764). Solís added that he found wolves on his trip between Goliad and San Antonio (Kress, 49).

During the late Pleistocene period, the large dire wolf, which had originated in North America south of the ice sheet, became extinct, and the smaller gray wolf became common in the archeological record at the beginning of the Holocene (Flannery, 216).

APPENDIX 2

SELECTED TREES AND OTHER PLANTS REPORTED ON SPANISH AND FRENCH EXPEDITIONS INTO TEXAS, 1528–1722

This appendix lists alphabetically selected wild and domesticated trees and other plants identified in diaries and other official documents relating to Spanish and French expeditions into Texas conducted between 1528 and 1722. Entries also include information from and citations to documents related to other European expeditions into the American Southwest and Southeast and information found in the historical work of Baltasar de Obregón, Fray Andrés Pérez de Ribas, Juan Bautista Chapa, Isidro Félix de Espinosa, Jean Louis Berlandier, Fray Alonso de Benavides, Alonso de León (the elder), and Herbert E. Bolton. Entries include the last name of the author, editor, or translator of the diary or history and a page notation.

The principal contemporary studies of flora in Texas and the Southwest consulted and cited include Robert A. Vines, *Trees Shrubs, and Woody Vines of the Southwest;* Scooter Cheatham and Marshall C. Johnson with Lynn Marshall, *Useful Wild Plants of Texas;* Nancy R. Morin, ed., *Flora of North America North of Mexico;* Charles C. Di Peso, John B. Rinaldo, and Gloria Fenner, *Casas Grandes;* William E. Doolittle, *Cultivated Landscapes of Native North America;* William W. Dunmire, *Gardens of New Spain;* Robert C. West, ed., *Natural Environment and Early Cultures.* Information from specific archeological sites is referenced by site identification in the text of the entry.

List of Plants

1. Agave
2. Amaranth
3. Apple
4. Ash
5. Beans
6. Blackberry and Dewberry
7. Bluewood condalia
8. Bois d'Arc
9. Cane
10. Catclaw
11. Cedar
12. Chestnut
13. Cotton
14. Cottonwood
15. Cypress
16. Elm
17. Grape
18. Hawthorn
19. Hemp
20. Huisache
21. Laurel
22. Madrone
23. Maize

24. Mesquite	30. Pecan	36. Prickly Pear
25. Mulberry	31. Persimmon	37. Tobacco
26. Oak	32. Peyote	38. Watermelon
27. Palm	33. Pine	39. Willow
28. Peach	34. Plum	40. Yucca
29. Pear	35. Pomegranate	

1. Agave (century plant, *mescal, maguey*)

Writing in the early 1600s, Fray Pérez de Ribas referred to agave as the "mescal plant" found in Sinaloa in northwest Mexico and near Laguna Grande de San Pedro in southern Coahuila (Pérez de Ribas, 6, 234). In northern Mexico the heads of agave were roasted in large pits and fermented to produce mescal or tequila (ibid., 6). Di Peso writes that Casas Grandes people baked agave hearts in their large ceremonial pit ovens (Di Peso, 2:619).

On Alarcón's 1718 expedition to Texas, the priest Mezquía reported finding maguey in Maverick County about twenty miles north of the Rio Grande (Hoffman, 313). Solís recorded maguey south of the Rio Grande in northern Coahuila (Forrestal 1931, 7, 8). Berlandier discusses the preparation of the plant to make pulque and mescal (Berlandier, 75, 528, 531).

Texas botanists Scooter Cheatham and Lynn Marshall review in detail the nine species of agave in Texas and the Southwest and provide maps illustrating the range of the several species in the United States and Mexico (Cheatham, Johnson, and Marshall, 1:135–169).

2. Amaranth (pigweed)

In 1535, on his march from the Rio Grande, crossing near Banderas below El Paso, westward across the northwestern Chihuahuan basin and range, Cabeza de Vaca visited people who for a third of the year ate nothing but "powdered grass," which was probably amaranth (Krieger, 224). In Oviedo's version of the same movement across Chihuahua, he wrote that Cabeza de Vaca's party ate powdered herbs (amaranth?) and killed many rabbits on their trek (ibid., 287). It should be noted that Spanish diarists in the 1530s were unfamiliar with and therefore could not identify many varieties of native North American plants such as amaranth.

In a recent archeological study of the area that Cabeza de Vaca traveled in northwest Chihuahua, researchers have uncovered evidence of domesticated amaranth under cultivation during the late Archaic period (Hard and Roney, 152).

Although Spanish expedition accounts seldom identify amaranth, ethnobotanists write that *amaranthus* species were among the most valuable seed plants in prehistoric cultures of North America. According to Cheatham, Johnson, and Marshall, domesticated and wild amaranth was found across northern Mexico, western Chihuahua (including Casas Grandes), New Mexico, and Texas (Cheatham, Johnson, and Marshall, 1:255–286). Di Peso writes that amaranth and cotton seed were grown at Casas Grandes for use in tamales (Di Peso, 2:618).

At the Watson Brake site in northern Louisiana, dated ca. 3400 BC, charred goosefoot (*chenopodium*), which, like amaranth, was a species later domesticated, was recovered during the excavation (Saunders, 1796–1799).

3. Apple (*manzano, pomme*)

In the spring of 1682 the French priest Zénobe Membré and La Salle's lieutenant, Henri de Tonty, reported finding apple trees at Acansa Indian villages near the junction of the Arkansas and Mississippi Rivers (Cox, 1:20, 141). Bolton writes that Spanish missions in northern Mexico cultivated apple trees along with other Old World fruit trees in the early 1600s (Bolton 1987, 20). Old World apple trees and other domesticated fruit trees found on the Mississippi and in East Texas by La Salle's chroniclers in the 1680s probably originated in Spanish mission orchards in northern Mexico and were traded across Texas along well-established Texas Indian trade routes that ran from Chihuahua and Nuevo León across South and Central Texas to the Caddo in East Texas and on to the Mississippi (Foster 2003, 40). Dunmire writes that Hernando Cortez ordered local Native workers in Mexico to plant apple orchards (Dunmire, 113).

4. Ash (*fresno*)

One of the earliest reports of ash along a Spanish expedition route was recorded in 1684 by Mendoza's diarist, who recorded the plant along Alamito Creek when his troops were marching from La Junta northward toward the Pecos River (Wade, 91). In January 1687 the French diarist Henri Joutel saw ash, along with oak and pecan, along the lower Navidad River about fifty miles north of Matagorda Bay (Foster 1998, 159).

The Spanish priest Isidro de Espinosa recorded ash growing in northern Mexico and in South Texas in the spring of 1709 (Tous, Mar. 1930, 3, 6). In 1768 Fray Gaspar de Solís found ash trees a few miles south of San Antonio in Bexar County (Kress, 53).

5. Beans (*haba, haricot*)

Spanish and French diarists and historians wrote that both wild beans and cultivated beans grew in the study area. In the fall of 1536 Cabeza de Vaca wrote that the Native people at La Junta grew maize, beans, squash, and gourds to hold water. He also wrote that La Junta people in West Texas cooked beans and squash in large gourds half filled with water heated by hot small stones from the campfire (Krieger, 222, 223). Cabeza de Vaca also found beans and maize cultivated by the Native people living near the Río Casas Grandes in northwestern Chihuahua (ibid., 225).

Pedro de Castañeda reported that the Teyas, whom Coronado met in the Texas Panhandle, had permanent large villages (one called Cona) where no maize or gourds were grown, but "grapes, beans, and plums" were available. As the grapes and plums were likely wild, the beans may have been as well. Coronado's chroniclers also recorded in Kansas that the Wichita Indians planted beans, maize, and melons but cultivated no cotton and kept no turkeys, as did the Pueblo people in New Mexico (Castañeda et al., 83, 84, 94, 112).

In June 1541 De Soto's chroniclers reported that in eastern Arkansas, Natives had maize, dried plums, wild beans, and squash and that the wild beans were large and better than the cultivated beans in Spain (Clayton, Knight, and Moore, 1:123, 128, 131, 133).

The chroniclers on the Chamuscado expedition in 1581 confirmed that beans, along with squash and some maize, were cultivated by the Indians at La Junta (Hammond and Rey 1966, 71). In the New Mexico pueblos located about 170 miles up the Rio Grande from present-day El Paso, Chamuscado wrote that Pueblo Indians cultivated large fields of beans, maize, squash, and cotton (ibid., 82).

Chroniclers on the Espejo expedition of 1582–1583 wrote that the La Junta Natives farmed their fields together, growing beans, maize, and squash. On Espejo's return trip to Parral in southern Chihuahua, the expedition was given beans, maize, and squash at a Native village located about twelve miles upstream on the Río Conchos from La Junta (ibid., 161, 172, 211, 216, 220).

The Spanish priest Andrés Pérez de Ribas recorded in the early 1600s that the Natives of Sinaloa in northwest Mexico cultivated a bean plant that was similar to the horse bean (*haba*) of Castile. He wrote that the Tepehuan were tillers of the soil and planted beans along with maize and pumpkins. He added that the Laguna Indians living near the Lagoon of San Pedro in southern Coahuila planted beans along with maize, pumpkins, chilies, and cotton (Pérez de Ribas, 6, 178, 226).

The Palaquechare Indians, who lived about twenty miles west of the present-day city of Navasota, told La Salle in 1687 that they planted beans along with maize when they were at a favorable location where they could remain for some time. While he was visiting the Hasinai Caddo, Joutel was fed a soup of beans "*de bresil*" (thought to be of a reddish brown color). Joutel added that he saw Assoni (Nasoni) men and women cultivating fields of beans, corn, and pumpkins and that the Caddo served the Frenchmen beans with bread and pumpkin (Foster 1998, 183, 207). On his journey from the Caddohadacho across Arkansas to the mouth of the Arkansas River, Joutel reported finding wild beans in the woods (ibid., 262).

On La Salle's trip down the Mississippi River in 1682, his lieutenant, Tonty, wrote that the Ojibwa women on the expedition found the same wild beans near the mouth of the Missouri River that they had known in New England (ibid., 98, 99, 102). On the same 1682 expedition, the priest Membré also commented on the large bean vines near the river (Cox, 1:155). Cheatham, Johnson, and Marshall note that North American Natives gathered at least two species of wild beans, the *Apios* and the *Amphicarpaea* (Cheatham, Johnson, and Marshall, 1:324, 384).

6. Blackberry and Dewberry (*zarzamora, mora, mûre*)

Spanish and French chroniclers seldom recognized the difference between the blackberry (*Rubus largus*), which grows above the ground on tall canes, and the dewberry (*Rubus texanus*), which grows on small vines near the ground. When Cabeza de Vaca visited the central Texas coast near Matagorda Bay, he wrote that he saw Indians eating berries (*moras*), probably dewberries (Krieger, 191). The Spanish historian Alonso de León (the elder) wrote that *zarzamoras* grew wild in Nuevo León near the Rio Grande (Duaine, 83).

Henri Joutel wrote that near Fort St. Louis "there are a great many wild berry bushes [probably dewberry] which in Normandy are called the 'Mulberry of the fox'" (Foster 1998, 125).

In the early 1700s the Spanish diarist Isidro de Espinosa identified *zarzamora* in northern Nuevo León (I. Espinosa, 673). In 1727 Rivera found *zarzamora* in Bexar County near San Antonio (Jackson, 112), and in 1767 Rubí reported wild berries at several locations in the Edwards Plateau (ibid., 111).

7. Bluewood Condalia (*brazil*, indigo)

Bluewood condalia or *brazil* (*Condalia obovata*) is a low bush or shrub with small bright and shiny green and reddish leaves and round black berries (Simpson, 110–111). The early Spanish historian Alonso de León listed *brazil* as one of the important food plants found in Nuevo León in the early 1600s (Duaine, 81). In 1716 Fray Espinosa recorded *brazil* near the Leona River south of present-day San Antonio (Tous, Apr. 1930, 7).

8. Bois d'Arc (Osage orange)

Bois d'arc (*Maclura pomifera*) was used by the Osage Indians and Indian tribes in northeast Texas to make bows. Joutel in 1687 wrote that the Caddohadacho in northeast Texas said that Indians from seventy-five miles away came to trade for bows that the Caddo made from the strong and colorful local bois d'arc wood (Foster 1998, 248). The tree has been in Texas for at least 8,000 years, according to a recent study at the Richard Beene site (41 BX 831) in Bexar County (Thoms and Mandel).

9. Cane (*otate, rotin*)

On La Salle's discovery expedition down the Mississippi in 1682, his chroniclers first recorded seeing an abundance of cane along the river on February 19 about thirty miles upriver from the mouth of the Ohio River. On April 6, about five miles upriver from the mouth of the Red River, La Salle's party cut large cane to construct an elevated platform to spend the night on the river. The Frenchmen did the same for overnight accommodations on April 13 near modern New Orleans. During La Salle's visit with the Taensa, his soldiers found the temple decorated with works made of cane and painted red inside. The diarist Nicolas de La Salle added: "Every night, two cane torches are lit inside" (Foster 2003, 96, 103, 111, 112, 114, 122).

On La Salle's expedition to Texas in 1685, Joutel wrote that east of Fort St. Louis the first large river (the modern Lavaca River) was named by the French "River of Canes" because of the heavy growth of cane along the riverbanks. As Joutel noted, La Salle himself later changed the name of the Cane River to the "Princess River" in honor of the young French girl called Princess whom Gabriel Minime, Sieur de Barbier, courted on the river and later married with La Salle's blessing. According to French tradition, the young teenage girls (often orphans) sent over by the government with French colonists and soldiers were called "The King's Daughters," thus, perhaps, the name "Princess."

On La Salle's last journey to the Caddo in 1687, Joutel described the thick cane brakes near the junction of the Navasota and the Brazos Rivers as "so thick they [La Salle's men] had to cut it in places to make an opening" (Foster 1998, 126, 155, 190).

On Captain Alonso de León's 1686 expedition to the mouth of the Rio Grande in search of La Salle, Chapa wrote that the party saw giant cane as thick as a man's leg (Chapa, 111). Governor Salinas Varona identified giant cane (*otate*) near the Trinity River in Leon County in 1693 (Foster and Jackson, 298). The Talon brothers said that the Karankawa made arrow shafts from the small cane on the Lavaca River (Weddle, 227).

10. Catclaw (*uña de gato*)

This shrub (*Acacia greggii*) is a thorny acacia found throughout the American Southwest. Terán reported it in 1691 about fifty miles south of the Rio Grande and again in Zavala County north of the river (Hatcher 11, 12). In December 1683 Mendoza found catclaw along with mesquite and lechuguilla along the route of his expedition down the Rio Grande near where the river borders present-day Jeff Davis County (Wade, 86). The Spanish priest Solís in 1768 recorded catclaw near Laredo (Kress, 34).

11. Cedar (*cedro, cedre*)

Joutel in 1687 reported that his small French party found groves of cedar along the lower Arkansas River that were similar to those found in Lebanon. He added that the Frenchmen at their post on the Arkansas River had constructed a house of juniper or cedar wood and had used cedar bark for roofing (Foster 1998, 264, 270).

Spanish expedition diarists noted that *cedro* was growing from Eagle Pass on the Rio Grande north to Kimble and Menard Counties and from there eastward to Bastrop County (Hatcher 14, 15, 61; Kinnaird, 144, 148, 149).

There is evidence that cedar has been a part of the Texas landscape for over 6,000 years, according to plant remains from the Varga site (41 ED 28; Quigg et al.).

12. Chestnut (chinquapin, *castaño*)

According to the historic record, American chestnut (*Castanea dentata*) was not found in Texas, but a species called chinquapin was reported, principally in East Texas. On De Soto's expedition in the 1540s the Gentleman from Elvas reported that across the Southeast, "Whenever there are mountains, there are chestnuts. They are somewhat smaller than those of Spain" (Clayton, Knight, and Moore, 1:170).

Espinosa described the chinquapin or chestnut tree and nut in some detail and wrote that the nut was small (I. Espinosa, 689). In 1718 Alarcón found *castaños* on the Trinity River, and three years later Aguayo reported the same (Hoffmann, 72). In 1768 Solís recorded seeing the tree near the Navasota River crossing and again near Nacogdoches (Kress, 59, 63).

13. Cotton (*algodonere*)

Botanists report that many centuries before Europeans explored the New World, domesticated cotton was cultivated in both the Old World and the Americas. New World cotton was grown in Mesoamerica in ca. 1700 BC, and by the first millennium or earlier, the plant was cultivated in the American Southwest (West, 439, 443).

Di Peso reports that cotton was grown and that cotton seeds were eaten at Casas Grandes (Di Peso, 8:314). Cotton was also used at Casas Grandes to fabricate textiles and to prepare cotton cordage and netting (ibid., 78). The cotton blankets (and copper bells) that the large trading party gave to Cabeza de Vaca in northern Coahuila likely originated in the Casas Grandes river valley (Krieger, 281). The cotton blankets (and turquoise) that Moscoso found among the Hasinai in 1542 also probably arrived via Indian trade connections along the same route from western Chihuahua across north-central Mexico and South Texas to the Hasinai Caddo (Clayton, Knight, and Moore, 1:148).

Coronado's chroniclers wrote that cotton was grown near Acoma and in other pueblo villages in the 1540s (Castañeda et al., 109). On the expeditions of Chamuscado in 1581 and Espejo in 1582–1583, cotton twine and cotton blankets were found among Indians living at La Junta and other settlements upriver along the Rio Grande in Texas, but no cotton was cultivated in Texas. In pueblo communities on the Rio Grande in New Mexico, expedition diarists recorded extensive cotton fields and cotton blankets (Hammond and Rey 1966, 74, 81, 82, 161, 172, 211).

In his history of the Native people of northwestern Mexico, the priest Ribas wrote that the Tepehuan dressed in either cotton or sisal fiber garments (Pérez de Ribas, 178). He also wrote that the Indians living near the Lagoon of San Pedro in southern Coahuila planted cotton along with maize, beans, pumpkins, and chilies (ibid., 226).

14. Cottonwood (*alamo*)

Cottonwood trees (*Populus fremontii*) were reported from northern Mexico to the Mississippi River. The Spanish historians Alonso de León (the elder) and Espinosa wrote that cottonwood trees were found in Nuevo León and Coahuila in the 1600s and 1700s (Duaine, 82; I. Espinosa 763). Bosque in 1675 identified cottonwood trees along with cedar, mesquite, and cypress on the Río Sabinas, which was named for the large cypress that today line the banks of the river in Coahuila (Wade, 28).

In 1682, about ten miles down the Mississippi River from the junction with the Arkansas River, La Salle saw a large number of trees that the diarist referred to as *trembles,* which were likely young cottonwoods (Foster 2003, 103, 105). Mendoza in 1683 reported cottonwood trees along his routes downstream on the Rio Grande in West Texas near Fort Hancock, a few days later near the Quitman Mountains, and again about seven miles upriver from modern-day Presidio (Wade, 83, 85, 89).

When Joutel reached the junction of the Arkansas and Mississippi Rivers in 1687, he identified the cottonwood as one of the trees growing along the riverbanks. Joutel wrote that "*cotonier* is called such because of a sort of cotton that falls on the water like down. Some of these grow very large" (Foster 1998, 278).

In 1691 Massanet recorded cottonwood in Bexar and Guadalupe Counties (Hackett, 54, 56). The same year, Captain Martínez wrote that cottonwood was growing on the Navidad River in Lavaca County. In 1716 Espinosa recorded the tree in Burleson County along the Brazos River and northeast in Nacogdoches County (Tous, Apr. 1930, 12, 13, 16).

15. Cypress (*sabina, savin, ciprés*)

Like cottonwood, cypress was reported during the study period from northern Mexico to the Mississippi. One of the earliest documentary recordings of cypress is found in Obregón's account of Ibarra's 1565 expedition to Casas Grandes. Obregón wrote that the Casas Grandes "is the most useful and beneficial of all the rivers we found in these provinces. Its shores are covered with beautiful and tall poplars, willows, and *savins.*" (Hammond and Rey 1928, 206). The historian Alonso de León (the elder) wrote that cypress was a prominent tree in Nuevo León in the early 1600s (Duaine, 82), and the historian's son reported cypress at the mouth of the Rio Grande (Chapa, 111). Espinosa described the *sabinas* along the major rivers in Coahuila (I. Espinosa, 761).

In May 1675 the Bosque diarist wrote that local Natives in northern Coahuila told him that the large, beautiful river they visited was called Río de las Sabinas (Wade, 29); the river has retained the name. In January 1684 Mendoza passed some *sabinas* along a creek a few miles south of present-day Marfa in the Trans-Pecos (ibid., 92).

Governor Alarcón in 1718 saw *sabinas* on the Medina River near San Antonio (Hoffman, 48), and in 1768 Fray Solís found cypress on the Brazos River in Burleson County (Kress, 57).

As an illustration of how long-term, cyclical climatic changes influence the range of trees, cypress trees grew as far north as St. Louis during the Medieval Warm period (ca. AD 900–1350), well beyond their current range (Foster 2003, 104n37).

16. Elm (*olmo, orme*)

La Salle's chroniclers noted that New England Loup Indians with La Salle's party constructed canoes of elm bark in early February 1682 while waiting to commence the expedition with the French party down the Mississippi River. On the expedition route in mid-March, La Salle found elm along with mulberry, peach, and plum trees near the junction of the Mississippi and Arkansas Rivers. The Old World peach trees were in bloom. By the time La Salle's party reached the area near Natchez in late March, the Loop Indians had made two more canoes of elm bark. On the lower Mississippi in present-day Louisiana, La Salle found elm, laurel, and mulberry trees with green mulberries (Foster 2003, 93, 102, 108, 114).

While La Salle was at Fort St. Louis on the central Texas coast in 1686, he asked a hunting party from the fort to secure some elm tree bark for use as roofing at the post. The hunting party found no elm that was rising or "in sap" at that time of year, so the bark could not be removed.

The following year, Joutel reported that another La Salle party found elm and pecan trees along the Navidad and Colorado Rivers and reported elm and aspen in East Texas (Foster 1998, 139, 159, 170, 234).

Espinosa wrote that *olmos* were in northern Coahuila in the early 1700s (I. Espinosa, 763). Captain Martínez found elm on the upper Navidad River in Fayette County in 1691. Later, in 1709, Espinosa reported the tree in Bexar and Travis Counties (Tous, Mar. 1930, 5, 7).

17. Grape (*parra, raisin*)

When Coronado visited the Texas Panhandle en route to Quivira, the Teyas Indians had wild grapes and "vineyards," which suggests that the grapes may have been cultivated. Coronado also saw grapes growing on the Arkansas River in central Kansas during his visit with the people of Quivira (Castañeda et al., 40, 43, 61, 117).

On De Soto's expedition, the Gentleman from Elvas compared the wild plum and grape found during the expedition. The chronicler claimed that local North American plums were better than those in Spain but that the grapes, although large, had large seeds and lacked cultivation (Clayton, Knight, and Moore, 1:170). One De Soto chronicler wrote that the local Indians dried grapes (raisins) for food on the lower Arkansas River (ibid., 2:422).

In 1565 Obregón wrote that wild grapes along with walnut trees, plum trees, and madrones were found along the Río Casas Grandes (Hammond and Rey 1928, 197). On Castaño's 1590 trek across West Texas, he found *parra* and some willow at a waterhole along the Pecos River near the New Mexico border (Schroeder and Matson, 63).

Ribas wrote that in the early 1600s *parras* grew between the community called Parras and San Pedro in southern Coahuila. This was in the land and lagoon area occupied by the Laguna Indians (Pérez de Ribas, 225). Espinosa said wild grapes were in Nuevo León in the early 1600s (I. Espinosa, 673).

In the spring of 1675, when the Basque expedition was in northern Coahuila, the party found "many stock of red grape . . . large like the ones in Castile." Mariah Wade, the translator and annotator of the expedition diary, suggests that the Spanish wording implies that there may have been purposeful pruning to produce larger fruit (Wade, 44).

Mendoza reported in 1684 that very beautiful grapevines were found on Alamito Creek about thirty miles north of the junction of the creek and the Rio Grande. When the expedition party reached the San Saba River near the present-day city of Menard, Mendoza's party again found wild grapes, along with wild plum and mulberry (ibid., 91, 115).

Grapes were reported by La Salle's chroniclers on his 1682 discovery expedition on the Mississippi River when the party reached the Acansa Indians near the junction of the Arkansas and Mississippi Rivers. The diarist Nicolas de La Salle wrote as follows: "They [the Acansa] gave us presents of maize, beans, and large quantity of dried fruit such as medlars, plums, and grapes for beverage. They crush the grapes in water and serve it as a drink" (Foster 2003, 102).

On his 1685 expedition to Texas, La Salle and his colonists found wild grapes near the fort on Matagorda Bay. Joutel wrote that "the grapes are pulpy and sour, unlike the ones in France." However, he added that colonists used the grape juice in preparing soups and stews. Joutel was probably referring to the mustang grape known as *Vitis mustangensis* (Foster 1998, 124). When Joutel reached the Acansa Indians, he mentioned that wild grapes grew in the area, confirming the earlier report by Nicholas de La Salle (ibid., 271).

18. Hawthorn (*tejocote*)

Joutel in 1685 described a tree that was near Fort St. Louis in Victoria County as bearing a small, rather mild-tasting red berry when ripe. Joutel added that the trees bore fruit up to twice a year. The hawthorn found near Matagorda Bay and inland has a small, edible red berry that ripens in May (see Vines, 334–387). The botanist Berlandier identified present-day Peach Creek in Gonzales County as Arroyo de los Tejocotes (Berlandier, 306–309).

The Spanish expedition leader Alarcón saw *tejocotes* in Burleson County in 1718 (Hoffman, 70). Today several species of hawthorn are found across Texas (Simpson, 128).

19. Hemp (*canamo*)

Hemp was reported growing wild from the Mississippi River west across much of Texas and Coahuila during the study period and into the 1700s. The fiber from the plant was used to make cloth and rope. The widely cultivated herb (*Cannabis sativa*) also forms the basis of the narcotic drug marijuana. The priest Membré wrote in 1682 that hemp was seen growing wild near the lower Mississippi River (Cox, 1:155). Fray Espinosa recorded hemp growing in open fields in Coahuila in the early 1700s (I. Espinosa, 763). Hemp was reported in Hays

County (Tous, Mar. 1930, 13), Zavala County (Hoffman, 45), and Wilson County (Kress, 53).

20. Huisache (*huisache, guisache*)

Several Spanish expedition accounts identify huisache (*Acacia farnesiana*) in northern Mexico. On the Bosque-Larios expedition of 1675, the diarist recorded *guisaches* about fifteen to eighteen miles northwest Eagle Pass (Wade, 31). Rivera in 1727 reported the plant in Chihuahua and Coahuila (Jackson, 21, 25). Solís in 1768 recorded huisache north of the Rio Grande in Texas near Laredo (Kress, 36), in Live Oak County (ibid.), and along the San Antonio River in Karnes, Wilson, and Bexar Counties (ibid., 48, 49).

21. Laurel (*laurel, laurier*)

French and Spanish diarists identify the mescal bean sophora (*Sophora ecundiflora*) as laurel. In the early 1600s Alonso de León (the elder) recorded *laureles* in northern Nuevo León (Duaine, 81). In 1682 the French diarist Nicolas de La Salle saw laurel with elm and mulberry trees along the Mississippi about twenty-five miles downstream from New Orleans (Foster 2003, 114). Solís in 1768 found the small tree along the Brazos River near the Burleson-Brazos county line (Kress, 57).

22. Madrone (*madroño*)

Obregón, who served as diarist on Ibarra's 1565 expedition into northwestern Chihuahua, identified the distinctive reddish madrone trees (Hammond and Rey 1928, 197), which are found in the same area today as well as in areas of West Texas (Cheatham, Johnson, and Marshall, 1:430–434). Espinosa recorded madrone in Nuevo León in the early 1700s (I. Espinosa, 723).

23. Maize (corn)

Some of the earliest dates for the domestication of maize in northern Mexico come from southern Tamaulipas, the modern Mexican state south of the Texas border along the Gulf of Mexico. The archeological record indicates that maize was cultivated in Tamaulipas in ca. 3000 BC and that maize cultivation continued in the region into the historic period (West, 431–432). In contrast, the historic and archeological record indicates that no maize or any other cultigen was cultivated north of Tamaulipas in South Texas.

It appears that maize cultivation spread north from Mesoamerica to the American Southwest by or before 1000 BC (Hard and Roney, 141). Maize was grown on the Mississippi River and in the northeast woodlands as early as 200 BC. However, tropical maize did not become a central part of the Mississippian diet until much later, perhaps by ca. AD 1200.

The spread of maize cultivation into the American Southwest is confirmed by the detailed archeological studies of the Casas Grandes region covering the period ca. AD 900–1500 (Di Peso et al., 8:247; 308–314, 320–321). The studies suggest that during the earlier phase, ca. AD 900 to 1200, maize was cultivated but that only after 1200 did maize become an important element in the diet of the Casas Grandes people.

Some of the earliest documentary references to maize cultivation in North America come from Cabeza de Vaca's trip across the continent between 1528 and 1536. Soon after landing on the west coast of Florida, Cabeza de Vaca and his soldiers found maize growing and stored in northern Florida (Krieger, 165). After moving along the Gulf Coast and arriving on the Texas coast, the Spaniards found no more maize under cultivation. It was not until September 1535, when Cabeza de Vaca's small four-man party crossed the Rio Grande into Coahuila, Mexico, that the Spaniards again were given maize; it had apparently been grown elsewhere toward the coast, perhaps in the Río Casas Grandes region. Several months later at the junction of the Río Conchos and Rio Grande, Cabeza de Vaca found Indians who cultivated maize, beans, and squash, as had the Florida Indians who lived about 1,300 miles to the east. The Spanish party thereafter found maize, beans, and squash cultivated in northwestern Chihuahua on the Río Casas Grandes and along his route farther west toward the Pacific (ibid., 216, 222, 225).

De Soto's expedition chroniclers confirmed that maize was cultivated not only across the Southeast and to the Mississippi but farther west up the Arkansas River to at least the Oklahoma state line. They also confirmed that maize was cultivated in East Texas but not west of the Colorado River. On Moscoso's return voyage along the Texas coast in 1543, when the Spaniards were sailing to Pánuco, some Indians, perhaps those living near Galveston Bay, also had maize to trade, suggesting that at that time some Indians in southeast Texas may have been cultivating maize (Clayton, Knight, and Moore, 1:111, 123, 133, 308).

While De Soto was searching for riches in the Southeast and East Texas, Coronado explored the Southwest and Central Plains. Coronado found maize cultivation in the Southwest and in central Kansas at Quivira. Although some researchers have interpreted passages in Coronado's accounts as suggesting horticulture was practiced in the Texas Panhandle at the time, there is no clear evidence that maize was being cultivated (Castañeda et al., 52, 56, 83, 84, 94, 104, 112).

The Spanish expeditions of the early 1580s in the Trans-Pecos and New Mexico by Chamuscado and Espejo confirm that maize was grown at La Junta and upriver but not along the lower Pecos River in Texas (Hammond and Rey 1966, 161, 162, 211, 172, 215, 216, 220).

In the early 1600s Ribas wrote that the Native people of Sinaloa and the Tepeguan living to the south of Sinoloa cultivated maize along with beans and pumpkins. Farther east, the Laguna Indians living in southern Coahuila were horticulturists who grew maize and other cultigens as well (Pérez de Ribas, 6, 178, 226).

On La Salle's discovery expedition down the Mississippi River in 1682, his several chroniclers detailed that maize was grown by Native tribes living from the Great Lakes area to the lower Mississippi River (Foster 2003, 92, 112, 117, 122). In 1686 La Salle brought maize that had been grown by the East Texas Caddo back to Fort St. Louis on the central Texas coast, where maize was not cultivated by Native people. Joutel's account suggests, however, that some Natives living one hundred miles or more inland from the coast between the Colorado and Brazos Rivers did on occasion plant maize (Foster 1998, 147).

24. Mesquite (*mezquite*)

One of the earliest references to mesquite in Spanish expedition documents was made during Cabeza de Vaca's crossing the Rio Grande into South Texas in August 1535 (Krieger, 278–279). When the 1581 Chamuscado expedition first reached the Rio Grande at La Junta, local Indians gave the Spaniards ground mesquite beans (Hammond and Rey 1966, 70, 71). In 1590 Castaño's party reported finding mesquite along the Pecos River near Sheffield, Texas (Schroeder and Matson, 57).

Ribas wrote that mesquite beans were an important form of sustenance for Natives living in Sinaloa, particularly during May and June of each year. The priest added that the Laguna Indians in southern Coahuila would grind mesquite beans into a flour for bread (Pérez de Ribas, 6, 226, 234).

The diarist on the Bosque 1675 expedition wrote that large groves of mesquite were along the Nadadores River in northern Coahuila, and Mendosa in 1683 reported mesquite along the Rio Grande near the Jeff Davis county line (Wade, 28, 86).

According to the Texas naturalist Roy Bedichek, mesquite is not native to Texas and was introduced into Texas from northern Mexico in the last 200 years. This comment is proven false by several Spanish expedition accounts, which report extensive concentrations of mesquite north of the Rio Grande over 300 years ago, some near Waco (over 300 miles north of the Rio Grande) in 1719 (Foster 1995, 254). A recent recovery of the remains of mesquite at the Varga site (41 ED 28) indicates that the plant has been a resident of Texas for over 6,000 years.

25. Mulberry (*moral*)

Coronado found groves of mulberry trees in the Texas Panhandle near the Teyas village called Cona. Coronado again found mulberry trees growing along with wild plum trees and grapevines among the Wichita villages in central Kansas (Castañeda et al., 40, 61).

Mulberry and wild plum trees were found at the same time by De Soto in Arkansas soon after crossing the Mississippi. Mulberry trees, the Gentleman from Elvas wrote, seemed to be set out in orchards and in a cleared grove. Later, in making the brigantine ships near the junction of the Arkansas and Mississippi Rivers, the Spaniards used rope made from the bark of local mulberry trees (Clayton, Knight, and Moore, 1:114, 152).

In the early 1600s Alonso de León (the elder) reported that mulberry trees (*morales*) were found in northern Nuevo León (Duaine, 83), and Espinosa recorded the tree in northern Coahuila in the early 1700s (I. Espinosa, 763). Spanish expedition diarists in the 1700s reported mulberry trees in the San Antonio area and on the lower Colorado River (Hatcher, 54, 61).

La Salle's chroniclers wrote that mulberry trees grew along with elm, domesticated peach, and domesticated plum trees close to the Acansa Indian villages near the junction of the Arkansas and Mississippi Rivers. Tonty and the French priest Membré said that the cottonlike material that the Taensa and Natchez Indians used for garments was made from mulberry tree bark (Cox, 1:21, 140). La Salle continued to find mulberry trees farther down the Mississippi until the party reached the area in which the river forms three branches (Foster 2003, 102, 114).

Joutel commented in 1687 that the area near the junction of the Navasota and Brazos Rivers would be suitable for raising silkworms because there were so many mulberry trees in the area. He added that the mulberry trees and leaves were much larger than those in France. Joutel also commented that the Indians used mulberry tree bark in the construction of huts as well as rope. When Joutel's party reached the Acansa, he again noted that mulberry trees were plentiful and the fruit very good (Foster 1998, 189, 271).

26. Oak (*encino*)

On Mendoza's 1684 expedition, his diarist recorded finding numerous very large *encinos* near Marfa and later near San Angelo. He said that the trees were so large at their base that wagon wheels could be made of the trunks (Wade, 92, 93, 106, 108).

On La Salle's trip down the Mississippi River in 1682, his diarist recorded finding oak trees between the Missouri River and Natchez (Foster 2003, 96, 99). With La Salle in 1687, Joutel recorded finding oaks from the central Texas coast to the Caddo country in East Texas, where Joutel said the oaks were smaller than those he had seen earlier because the soil was better near the coast (Foster 1998, 169, 204).

Spanish expedition diarists in the late 1600s and early 1700s recorded oaks from Zavala County near the Rio Grande to the San Antonio area (Hatcher, 14; Tous, Mar. 1930, 3, 4, 5).

Recent archeological studies from the Varga site (41 ED 28) indicate that oak was present in Texas as early as 4000 BC.

27. Palm (*palma*)

On the La Salle expedition down the Mississippi River in 1682, the accompanying priest Membré noted that where the Taensa lived in northeast Louisiana "the whole country is covered with palm trees" (Cox, 1:141). This may be a reference to the small, low dwarf palm found in the area today.

On La Salle's expedition to Texas, Joutel wrote of seeing many palm trees on the Cuban island he called "The Island of Pines" and later on the central Texas coast. Cheatham, Johnson, and Marshall comment that Joutel's description of palm trees on Garcitas Creek near Matagorda Bay may refer to *Sabal texana* (Foster 1998, 64, 124).

Chapa wrote that De León found large *palmas* near the mouth of the Rio Grande in 1686 (Chapa, 130). Both Espinosa and Solís use the Spanish word *palmito* to identify the trunkless palmetto (Kress, 34, 36; I. Espinosa, 763). The frequent recovery of petrified trunks of palm on the lower Colorado River suggests that the plant is a long-term resident of Central Texas.

28. Peach

Peach trees mentioned in Spanish and French expedition documents refer to Old World domesticated fruit trees brought to North America by Spaniards and other Europeans in the early 1500s. Peach trees are not native to the Americas. As Benavides wrote, European peach trees were planted in the early 1600s at Catholic missions in northern Mexico (Ayer, 36). Dunmire notes that peach trees were planted at Texas missions as well (Dunmire, 230).

On La Salle's trip down the Mississippi in 1682, the explorer found that peach trees, along with plum and mulberry trees, were cultivated by the Acansa Indians near the junction of the Arkansas and Mississippi Rivers. According to the priest Membré, the Taensa Indians, who also lived on the west side of the Mississippi River, had peach orchards (Cox, 1:155, 156). Joutel in 1687 confirmed La Salle's 1682 reports of peach orchards at Acansa villages on the Mississippi (Foster 1998, 270, 277, 280).

29. Pear

The priest Membré wrote that the Taensa Indians living on the west side of the lower Mississippi River had domesticated Old World pear trees as well as apple and peach trees (Cox, 1:141). According to Bolton, pear, apple, and peach trees were grown in Spanish missions in northern Mexico and New Mexico (Bolton 1916, 58, 59). Dunmire says that Cortez directed Indian workers to plant pear, peach, apple, and plum orchards (Dunmire, 113).

30. Pecan (*nogal, nueces*)

In most sixteenth- and seventeenth-century Spanish and French expedition documents, the diarists do not identify which species of the nut tree—pecan, walnut, or hickory—was observed. For example, Cabeza de Vaca wrote, when he was living along the lower Guadalupe River, that for two months of each year the local Indians ate primarily local nuts (probably pecans) as their food. He said that the nut trees were very large and numerous but that they bore nuts only every other year (Krieger, 189, 190). In 1541 Coronado found nut trees, probably walnut, in the Texas Panhandle (Castañeda et al., 40). Remains of both pecan and walnut have been recently found at the Varga site (41 ED 28), dated ca. 4000 BC.

On the De Soto expedition in 1542, diarists recorded many nut trees with "soft nuts shaped like acorns" about twenty miles west of the Mississippi River in Arkansas. The Spaniards also wrote that Indians stored nuts along with maize and dried wild plums for use during the winter (Clayton, Knight, and Moore, 1:141, 128).

Governor De León in 1690 recorded finding nut trees (*nueces*) along the Nueces River (Chapa, 157). Bosque saw nut trees near the Rio Grande crossing in 1675, and Mendoza's party in 1684 reported that on the middle Concho River they saw their first nut trees of the expedition (Wade, 48, 106). Nut trees were frequently seen in the area thereafter.

On his 1682 expedition down the Mississippi, La Salle's party reported nut trees with maple and wild plum trees along the Mississippi River about fifty miles below the mouth of the Missouri River (Foster 2003, 96). During La Salle's expedition to Texas in 1684–1687, his party found nut trees along Cummins Creek in Fayette County, near the Trinity River in Houston County, and again in the Neches River area (Foster 1998, 181, 234, 236).

Spanish historians report that nut trees (*nogales*) grew in both northern Nuevo León and Coahuila (Duaine, 83; I. Espinosa, 763). Spanish diarists wrote that *nogales* were seen along the San Antonio River in Karnes County, on the Llano River in the Edwards Plateau, on the Trinity River near Nacogdoches, and near Los Adaes in western Louisiana (Bolton 1987, 393; Hoffmann, 47, 71, 80, 81; Kinnaird, 149).

31. Persimmon (medlar, *níspero, zapote, chapote*)

The small persimmon tree (*Diospyros*), called "medlar" or *níspero,* is a native fruit tree that was reported across northern Mexico and Texas and on eastward to the Mississippi River. In 1682 La Salle and his men referred to the tree as a medlar when they saw it near the mouth of the Arkansas River (Foster 2003, 102). Joutel wrote that the Acansa called a French medlar-looking tree a *pia-guiminia,* which he said was better-tasting and more delicate than the French version (Foster 1998, 271).

Espinosa wrote that *nísperos* were in northern Coahuila, and he identified some small fruit trees in Central Texas as similar to *nísperos* in Spain (I. Espinosa, 763; Tous 1930, 11). Solís recorded *nísperos* near the Brazos crossing in Burleson County and again later when he crossed the Sabine River into Louisiana (Kress, 57, 63).

32. Peyote

A 2003 study of rock art on the lower Pecos includes a map reflecting the current range of peyote in North America. The map indicates that peyote is presently found growing wild along the Rio Grande from La Junta east to Corpus Christi and southward to Torreón, San Luis Potosí, and Monterrey in Mexico (Boyd, 71). According to studies of peyote prepared for Di Peso, the range of peyote in the 1200s extended farther west to include Deming, New Mexico (Di Peso, 1:220n2).

The early Spanish historian Fray Pérez de Ribas described the use of peyote during the early decades of the 1600s among the Laguna Indians in southern Coahuila. The padre wrote: "To all of these orgies must be added their habit of drinking, which was much practiced by them during their long period of spiritual darkness. Into this drinking they had introduced the use of the herb called peyote, before referred to, which is very celebrated among the Indians of the Nations of New Spain and which, although considered to hold certain medicinal properties when taken in moderation, when taken in excess causes derangement of the mind, bringing diabolical fantasies to the imagination" (Pérez de Ribas, 227).

According to the anthropologist and ethnohistorian Mariah Wade, the native population in Coahuila at the mission San Buenaventura de las Quarto Ciénegas in the 1670s danced and drank a beverage made of peyote and a small bean, or *peyote y frijolillo* (Wade, 64).

Di Peso writes that the Suma Indians who lived on the Rio Grande between El Paso and La Junta and along the Río Casas Grandes in the late 1600s "were known to be prone to peyote and used it in many of their ceremonials and at a number of their dances" (Di Peso, 3:915). The same was written about the Chichimecans living farther south (ibid., 1:220).

The Spanish historian Bernardino de Sahagún wrote in 1569 that peyote was a discovery of the Aztec. He says the Aztec people preferred peyote to wine or mushrooms. Peyote came from the desert, Sahagún wrote, and there the people ate it and danced and sang all night (ibid.).

Di Peso also notes that the peyote motif was used by Casas Grandes potters to decorate their polychrome bowls. He adds that the "ticked, counterclockwise spiral found on Casas Grandes pottery is today a peyote symbol among the Huichol" (ibid., 2:573).

33. Pine (*pino*)

Cabeza de Vaca reported finding small pine trees (*Pinus*) in northern Coahuila, and he wrote that the trees had better nuts than those of Castile because of their very thin shells. This passage and description of the pine nut has helped identify Cabeza de Vaca's route in Coahuila (Krieger, 217, 282).

Coronado's diarist reported that the Cibola (Zuni) gathered pine nuts each year and stored them. The diarist made the same remark regarding the Pueblo people living along the upper Rio Grande (Castañeda et al., 52, 55, 56). In the 1620s Benavides wrote that the pine trees and nuts in New Mexico were different from those in Spain, where the pine trees were larger but the nuts not as large and not as easy to crack (Ayer, 36).

A number of Spanish expedition diarists recorded rich, tall pine forests in East Texas (Bolton 1916, 415; Santos, 52). Governor Alonso de León in 1687 noted pine trees (*pinos*) near the mouth of the Rio Grande (Chapa, 111). On Mendoza's expedition to the Edwards Plateau in 1684, his diarist recorded finding many pine trees at an encampment that has been located on a west-flowing tributary of the North Llano Draw (Wade, 119).

A recent archeological study at the Varga site (41 ED 28) indicates that pine was present in Texas at least 6,000 years ago.

34. Plum (*ciruela*)

Wild plum trees (*Prunus mexicana*) are native to North America and were reported from the Southeast across Texas to northern Mexico and New Mexico. In 1542 Castañeda wrote that wild plum trees were found in the country of the Teyas in the Texas Panhandle, and Coronado's party found more in central Kansas with the Wichita Indians at Quivira (Castañeda et al., 40, 41, 61, 117). Pierre Le Moyne d'Iberville saw wild plum soon after landing in Louisiana (Mc-Williams, 43).

Farther south, near Casas Grandes, Obregón reported finding wild plum trees in 1565 along with large madrone trees and wild grapes (Hammond and Rey 1928, 197). Benavides wrote that domesticated plum trees were planted at missions in New Mexico in the 1620s (Ayer, 36).

On De Soto's travels across the Southeast, his diarist, the Gentleman from Elvas, recorded finding wild plum trees, and after crossing the Mississippi River, the diarist again identified wild plum groves in Arkansas (Clayton, Knight, and Moore, 1:112, 114, 120, 170).

On La Salle's 1682 trip down the Mississippi River, his party discovered wild plum trees on the riverbanks about fifty miles south of the mouth of the Missouri River and later at the junction of the Arkansas and Mississippi Rivers (Foster 2003, 96, 102). Both the Frenchman Tonty and the priest Membré confirmed that domesticated plum trees and fruit tree orchards were cultivated by the Acansa Indians near the Arkansas River and by the Taensa Indians (Cox, 1:20, 137, 141).

Mendoza in 1684 found numerous groves of wild plum trees on the Texas San Saba River and on the North Llano Draw (Wade, 115, 119).

On La Salle's 1685–1687 expedition to Texas, his diarist, Joutel, wrote that when he reached the Acansa Indians on the Mississippi, he found "a large number of plum trees; in France I have seen many places where the plums were not as good" (Foster 1998, 270, 277, 280).

35. Pomegranate (*granaditas de China*)

Pomegranate trees (*Punicaceae*) are native to China and known throughout the Old World. The plant was brought, along with other Old World fruit, to the Americas by the Spaniards, who planted pomegranate trees in mission orchards and Spanish outposts in northern Mexico (Bolton, 20). William W. Dunmire writes that pomegranate seeds were brought to Mexico and planted in the city of Pueblo in the 1530s. The author says the plant became the national emblem of

Spain and was planted in St. Augustine, Florida, in the 1560s (Dunmire, 116, 133, 292).

One of the most intriguing discoveries by La Salle on his 1682 expedition down the Mississippi was that Native Americans were growing European fruit trees, including pomegranate, before French explorers arrived. The priest Membré wrote that pomegranate trees along with peach trees were cultivated by the Acansa Indians (Cox, 1:165). In 1673, nine years before La Salle's expedition, the French explorer Louis Jolliet and the priest Jacques Marquette canoed down the Mississippi as far as the Arkansas River and reported finding pomegranate along with apple and plum trees being grown by Indians near the Arkansas River (Margry, 1:259–270).

Bolton writes that the East Texas Hasinai Caddo grew pomegranates (Bolton 1987, 96). Solís, who visited the area in 1768, gave several reports of pomegranates in East Texas. He observed "pomegranates in abundance" along the Camino Real on April 23, 1768, and again near the crossing of the Brazos River on April 25. Moving farther eastward on April 27, he recorded crossing the Navasota River and again finding pomegranate trees. After arriving at the Hasinai village, he reported that they had pomegranates, peaches, and plums in their orchards (Kress, 53–56). These recorded sightings of pomegranate trees along the Camino Real may represent present-day physical evidence of the Camino Real route because apparently pomegranate trees in the wild sponsor independent growth from fallen fruit.

36. Prickly pear (*nopal*)

Cabeza de Vaca wrote that the fruit (tuna) of the prickly pear cactus (*Opuntia lindheimeri*) was the size of an egg, red and black in color, and very good in flavor. He added that in South Texas the Indians ate tuna and nothing else for three months each year (Krieger, 190, 195). Ribas reported that the prickly pear found in Sinaloa was similar to the fruit in Spain, called "figs of the Indies." The priest said that in the Central Plateau of Mexico, near Mapimi, the Natives ate the fruit of the *nopal* and yucca, roasted mescal beans, and pods of the mesquite tree (Pérez de Ribas, 6, 234).

Alonso de León (the elder) wrote that the Indians in Nuevo León ate the fruit of the *nopal* (Duaine, 67). Joutel wrote about the prickly pear in the Texas coastal area and said the plant was of the same species as cactus found in France and the West Indies. He added that the pads of the prickly pear were called *raquettes* in French because of their racket shape. One French soldier at Fort St. Louis died from eating the fruit without first wiping it to remove the small thorns (Foster 1998, 124).

Recent studies indicate that prickly pear has been present in Texas for over 6,000 years (Quigg et al.).

37. Tobacco (*piciete, nicotina*)

Espejo in 1593 wrote that the Piro Indians in central New Mexico planted tobacco along with corn, beans, and calabashes (Hammond and Rey 1966, 220). Espinosa reported that the Hasinai cultivated tobacco (Tous 1930, 20). Joutel wrote that the Frenchmen in his party were offered tobacco to smoke at several Caddo villages and by the Acansa Indians on the Mississippi (Foster 1998, 254, 264, 272).

38. Watermelon (*sandía*)

Watermelon is one of several melons brought to the New World by Spanish explorers. Spanish missions and outposts in Nueva Vizcaya in the 1560s cultivated watermelons, and local Conchos Indians, who worked in mission orchards, were also cultivating watermelons on the upper Río Conchos by the 1580s (Hammond and Rey 1966, 215). Benavides confirmed that watermelons were grown in New Mexico in the early 1600s (Ayer, 36). Joutel reported that watermelon was cultivated by the Caddo and the Acansa on the Mississippi in 1687 (Foster 1998, 147, 263).

39. Willow (*sauz, sauce, mimbre*)

When Obregón visited Casas Grandes in northwest Chihuahua in 1565, the diarist recorded tall willows and cypress along the Río Casas Grandes (Hammond and Rey 1928, 206). In 1590 Castaño discovered some extremely large willows (*mimbres*) around a pond near the Texas-New Mexico state line (Hammond and Rey 1966, 261).

In 1581 Chamuscado's party observed that the La Junta Indians on the Rio Grande built their granaries of willow, "after the fashion of the Mexicans [Aztec]" (ibid., 75). On the 1675 Bosque expedition, the party found willows at the lower Rio Grande crossing near modern Normandy, Texas (Wade, 31).

On his 1685 expedition to Texas with La Salle, Joutel wrote of finding willows near the French fort on Garcitas Creek, at the Colorado River crossing in Fayette County, and also near the junction of the Arkansas and Mississippi Rivers (Foster 1998, 148, 170, 278).

40. Yucca (Spanish dagger, *palma pita*)

The Spanish priest Ribas, writing in the early 1600s, said that the Indians of the Laguna Grande de San Pedro in southern Coahuila, near the border with Chihuahua, ate the fruit of the yucca and the *nopal* cactus (Pérez de Ribas, 233, 234).

Joutel described the yucca found near the fort on Matagorda Bay as follows: "The leaves are pointed and stiff, formed like spouts, and they must not be approached abruptly because they pierce material and skin. This tree has a tall stalk which flowers and forms a rather beautiful cluster of white flowers with a tinge of yellow" (Foster 1998, 124, 125).

Di Peso writes that the Casas Grandes people used yucca fiber as a brush to paint ceramic vessels (Di Peso, 2:534).

NOTES

Introduction

1. Klein and Edgar, *The Dawn of Human Culture*, 235–237. The conclusion that the ancestors of Native Americans or Indians immigrated to North and South America is widely accepted by contemporary anthropologists, archeologists, geneticists, linguists, and other scientists. However, it is recognized that this conclusion is not accepted by some Native Americans or by others who subscribe to an incompatible world view.

2. For purposes of this study, the following chronological time periods will be observed: Paleo-Indian (ca. 11,500 BC to 8,000 BC); Early, Middle, and Late Archaic (ca. 8,000 BC to AD 800); and Prehistoric (ca. AD 800 to 1500).

3. Dillehay, *The Settlement of the Americas*, 14.

4. Ibid., 12.

5. Klein, *The Human Career*, 540, 542.

6. Ibid., 409–415, 520, 542. See Klein and Edgar, *The Dawn of Human Culture*, 238. Brian M. Fagan concludes that the Clovis tool kit and Clovis core and blade technology came from modern *H. sapiens* in Europe. Fagan, *People of the Earth*, 9th ed. (New York: Addison Wesley Longman, 1997), 130, 190. More cautiously, Michael B. Collins writes as follows: "It seems plausible that Clovis blade technology is ultimately derived from the often very similar ones in Upper Paleolithic cultures of Eurasia, even though independent invention is not an impossibility." Collins, *Clovis Blade Technology*, 179.

7. Tattersall and Schwartz, *Extinct Humans*, 239–241.

8. Ibid., 237–239.

9. Ibid., 238–239.

10. Olson, *Mapping Human History*, 86–89. Tattersall and Schwartz, *Extinct Humans*, 236–237.

11. Arsuaga, *The Neanderthal Necklace*, 294.

12. See ibid., 292; Olson, *Mapping Human History*, 86.

13. A recent study of sea-level history in the Gulf of Mexico indicates that about 20,000 years ago the sea level was about 125 meters lower than it is today. See Balsillie and Donoghue, *High Resolution Sea-Level History*, Figs. 8 and 9, 9–16. If true, the central Texas Gulf coastline of 20,000 years ago was along a line that was over 200 miles seaward from the current coastline off Galveston and about 100 miles off Brownsville. See U.S. Department of Commerce, National Oceanic and Atmospheric Administration,

National Ocean Service, "Galveston to Rio Grande," United States Coast Survey Nautical Chart 11300. Washington, D.C., N.d.

14. Perttula, ed., *The Prehistory of Texas*, 16–17.

15. See Quigg et al., *The Varga Site*; and Thoms and Mandel, eds., *Archeological and Paleoecological Investigations at the Richard Beene Site 41BX831*.

16. Flannery, *The Eternal Frontier*, 194–205.

17. Elias, *Rocky Mountains*, 33–36, 88–95. For a list of the types of animals inhabiting Europe, the Middle East, and Asia during the last Ice Age, see Stringer and Gamble, *In Search of the Neanderthals*, 53.

18. Flannery, *The Eternal Frontier*, 218–229.

19. Harris, *Late Pleistocene Vertebrate Paleoecology of the West*, 184, 185, 189, 191.

20. Flannery, *The Eternal Frontier*, 124, 138, 142, 162, 164, 172, 222.

21. Ibid., 161.

22. Davis and Schmidly, *The Mammals of Texas*, 255–263.

23. Dillehay comments on the synchronized global timing of the development of agriculture as follows: "What makes the New World so fascinating is that the first impulse of human civilization developed within just a few millennia after human arrival. It is a curious and provocative fact of world prehistory that agriculture and early civilization appears independently in China, Mesopotamia, South and Southeast Asia, and parts of the Americas at almost the same time." Dillehay, *The Settlement of the Americas*, 287–288.

24. Wells, *The Journey of Man*, 148–151.

25. See Saunders et al., "A Mound Complex in Louisiana at 5400–5000 years Before the Present," 1796–1799. For a review of Watson Brake site in the larger contest of mound construction in the Southeast in the Middle Archaic, see Michael Russo, "Southeastern Archaic Mounds," in *Archeology of the Mid-Holocene Southeast*, ed. Kenneth E. Sassaman and David G. Anderson (Gainesville: University Press of Florida: 1996), 279–285.

26. See Jay K. Johnson, "Beads, Microdrills, Bifaces, and Blades from Watson Brake," *Southeastern Archaeology* 19, no. 2 (2000): 95–104. See also Samuel O. Brookes, "Cultural Complexity in the Middle Archaic of Mississippi," in Gibson and Carr, eds., *Signs of Power*, 97–113.

27. Recent studies indicate that tropical domesticated cultigens, including maize and amaranth from central Mexico, reached the American Southwest by ca. 1200 BC or earlier. See Hard and Roney, "The Transition to Farming on the Rio Casas Grandes and in the Southern Jornada Mogollon Region," 141–186.

28. See Neitzel, ed., *Great Towns and Regional Polities*, 3–4.

29. Ibid., 3–38.

30. Timothy R. Pauketat projects that greater Cahokia had a population of about 31,000 in ca. AD 1100; Stephen H. Lekson et al. project that great Casas Grandes had a population of about 95,000 in ca. AD 1400. See Pauketat, *Ancient Cahokia and the Mississippians*, 96, 108, and Stephen H. Lekson, Michael Bletzer, and A. C. MacWilliams, "Pueblo IV in the Chihuahua Deserts," in Adams and Duff, eds., *The Protohistoric Pueblo World*, 60–61.

31. See George R. Holley and Stephan H. Lekson, "Comparing Southwestern and Southeastern Great Towns," in Neitzel, ed., *Great Towns and Regional Polities*, 39–44.

32. See Vivian, *The Chacoan Prehistory of the San Juan Basin*.

33. See Di Peso, Rinaldo, and Fenner, *Casas Grandes*, 4:123–471.

34. Doolittle, *Canal Irrigation in Prehistoric Mexico*, 84–90. See also Doolittle, *Cultivated Landscapes of Native North America*, 388–389.

35. Brody, *Mimbres Painted Pottery*.

36. See Di Peso, *Casas Grandes*, 2:407–409, and Sally A. Chappell, *Cahokia, Mirror of the Cosmos* (Chicago: University of Chicago Press, 2002), 158–160.

37. For a discussion of interregional trade between the Southwest and the Mississippi centers during the late prehistoric, see Foster, *The La Salle Expedition on the Mississippi River*, 32–89.

38. Diamond, *Collapse*, 219. Steven LeBlanc reviews the arguments that the Medieval Warm period and the Little Ice Age had a direct bearing on the Native population and cultural centers in the Southwest. See LeBlanc, *Prehistoric Warfare in the American Southwest*, 34–36.

39. LeBlanc, *Constant Battles*, 149. See also Burroughs, *Climate Change in Prehistory*, 239.

40. A 2004 study of the history of sea-level change over the past 20,000 years in the Gulf of Mexico and along the Texas coast clearly indicates that the Medieval Warm period and the Little Ice Age impacted the climate in Texas. See Balsillie and Donoghue, *High Resolution Sea-Level History*, Figs. 11 and 20. The study pinpoints the dates of the Medieval Warm period and the Little Ice Age on the Gulf Coast. The study indicates that the sea level in the Gulf of Mexico rose about six feet during the Medieval Warm period (ca. AD 900–1300) and fell about ten feet during the Little Ice Age (ca. AD 1350–1850). The authors note that information on sea-level change in the Gulf of Mexico is almost identical to reports on sea-level change during the same time periods at locations on the Red Sea.

41. For a different interpretation, see Huebner, "Late Prehistoric Bison Populations in Central and Southern Texas," 343.

42. We have two recent and excellently annotated translations of Cabeza de Vaca's journal. See Krieger, *We Came Naked and Barefoot*; and Adorno and Pautz, trans., *Álvar Núñez Cabeza de Vaca*. Unlike the Adorno and Pautz study, Krieger's work includes an English translation of a report of the journey prepared by Gonzalo Fernández de Oviedo y Valdez based on interviews with the other two Spaniards, Alonso del Castillo and Andrés Dorantes, who accompanied Cabeza de Vaca. In my opinion, any study of Cabeza de Vaca's journey is incomplete without a careful consideration of Oviedo's work.

43. There are two recent works covering the Coronado expeditions. See Flint and Flint, eds. and trans., *Documents of the Coronado Expedition*; and Morris, *Narrative of the Coronado Expedition*.

44. Moscoso's visit to Texas is covered in Clayton, Knight, and Moore, eds., *The De Soto Chronicles*, 1:143–150. See also Charles Hudson's study of Moscoso's visits to East Texas and the central Texas coast in Hudson, *Knights of Spain*, 359–403.

45. See Hammond and Rey, eds. and trans., *Obregón's History of 16th Century Explorations in Western America*, 196–208.

46. The first expedition (1581–1582) was led by Francisco Sánchez Chamuscado; the second (1582–1583), by Antonio de Espejo. See Hammond and Rey, *The Rediscovery of New Mexico*, 67–114, 153–231.

47. See Schroeder and Matson, *A Colony on the Move*; and Hammond and Rey, *The Rediscovery of New Mexico*, 245–295.

48. Juan de Oñate's journey to New Mexico and across far West Texas in 1598 is covered in Simmons, *The Last Conquistador*, 91–111.

49. See Craddock, ed., *Zaldívar and the Cattle of Cibola*.

50. See Simmons, *The Last Conquistador*, 156–164.

51. See George P. Hammond and Agapito Rey, eds., *New Mexico in 1602: Juan de Montoya's Relation of the Discovery of New Mexico* (New York: Arno Press, 1967).

52. See Ayer, trans., *The Memorial of Fray Alonso de Benavides, 1630*.

53. Pérez de Ribas, *My Life among the Savage Nations of New Spain.*

54. See Duaine, *Caverns of Oblivion.*

55. Chapa, *Texas and Northeastern Mexico.*

56. Ibid., 53–56.

57. Wade, *The Native Americans of the Texas Edwards Plateau,* 24–25.

58. Ibid., 68–133. See also Imhoff, ed., *The Diary of Juan Dominguez de Mendoza's Expedition into Texas (1683–1684).*

59. See Foster, ed., *The La Salle Expedition to Texas;* and Cox, ed., *The Journeys of René Robert Cavelier.*

60. Governor Alonso de León's 1689 and 1690 expedition diaries are found in Bolton, ed., *Spanish Exploration in the Southwest,* 388–422. A revised and expanded version of De León's 1690 expedition diary is included in Chapa, *Texas and Northeastern Mexico,* 155–172.

61. An English translation of Governor Terán's diary account of the 1691 expedition is found in Hatcher, trans., *The Expedition of Don Domingo Terán de los Ríos into Texas,* 10–48. A second diary covered only the side trip by Captain Martínez from Terán's base camp near the Colorado River to Matagorda Bay to rescue the last French survivors from Fort St. Louis. For a translation of this expedition diary account, see Foster, ed., *Save the Young.*

62. See Foster and Jackson, eds., "The 1693 Expedition of Governor Salinas Varona to Sustain the Missionaries among the Tejas Indians," 264–311.

63. The 1709 expedition was led by Fray Isidro de Espinosa, who prepared a diary account of the trip. See Gabriel Tous, *Preliminary Studies of the Texas Catholic Historical Society* 1, no. 3 (March 1930). 3–14.

64. Both Captain Diego Ramón and Fray Isidro Espinosa maintained diary accounts on the 1716 expedition. See an English translation of Espinosa's diary in Tous, *The Ramón Expedition,* 4–24; and Ramón's diary in Foik, *Captain Don Domingo Ramón's Diary of His Expedition into Texas in 1716,* 3–23. A fresh translation of Ramón's 1716 diary is found in Debbie S. Cunningham, ed., "The Domingo Ramón Diary of the 1716 Expedition into the Province of the Tejas Indians: An Annotated Translation," *Southwestern Historical Quarterly* 110 (July 2006): 39–68.

65. The 1718 expedition was led by Governor Martín de Alarcón. We have two translations of Alarcón's expedition accounts. See Fray Francisco Celíz's account in Fritz Leo Hoffman, *Diary of the Alarcón Expedition into Texas, 1718–1719* (Los Angeles: Quivira Society, 1935). Fray Pedro Perez de Mezquía's account of the expedition, which describes only a part of the journey, is covered in Hoffman, "The Mezquía Diary of the Alarcón Expedition into Texas, 1718."

For the 1721–1722 Aguayo expedition, we have two English translations of Juan Antonio de la Peña's account. See Forrestal, trans., *Pena's Diary of the Aguayo Expedition,* 3–68; and Santos, *Aguayo Expedition into Texas.*

66. See note 42.

67. See note 57.

68. See note 55.

69. See note 43.

70. See note 49.

71. See note 58.

72. Jack Jackson, ed., *Imaginary Kingdom: Texas as Seen by the Rivera and Rubí Military Expeditions, 1727 and 1767* (Austin: Texas State Historical Association, 1995).

73. See note 59.

74. Foster, ed., *The La Salle Expedition on the Mississippi River.*

75. See note 62.

76. Cunningham, ed., "The Domingo Ramón Diary," 39–68.

77. Perttula, ed., *The Prehistory of Texas.*

Chapter One

1. See the letter dated April 1, 1767, to the governor from Orobio Basterra, Bexar Archives Translations, XVII, 74, Center for American History, University of Texas at Austin.

2. Foster, ed., *The La Salle Expedition to Texas,* 172.

3. See the discussion of Apache occupation of the area north and northwest of the upper Colorado River crossing in Foster, *Spanish Expeditions into Texas,* 103.

4. See Krieger, *We Came Naked and Barefoot,* 178–197.

5. See Clayton, Knight, and Moore, eds., *The De Soto Chronicles,* 1:142–150, 2:527–528.

6. See Cox, ed., *The Journeys of René Robert Cavelier,* 1:222–248; and Foster, ed., *The La Salle Expedition to Texas,* 153–203.

7. See Chapa, *Texas and Northeastern Mexico,* 155–172.

8. See Hatcher, trans., *The Expedition of Don Domingo Terán de los Ríos into Texas.*

9. See William C. Foster and Jack Jackson, eds., "The 1693 Expedition of Governor Salinas Varona to Sustain the Missionaries among the Tejas Indians," *Southwestern Historical Quarterly* 97 (Oct. 1993): 264–311.

10. See Tous, *The Espinosa-Olivares-Aguirre Expedition of 1709.*

11. Krieger, *We Came Naked and Barefoot,* 178. For a review of the origin and early period of the Narváez expedition, see Schneider, *Brutal Journey.*

12. Krieger, *We Came Naked and Barefoot,* 184.

13. Ibid., 259–260.

14. Ibid., 260–261.

15. Ibid., 187–188.

16. Ibid., 208–210.

17. Clayton, Knight, and Moore, eds., *The De Soto Chronicles,* 1:148.

18. Ibid., 2:527–528.

19. Hudson, *Knights of Spain,* 402.

20. Ibid.

21. Ibid., 304.

22. The diary account of La Salle's 1682 discovery expedition on the Mississippi is found in Foster, *The La Salle Expedition on the Mississippi River.*

23. Henri Joutel's diary account of La Salle's 1685 expedition to Texas is found in Foster, ed., *The La Salle Expedition to Texas.*

24. Foster, ed., *The La Salle Expedition on the Mississippi River,* 96, 104.

25. Anastase Douay's account of La Salle's 1686 expedition to the Hasinai Caddo in East Texas is found in Cox, ed., *The Journeys of René Robert Cavelier,* 1:222–237.

26. Foster, ed., *The La Salle Expedition to Texas,* 172.

27. See Kotter et al., *Final Report of Cultural Resource Investigations at the Cummins Creek Mine.*

28. Ibid., 182–183.

29. Ibid., 183–184.

30. Ibid., 183. La Salle's lieutenant, Henri de Tonty, calls the Chickasaw "Flatheads." Cox, ed., *The Journeys of René Robert Cavelier,* 1:18. The cultural practice of intentionally

flattening the human head (called cranial modeling or cranial deformation by archeologists) was found across North America and Mesoamerica. For accounts of cranial modeling in the Southeast, see Swanton, *The Indians of the Southeastern United States*, 537–541. For reports of cranial modeling in Mesoamerica, see Pohl, *Exploring Mesoamerica*, 25, and in northwest Chihuahua at Paquimé, see Di Peso, Rinaldo, and Fenner, *Casas Grandes*, 8:331–338.

31. Alan Gallay writes that the Native people west of the Mississippi who interacted with the French were "subject to slave raids inspired by English Carolina." He adds: "These Mississippi River people had little direct contact with the Creek and other Indians east of the Choctaw and Chickasaw." Gallay, *The Indian Slave Trade*, 14.

32. In 1981 Grant D. Hall completed a study of the cultural prehistory of the lower Brazos River valley. The study suggests that between ca. 650 BC and AD 500 Native groups on the lower Brazos maintained periodic long-distance interaction and trade networks with tribes residing in East Texas, Arkansas, and possibly the Southeast. See Grant D. Hall, *A Study in the Cultural Prehistory of the Lower Brazos River Valley, Texas*, Research Report No. 61 (Austin: Texas Archeological Survey, 1981).

33. For a review of Alonso de León's 1689 expedition and references to expedition diaries and documents related to the expedition, see Foster, ed., *Spanish Expeditions into Texas*, 17–31.

34. The revised and more complete diary account of De León's 1690 expedition to Texas is found in Chapa, *Texas and Northeastern Mexico*, 154–172.

35. See the review of Governor Domingo Terán's 1691–1692 expedition to Texas in Foster, *Spanish Expeditions into Texas*, 51–75.

36. The diary of Governor Salinas Varona is found in Foster and Jackson, eds., "The 1693 Expedition of Governor Salinas Varona to Sustain the Missionaries among the Tejas Indians," 264–311.

37. A review of the 1709 Espinosa expedition to the Colorado River is given in Foster, *Spanish Expeditions into Texas*, 95–108.

38. See Robert A. Ricklis and Michael B. Collins, *Archaic and Late Prehistoric Human Ecology in the Middle Onion Creek Valley, Hays County, Texas*, Studies in Archeology 19 (Austin: Texas Archeological Research Laboratory, 1994).

39. T. N. Campbell, "Espinosa, Olivares, and the Colorado Indians, 1709," *Sayersville Historical Association Bulletin* 3 (1983): 2–16.

40. For a review of the three expeditions and the associated documentary records, see Foster, *Spanish Expeditions into Texas*, 109–162.

Chapter Two

1. Although several expedition diarists, including Henri Joutel, gave firsthand accounts of bison remaining in Area II throughout the year during the study period, contemporary historians often have written to the contrary and have suggested, mistakenly I believe, that bison were generally absent from Central Texas during the winter months and that bison did not significantly contribute to the subsistence of Central Texas Indians. For example, see William W. Newcomb Jr., "Historic Indians of Central Texas," *Bulletin of the Texas Archeological Society* 64 (1993): 49.

A contrary and, I think, more accurate interpretation of the early historic and prehistoric record of bison population in Central Texas is found in Tom D. Dillehay's study of bison population changes on the Southern Plains. Dillehay projects that bison herds were often absent from the Southern Plains between AD 500 and 1300 but were present without interruption on the Southern Plains between ca. AD 1300 and 1550. Dillehay argues that the presence or absence of bison on the Southern Plains fluctuates according to climatic changes.

As noted earlier, the global Medieval Warm period (ca. AD 900 to 1350) contributed to the relative absence of bison on the Southern Plains and in Area II during the period of absence noted by Dillehay. The global mesic-hydric Little Ice Age (ca. AD 1350–1850) extended the rich grazing grasslands southward on the Southern Plains and the presence of large bison herds in Area II during the study period. See Thomas D. Dillehay, "Late Quaternary Bison Population Changes on the Southern Plains," *Plains Anthropologist* 19, no. 65 (Aug. 1974): 180–196.

2. In his study of the natural history of the Rocky Mountains published for the Smithsonian Institution in 2002, Scott A. Elias writes that during the Little Ice Age (dated AD 1400 to 1900 by the author), the glaciers in Glacier National Park "were bigger than they had been in the past 10,000 years." Elias, *Rocky Mountains,* 12, 13.

3. In his study of the historic Indians of Central Texas, William Newcomb writes that the river called by the French the "Maligne" was the Brazos River rather than the Colorado River. Newcomb, "Historic Indians of Central Texas," 14. This mistake leads to Newcomb's inaccurate projections of the homeland of the over forty Central Texas tribes. This same mistake was made by Robert A. Ricklis and Michael B. Collins, who relied on an unauthorized version of Henri Joutel's journal found in Cox, ed., *Journeys of René Robert Cavelier,* 2:145–146. See Ricklis and Collins, *Archaic and Late Prehistoric Human Ecology in the Onion Creek Valley,* 18.

4. The recent publication of two fully annotated translations of Cabeza de Vaca's narrative account provides relevant information on the Native peoples of Texas. See Krieger, *We Came Naked and Barefoot;* and Adorno and Pautz, *Álvar Núñez Cabeza de Vaca.*

5. For a translation of Henri Joutel's unabridged journal account of La Salle's expedition to Texas, see Foster, ed., *The La Salle Expedition to Texas.*

6. A detailed review of the diary accounts of these five Spanish expeditions is found in Foster, *Spanish Expeditions into Texas,* 17–108.

7. Ibid., 109–162.

8. The review of Cabeza de Vaca's visit to Area II is based primarily on the translation of the narrative of Cabeza de Vaca and the report of Oviedo y Valdez found in Krieger, *We Came Naked and Barefoot,* 193–205, 261–275.

9. The account describing Moscoso's visit with the Hasinai Caddo and the scouting expedition into Area II is found in Clayton, Knight, and Moore, eds., *The De Soto Chronicles,* 1:145–150.

10. The review of La Salle's marine expedition to Texas and his two overland expeditions from Fort St. Louis to the Hasinai Caddo through Area II is based primarily on Henri Joutel's narrative found in Foster, *The La Salle Expedition to Texas,* 111–176.

11. W. W. Newcomb Jr. writes that the Karankawa carried their "eighteen foot long" hut poles with each move. Newcomb, *The Indians of Texas from Prehistory to Modern Times* (Austin: University of Texas Press, 1961), 68. For an expedition account of finding an abandoned Indian encampment with numerous pole structures left standing, see Foster, *Spanish Expeditions into Texas,* 133.

12. Foster, ed., *The La Salle Expedition to Texas,* 162.

13. Clark, *The Indian Sign Language,* 183.

14. Elaine Costello, *American Sign Language,* 177.

15. Foster, *Spanish Expeditions into Texas,* 314n23.

16. Linguists who prepared a comprehensive study of North American Indian languages published by Smithsonian Institution in 1996 included a review of nonspeech

communication systems such as Indian sign language and smoke signals. Allan R. Taylor writes that the Indian sign language was by far the most sophisticated of the nonspeech communication systems employed by North American Indians. Taylor says that the use of signs was not a secondary system based on a particular Indian language but an independently structured primary system. Taylor adds that sign language may have "originated in the extreme southern fringe of the Plains, or on the Texas Gulf coast," citing the volume editor Ives Goddard. This suggests that sign language may have originated in and around Area II among the numerous tribes with different languages, each eager to trade with each other and with the Plains Indians when they arrived to hunt bison. See Taylor, "Nonspeech Communication Systems," 17:275–282; Foster, *Spanish Expeditions into Texas,* 104, 208–209, 230, 314n23.

17. Foster, ed., *The La Salle Expedition to Texas,* 171–172.

18. See LeRoy Johnson and T. N. Campbell, "Sanan: Traces of a Previously Unknown Aboriginal Language in Colonial Coahuila and Texas," *Plains Anthropologist* 37, no. 140 (1992): 185–212.

19. Robert Ricklis, "Prehistoric Occupation of the Central and Lower Texas Coast," in Perttula, ed., *The Prehistory of Texas,* 171.

20. See Hackett, ed., *Historical Documents,* 2:251–281.

21. Ibid., 271, 279.

22. Newcomb, *The Indians of Texas,* 59.

23. See Chapa, *Texas and Northeastern Mexico,* 155–172.

24. Letter from Fray Massanet to Viceroy, September 1690, included in typescript of "Testimony of the Activities and Their Results of the Entrada by Land to the Parajes to the Bay of Espiritu Santo, 1691," Manuscript Division, Library of Congress, Sevilla, México, 61-6-21, 75–84.

25. Foster, *Spanish Expeditions into Texas,* 57–60.

26. See an English translation of the Martínez diary in Foster, ed., *Save the Young.*

27. See Foster, *Spanish Expeditions into Texas,* 208–209.

28. Ibid., 112.

29. A comprehensive review of the three expeditions is found in ibid., 109–162.

Chapter Three

1. Robert A. Ricklis, *The Karankawa Indians: An Ecological Study of Cultural Transition and Change* (Austin: University of Texas Press, 1996), 5–12; and Ricklis, "Prehistoric Occupation of the Central and Lower Texas Coast," in Perttula, ed., *The Prehistory of Texas,* Fig. 5.1, "Map of the Texas coast delimiting the central and lower coastal zones," 156.

2. Pedro de Rivera includes the Karankawa (Carancaguaze) in his list of tribes in Texas at the time of his expedition trip in 1727–1728. See Jackson and Foster, eds., *Imaginary Kingdom,* 43.

3. In his *Dictamen* of 1768, the Marqués de Rubí refers to the Carancaguazes as Central Texas residents, along with the "Cojanes, Piguicanes, and Jaranames." Ibid., 188.

4. For a review of Cabeza de Vaca's travels in Area III, I use his account found in Krieger, *We Came Naked and Barefoot,* 186–211.

5. There is some confusion regarding the war between the Doguene and the Quevene. First, Cabeza de Vaca injects the account late in his narrative after he has left Areas I, II, and III. Secondly, Krieger's editor fails to note that "Aguenes" is a variant of "Deagunes." But Adorno and Pautz correctly recognize this. See Adorno and Pautz, *Álvar Núñez Cabeza de Vaca,* 1:181n2.

6. Ricklis, "Prehistoric Occupation of the Central and Lower Texas Coast," 156.

7. Moscoso's voyage along the Texas coast in 1543 is described in the account by a Gentleman from Elvas, found in Clayton, Knight, and Moore, eds., *The De Soto Chronicles,* 1:161–164; and the account by the Inca, found in ibid., 2:526–529.

8. See Foster, ed., *The La Salle Expedition to Texas,* 69–176.

9. Oviedo describes the high sand mounds as "cliffs of white sand." Krieger, *We Came Naked and Barefoot,* 261.

10. For an English translation of the testimony of Pierre and Jean Talon, see R. T. Huntington, trans., "Expedition to the Mississippi River by Way of the Gulf of Mexico," *Iowa Review* 15, no. 2 (1985): 99–131.

11. For the 1686 Barroto diary, see Weddle, ed., *La Salle, the Mississippi, and the Gulf,* 149–171.

12. For a report on the investigation, see Hackett, ed., *Historical Documents,* 1:251–281.

13. For an English translation of De León's 1689 diary, see Bolton, *Spanish Exploration in the Southwest,* 388–404.

14. For De León's revised 1690 diary, see Chapa, *Texas and Northeastern Mexico,* 155–172.

15. For an English translation of Terán's personal diary account, see Hatcher, trans., *The Expedition of Don Domingo Terán de los Ríos into Texas,* 10–48.

16. For an English translation of the 1690 Martínez diary, see Foster, ed., *Save the Young.*

17. An English translation of the 1718 diary account of Fray Pedro Perez de Mezquía on Alarcón's journey, see Hoffmann, "The Mezquía Diary of the Alarcón Expedition into Texas, 1718."

18. For an English translation of Béranger's 1720 voyage, see W. Carrol, trans., *Béranger's Discovery of Aransas Pass* (Corpus Christi: Corpus Christi Museum, 1983).

19. Ibid., 22.

20. Fray Juan Antonio de la Peña's diary account of Governor Aguayo's visit to Area III is found in Santos, *Aguayo Expedition into Texas,* 76–79.

21. See Albert S. Gatschet, *The Karankawa Indians: The Coast People of Texas* (Cambridge: Peabody Museum of Harvard University, 1891).

22. See Richard A. Weinstein, *Archaeology and Paleogeography of the Lower Guadalupe River/San Antonio Bay Region* (Baton Rouge: Coastal Environments, Inc., 1992).

23. Richard A. Weinstein, *Archaeological Investigations along the Lower Lavaca River, Jackson County, Texas* (Baton Rouge: Coastal Environments, Inc., 1994).

Chapter Four

1. The following counties or parts of counties are included in Study Area IV: Val Verde, Kinney, Maverick, Uvalde, Zavala, Dimmit, Webb, Medina, Frio, La Salle, Zapata, Jim Hogg, Starr, Bexar, Wilson, Atascosa, Karnes, Live Oak, McMullen, Duval, Jim Wells, Nueces, San Patricio, Bee, Goliad, Refugio, Kleberg, Brooks, Kenedy, Hidalgo, Willacy, and Cameron. Contemporary ethnohistorians occasionally use the term "Coahuiltecans" to identify collectively the hunter-gatherers in Area IV and northern Coahuila. As this toponym arose in the ethnographic record after the close of the study period, it is not used in the present study.

2. Some Spanish chroniclers considered the Guadalupe River to be a cultural boundary. See Foster, *Spanish Expeditions into Texas,* 58.

3. Cabeza de Vaca's journey cannot be understood fully without consulting both

Cabeza de Vaca's own account and the report of the journey prepared by Gonzalo Fernández de Oviedo y Valdez. For a recent translation of the two documents, see Krieger, *We Came Naked and Barefoot*.

4. Ibid., 276, 278.

5. Spanish chroniclers used the term "leguas grandes" (long league) to indicate a distance that was slightly more than indicated by the customary league of 2.6 miles. See Foster and Jackson, eds., "The 1693 Expedition of Governor Salinas Varona to Sustain the Missionaries among the Tejas Indians," 306, 308.

6. Krieger, *We Came Naked and Barefoot*, 65.

7. It appears that Estevan kept the gourd because he reportedly took a gourd and a white and red (scarlet macaw?) feather as evidence of his authority on his return trip to the Southwest with Fray Marcos de Niza. See Schneider, *Brutal Journey*, 315.

8. Alex Krieger considers the Río Salado as an alternate route taken by Cabeza de Vaca. Krieger, *We Came Naked and Barefoot*, 64.

9. Di Peso illustrates several types of styles of cast copper bells traded from Paquimé, including Type ICIa, which, Di Peso writes, "was set apart from the others by the fact that on one side of its body it had a small anthropomorphic face resembling Tlaloc [an Indian god of rain and fertility] with two raised round eyes and a squared large toothed mouth." Di Peso, Rinaldo, and Fenner, *Casas Grandes*, 7:526. Di Peso also notes that two other types of Casas Grandes copper bells were recovered at the Pavón site in Huasteca. See ibid., Fig. 640.7.

10. Di Peso identifies several copper-mining sites near Casas Grandes, one about five miles from downtown Paquimé. See the survey map in ibid., 5:Figs. 284–285.

11. See ibid., 8:271.

12. Ibid., 2:600, 734n13.

13. Hard and Roney, "The Transition to Farming on the Rio Casas Grandes and in the Southern Jornada Mogollon Region," 152–153.

14. Hammond and Rey, eds. and trans., *Obregón's History of 16th Century Explorations in Western America*, 207, 208.

15. For an English translation of Alonso de León's work, see Duaine, *Caverns of Oblivion*, 8–142.

16. See the English translation of Chapa's work in Chapa, *Texas and Northeastern Mexico*, 25–154.

17. Ibid., 98–100.

18. Krieger, *We Came Naked and Barefoot*, 65.

19. Ibid., 65.

20. Wade, *The Native Americans of the Texas Edwards Plateau*, 24–26.

21. Ibid., 12, 13.

22. Mariah Wade translates the diary account of Bosque in ibid., 26–52.

23. For an English translation of Henri Joutel's account of La Salle's expedition to Texas, see Foster, ed., *The La Salle Expedition to Texas*, 49–282.

24. The interrogations are translated in Hackett, ed., *Historical Documents*, 1:251–281.

25. For an English translation of Alonso de León's 1688 expedition to South Texas to capture the Frenchman Géry, see O'Donnell, ed., *La Salle's Occupation of Texas*, 12–15.

26. Ibid., 13.

27. See Bolton, ed., *Spanish Exploration in the Southwest*, 388–404.

28. De León's 1686 expedition diary is included in Juan Bautista Chapa's history of Nuevo León and Coahuila; see Chapa, *Texas and Northeastern Mexico*, 104–113.

29. Juan Bautista Chapa lists the Indian tribes loyal to the Frenchman Jean Géry. See ibid., 135.

30. Bolton, ed., *Spanish Exploration in the Southwest,* 388–404.

31. See Chapa, *Texas and Northeastern Mexico,* 156.

32. See Hatcher, trans., *The Expedition of Don Domingo Terán de los Ríos into Texas,* 10–48.

33. See Foster and Jackson, eds., "The 1693 Expedition of Governor Salinas Varona to Sustain the Missionaries among the Tejas Indians," 264–311.

34. See Tous, *The Espinosa-Olivares-Aguirre Expedition of 1709,* 3–14.

35. See Thomas N. Campbell's entry "Sijame Indians" in Tyler et al., *The New Handbook of Texas,* 5:146.

36. For a translation of Fray Espinosa's diary account, see Tous, *The Ramón Expedition,* 4–24.

37. For a diary account of the Alarcón trip by Fray Francisco de Celíz, see Fritz Leo Hoffman, *Diary of the Alarcón Expedition into Texas, 1718–1719* (Los Angeles: Quivira Society, 1935).

38. See Santos, *Aguayo Expedition into Texas.*

39. See Duaine, *Caverns of Oblivion.*

40. See T. N. Campbell and T. J. Campbell, *Historic Indian Groups of the Choke Canyon Reservoir and Surrounding Area, Southern Texas,* Choke Canyon Series Vol. 1 (San Antonio: Center for Archeological Research, University of Texas at San Antonio, 1981).

41. Salinas, *Indians of the Rio Grande Delta.*

42. See Perttula, ed., *The Prehistory of Texas.*

43. Ibid., 127–154.

44. Ibid., 155–180.

45. Ibid., 266–282.

46. For a recent, comprehensive study of rock art on the lower Pecos River, see also Boyd, *Rock Art of the Lower Pecos.*

Chapter Five

1. See map captioned "Key to Tribal Territories," in William C. Sturtevant, gen. ed., *Handbook of North American Indians,* vol. 9, *Southwest,* ed. Alfonso Ortiz (Washington, D.C.: Smithsonian Institution, 1979), ix.

2. For a map that illustrates the division of the Trans-Pecos counties into the eastern Trans-Pecos and the western Trans-Pecos/Jornada Mogollon, see Miller and Kenmotsu, "Prehistory of the Jornada Mogollon and Eastern Trans-Pecos Regions of West Texas," in Perttula, ed., *The Prehistory of Texas,* Fig. 7.1, 206.

3. A series of Cabeza de Vaca route projections prepared by Alex D. Krieger are found in Krieger, *We Came Naked and Barefoot;* Cabeza de Vaca routes projected by Rolena Adorno and Patrick Pautz are found in Adorno and Pautz, *Álvar Núñez Cabeza de Vaca.*

4. A projection of Cabeza de Vaca's route that deviates substantially from that prepared by Rolena Adorno and Patrick Pautz, Alex Krieger, Thomas Campbell, Thomas Hester, and other scholars is found in Hickerson, *The Jumanos,* Map 1, "Route of Cabeza de Vaca (1533–1535)," 9.

5. For a brief but careful review of the life and work of Gonzalo Fernández de Oviedo y Valdez, including Oviedo's report regarding the journey of Cabeza de Vaca, see Flint and Flint, eds., *Documents of the Coronado Expedition,* 89, 90, 311, 314.

6. See the discussion of amaranth grown in northwestern Chihuahua during the pre-

Columbian period in Cheatham, Johnson, and Marshall, *The Useful Wild Plants of Texas,* 1:255–287. See also Foster, ed., *The La Salle Expedition on the Mississippi River,* 71–72.

7. See Krieger, *We Came Naked and Barefoot,* 108; and Adorno and Pautz, *Álvar Núñez Cabeza de Vaca,* 1:229.

8. Hammond and Rey, eds. and trans., *Obregón's History of 16th Century Explorations in Western America,* 205, 206.

9. Mural paintings are found at El Tajín (ca. AD 300–1150) near Tampico on the Gulf of Mexico and at Cacaxtla (ca. AD 650–850) in central Mexico. See Pohl, *Exploring Mesoamerica,* 132–140, 141–149. For a study of wall paintings at selected sites of the Southwest, see Lister, *Behind Painted Walls.* The Polvo site in the Texas Big Bend country had "smooth plastered interior walls with designs painted in yellow, black, red, and white colors." William A. Cloud, *Archeological Testing at Sites 41PS800 and 41PS801, Presidio County, Texas* (Austin: Texas Department of Transportation and Center for Big Bend Studies, 2001), 23.

10. Doolittle, *Canal Irrigation in Prehistoric Mexico,* 84–90. See also Doolittle, *Cultivated Landscapes in Native North America,* 388, 389.

11. Hammond and Rey, eds. and trans., *Obregón's History of 16th Century Explorations in Western America,* 208.

12. Richardson B. Gill, *The Great Maya Droughts* (Albuquerque: University of New Mexico Press, 2000), 22.

13. Rivera's 1727 diary account is well known to scholars, but an English translation of Rivera's journey through Casas Grandes has never been published. A Spanish version of Rivera's diary is found in Pedro de Rivera, *Diario y Derrotero de lo caminado, visto, y obcervado. . . .* (Mexico City: Porrua, 1945). For a history of the publication of Rivera's diary, see Thomas H. Naylor and Charles W. Polzer, *Pedro de Rivera and the Regulations for Northern New Spain, 1724–1729* (Tucson: University of Arizona Press, 1988), 18, 19.

14. Rubí's 1766–1767 diary account is not well known to scholars. The diary passage covering Rubí's visit to Casas Grandes has not appeared in English. A manuscript copy of Rubí's diary account is held by the Center for American History at the University of Texas at Austin.

15. See Lawrence Kinnaird, *The Frontiers of New Spain,* 99.

16. Di Peso, Rinaldo, and Fenner, *Casas Grandes,* 8:182–185. For a discussion of the source of scarlet macaw imported into the Southwest from northeast Mexico, see Foster, ed., *The La Salle Expedition on the Mississippi River,* 54–65.

17. See Hammond and Rey, *The Rediscovery of New Mexico,* 67–114. Other more cursory accounts of the expedition should also be noted. On the same day that Gallegos testified in Mexico City, Pedro de Bustamante, also a soldier in the expedition party, testified and gave his brief rendition of the expedition. In October of the same year, the viceroy requested testimony from another member of the expedition party, Hernando Barrado, on the circumstances surrounding the murder of the priest as reported by a Conchos Indian called Geronimo, whom Barrado had taken as a servant on the expedition. In March 1583 Barrado and Felipe de Escalante (another member of the expedition) prepared a brief supplementary account that provides few new insights on the trip.

18. See Mallouf, "Late Archaic Foragers of Eastern Trans-Pecos Texas and the Big Bend," 226.

19. Hammond and Rey, *The Rediscovery of New Mexico,* 78.

20. See Blake, *Birds of Mexico,* 191–192; and Hargrave, *Mexican Macaws.*

21. See Foster, *The La Salle Expedition on the Mississippi River,* 54–60.

22. See the map of northwest Mexico in *Webster's New Geographical Dictionary* (Springfield, Mass.: Merriam-Webster, 1988), 767.

23. See Hammond and Rey, *The Rediscovery of New Mexico,* 153–212.

24. Ibid., 213–231.

25. Foster, ed., *The La Salle Expedition to Texas,* 263, 269, 275, 277, 280.

26. See Duaine, *Caverns of Oblivion,* 26; Hammond and Rey, eds. and trans., *Obregón's History of 16th Century Explorations in Western America.*

27. Two translations of Castaño's 1590 expedition diary were consulted in this study. See Hammond and Rey, eds., *The Rediscovery of New Mexico,* 245–295; and Schroeder and Matson, *A Colony on the Move.*

28. See the discussion of Francisco Leyva de Bonilla and Antonio Gutiérrez de Humaña in Weber, *The Spanish Frontier in North America,* 79.

29. For a review of Oñate's 1598 expedition, see Simmons, *The Last Conquistador,* 48–113.

30. We have two recent excellent studies of the 1684 Mendoza expedition. See Imhoff, ed., *The Diary of Juan Domínguez de Mendoza's Expedition into Texas,* and Wade, *The Native Americans of the Texas Edwards Plateau,* 68–133.

31. Hackett, ed., *Historical Documents,* 2:251–289.

32. An English translation of the 1715 diary of Sergeant Major Don Juan Antonio de Trasviña y Retis is found in Reginald C. Reindorp, trans., *The Founding of Missions at La Junta de los Ríos,* Texas Catholic Historical Society Supplementary Studies 1, no. 1 (Austin: St. Edward's University, April 1938).

Chapter Six

1. A recently published compilation of documents relating to the Coronado expedition is found in Flint and Flint, eds. and trans., *Documents of the Coronado Expedition.* For a fresh translation of the narrative of Coronado's expedition with an extensive introduction and notes, see Morris, ed., *Narrative of the Coronado Expedition.* See also Castañeda et al., *The Journey of Coronado.*

2. Coronado's chronicler, Pedro de Castañeda, writes that the Rio Grande and Pecos River were frozen over with a thick layer of ice and snow for almost four months during the winter of 1540–1541. Morris, ed., *Narrative of the Coronado Expedition,* 187.

3. See Flint and Flint, eds. and trans., *Documents of the Coronado Expedition,* 320; Castañeda et al., *The Journey of Coronado,* 116.

4. For an analysis of copper artifacts, including crotals recovered at Casas Grandes, see Di Peso, Rinaldo, and Fenner, *Casas Grandes,* 7:500–532.

5. See ibid., 524–526.

6. Foster, ed., *The La Salle Expedition on the Mississippi River,* 124.

7. Brooks, "From Stone Slab Architecture to Abandonment," 342.

8. See Flint and Flint, eds. and trans., *Documents of the Coronado Expedition,* 508–524.

9. See Hammond and Rey, eds. and trans., *Obregón's History of 16th Century Explorations in Western America,* 200–208.

10. See Elias, *Rocky Mountains,* 12.

11. See Hammond and Rey, *The Rediscovery of New Mexico,* 16–114.

12. McKusick, *Southwest Birds of Sacrifice,* 46–47, 74.

13. A map that identifies the range of the scarlet macaw in Mexico and the closest source of premature scarlet macaw available for Casas Grandes traders in the Late Pre-

historic period is found in Foster, ed., *The La Salle Expedition on the Mississippi River*, 59.

14. See Hammond and Rey, *The Rediscovery of New Mexico*, 213–231.

15. See the English translation of Alonso de León's history in Duaine, *Caverns of Oblivion*, 26.

16. For an English translation of a journal account of Castaño's 1590 expedition to New Mexico, see Hammond and Rey, *The Rediscovery of New Mexico*, 245–295. See also Schroeder and Matson, *A Colony on the Move*.

17. Oakah L. Jones Jr. identifies the Tepeguan homeland and comments on the tribe's travels in Jones, *Nueva Vizcaya*, Map 3, "Amerinds of Nueva Vizcaya on Spanish Contact, about 1550," xix.

18. See Chapa, *Texas and Northeastern Mexico*, 188.

19. Regarding the Morlete expedition, see Hammond and Rey, *The Rediscovery of New Mexico*, 47, 48.

20. See George P. Hammond and Agapito Rey, *New Mexico in 1602: Juan de Montoya's Relation of the Discovery of New Mexico* (Albuquerque: Quivira Society, 1938).

21. Ibid., 42.

22. Hammond and Rey, *The Rediscovery of New Mexico*, 48.

23. Duaine, *Caverns of Oblivion*, 73, 74. See also Genaro García, *Documentos ineditos o muy raros para la historia de México*, (Mexico City: Librería de la Vda. de Ch. Bouret, 1909), 25:94–95.

24. Ibid., 95.

25. Hammond and Rey, *The Rediscovery of New Mexico*, 48. See also Weber, *The Spanish Frontier in North America*, 390n83.

26. For recent examples of this mistaken interpretation, see Riley, *Becoming Aztlan*, 192; and Simmons, *The Last Conquistador*, 101.

27. A review of Oñate's 1598 expedition is found in Simmons, *The Last Conquistador*, 156–164.

28. See Craddock, ed., *Zaldívar and the Cattle of Cíbola*.

29. Hammond and Rey, *The Rediscovery of New Mexico*, 169.

30. See Klein, *The Human Career*, 520, 526.

31. Abbé Jean Cavelier writes that mounted bison hunters were encountered about forty miles north of Fort St. Louis in 1687 and were armed with bone-tipped spears. Jean Delangers, *The Journal of Jean Cavelier* (Chicago: Institute of Jesuit History, 1938), 3–35.

32. See Simmons, *The Last Conquistador*, 160–164.

33. Thomas N. Campbell suggests that the Escanjaque may have been a Wichita group, possibly the same as the Yscani. See Tyler et al., eds., *The New Handbook of Texas*, 2:889.

34. Simmons, *The Last Conquistador*, 178–194.

35. These efforts by Hernando Martín and Diego del Castillo are mentioned in Chipman, *Spanish Texas*, 62.

36. For a brief study of the three tribes, see W. W. Newcomb and T. N. Campbell, "Southern Plains Ethnohistory: A Re-examination of the Escanjaques, Ahijados, and Cuitoas," in *Pathways to Plains Prehistory*, ed. Don G. Wyckoff and Jack L. Hofman, Oklahoma Anthropological Society Memoir 3 (Duncan, Okla., 1982), 29–43.

37. A recent fully annotated English translation of the 1684 Mendoza expedition is found in Wade, *The Native Americans of the Texas Edwards Plateau*, 68–134. See also Imhoff, ed., *The Diary of Juan Domínguez de Mendoza's Expedition into Texas*.

38. Mariah F. Wade offers helpful comments on the Arcos Tuertos and Arcos Fuertes

and suggests that their special bows may have been the same as those referred to as "Turkish bows" in Spanish diary accounts from the late 1600s. Wade, *The Native Americans of the Texas Edwards Plateau*, 248n44.

Steven A. LeBlanc reviews the prehistoric bow and arrow technology in the Southwest and notes the advances made by the sinew-reinforced (i.e., sinew twisted around the bow for support) and recurved bows. See LeBlanc, *Prehistoric Warfare in the American Southwest*, 99–104.

39. Wade, *The Native Americans of the Texas Edwards Plateau*, 115.

40. See Tom D. Dillehay, "Late Quaternary Bison Population Changes on the Southern Plains," *Plains Anthropologist* 19, no. 65 (Aug. 1974): 180–196.

41. Dillehay writes as follows: "It appears that there are no postulated climatic periods (such as the Altithermal) which could possibly explain the 700 to 800 year bison gap for the Absence Period II [AD 500 to 1200–1300]." Ibid., 185.

42. Dendrochronolgy and sea-level studies establish the Medieval Warm period chronology applicable to North America, including Texas. See Jan Esper, Edward R. Cook, and Fritz H. Schweingrubar, "Low-Frequency Signals in Long Tree-Ring Chronologies for Reconstructing Past Temperature Variability," *Science* 295 (March 22, 2002): 2250–2253. The chronology of climate changes during the past millennium that influenced North America (including the study area) is found in a Smithsonian Natural History Series publication authored by Scott A. Elias. Elias writes as follows: "Between 1100 and 1300 the Medieval Warm Period began to subside and was replaced by the Little Ice Age, a time of intense cold in the Northern Hemisphere." Elias, *Rocky Mountains*, 133.

43. Balsillie and Donoghue, *High Resolution Sea-Level History for the Gulf of Mexico since the Last Glacial Maximum*.

44. Oakah L. Jones identifies the homeland of the Salinero east of Tepeguan and between Parral to the north and Durango to the south. See Jones, *Nueva Vizcaya*, xix.

45. Christopher Lintz prepared the entry "Antelope Creek Phase" for *The New Handbook of Texas*. See Tyler et al., eds., *The New Handbook of Texas* 1:203–205. See also Brooks, "From Stone Slab Architecture to Abandonment," 332.

46. Brooks, "From Stone Slab Architecture to Abandonment," 339.

47. LeBlanc, *Prehistoric Warfare in the American Southwest*, 34. For another interpretation of the climatic change and the bison influx that occurred in Area VI and Central Texas during the late prehistoric and historic periods, see Robert A. Ricklis and Michael B. Collins, *Human Ecology in the Middle Onion Creek Valley, Hays County, Texas* (Austin: Texas Archeological Research Laboratory, 1994), 322, 323.

Chapter Seven

1. See Timothy K. Perttula, "The Prehistoric and Caddoan Archeology of the Northeastern Texas Pineywoods," Fig. 13.1, "The Caddoan archeological area, physiographic zones (from Fenneman 1938), and the location of the study area," in Perttula, ed., *The Prehistory of Texas*, 371. See also the map of the Late Caddoan area (ca. AD 1400–1680), Fig. 13.26, 394.

2. All or part of the following counties are included in Study Area VII: Wichita, Clay, Montague, Cook, Grayson, Fannin, Lamar, Red River, Bowie, Archer, Young, Jack, Wise, Denton, Collin, Rock, Hunt, Delta, Hopkins, Rains, Wood, Franklin, Titus, Camp, Morris, Marion, Cass, Upshur, Gregg, Harrison, Tarrant, Dallas, Rockwall, Kaufman, Van Zandt, Panola, Johnson, Ellis, Hill, Navarro, Henderson, Cherokee, Anderson, Nacogdoches, Shelby, San Augustine, Sabine, Hill, Limestone, Leon, Houston, Angelina, Trinity, Madison, Grimes, Walker, Montgomery, San Jacinto, Polk, Jasper, and Newton.

3. An English translation of accounts of Hernando de Soto's expedition is found in Clayton, Knight, and Moore, eds., *The De Soto Chronicles.*

4. Ibid., 1:239. Timothy K. Perttula writes that mounds were constructed by the Native population in Area VII after ca. AD 900 and that the cultivation of maize became significant after ca. AD 1300–1450. Perttula, "The Prehistoric and Caddoan Archeology of the Northeastern Texas Pineywoods," 383.

5. Clayton, Knight, and Moore, eds., *The De Soto Chronicles,* 2:295–297.

6. Ibid., 1:241.

7. See ibid., 2:422.

8. Ibid., 1:143–145.

9. This part of Moscoso's expedition is covered in Hudson, *Knights of Spain,* 353–373.

10. Timothy Perttula writes that during the Late Caddoan period (ca. AD 1400–1680), Edwards chert from Central Texas was obtained by Caddoan people from non-Caddoan people living more than 150 kilometers to the west and southwest of the Pineywoods. Perttula, "The Prehistoric and Caddoan Archeology of the Northeastern Texas Pineywoods," 406.

11. Ibid., 367–370. See also Young and Hoffman, eds., *The Expedition of Hernando de Soto West of the Mississippi,* 152, 153.

12. For a different interpretation of Moscoso's route from the Hasinai to the Colorado River, see Bruseth and Kenmotsu, "From Naguatex to the River Daycao: the Route of the Hernando de Soto Expedition through Texas," 199–225.

13. See Clayton, Knight, and Moore, eds., 2:470–471.

14. For an English translation of Nicolas de La Salle's diary account of La Salle's 1682 expedition, see Foster, ed., *The La Salle Expedition on the Mississippi River.*

15. For an English translation of Henri Joutel's account of La Salle's 1684 expedition to Texas, see Foster, ed., *The La Salle Expedition to Texas.*

16. See Cox, *The Journeys of René Robert Cavelier,* 1:222–247.

17. See Wade, *The Native Americans of the Texas Edwards Plateau,* 69–70, 130, 218.

18. Ibid., 233.

19. Ibid., 233.

20. This segment of La Salle's expedition is recorded by his chronicler Joutel as a diary account in which the distance and direction taken each day is recorded. See Foster, ed., *The La Salle Expedition to Texas,* 151–281.

21. Ibid., 241–243. Timothy Perttula notes that a central part (the Titus Phase) of the Pineywoods was virtually abandoned at some time after Moscoso's men left in 1542. Perttula, "The Prehistoric and Caddoan Archeology of the Northeastern Texas Pineywoods," 406. Joutel's account supports the conclusions of Perttula.

22. Henri de Tonty, La Salle's lieutenant, refers to the "Chickasas" as having flat heads. Cox, *The Journeys of René Robert Cavelier,* 1:18.

23. A study by Alan Gallay concerning the British-inspired Indian slave trade on the lower Mississippi in the late 1600s suggests that Chickasaw Indians raided tribes west of the Mississippi allied with the French such as the Taensa, Acansa, and Caddo. Gallay, *The Indian Slave Trade,* 296, 297.

24. La Salle's lieutenant, Henri de Tonty, also mentions that the Caddohadacho produced superb bows for long-distance trade. Cox, *The Journeys of René Robert Cavelier,* 1:47–48.

25. Nicolas de La Salle records that on March 18, 1682, at a location near the mouth of the Yazoo River, the French party passed a village of "Tonica" (Tunica), who the Acansa

guides said were their enemies. Foster, ed., *The La Salle Expedition on the Mississippi River*, 105 and 105n38.

26. Foster, ed., *The La Salle Expedition to Texas*, 263.

27. Cox, *The Journeys of René Robert Cavelier*, 1:31–65.

28. For an English translation of De León's revised and unabridged 1690 expedition account, see Chapa, *Texas and Northeastern Mexico*, 155–172.

29. For an English translation of Fray Massanet's account, see Bolton, ed., *Spanish Exploration in the Southwest*, 353–387.

30. Both De León and Massanet report being served corn tamales by the Hasinai in 1690. Bolton, ed., *Spanish Exploration in the Southwest*, 376, 415. Joutel describes the corn dish as being wrapped in corn shucks and boiled. Foster, ed., *The La Salle Expedition to Texas*, 220. The cited reports, which suggest that tamales were served by the Caddo and in the Southwest before the arrival of the first Spanish explorers, conflict with the conclusions reached by William W. Dunmine, who writes that Spanish colonists introduced tamales to the Pueblo people. See Dunmine, *Gardens of New Spain*, 280, 281.

31. The American geographer William E. Doolittle explains that Old World fruit trees and other plants were traded by Native horticultural villages inland and frequently were under cultivation before European explorers came on the scene. Doolittle, *Cultivated Landscapes of Native North America*, 139, 156–158.

32. Foster, *Spanish Expeditions into Texas*, 46.

33. See Schneider, *Brutal Journey*, 149.

34. See Hatcher, trans., *The Expedition of Don Domingo Terán de los Ríos into Texas*, 10–48.

35. Foster and Jackson, eds., "The 1693 Expedition of Governor Salinas Varona to Sustain the Missionaries among the Tejas Indians," 264–311.

36. Ibid., 302–303.

37. Ibid., 303.

38. Ibid., 304.

39. For a reference to the use of Hasinai guides by Ramón and Espinosa when crossing the middle Brazos River, see Foster, ed., *Spanish Expeditions into Texas*, 118.

40. See ibid., 119.

41. Ibid.

42. The archeological evidence of a Late Prehistoric presence of Caddoan interaction in the middle Brazos River valley is covered in Gadus, Fields, and Kibler, *Data Recovery Excavations at the J. B. White Site (41MM341)*, 29–32; 177–182.

43. Kress, trans., "Diary of a Visit of Inspection of the Texas Missions Made by Fray Gaspar José de Solís," 61.

44. See the reference to the use of Hasinai Caddo (Tejas) guides by Alarcón when leaving San Antonio in ibid., 119.

45. Ibid., 125.

46. See Smith, trans., "Account of the Journey of Bénard de La Harpe." With respect to the relationship between the Caddo- and the Wichita-speaking groups called the Norteños, with whom La Harpe met, Timothy Perttula writes that there is some archeological evidence of interaction between the two toward the close of the Late Caddoan period (ca. AD 1400–1680). Perttula, "The Prehistoric and Caddoan Archeology of the Northeastern Texas Pineywoods," 406.

47. See Perttula, "The Prehistoric and Caddoan Archeology of the Northeastern Texas Pineywoods," 375, 376.

48. Saunders et al., "A Mound Complex in Louisiana at 5400–5000 years Before the Present," 1796–1799.

Chapter Eight

1. See John R. Swanton, *Indian Tribes of the Lower Mississippi Valley and Adjacent Coast of the Gulf of Mexico* (Washington, D.C.: U.S. Government Printing Office, 1911), front endpaper map, reduced in the Dover 1998 edition of the original foldout format. In 1979 Lawrence Edward Aten prepared his Ph.D. dissertation for the University of Texas at Austin entitled "Indians of the upper Texas Coast: Ethno-historic and Archeological Frameworks."

2. All or part of the following counties are included in Study Area VIII: Fort Bend, Brazoria, Galveston, Chambers, Jefferson, Liberty, Hardin, Orange, Newton, Jasper, Tyler, Polk, San Jacinto, Montgomery, Harris, Grimes, and Waller.

3. See Krieger, *We Came Naked and Barefoot;* and Adorno and Pautz, trans., *Álvar Núñez Cabeza de Vaca.*

4. Oviedo reports that there were 200 rather than 100 bowmen. Krieger, *We Came Naked and Barefoot,* 255.

5. W. W. Newcomb Jr., *The Indians of Texas from Prehistory to Modern Times* (Austin: University of Texas Press, 1961), 59.

6. Krieger, *We Came Naked and Barefoot,* 258.

7. See Bolton, *The Hasinais,* 125.

8. The most detailed account of this leg of Moscoso's journey is found in Garcilaso de la Vega, the Inca, "La Florida," in Clayton, Knight, and Moore, eds., *The De Soto Chronicles,* 2:523–530.

9. Ibid., 524–525.

10. Ibid., 524.

11. Mallouf, "Late Archaic Foragers of Eastern Trans-Pecos Texas and the Big Bend," 226.

12. Clayton, Knight, and Moore, eds., *The De Soto Chronicles,* 527.

13. Ibid., 527–528.

14. Ibid., 528.

15. See Hudson, *Knights of Spain,* 304, 401–403.

16. Ibid., 409.

17. For an annotated translation of the most complete diary account of La Salle's 1682 expedition on the Mississippi, see Foster, ed., *The La Salle Expedition on the Mississippi River.*

18. Foster, ed., *The La Salle Expedition to Texas,* 66.

19. For a detailed account of La Salle's route from Matagorda Bay to the crossing of the Brazos River a few miles northwest of Area VIII, see ibid., 151–193.

20. For an English translation of the Bellisle's *Relation,* see Henri Folmer, "De Bellisle on the Texas Coast," *Southwestern Historical Quarterly* 44 (Oct. 1940): 204–224. See also Robert S. Weddle and Patricia R. Lemee, "Exploring the Texas Coast: Bellisle, Béranger, and La Harpe, 1719–1721," in Lagarde, ed., *The French in Texas,* 20–34.

21. Folmer, "De Bellisle on the Texas Coast," 219.

22. Reports of cannibalism among Neanderthal are found in Klein and Edgar, *The Dawn of Human Culture,* 198–200.

23. See Klein, *The Human Career,* 469, citing Arens, *The Man-eating Myth.*

24. Folmer, "De Bellisle on the Texas Coast," 225.

25. Ibid, 228–231.

26. Ibid., 225–231.

27. See Don Joachín de Orobio Basterra, "Investigation of a French Settlement Con-

ducted by Don Joaquin de Orobio, Captain of La Bahia," Bexar Translations, 17:33–80, Center for American History, University of Texas at Austin.

28. See Jackson, ed., *Imaginary Kingdom,* 134–135n90.

29. Ibid., 134.

30. Foster, ed., *Spanish Expeditions into Texas,* 189.

Conclusions

1. The impact of the Medieval Warm period on horticultural areas in the Southwest is discussed in LeBlanc, *Prehistoric Warfare in the American Southwest,* 32–41. The positive economic and cultural impact of the Medieval Warming period in Europe is described by Eugene Linden as follows: "The Medieval Warming or the Climate Optimum saw significantly warmer temperatures through much of the North Atlantic. Farmers grew grapes in the United Kingdom, and population and trade expanded throughout Europe. Significantly for the New World, this warming period had a dramatic effect. In parts of southwestern Greenland, the growing season lengthened to allow the planting of crops, while lush meadows supported goats, sheep and cattle." Linden, *The Winds of Change,* 13.

2. See LeBlanc, *Prehistoric Warfare in the American Southwest,* 32–41.

3. See LeBlanc, *Constant Battles,* 149.

4. Taylor, "Nonspeech Communication Systems," 275.

5. Adorno and Pautz, trans., *Álvar Núñez Cabeza de Vaca,* 1:233.

6. See Kress, trans., "Diary of a Visit of Inspection of the Texas Missions Made by Fray Gaspar José de Solís, 58.

7. See Foster, *Spanish Expeditions into Texas,* 314n23. See also Clark, *The Indian Sign Language.*

8. For evidence of human retainer sacrifices at Cahokia, see Pauketat, *Ancient Cahokia and the Mississippians,* 91–92; at the East Texas Caddo Belcher site, see Timothy K. Pertula, *The Caddo Nation* (Austin: University of Texas Press, 1992), 122–124; and at Paquimé in northwest Mexico, see Di Peso, Rinaldo, and Fenner, *Casas Grandes,* 8:329–332.

9. Foster, ed., *The La Salle Expedition to Texas,* 245.

10. Hammond and Rey, *The Rediscovery of New Mexico,* 78.

11. Pérez de Ribas, *My Life among the Savage Nations of New Spain,* 227.

12. See Turpin's comments in the Foreword to *Bison Hunting at Cooper Site,* xvi.

13. Dillehay, *The Settlement of the Americas,* 12.

14. David Lewis-Williams reviews the origin of Paleolithic art that emerged in Europe in Lewis-Williams, *The Mind in the Cave,* 18–40.

15. Tattersall and Schwartz, *Extinct Humans,* 236.

16. Tankersley, "The Concept of Clovis and the Peopling of North America," 49–63; Collins, *Clovis Blade Technology,* 179.

17. Klein and Edgar describe the "sinkers" as "grooved stone net sinkers" that "recall ethnographically recorded fishing and fowling gear." Klein and Edgar, *The Dawn of Human Culture,* 238.

18. The "sinker" used by Texas Indians and also Native people in the Southeast is described by Turner and Hester as medium-size stone artifacts with either ground or chipped notches in the ends and as "skillfully shaped objects of highly specialized form." The authors acknowledge that the use of the sinker is uncertain, but say that some suggest that it may have served as "sinker weights" or as "bolas" stones. Turner and Hester, *A Field Guide to Stone Artifacts,* 316–317.

19. See Klein and Edgar, *The Dawn of Human Culture,* 249, 265–266. Randall White,

an associate professor of anthropology at New York University, has published extensively on Upper Paleolithic personal adornment in various regions of Europe. See Randall White, "Technological and Social Dimensions of 'Aurignacian Age' Body Ornaments across Europe," in *Before Lascaux: The Complete Record of the Early Upper Paleolithic,* ed. Heidi Knecht, Anne Pike-Tay, and Randall White (Boca Raton, Fla.: CRC Press, 1993), 277–300.

BIBLIOGRAPHY

Adams, E. Charles, and Andrew I. Duff, eds. *The Protohistoric Pueblo World, AD 1275–1600.* Tucson: University of Arizona Press, 2004.

Adorno, Rolena, and Patrick Charles Pautz, trans. *Álvar Núñez Cabeza de Vaca: His Account, His Life, and the Expedition of Pánfilo de Narváez.* 3 vols. Lincoln: University of Nebraska Press, 1999.

Arens, W. *The Man-Eating Myth: Anthropology and Anthropophagy.* Oxford: Oxford University Press, 1979.

Arsuaga, Juan Luis. *The Neanderthal Necklace.* New York: Four Walls Eight Windows, 2002.

Ayer, Mrs. Edward E., trans. *The Memorial of Fray Alonso de Benavides, 1630.* Albuquerque: Horn and Wallace, 1965.

Balsillie, James H., and Joseph F. Donoghue. *High Resolution Sea-Level History for the Gulf of Mexico since the Last Glacial Maximum.* Report of Investigations No. 103. Tallahassee: Florida Geological Survey, 2004.

Baugh, Timothy G., and Jonathan E. Ericson, eds. *Prehistoric Exchange Systems in North America.* New York: Plenum Press, 1994.

Berlandier, Jean L. *Journey to Mexico.* 2 vols. Austin: Texas State Historical Association, 1980.

Blake, Emmet R. *Birds of Mexico: A Guide for Field Identification.* Chicago: University of Chicago Press, 1953.

Bolton, Herbert E. *The Hasinais: Southern Caddoans as Seen by the Earliest Europeans.* Edited by Russell M. Magnaghi. Norman: University of Oklahoma Press, 1987.

———. "The Mission as a Frontier Institution in the Spanish-American Colonies." *American Historical Review* 23 (Oct. 1917): 42–61.

———, ed. *Spanish Exploration in the Southwest, 1542–1706.* New York: Charles Scribner's Sons, 1916.

Boyd, Carolyn E. *Rock Art of the Lower Pecos.* College Station: Texas A&M University Press, 2003.

Bradley, Raymond S., and Philip D. Jones, eds. *Climate since AD 1500.* New York: Routledge, 1992.

Brody, J. J. *Mimbres Painted Pottery.* Albuquerque: University of New Mexico Press, 1977.

Brooks, Robert L. "From Stone Slab Architecture to Abandonment: A Revisionist's View of the Antelope Creek Phase." In Perttula, *The Prehistory of Texas*, 331–344.

Brown, James A. *The Spiro Ceremonial Center*. 2 vols. Memoirs of the Museum of Anthropology, no. 29. Ann Arbor: Museum of Anthropology, University of Michigan, 1996.

Bruseth, James E., and Nancy A. Kenmotsu. "From Naguatex to the River Daycao: The Route of the Hernando de Soto Expedition through Texas." *North American Archeologist* 14, no. 3 (1998): 199–225.

Burroughs, William J. *Climate Change in Prehistory*. Cambridge: Cambridge University Press, 2005.

Campbell, Thomas N. "Archeological Materials from Five Islands in Laguna Madre, Texas Coast." *Bulletin of the Texas Archeological Society* 28 (1956): 41–46.

Castañeda, Pedro de, et al. *The Journey of Coronado*. Edited and translated by George Parker Winship. New York: Dover Publications, 1990.

Chapa, Juan Bautista. *Texas and Northeastern Mexico, 1630–1690*. Edited by William C. Foster; translated by Ned F. Brierley. Austin: University of Texas Press, 1997.

Cheatham, Scooter, and Marshall C. Johnson with Lynn Marshall. *The Useful Wild Plants of Texas, the Southeastern and Southwestern United States, the Southern Plains, and Northern Mexico*. 2 vols. Austin: Useful Wild Plants, Inc., 1995.

Chipman, Donald E. *Nuño de Guzmán and the Province of Pánuco in New Spain, 1518–1533*. Glendale, Calif.: Arthur H. Clark, 1967.

———. *Spanish Texas, 1519–1821*. Austin: University of Texas Press, 1992.

Clark, W. P. *The Indian Sign Language*. New York: Random House, 1998.

Clayton, Lawrence A., Vernon James Knight Jr., and Edward C. Moore, eds. *The De Soto Chronicles: The Expedition of Hernando De Soto to North America in 1539–1543*. 2 vols. Tuscaloosa: University of Alabama Press, 1993.

Cloud, William A., Robert J. Mallouf, Patricia A. Mercado-Allinger, Catheryn A. Hoyt, Nancy A. Kenmotsu, Joseph M. Sanchez, and Enrique R. Madrid. *Archeological Testing at the Polvo Site, Presidio County, Texas*. Austin: Texas Historical Commission, 1994.

Collins, Michael B. *Clovis Blade Technology*. Austin: University of Texas Press, 1999.

Cordell, Linda. *Archaeology of the Southwest*. Reprint. Boulder: Academic Press, 1997.

Costello, Elaine, *American Sign Language*. New York: Random House, 1998.

Cox, Isaac J., ed. *The Journeys of René Robert Cavelier, Sieur de La Salle*. 2 vols. New York: A. S. Barnes and Company, 1905.

Craddock, Jerry R., ed. *Zaldívar and the Cattle of Cibola: Vicente de Zaldívar's Expedition to the Buffalo Plains in 1598*. Dallas: William P. Clements Center for Southwest Studies, Southern Methodist University, 1999.

Davis, William B., and David J. Schmidly. *The Mammals of Texas*. Rev. ed. Austin: Texas Parks and Wildlife, 1994.

Diamond, Jared. *Collapse: How Societies Choose to Fail or Succeed*. New York: Penguin Group, 2005.

Dillehay, Thomas D. *The Settlement of the Americas*. New York: Basic Books, 2000.

Di Peso, Charles C. *Casas Grandes: A Fallen Trading Center at the Gran Chichimeca*. 3 vols. Flagstaff: Amerind Foundation and Northland Press, 1974.

———, John B. Rinaldo, and Gloria Fenner. *Casas Grandes: A Fallen Trading Center of the Gran Chichimeca*. 5 vols. Flagstaff: Amerind Foundation and Northland Press, 1974.

Doolittle, William E. *Canal Irrigation in Prehistoric Mexico*. Austin: University of Texas Press, 1990.

————. *Cultivated Landscapes of Native North America*. Oxford: Oxford University Press, 1990.

Duaine, Carl L. *Caverns of Oblivion*. Corpus Christi: privately printed, 1971.

Dunmire, William W. *Gardens of New Spain: How Mediterranean Plants and Foods Changed America*. Austin: University of Texan Press, 2004.

Elias, Scott A. *Rocky Mountains*. Smithsonian Natural History Series. Washington, D.C.: Smithsonian Institution Press, 2002.

Emerson, Thomas E., and R. Barry Lewis, eds. *Cahokia and the Hinterlands: Middle Mississippian Cultures of the Midwest*. Urbana: University of Illinois Press, 1991.

Espinosa, Isidro Félix de. *Crónica de los colegios de propaganda fide de la Nueva España*. Edited by Lino Gómez Canedo. Washington, D.C.: Academy of American Franciscan History, 1964.

Espinosa, J. Manuel. *The Pueblo Indian Revolt of 1696 and the Franciscan Missions of New Mexico*. Norman: University of Oklahoma Press, 1988.

Fagan, Brian. *Ancient North America*. New York: Thames and Hudson, 1995.

————. *The Little Ice Age: How Climate Made History, 1300–1850*. New York: Perseus, 2000.

Fiedel, Stuart J. *Prehistory of the Americas*. Cambridge: University of Cambridge, 1992.

Flannery, Tim. *The Eternal Frontier: An Ecological History of North America and Its People*. London: William Heinemann, 2001.

Flint, Richard, and Shirley Cushing Flint, eds. and trans. *Documents of the Coronado Expedition, 1539–1542*. Dallas: Southern Methodist University Press, 2005.

Foik, Paul J. *Captain Don Domingo Ramon's Diary of His Expedition into Texas in 1716*. Preliminary Studies of the Texas Catholic Historical Society 2, no. 5. Austin: Texas Knights of Columbus Historical Commission, April 1933.

Forrestal, Peter P., trans. *Peña's Diary of the Aguayo Expedition*. Preliminary Studies of the Texas Catholic Historical Society 2, no. 7. Austin: Texas Knights of Columbus Historical Commission, January 1935.

————, trans. *The Solís Diary of 1767*. Preliminary Studies of the Texas Catholic Historical Society, vol. 1, no. 6. Austin: Texas Knights of Columbus Historical Commission, March 1931.

Foster, William C. *Spanish Expeditions into Texas, 1689–1768*. Austin: University of Texas Press, 1995.

————, ed. *The La Salle Expedition on the Mississippi River: A Lost Manuscript of Nicolas de La Salle, 1682*. Translated by Johanna S. Warren. Austin: Texas State Historical Association, 2003.

————, ed. *The La Salle Expedition to Texas: The Journal of Henri Joutel, 1684–1687*. Translated by Johanna S. Warren. Austin: Texas State Historical Association, 1998.

————, ed. *Save the Young*. Corpus Christi: privately printed, 2004.

————, and Jack Jackson, eds.; Ned F. Brierley, trans. "The 1693 Expedition of Governor Salinas Varona to Sustain the Missionaries among the Tejas Indians." *Southwestern Historical Quarterly* 97 (Oct. 1993): 264–311.

Gadus, E. Frances, Ross C. Fields, and Karl W. Kibler. *Data Recovery Excavations at the J. B. White Site (41MM341), Milam County, Texas*. Archeological Studies Program, Report No. 87. Austin: Texas Department of Transportation, Environmental Affairs Division, 2006.

Gallay, Alan. *The Indian Slave Trade: The Rise of the English Empire in the American South, 1670–1717*. New Haven: Yale University Press, 2002.

Gibson, Jon L. *Poverty Point: A Terminal Archaic Culture of the Lower Mississippi Valley*.

Rev. ed. Baton Rouge: Louisiana Archaeological Survey and Antiquities Commission, 1999.

———, and Philip J. Carr, eds. *Signs of Power: The Rise of Cultural Complexity in the Southeast.* Tuscaloosa: University of Alabama Press, 2004.

Grove, Jean M. *The Little Ice Age.* New York: Methuen, 1988.

Hackett, Charles W., ed. *Historical Documents Relating to New Mexico, Nueva Vizcaya, and Approaches Thereto, to 1773.* 3 vols. Washington, D.C.: Carnegie Institution of Washington, 1926.

Hammond, George P., and Agapito Rey. *The Rediscovery of New Mexico, 1580–1594.* Albuquerque: University of New Mexico Press, 1966.

———, eds. and trans. *Obregón's History of 16th Century Explorations in Western America.* Albuquerque: University of New Mexico Press, 1928.

Hard, Robert J., and John R. Roney. "The Transition to Farming on the Rio Casas Grandes and in the Southern Jornada Mogollon Region." In Vierra, ed., *The Late Archaic across the Borderlands,* 141–186.

Hargrave, Lyndon L. *Mexican Macaws: Comparative Osteology and Survey of Remains from the Southwest.* Tucson: University of Arizona Press, 1970.

Harris, Arthur H. *Late Pleistocene Vertebrate Paleoecology of the West.* Austin: University of Texas Press, 1985.

Hatcher, Mattie Austin, trans. *The Expedition of Don Domingo Terán de los Ríos into Texas.* Preliminary Studies of the Texas Catholic Historical Society, vol. 2, no. 1. Austin, January 1932.

Hester, Thomas R. "Artifacts, Archeology, and Cabeza de Vaca in Southern Texas and Northeastern Mexico." *Bulletin of the Texas Archeological Society* 70 (1999): 17–28.

———, Harry J. Shafer, and Kenneth L. Felder. *Field Methods in Archeology.* 7th ed. Mountain View, Calif.: Mayfield, 1997.

Hickerson, Nancy P. *The Jumanos: Hunters and Traders of the South Plains.* Austin: University of Texas Press, 1994.

Hoffman, Fritz Leo, ed. "The Mezquía Diary of the Alarcón Expedition into Texas, 1718." *Southwestern Historical Quarterly* 41 (Apr. 1938): 312–323.

Hudson, Charles. *Knights of Spain, Warriors of the Sun: Hernando de Soto and the South's Ancient Chiefdoms.* Athens: University of Georgia Press, 1997.

Huebner, Jeffery A. "Late Prehistoric Bison Populations in Central and Southern Texas." *Plains Anthropologist* 36 (1991): 343–356.

Imhoff, Brian, ed. *The Diary of Juan Domínguez de Mendoza's Expedition into Texas (1683–1684).* Dallas: William P. Clements Center for Southwest Studies, Southern Methodist University, 2002.

Jackson, Jack, ed. *Imaginary Kingdom: Texas as Seen by the Rivera and Rubí Military Expeditions, 1727 and 1767.* Barker Texas History Center Series, no. 4. Austin: Texas State Historical Association, 1995.

Jones, Oakah L., Jr. *Nueva Vizcaya: Heartland of the Spanish Frontier.* Albuquerque: University of New Mexico Press, 1988.

———. "San José del Parral: Colonial Trade of Parralenses with Nuevo México and El Paso del Río del Norte. *Journal of Big Bend Studies* 13 (2001): 11–26.

Kelly, J. Charles. "The Historic Indian Pueblos of La Junta de los Ríos." *New Mexico Historical Review* 27 (Oct. 1952): 257–295.

———. *Jumano and Patarabueye: Relations at La Junta de los Ríos.*" Anthropological Papers, No. 77. Ann Arbor: Museum of Anthropology, University of Michigan, 1986.

Kinnaird, Lawrence. *The Frontiers of New Spain: Nicolas de Lafora's Description, 1766–1768.* Berkeley, Calif.: Quivira Society, 1958.

Klein, Richard G. *The Human Career.* Chicago: University of Chicago Press, 1999.

———, and Blake Edgar. *The Dawn of Human Culture.* New York: John Wiley and Sons, 2002.

Kotter, Steven M., Patience E. Patterson, Dan K. Utley, and Henry B. Moncure. *Final Report of Cultural Resource Investigations at the Cummins Creek Mine, Fayette County, Texas.* Studies in Archeology 11. Austin: Texas Archeological Research Laboratory, University of Texas at Austin, 1991.

Kress, Margaret K., trans. "Diary of a Visit of Inspection of the Texas Missions Made by Fray Gaspar José de Solís in the Year 1767–1768." *Southwestern Historical Quarterly* 35, no. 1 (July 1931): 28–76.

Krieger, Alex D. *We Came Naked and Barefoot: The Journey of Cabeza de Vaca across North America.* Austin: University of Texas Press, 2002.

Lagarde, François, ed. *The French in Texas: History, Migration, Culture.* Austin: University of Texas Press, 2003.

Lamb, H. H. *Climate, History, and the Modern World.* 2d ed. New York: Routledge, 1995.

La Vere, David. *The Caddo Chiefdoms: Caddo Economics and Politics, 700–1835.* Lincoln: University of Nebraska Press, 1998.

LeBlanc, Steven A. *Constant Battles: Why We Fight.* New York: St. Martin's Press, 2003.

———. *Prehistoric Warfare in the American Southwest.* Salt Lake City: University of Utah Press, 1999.

Lewis-Williams, David. *The Mind in the Cave: Consciousness and the Origins of Art.* London: Thames and Hudson, 2002.

Linden, Eugene. *The Winds of Change: Climate, Weather, and the Destruction of Civilizations.* New York: Simon and Schuster, 2006.

Lintz, Christopher. "Antelope Creek Phase," In Tyler et al., *The New Handbook of Texas,* 1:203.

Lister, Florence C. *Behind Painted Walls.* Albuquerque: University of New Mexico Press, 2000.

McKusick, Charmion R. *Southwest Birds of Sacrifice.* Arizona Archaeologist 31. Globe, Ariz.: Arizona Archeological Society, 2001.

———. *Southwest Indian Turkeys: Prehistory and Comparative Osteology.* Globe, Ariz.: Southwest Bird Laboratory, 1986.

McWilliams, Richebourg G., ed. and trans. *Iberville's Gulf Journals.* Tuscaloosa: University of Alabama Press, 1981.

Mallouf, Robert J. "Arroyo de las Burras: Preliminary Findings from the 1992 SRSU Archeological Field School," *Journal of Big Bend Studies* 7 (Jan. 1995): 3–41.

———. "Comments on the Prehistory of Far Northeastern Chihuahua, the La Junta District, and the Cielo Complex." *Journal of Big Bend Studies* 11, (Jan. 1999): 49–92.

———. "Late Archaic Foragers of Eastern Trans-Pecos Texas and the Big Bend." In Vierra, *The Late Archaic across the Borderlands,* 219–246.

Margry, Pierre. *Decouvertes et etablissements des Francais dans l'ouest et dans le sud de l'Amérique Septentrionale, 1614–1754.* 6 vols. Paris: D. Jouaust, 1876–1886.

Milner, George R. *The Cahokia Chiefdom: The Archaeology of a Mississippian Society.* Washington, D.C.: Smithsonian Institution Press, 1998.

Morris, John Miller, ed. *Narrative of the Coronado Expedition.* Chicago: Lakeside Press, 2002.

Neitzel, Jill E., ed. *Great Towns and Regional Polities in the Prehistoric American South-*

west and Southeast. Amerind Foundation New World Studies, No. 3. Albuquerque: University of New Mexico Press, 1999.

O'Donnell, Walter J., ed. *La Salle's Occupation of Texas.* Preliminary Studies of the Texas Catholic Historical Society 3, no. 2. Austin: Texas Knights of Columbus Historical Commission, April 1936.

Olson, Steve. *Mapping Human History: Discovering the Past through Our Genes.* Boston: Houghton Mifflin, 2001.

Pauketat, Timothy R. *Ancient Cahokia and the Mississippians.* Cambridge: Cambridge University Press, 2004.

Pérez de Ribas, Andrés. *My Life among the Savage Nations of New Spain.* Translated by Tomás A. Robertson. Los Angeles: Ward Ritchie Press, 1968.

Perttula, Timothy K., ed. *The Prehistory of Texas.* College Station: Texas A&M University Press, 2004.

——, and James E. Bruseth, eds. *The Native History of the Caddo: Their Place in Southeastern Archeology and Ethnohistory.* Studies in Archeology 30. Austin: Texas Archeological Research Laboratory, University of Texas at Austin, 1998.

Pohl, John M. D. *Exploring Mesoamerica.* Oxford: Oxford University Press, 1999.

Quigg, J. Michael, et al. *The Varga Site: A Multicomponent, Stratified Campsite in the Canyonlands of Edwards County, Texas.* Technical Report No. 35319. Austin: TRC Inc., 2005.

Riley, Carroll L. *Becoming Aztlan: Mesoamerican Influence in the Greater Southwest,* AD 1200–1500. Salt Lake City: University of Utah Press, 2005.

——. *Rio del Norte: People of the Upper Rio Grande from Earliest Times to the Pueblo Revolt.* Salt Lake City: University of Utah Press, 1995.

Salinas, Martin. *Indians of the Rio Grande Delta.* Austin: University of Texas Press, 1990.

Santos, Richard G. *Aguayo Expedition into Texas, 1721: An Annotated Translation of the Five Versions of the Diary Kept by Br. Antonio de le Peña.* Austin: Jenkins Publishing, 1981.

Saunders, Joe W., et al. "A Mound Complex in Louisiana at 5400–5000 years Before the Present." *Science* 277 (Sept. 19, 1997): 1796–1799.

Schaafsma, Curtis F., and Carroll L. Riley, eds. *The Casas Grandes World.* Salt Lake City, University of Utah Press, 1995.

Schneider, Paul. *Brutal Journey: The Epic Story of the First Crossing of North America.* New York: Henry Holt, 2006.

Schroeder, Albert H., and Dan S. Matson. *A Colony on the Move: Gaspar Castaño de Sosa's Journal, 1590–1591.* Santa Fe, N.M.: School of American Research, 1965.

Simmons, Marc. *The Last Conquistador: Juan de Oñate and the Settling of the Far Southwest.* Norman: University of Oklahoma Press, 1991.

Simpson, Benny J. *Texas Trees.* Austin: Texas Monthly Press, 1988.

Smith, Bruce D. *The Emergence of Agriculture.* New York: Scientific American Library, 1995.

Smith, F. Todd. *The Wichita Indians: Traders of Texas and the Southern Plains, 1540–1845.* College Station: Texas A&M University Press, 2000.

Smith, Larry L., and Robin W. Doughty. *The Amazing Armadillo.* Austin: University of Texas Press, 1984.

Smith, Ralph A., trans. "Account of the Journey of Bénard de La Harpe: Discovery Made by Him of Several Nations Situated in the West." *Southwestern Historical Quarterly* 62 (July 1958): 75–86; (Oct. 1958): 246–259; (Jan. 1959): 371–385; (Apr. 1959): 525–541.

Stringer, Christopher, and Clive Gamble. *In Search of the Neanderthals.* New York: Thames and Hudson, 1993.

Swanton, John R. *The Indians of the Southeastern United States*. Washington, D.C.: Smithsonian Institution, 1946.

Tankersley, Kenneth B. "The Concept of Clovis and the Peopling of North America." In *The Settlement of the American Continents: A Multidisciplinary Approach to Human Biogeography*. Edited by C. Michael Barton et al. Tucson: University of Arizona Press, 2004.

Tattersall, Ian, and Jeffrey Schwartz. *Extinct Humans*. Boulder, Colo.: Westview Press, 2001.

Taylor, Allan R. "Nonspeech Communication Systems." In *Handbook of North American Indians*. Vol. 17. Edited by Ives Goddard, 275–282. Washington, D.C.: Smithsonian Institution, 1996.

Thoms, Alston V., and R. D. Mandel, eds. *Archeological and Paleoecological Investigations at the Richard Beene Site, 41BX831: South-Central Texas*. College Station: Center for Ecological Archaeology, Texas A&M University, 2005.

Tous, Gabriel. *The Espinosa-Olivares-Aguirre Expedition of 1709*. Preliminary Studies of the Texas Catholic Historical Association, vol. 1, no. 3. Austin: Texas Knights of Columbus Historical Commission, March 1930.

———. *The Ramón Expedition: Espinosa's Diary of 1716*. Preliminary Studies of the Texas Catholic Historical Society, vol. 1, no. 4. Austin: Texas Knights of Columbus Historical Commission, April 1930.

Turner, Ellen Sue, and Thomas R. Hester. *A Field Guide to Stone Artifacts of Texas Indians*. Houston: Gulf Publishing, 1985.

Turpin, Solveig A., ed. *Papers on Lower Pecos Prehistory*. Studies in Archeology 8. Austin: Texas Archeological Research Laboratory, University of Texas at Austin, 1991.

———. Foreword to *Bison Hunting at Cooper Site: Where Lightning Bolts Drew Thundering Herds*, by Leland C. Bement. Norman: University of Oklahoma Press, 1999.

Tyler, Ron, et al., eds. *The New Handbook of Texas*. 6 vols. Austin: Texas State Historical Association, 1996.

Vierra, Bradley J., ed. *The Late Archaic across the Borderlands: From Foraging to Farming*. Austin: University of Texas Press, 2005.

Vines, Robert A. *Trees, Shrubs, and Woody Vines of the Southwest*. Austin: University of Texas Press, 1960.

Vivian, R. Gwinn. *The Chacoan Prehistory of the San Juan Basin*. Tucson: Academic Press, 1990.

Wade, Mariah F. *The Native Americans of the Texas Edwards Plateau, 1582–1799*. Austin: University of Texas Press, 2003.

Weber, David J. *The Spanish Frontier in North America*. New Haven: Yale University Press, 1992.

Weddle, Robert S., ed. *La Salle, the Mississippi, and the Gulf: Three Primary Documents*. College Station: Texas A&M University Press, 1987.

Wells, Spencer. *The Journey of Man: A Genetic Odyssey*. Princeton, N.J.: Princeton University Press, 2002.

West, Robert C., ed. *Natural Environment and Early Cultures*. Vol. 1 of *Handbook of Middle American Indians*. Edited by Robert Wauchope. Austin: University of Texas Press, 1964.

Young, Gloria A., and Michael P. Hoffman, eds. *The Expedition of Hernando de Soto West of the Mississippi, 1541–1543*. Fayetteville: University of Arkansas Press, 1993.

INDEX

Page numbers in italics refer to maps.

bison-hide robes, 141; and Cabeza de Vaca expedition, 25, 53–54, 255; and Caux Indians, 224–225; in Central Texas Coast, 53–54, 86; and Chamuscado expedition, 149; and climate change, 7, 8, 51, 108, 143, 174, 186, 188, 234, 238, 240, 291n.1; and De León expedition, 34; and De Soto expedition, 255; and Ebahamo Indians, 57, 77; and Espinosa expedition, 35, 71, 123; extinction of larger bison, 3, 247, 256; as food source, 71, 148, 177, 181, 185, 224, 255; and Hasinai Caddo, 71; hump on, 71; and Jumano Indians, 164; jump technique for killing of, 126; and La Junta Indians, 140, 161; and La Salle expedition, 29, 31, 32, 53, 86, 90, 99, 100, 256; between Lower Brazos and Lower Colorado Rivers, 25, 29, 31, 32, 34, 35; between Lower Colorado and San Antonio Rivers, 51, 71, 72, 290n.1; and Mendoza expedition, 184, 185–186, 187; nomadic lifestyle of bison hunters, 234; in Northeast Texas, 210; and Plains Indians, 8, 241–242, 292n.16; in prehistoric period, 3, 125, 126, 256, 290–291n.1; and Querechos, 12, 138, 143, 165–166, 171, 173–174, 191, 244, 255, 258; and Quivira Indians, 191; size of bison herds, 108, 234; in Southern Plains, 7–8, 72, 173–174, 178, 180–188, 192, 255, 290–291n.1; in South Texas, 108, 116, 117, 120, 127; Spanish and French explorers on generally, 11, 255–256; trade of bison hides and meat, 54, 148, 177, 234; in Trans-Pecos, 138, 143, 149, 150, 152, 157, 192; in Upper Texas Coast, 224–225, 230; uses of different parts of, 71, 181; and Wichita Indians, 169, 192; Zaldívar's bison-hunting expedition, 12, 138, 170, 180–181
blackberry, 269
Blackland Prairies, 19, 195
black people, 151, 174
Blanco Canyon, 171
Blanco Indians, 120
Blue Bayou site, 99
bluewood condalia, 269
boats and ships, 27, 31, 97, 200, 202, 221–222, 273, 277. See also canoes

bobcats, 4, 125, 127, 248, 256
Bobida Indians. See Bidai/Bobida Indians
Bobole Indians, 115, 116, 129, 225
bois d'arc, 203, 205, 269
bolas or sinkers, 249, 303n.18
Bolton, Herbert E., 39, 101, 128, 211, 214, 221, 267, 279, 283
Bonilla, Francisco Leyva de, 155–156, 170, 190
Borrodo Indians, 114, 129
Bosque expedition: and fish, 259; on Native tribes, 129–135; publication on, 15; and rescue of Spanish boy held captive by Native tribe, 117; in South Texas (Study Area 4), 13, 47, 109, 116–117; on trees and plants, 117, 272, 274, 275, 277, 280, 284
bow and arrow, 5, 127, 141, 146, 150, 181, 203, 221, 239, 248, 269, 270, 299n.38, 300n.24. See also hunting
Brazos River: and Aguayo expedition, 37, 72; and Alarcón expedition, 209; alligators in, 252; as boundary of Upper Texas Coast, 219; and Cabeza de Vaca expedition, 24; cane brakes near, 270; crossing area of, 208; and De León expedition, 34; and Dorantes party, 24; and La Salle expedition, 30–32, 34, 223; location of, 10, 18, 168, 169, 194, 196, 218; misidentification of, as Maligne River, 51, 291n.3; and Ramón expedition, 37, 208; and Rubí expedition, 229; trees along, 33–34, 272, 275, 278, 280, 283. See also Lower Brazos River to Lower Colorado River (Study Area 1)
Bréman, Eustache, 97, 225
Brooks, Robert, 173, 187–188
Buckner's Creek, 32, 50, 59
buffalo. See bison or buffalo
burial practices, 2, 22, 127, 235, 240, 246
Bustamante, Pedro de, 149, 296n.17

Cabeza de Vaca expedition: and bison, 25, 53–54, 255; on cannibalism, 127; in Central Texas Coast (Study Area 3), 82, 84, 85–86; in Chihuahua, Mexico, 138, 141, 255; and copper bell, 172–173, 198; and Cow People, 140, 165; deaths of members of, 22; detail in expedition narrative of, 149; on food, 54; on Galveston

Island, 21–23, 220–221; on horticulture, 267, 276; and La Junta, 11, 138, 139–140, 151, 154; in Lower Brazos River to Lower Colorado River (Study Area 1), 21–26; in Lower Colorado River to San Antonio River (Study Area 2), 52, 53–55, 118; and Maize People, 141–142, 155; map and route of, *10*, 11, 20–21, 154, 170, 197, 220; and Mariame Indians, 53, 85–86, 110, 139; and Native tribes, 21–26, 31, 40–42, 44, 53, 85–86, 110, 125, 128–134, 139, 154, 220–221, 225, 231, 237, 239; on plants and trees, 266, 269, 277, 279, 281, 283; publications on, 15, 287n.42; and Quevene Indians, 26, 44–45, 53, 85; and rabbits, 262; and Rio Grande, 11, 111, 138, 140–141, 154, 176; on shamans, 22, 225, 240, 246; on sign language, 241; and silver received from Natives, 176; in South Texas (Study Area 4), *106*, 109, 110–113; and trade, 23, 24–25, 111–112, 127, 142, 198, 221, 261, 271; in Trans-Pecos (Study Area 5), *136*, 138, 139–142, 148, 170; travel time and distances for, 141; in Upper Texas Coast (Study Area 8), 11, *218*, 219–221; on warfare between Indian tribes, 25–26; and Yguase, 53

Cabeza Indians, 117, 129, 158, 163

Cabri Indians, *136*, 146, 160, 163

Cacalote Indians, 160, 163

Cacase Indians, 122

Cacaxtle/Cacaxles Indians: enemies of, 225; location of, 75, *106*; and Salinas Varona expedition, 69, 75, 122, 243; Spanish military expeditions against, 12–13, 69, 115–116, 129, 134

Cacquite Indians, 69–70

Cacuytattom Indians, 163

Cadadaquis Indians. *See* Caddohadacho Indians

Cadaquis Indians, 212

Caddohadacho Indians: allies and enemies of, 211–217; cosmopolitan lifeways of, 203; and horses, 205; Joutel on, 202–203, 205, 211–217, 268; and La Harpe, 209; map location of, *194*; and tattoos, 205; and Terán expedition, 207; and Tonty, 205, 208, 300n.24; trade of bows by, 205, 269, 300n.24

Caddo Indians: allies of, 45, 77, 102, 170, 211; and Cabeza de Vaca expedition, 24; capture of, by Chickasaw, 33; Catholic missionaries driven out of East Texas by, 13, 52, 71, 122; Clamcoeh raid against, 92; cosmopolitan lifeways of, 201, 206, 207–208, 209, 210–211, 236, 244; and De León expedition, 94; and Edwards chert, 300n.10; enemies of, 60, 92, 100, 195, 225; and Espinosa expedition, 43; and horticulture, 210, 235–236, 284; huts of, 182; and La Salle expedition, 30; list of tribes in Northeast Texas, 211–217; location of, 70, 195; and Mississippian cultural tradition, 7, 235; and Moscoso expedition, 11; and mounding building, 210; slave raids against, 203, 300n.23; Spanish military and clerical expeditions to, 122–123; and tobacco, 284; trade and travel by, 127, 201, 207–208, 210–211, 235; and warfare, 209, 244; and weapons, xii. *See also* Hasinai Caddo

Cagremoa Indians, 120, 129

Caguate Indians, 151, 160, 163, 165, 166

Cahaynihoua Indians. *See* Cahinno/Cahinio/Cahaynihoua Indians

Cahinno/Cahinio/Cahaynihoua Indians, 203–204, 212

Cahokia, 6, 7, 8, 234–235, 258, 286n.30

Caiasban Indians, 212

Caisquetebanna Indians, 65, 75, *82*, 94, 102

Caitsodammo Indians, 212

calumet ceremony, 206, 209–210

camels, 3

Camino Real, xi, 50, 227, 260, 283

Camole Indians, 110, 129

Campbell, Thomas N., 35, 36, 39, 41–47, 53, 61, 65, 74, 75, 77, 80, 102–104, 125, 189, 190, 191, 230–232

Campbell, T. J., 125

Canada, 200, 204

Canadian River: animals along, 252, 256; Antelope Creek people along, 187, 190; and Coronado expedition, 192; gathering of Native tribes along, 209–210; horticulture along, 234; and La Harpe, 209–210; location of, *10*, 168, 169; Native tribes along, 211, 213, 214, 216, 217; and Oñate expedition, 181–182

Cancy Indians. *See* Apache Indians
cane, 269–270
Caney Creek, 20, 24
Cannaha Indians, 212
Cannahio Indians, 212
cannibalism, 92, 116, 124, 127, 210, 211,
   216–217, 225, 231, 232, 258, 259
Cannohatinno Indians. *See* Canoatinno/
   Cannohatinno/Kanoatinno Indians
Canoatinno/Cannohatinno/Kanoatinno
   Indians, 32, 212
canoes, 83, 87, 88–89, 91, 97, 98, 104, 224,
   273. *See also* boats and ships
Canohatino Indians. *See* Quansatinno
   Indians
Cantey Indians, 212
Cantona Indians: on Colorado River as
   boundary, 19; and De León expedition,
   65; and Espinosa expedition, 43; and
   Hasinai Caddo, 236; and La Salle expe-
   dition, 40, 60; location of, *48*, 75; and
   Ramón Indians, 36; and Salinas Varona
   expedition, 69, 207; and Terán expedi-
   tion, 66–67
Caocose Indians. *See* Cascosi/Caocose
   Indians
Caomopac Indians, 120, 129
Capoque Indians, *18*, 21–24, 26, 31, 40,
   220. *See also* Coco Indians
Cappa Indians, 203, 204, 212. *See also*
   Acansa Indians
captives held by Native tribes, 65, 67–68,
   95, 117, 129, 206
Caquate Indians, *136*
Carancaguaze Indians. *See* Karankawa
   Indians
Carib Indians, 84
Carretero, Don Nicolas de, 115
Carvajal y de la Cueva, Don Luis, 113,
   175–176
Casas Grandes: animals near, 253, 255,
   257, 262; and Cabeza de Vaca, 138,
   141–142; copper bells from, 6, 7, 112,
   202, 237, 294n.9; copper mining near,
   294n.10; and cotton, 140, 237; decline
   of, 8; food at, 266–267, 271, 276; horticulture at, 112, 235, 275–276; houses
   of, 142–144; and Ibarra expedition, 138,
   142–143, 174; and parrots, 142, 144, 237;

261; plants and trees near, 266, 267,
   271, 272, 275–276, 282, 284; population of, 286n.30; and pottery, 281, 284;
   and Rivera expedition, 143–144; and
   Rubí expedition, 144; and trade, 6–7,
   111–112, 142, 147, 172–173, 192, 198, 237;
   and turkeys, 237; water control system
   at, 143
Casas Grandes people, 163. *See also* Casas
   Grandes
Cascosi/Caocose Indians, *82*, 94, 97, 99,
   101, 102. *See also* Karankawa Indians
Casqueza Indians, 66–67, 69, 75
Cassia Indians, 212
Castañeda de Nájera, Pedro de: on animals, 252, 253; on copper pendant, 172;
   on Coronado's expedition generally,
   173; on frozen rivers, 297n.2; on plants
   and trees, 183, 192, 267, 273, 282, 284; on
   Querecho Indians, 171, 191
Castaño de Sosa expedition: on animals,
   257, 258, 263; attack against, by Native
   Americans, 177; criminal trial and
   exile of Castaño, 178, 179; and death of
   Castaño, 178, 179; and fish, 259; food
   for, 177–178; map of, *10*; and Native
   tribes, 176–178, 188, 192, 242; in New
   Mexico, 138, 155, 176, 178; number of
   colonists with, 176; on plants, 277;
   route of, 12, 109; and search for silver
   in northeast Mexico, 176; in Southern
   Plains (Study Area 6), *168*, 170, 175–179,
   188, 192; in South Texas (Study Area 4),
   109; in Trans-Pecos (Study Area 5), 138,
   155, 167; warfare between Pueblo Indians and, 178
Castile melons, 153
Castillo, Alonso del, 21, 23, 81, 128,
   287n.42
Castillo, Diego del, 190
Catcho Indians, 212
catclaw, 270
Catholic missionaries: and banners and
   crosses carried by Native tribes, 185;
   and Caddo Indians, 13, 52, 71, 122, 206,
   207; clothing of Franciscan priests
   in possession of Native Americans,
   62–63, 159; in Coahuila, Mexico, 116;
   and Conchos Indians, 160; deaths of,

in New Mexico, 145, 149, 175; and La Bahía mission, 100, 101; and La Junta Indians, 159–160, 201; in Northeast Texas, 214; and Oñate expedition to Kansas, 181; and Pueblo revolt (1680), 201; in Quivira, Kansas, 174; and San Juan Bautista mission, *106*, 122, 123; and sign language, 68, 241; in Southern Plains, 184

Catouinayo Indians, 212

Catqueza/Saquita Indians, 67, 69, 75–76, 122, 133, 207, 243

Catujano Indians, 117, 129, 131, 134

Caudacho Indians, 227

Caula Indians, 157, 163

Caumuche Indians. *See* Comanche Indians

Cauquesi/Caucosi Indians, 87–88

Caurame Indians, 129

Caux Indians, *218*, 224–226, 230, 231, 232, 236

Cava Indians: and De León expedition, 62–63, 64, 66, 76, 240; destruction of Fort St. Louis by, 62–63; and dogs, 62, 240; and Emet Indians, 76; and Géry, 63, 66; language of, 61; between Lower Colorado and San Antonio Rivers, 65, 66, 76; and Mendoza expedition, 76, 187, 189; as same as Kabaye Indians, 42, 76

Cavelier, Abbé Jean, 31, 44, 47, 55, 56, 79, 196, 200, 204

cedar trees, 3, 157, 270

Cenis Indians. *See* Hasinai Caddo

Central Texas Coast (Study Area 3): Aguayo expedition in, *82*, 85, 98; Alarcón expedition in, *82*, 85, 97; archeological and anthropological studies on, 98–100; Béranger in, 85, 97–98; bison in, 53–54; boundaries of, 83; Cabeza de Vaca expedition in, *82*, 84, 85–86; counties in, 83; De León expedition in, *82*, 84, 93–95, 96; Dorantes in, 84; hunting parties from the Plains travel to, 54; La Salle expedition in, *82*, 84, 86–91; maps of, *14, 82*; Moscoso expedition in, 86; Native tribes in, *82*, 83–84, 100–104, 241; Rívas in, 92–93; sign language by Native Americans in, 87, 90, 93; Talon

brothers in, 91–92; Terán expedition in, *82*, 84–85, 95–97

century plant. *See* agave

Cepeda, Ambrosio de, 115

ceramics: animal images on, 254; and Antelope Creek People, 238; at beginning of Prehistoric period, 5; Caddoan pottery, 161; Casas Grandes pottery, 161, 281; for cooking, 61; El Paso pottery and polychrome ceramics, 161; and horticultural lifestyle, 248; Huastecan pottery, 125; and hunter-gatherers, 239; painting on, 6, 284; and Pueblo Indians, 148; Rockport pottery, 83; from San Antonio Bay site, 99; from South Texas, 125; Southwestern ceramics at Antelope Creek sites, 173; as trade good, 180, 238; yucca brush for painting, 284

Cerralvo, Mexico, 113, 114

Chaco Canyon, 6, 8, 235

Chaguan Indians, 129

Chaguantapan Indians, 66, 76

Chalome Indians, 67, 76, 243

Chamuscado expedition: on animals, 261, 262; and bison hunt, 149; dates of, 287n.46; and death of Chamuscado, 145; and horses, 145; on maize cultivation, 276; map of, *10*; and Native tribes, 145–149, 166, 185; in New Mexico, 138, 145, 148–149, 152, 174–175; on plants and trees, 268, 271, 277, 284; in Trans-Pecos (Study Area 5), *136*, 138, 145–149, 174–175

Chancre Indians, 60, 76

Chapa, Juan Bautista: on Azcué military expedition, 115–116; on cannibalism, 225; on De León's 1689 and 1690 expeditions in Texas, 15, 120; on European diseases impacting Native Americans, 108, 113, 245; on French post on Garcitas Creek, 64; history of northeastern Mexico and Texas by, 12; on Native tribes, 45, 69, 77, 79–80, 101–103, 108, 109, 113, 120, 128–135, 192, 242; on Native tribes loyal to Géry, 120, 128, 295n.29; on Nuevo León, Mexico, 12, 108, 113–115, 192; on plants and trees, 270, 279

Chaquash Indians, 122

Charruco Indians, *18,* 24, 25, 26, 31, 40, 221

Chaularame Indians, 70. *See also* Xarame Indians

Chaumene Indians, 40

Chavavare Indians. *See* Avavare/Chavavare Indians

Chaye Indians, 212

Chaymaya Indians, 67, 76, 243

Cheatham, Scooter, 266, 268, 279

Chepoussa Indians. *See* Chickasaw Indians

chestnut trees, 270–271

Chichimeca Indians, 114, 129, 281

Chichitame Indians, 158, 163, 165

Chickasaw Indians: enemies of, 209, 212; as Flatheads, 77, 203, 244, 300n.22; and La Salle expedition, 212; slave-raiding by, 33, 37, 203, 244, 300n.23; and warfare, 203, 209, 244. *See also* Flathead tribes

Chicolete Prairie, 95

Chihuahua, Mexico: bison herds in, 8, 143; Cabeza de Vaca in, 138, 141, 255; Chamuscado expedition in, 145, 148; copper in, 154; grasslands of, 126; horticulture in, 5, 153, 268, 276; Ibarra expedition in, 11; Indian raids on Spanish settlements in, 167; invasion of, by Hijos de las Piedras Indians, 164; Native scouts and hunting parties from, 8, 102; Native tribes in, 8, 67, 102, 114, 160–161, 163, 164, 186, 242; parrots in, 261; plants and trees in, 266, 267, 275; pottery in, 161; revolts of Native tribes in, 163, 164, 165, 167; Ribas in, 12; silver mines in, 113, 117, 139, 158, 159; trade routes in, 114, 208, 267, 271. *See also* Casas Grandes; Paquimé, Mexico

Chihuahuan Desert, 8, 143, 174

Chile Indians, 120, 130

Chinarra Indians, 160, 163, 166, 167

chinquapin. *See* chestnut trees

Chisos Indians, 158, 160, 161, 163, 164, 165, 166

Cholome Indians, 158, 160, 163, 164, 165, 167. *See also* Jumano Indians

Chomene Indians, 130

Chouman/Choumay Indians. *See* Jumano Indians

Cibola/Cibolo/Sibola Indians: allies and enemies of, 67, 76; gifts for, from French explorers, 159; and Hasinai Caddo, 236; hunting by, 163; and La Salle expedition, 30, 159; location of, 76, *136,* 161; Miguel as leader of, 159; revolt of, near Parral (1684), 163, 164, 165, 167; and Sabeata, 158; as Spanish scouts in search of French colony, 61–63, 93, 102, 166; and Terán expedition, 66–67, 76, 243; trade and travel by, 57, 76, 127, 163

Clamcoeh/Clamcoet Indians, 80, *82,* 91–92

Clark, W. P., 57

Classic period, 5–8, 235

Clayton, Lawrence A., 39

climate change: and bison, 7, 8, 51, 143, 174, 186, 188, 234, 238, 291n.1; dating of, 299n.42; and De Soto expedition, 198; and drought, 54, 140; and extinction of animals, 247–248; and Glacier National Park, 291n.2; and horticulture, 4–5, 7, 54, 187–188, 210, 234–235, 238–239, 303n.1; and Native peoples, 2, 4, 7–8, 287n.38; and sea level in Gulf of Mexico, 186, 287n.40, 299n.42; in Southern Plains, 180–181; in South Texas, 107–108, 113, 116, 117, 124, 126; and trees, 272; and warfare, 188, 238, 239; and winter weather, 124, 151–152, 171, 198, 200, 220–221, 297n.2. *See also* Little Ice Age; Medieval Warm Period

clothing: bison-hide robes, 141; of Capoque Indians, 22; ceremonial dress and feather headdresses, 151, 202, 203, 237, 249, 261; cotton clothing, 142, 151, 271; deerskin clothing, 88, 140, 142, 150; of Franciscan priests, 62–63, 159; of French settlers at Fort St. Louis, 62, 158–159; gifts of, by French and Spanish explorers, 97, 120; of Jumano Indians, 152; of Karankawa Indians, 98; of La Junta Indians, 139–140, 150; leather shoes, 177; of Lower Colorado River to San Antonio River tribes, 61; of Maize People (Casas Grandes), 142; from mulberry tree bark, 278; of Natchez Indians, 278; in prehistoric period, 249; of Pueblo Indians, 146, 155; of South Texas tribes, 127; of Taensa Indians, 278; of

lurgy, 172–173, 191, 199; execution of the Turk (Indian guide) by, 172; guides for, 171–172, 192; and horses, 259; on maize cultivation, 276; map and route of, *10, 11*, 142, 198; on Native lifeways generally, xii; and Native tribes, 171–174, 191, 192, 198; in New Mexico, 170, 171, 191, 255; on plants and trees, 267–268, 271, 273, 277, 279, 281, 282; publications on, 15, 287n.43; and Querechos, 12, 171, 173–174, 191, 244; to Quivira, Kansas, 11, 170, 171, 172, 173; in Southern Plains (Study Area 6), *168*, 170, 171–174

Corpus Christi Bay, *82*, 84, 93, 103

Cortez, Hernando, 267, 279

Cosmojoo Indians, 120, 130

cosmopolitan lifeways: of Caddohadacho Indians, 203; of Caddo Indians, 201, 206, 207–208, 209, 210–211, 236, 244; and common traditions in Texas Indian cultures, 243–245; definition of, xi; and diseases, 243; and diversity of Texas Indian cultures, xi, 233–243; of Ebahamo Indians, 73; of Karankawa Indians, 100; of Lower Colorado River to San Antonio River Native tribes, 57, 73, 84; of Native tribes in Texas generally, 9; of South Texas Native tribes, 114, 123, 127–128; of Trans-Pecos Native tribes, 159, 161, 244. *See also* trade; trade routes and travel corridors

Costello, Elaine, 57

cotton and cotton goods: and Casas Grandes, 140, 141; and Hasinai Caddo, 202; and Jumano Indians, 154; and Pueblo Indians, 148, 173, 175, 191, 237; Spanish and French explorers on, 198, 271; trade of, 112, 127, 140, 141, 142, 147, 148, 198, 199, 201, 202

cottontail rabbits. *See* rabbits

cottonwood trees, 117, 123, 152, 155, 157, 180, 271–272

cougars, 4, 51, 71, 123, 126, 248, 256–257

Council of the Indies, 178, 179

Cow People, 140, 165

Cox, Isaac J., 39, 101

Coyabsqux Indians, 60, 76

coyotes, 250

Craddock, Jerry R., 189

cremation, 22, 225, 240, 246

Cuajin Indians, 120, 130

Cuba, 252, 262, 279

Cuba Indians, 120

Cuchendado Indians, 110, 130

Cuita/Cuitoa/Cuytoa Indians, 184, 189, 190–191

Cujaco Indians, 157

Cujalo Indians, 157, 164

Cujane/Cojame Indians, 101, 103–104, 228, 231

Cummins Creek, 20, 31, 32, 280

Cummins Creek Mine site, 31

Cunquebaco Indians, 157, 164

Curmicai Indians, 37, 41, 44

Cuthalchuche Indians, 110, 130

Cuytoa Indians. *See* Cuita/Cuitoa/Cuytoa Indians

cypress trees, 3, 127, 272, 284

dancing and singing: by Capoque Indians, 23; by Central Texas Coast tribes, 91; by Guadalupe Valley Indians, 62; and peyote, 124, 127, 247, 281; by Pueblo Indians, 155; by Querecho Indians, 143, 174; religious practice of, 246–247; by South Texas tribes, 111, 124, 127; by Trans-Pecos tribes, 147, 151. *See also* musical instruments

Daquinatinno Indians, 213

Daquio Indians, 213

Datcho Indians, 213

Davis (George C.) site, 6

Deadose/Ygodsa Indians, 209, 212, 213, *218*, 231, 239

Deaguane/Doguene Indians: and Cabeza de Vaca expedition, 25–26, 31, 41, 53, 85, 103; location of, *18*, 41, 85; warfare between Quevene and, 25–26, 41, 44–45, 85, 103, 104

deer: clothing of deerskin, 88, 140, 142, 150; and De León expedition, 34; as food source, 224, 248, 257; and Hasinai Caddo, 71; hunting of, 123, 127, 153, 157, 199, 248, 250, 257; and La Salle expedition, 32, 86, 100; between Lower Brazos and Lower Colorado Rivers, 32, 34; between Lower Colorado River and San Antonio Rivers, 51, 54, 55; in Northeast

Texas, 210; in prehistoric period, 3; in rock art, 126; in Southern Plains, 178, 182, 185; in South Texas, 123, 124, 127; Spanish and French explorers on, 257; in Upper Texas Coast, 224

Deguene Indians. *See* Deaguane/Doguene Indians

De León, Captain Alonso (the elder): on animals, 114, 124–125, 252, 257, 259, 261; on Cabeza de Vaca, 111, 113, 176; on Carvajal, 113; on Castaño de Sosa, 178–179; expedition of, 12; on Native tribes, 108, 109, 113, 114, 124, 130, 134, 240; on religious beliefs and practices of Native tribes, 245, 246; on trade routes, 114; on trees and plants, 113–114, 269, 271–272, 275, 278, 283; on weather conditions, 113

De León, Governor Alonso (the younger): attacks by Matagorda Bay Indians against, 94; in Central Texas Coast (Study Area 3), *82*, 84, 93–95, 96; and dogs, 258; and food, 301n.30; and Fort St. Louis, 13, 21, 34, 64–65, 115, 119; and Garcitas Creek, 96; Géry as guide and interpreter for, 62, 63, 93–94, 119–120; Géry captured by, 93–94, 108, 117–119, 240; guides for, 62, 63, 78, 80, 93–94, 103, 119–120, 131, 133; and horses, 64, 121–122; in Lower Brazos River to Lower Colorado River (Study Area 1), *18*, 21, 34; in Lower Colorado River to San Antonio River (Study Area 2), *48*, 52, 62–66; maps and route of, 13, *18*, *48*; and Monument Hill, 20; and Native tribes, 34, 40, 41, 45, 46, 57, 62–66, 69, 74–78, 81, 94, 120, 129, 131, 132, 206, 215, 242; in Northeast Texas (Study Area 7), *194*, 196, 206; on plants and trees, 270, 272, 280–282; publications on, 15, 288n.60; and rescue of Talon children from Cascosi Indians, 94–95, 96, 99, 102; and Rio Grande, 62, 65–66, 69, 120, 121; search for La Salle by, 62–65; in South Texas (Study Area 4), *106*, 116, 117–122, 129, 131; on wildlife, 127, 257, 260; and Zacatil leader, 135

Depesguan Indians. *See* Tepeguan/Tepehuan/Depesguan Indians

Derbanne, François, 44, 74, 78–79, 190

De Sosa expedition. *See* Castaño de Sosa expedition

De Soto/Moscoso expedition: on animals, 254–257, 262, 263; and death of De Soto, 21, 26, 198, 245; and fish, 258–259; in Florida, 26, 170–171, 197; and horses, 259; on maize cultivation, 276; map and route of, *10*, *18*, 21, 142, 221, 222; on Native lifeways generally, xii, 8; in Northeast Texas (Study Area 7), 197–198; on plants and trees, 268, 271, 273, 277, 280, 282. *See also* Moscoso expedition

Detobiti Indians, 189

Devils River, 176

dewberry, 250, 269

Diamond, Jared, 7

Diju Indians, 189

Dillehay, Thomas D., 1, 185–186, 248, 250, 286n.23, 290–291n.1, 299n.41

Di Peso, Charles C., 144, 266–267, 271, 280–281, 284, 294nn.9–10

diseases, xii, 12, 22, 91, 108, 113, 124, 207, 245

dogs: and Apache Indians, 212; and Cava Indians, 62, 240; and dog trains, 171, 177, 180, 240, 241; domestication of, by Natives, 29, 248, 249, 257–258; and Emet Indians, 62, 240; as food source, 258; and Plains Indians, 177, 240, 241, 258; and Pueblo Indians, 148, 175, 191; and Querecho Indians, 171, 174, 180, 191, 258; Spanish and French explorers on, 257–258; and Vaquero Indians, 180

Doguene Indians. *See* Deaguane/Doguene Indians

dolphins, 88

Doolittle, William E., 143, 206, 301n.31

Dorantes, Andrés: and Cabeza de Vaca expedition, 287n.42; in Central Texas Coast (Study Area 3), 84; and Jumano Indians, 154; in Lower Brazos River to Lower Colorado River (Study Area 1), 21–24, 26; in Lower Colorado River to San Antonio River (Study Area 2), 52, 53, 75; and Narváez expedition, 84; and Quevene Indians, 86; as slave of Mariame Indians, 85–86

Dotchetonne Indians, 213

Douay, Fray Anastase: in Central Texas
Coast (Study Area 3), 84, 90, 101; on
horticulture, 239; in Lower Brazos
River to Lower Colorado River (Study
Area 1), 30, 31, 33, 34, 39–40, 42–46; in
Lower Colorado River to San Antonio
River (Study Area 2), 55, 56, 74, 79; and
Mississippi River, 196; on Native tribes,
101, 102, 104, 196, 212–215, 244; in
Northeast Texas, 196, 200–201, 212–215
Douesdonqua Indians, 213
dress. *See* clothing
drought, 54, 140
drunkenness, 91, 281
Duaine, Carl L., 128
Dunmire, William W., 267, 279, 282–283,
301n.30
Durango, Mexico, 9, 114, 128, 138, 161, 167,
177, 188, 242

Ebahamo Indians, 32, 56–57, 75–77, 102
Echancote Indians, 189
Edwards Plateau: animals on, 252, 253,
256, 257; bison hunting on, 161; and
Mendoza expedition, 163–167, 170, 184–
185; and Native tribes, 67, 161–167, 187,
199; plants in, 269; trees in, 280, 282
eels, 117
eggs, 224
Ehrlich, Paul, 1
Elias, Scott A., 291n.2, 299n.42
elm trees, 123, 273
Emet/Emot Indians: and Alarcón expedition, 37, 41, 45, 46; allies of, 46; and
Cava Indians, 76; and De León expedition, 41, 57, 62–64, 66, 77, 240; destruction of Fort St. Louis by, 62–63; and
dogs, 62, 240; and Géry, 63, 66, 77, 120;
and Hasinai Caddo, 236; language of,
61; location of, 41, 66, 76; messengers
from, 57, 64
Emot Indians. *See* Emet/Emot Indians
Enagado Indians. *See* Anagado/Enagado
Indians
Enoqua Indians, 213
Enríquez Barroto, Juan, 92–93
Erigoanna Indians, 101
Ervipiame Indians, 36, 46. *See also* Yeripiama Indians

Escalante, Felipe de, 145, 296n.17
Escanjaque/Aquacane Indians, *168*, 182,
184, 189, 191
Espejo expedition: on animals, 254–255,
261, 262; on bows and arrows, 181; dates
of, 287n.46; guides for, 150, 151, 152, 153;
on maize cultivation, 276; and Native
tribes, 149–155, 164, 165, 167, 185, 237;
in New Mexico, 151–152; on plants and
trees, 155, 268, 271; in Southern Plains
(Study Area 6), 170, 175; on tobacco,
283–284; in Trans-Pecos (Study Area 5),
136, 149–155
Espinosa expedition: and animals, 123,
252, 254, 257, 263; in Lower Brazos
River to Lower Colorado River (Study
Area 1), 21, 34–37, 40, 43–47, 72, 185; in
Lower Colorado River to San Antonio
River (Study Area 2), *48*, 52, 70–72; and
Native tribes, 40, 43–47, 70–71, 78, 81,
123, 131, 132, 214, 215; in Northeast Texas
(Study Area 7), 208, 214, 215; on plants
and trees, 267, 269, 271–275, 278–280;
publication on, 16, 288n.64; in South
Texas (Study Area 4), *106*, 123; on to-
bacco cultivation, 284
Espiritu Santo, 24, 26, 85. *See also* Mata-
gorda Bay
Estevan, 81, 111, 140, 294n.7
Estevanico, 81
Etayax Indians, 120, 130
Etowah, 235
Exepiahoke Indians, 41
extinct animals, 3, 125, 126, 247, 256, 259,
263

Fagan, Brian M., 285n.6
farming. *See* horticulture
feathers of macaw parrots. *See* parrots and
parrot feathers
fish: as food source, 97, 116, 149, 152, 210,
259; between Lower Colorado and San
Antonio Rivers, 54; in South Texas, 117;
Spanish and French explorers on, 100,
258–259; in Trans-Pecos, 146, 149, 151,
152; in Upper Texas Coast, 229
Flannery, Tim, 4, 248
Flathead tribes: and cranial modeling
or cranial deformation, 290n.30; and

La Salle expedition, 33, 37, 103, 213, 289n.30; and maize (corn), 33, 37, 77; warfare against, 60, 77, 88, 100, 103, 203, 244

flax, 174

Flechas Chiquitas Indians, 189

Flint, Richard, 189

Flint, Shirley Cushing, 189

flint tools, 191

Florida: Apalache in, 235; De Soto expedition in, 26, 170–171, 197; maize cultivation in, 276; Native tribes in, 206; pomegranate in, 283; turkeys in, 262

Folmer, Henri, 230

food: of Acansa Indians, 274; agave as, 266; amaranth as, 266; antelopes as source of, 248; armadillos as food source, 253; barbecued beef, 121; beans as, 140, 141, 152, 208, 267–268; bison meat, 71, 148, 177, 181, 185, 224, 255; of Capoque Indians, 21, 22, 23; of Casas Grandes people, 266–267, 271; of Caux Indians, 224; of Conchos Indians, 146; cooking vessels for, 61, 140, 141, 267; corn tamales, 301n.30; deer as food source, 224, 248, 257; dogs as food source, 175, 258; eggs as, 224; fish as, 97, 116, 149, 152, 210, 259; for Fort St. Louis, 202; of Hasinai Caddo, 206, 208, 268, 301n.30; of Karankawa Indians, 54; of La Junta people, 140, 267; lechuguilla as, 114; maize as, 208, 275–276; mesquite beans as, 146, 177, 277, 283; prickly pear as, 54, 55, 78, 146, 244, 283, 284; of Pueblo Indians, 148, 206; sotol as, 114; for Spanish and French explorers, 27, 28, 59, 97, 177–178, 181, 185, 199, 208, 222, 274; of Tanpachoa Indians, 151; tidal food sources between Lower Colorado and San Antonio Rivers, 54; of Trans-Pecos Native people, 152; turkeys as food source, 175; yucca as, 114, 284. *See also specific foods*

Fort Hancock, 272

Fort Lancaster, 167

Fort Natchitoches, 226

Fort St. Louis: and De León expedition, 13, 21, 34, 64–65, 115, 119; destruction of, by Native Americans, 62–63, 64,

158–159, 163, 205; and fishing, 259; food for, 202, 283; horses at, 202; Joutel at, 56; and La Salle expedition, 13, 21, 30, 31, 52, 84, 201–202; and maize cultivation, 277; map location of, *10, 48;* number of soldiers and colonists at, 90; plants and trees near, 270, 274; rescue of French survivors from, 52, 67–68, 95–97, 288n.61; roofing for, 273; Spanish fort on site of, 98; Spanish search for, 61–63, 92–94, 102, 103; water supply for, 96

Foster, William C., 39, 74, 101, 128, 162, 211, 230

foxes, 71

French expeditions: animals reported by, 251–263; in Canada, 200; diaries from, 9, 11; map of expedition routes of, *10;* in Mississippi Valley generally, 200; overview of, 13–14; publications on, 15–16; on trees and other plants, 265–284. *See also specific expeditions*

Frio River: animals near, 127; crossing area for, 34, 69, 108, 121; and De León expedition, 121; and Espinosa expedition, 34–35; map location of, *106;* Native tribes along, 66, 122, 128, 129, 134; in Nueces River system, 107; and Salinas Varona expedition, 69, 133; and Terán expedition, 122, 128, 132, 133; white rock with carved cross on, 121

fruit trees. *See specific types of trees*

Gallay, Alan, 244, 290n.31, 300n.23

Gallegos, Hernán, 145–149, 154, 162–164, 166, 246, 254

Galveston Bay, 28, *218,* 221–224, 226, 229, 276

Galveston Island, 21–24, 28, 40, 85, 219, 220–221

García Larios, Francisco, 227

Garcilaso de la Vega (the Inca), 27, 28, 221–222

Garcitas Creek: and De León expedition, 94, 96; distance between Lavaca River and, 95–96; Fort St. Louis on, 30, 31, 64, 84, 201; and Martínez, 95–96; and Matagorda Bay, 50; plants and trees near, 279, 284. *See also* Fort St. Louis

Garza, Juan de la, 115

Gatschet, Albert S., 98
Gavilan Indians, 164
Gediondo Indians. *See* Jediondo/
  Gediondo Indians
Geniocane Indians, 117, 130
Gentleman from Elvas, 27, 198, 271, 273,
  277, 282
George C. Davis site, 6
Georgia, 235
Géry, Jean: capture of, by De León, 93–94,
  108, 117–119, 240; as De León's guide
  and interpreter, 62, 63, 93–94, 119–120;
  and Native languages, 63, 118; and
  Native tribes, 45, 46, 63, 66, 77, 118–120,
  128–135, 295n.29; physical appearance
  of, 118–119; wife and children of, 118,
  119, 121
Gill, Richardson B., 143
Gilmore Corridor, xi
Giora Indians, 116
Glacier National Park, 291n.2
goats, 178, 263
Goddard, Ives, 73, 241, 292n.16
goosefoot, 5
gourds, 111, 124, 140, 150, 237
grapes: and Espinosa expedition, 35, 123;
  in Kansas, 174; in modern-day Texas,
  250; in Southern Plains, 185, 192; Spanish and French explorers on, 273–274,
  282; in Trans-Pecos, 152, 155, 157
graves. *See* burial practices
Great Lakes, 204
Grollet, Jacques, 95
Guachachile/Hatachichile Indians, 114, 130
Guadalajara, Diego de, 189, 190
Guadalupe Bay, 84
Guadalupe River: and Alarcón expedition,
  209; and Cabeza de Vaca expedition, 53;
  and De León expedition, 62, 64, 65, 95,
  240; dog trains near, 258; and Espinosa
  expedition, 70; and Guadalupe Bay and
  San Antonio Bay, 84; and Jumano and
  Cibola Indians scouting party, 62; La
  Bahía presidio along, 226; map location
  of, *48, 82*; naming of, 62; Native tribes
  near, 66, 74; pecan gathering by Native
  Americans on, 45, 54, 80, 81, 85, 279;
  trees along, 279
Guapite Indians. *See* Coapite/Guapite
  Indians

Guasco Indians, *194*, 198, 213. *See also*
  Hasinai Caddo
Guaycone Indians, 110, 129, 130
Gueiquesale Indians, 116
Guevene Indians. *See* Quevene Indians
Gulf Coast. *See* Central Texas Coast
  (Study Area 3); Upper Texas Coast
  (Study Area 8)
Gulf of California, 6, 142, 161
Gulf of Mexico: birds along, 255; fish in,
  259; and La Salle expedition, 28, 200;
  map location of, *82, 218*; and Moscoso
  expedition, 27, 200; Natives swimming
  in, 29; rivers and creeks flowing into,
  20, 196, 228; sea-level history in, 186,
  285n.13, 287n.40
Gutiérrez, Jusepe, 180, 181, 190
Gutiérrez de Humaña, Antonio, 190

Hall, Grant D., 290n.32
Hammond, Charles A., 98
Hammond, George P., 162, 179, 189
Hanacine/Hanasine Indians, 157, 164
Handbook of North American Indians,
  137, 241
hand signs. *See* sign language
Han Indians, 21–22, 23, 31, 220, 231
Hape Indians. *See* Ape/Api/Hape Indians
Haqui Indians, 213
Hasinai Caddo: and Aguayo expedition,
  40, 209; and Alarcón expedition, 72,
  209; allies of, 32, 57, 62, 67, 80, 161, 195,
  201, 244; Bellisle rescued by, 225–226,
  231; and calumet ceremony, 206, 209–
  210; cannibalism of, 225; and Catholic
  missionaries and missions, 13, 52, 71,
  206, 207, 214; clothing of, 202; cosmopolitan lifeways of, 201, 206, 207–211,
  236, 244; and De León expedition, 34,
  40, 64, 65, 206; and Ebahamo Indians,
  56–57, 75; enemies of, 67, 212, 213, 214,
  225, 227, 244; and epidemic, 207; and
  Espinosa expedition, 40, 46, 208; food
  of, 206, 208, 268, 301n.30; Frenchmen
  living with, 32, 205–206; and horses, 33,
  201, 206, 227, 237; horticulture by, 153,
  206, 208, 209, 210, 235–236, 237, 283,
  284; houses of, 206; hunting by, 33, 34,
  38, 40, 55, 70–71, 75, 199, 206, 207, 236,
  308; and Jumano Indians, 42, 156, 159,

161, 166, 201, 210, 212–213, 244, 326; and La Harpe, 209–210; and La Salle expedition, 21, 32, 40, 45, 89, 196, 200–206, 213; location of, 31, 56, *194*, 208; and Mendoza expedition, 184, 187, 189; and Moscoso expedition, 11, 26–27, 55, 196, 198–199, 271; pipe-smoking ceremony of, 208; and Ramón expedition, 13, 36, 208; religious practices of, 246; and Salinas Varona expedition, 40, 69, 80, 207; and Spanish expeditions generally, 213; and Terán expedition, 207; tobacco cultivation by, 284; and Tonty, 205–206; trade and travel by, 26–27, 35, 37, 156, 161, 195, 198, 201, 202, 207–211, 227, 235, 271; and warfare, 209, 244; and women's status, 208

Hatachichile Indians. *See* Guachachile/ Hatachichile Indians

hawthorn trees, 274

Haychis Indians, 213

hemp, 274–275

Hester, Thomas R., 125, 303n.18

Hianagouy Indians, 213

Hiantatsi Indians, 213

Hidalgo, Mexico, 125

Hijos de las Piedras Indians, 164

Hinchi Indians, 157, 164

Hinsa Indians, 189

Hispanola, 262

Holocene period, 3, 248, 252, 253, 261, 263

Homo Erectus, 2

homosexuals and cross-dressers, 204

Hondo Creek, *106*, 122

Hondo River, 107, 127, 133

Honecha Indians. *See* Waco/Honecha Indians

horses: and Akokisa Indians, 230; and Apache Indians, xii, 212, 243, 260; and Caddohadacho Indians, 205; of Cahinno Indians, 203–204; and Caux Indians, 224; and Chamuscado expedition, 145; and De León expedition, 64, 121–122; exchange of French captives for, 68; extinction of, in prehistoric period, 3, 259; and Hasinai Caddo, 33, 201, 206, 227, 237; and Jumano Indians, 32–33, 153, 201, 237, 260; and Karankawa Indians, 102, 214; and La Salle expedition, 33, 89, 104, 202, 260; for leaders of

Native tribes, 243; and Ramón Indians, 36; with saddles and stirrups, 67; sale of, by Quoaque Indians, 104; Spanish and French explorers on, 259–260; and Taraha Indians, 45; and Teao Indians, 32; theft of and raids for, 67, 69, 70, 114–115, 121–122, 214, 227, 229, 259

horticulture: and Antelope Creek People, 171, 187–188, 190, 238–239; and Bidai Indians, 230, 239; and Casas Grandes people, 112, 235, 275–276; in Chihuahua, Mexico, 5, 153, 268, 276; and climate change, 4–5, 7, 54, 187–188, 210, 234–235, 238–239, 303n.1; in Coahuila, Mexico, 268, 271; and Conchos Indians, 146, 149, 153, 155, 164, 284; and drought, 54, 140; and Flathead tribes, 33, 37, 77; global timing of development of, 1, 286n.23; and Hasinai Caddo, 153, 206, 208, 209, 210, 235–236, 237, 283, 284; and irrigation, 155, 160, 248; and Jumano Indians, 160; in Kansas, 169, 182, 183, 190, 268, 276; and Kirona Indians, 30; and La Junta Indians, 140, 146, 161, 183, 234, 236–237, 267, 268, 276; between Lower Brazos and Lower Colorado Rivers, 30, 33, 37; and Mississippian tribes, 197, 199, 210, 235, 237; Moscoso expedition on, 33; in Northeast Texas, 196, 204, 206, 215; in Oklahoma, 169, 190, 276; and Otomoaco Indians, 150; and Palaquechare Indians, 33, 268; in prehistoric period, 4–5; and Pueblo Indians, 146, 148, 155, 169, 173, 175, 180, 191, 237, 268; and Quivira Indians, 191; summary of horticultural lifestyle, 233, 234–239, 248; and Tanpachoa Indians, 151; and Teyas Indians, 267–268; in Trans-Pecos, 140, 146, 148, 150, 151, 157, 160, 161, 163, 164, 234, 268; in Upper Texas Coast, 222, 229, 230; and Wichita Indians, 169, 183, 190, 192, 268. *See also* beans; maize (corn)

Houaneiha Indians, 214

houses: of Antelope Creek people, 187, 238; Conchos Indians on, 154; of Hasinai Caddo, 206; of Jumano Indians, 154, 164; of La Junta Indians, 139, 146–147, 150; of Paquimé (Casas Grandes), 6, 142–144; of Pueblo Indians, 146, 148,

150, 152, 155, 173, 175, 191; and stone architecture, 248; of Taensa Indians, 205; of Wichita Indians, 182–183, 192. *See also* huts

Huasteca and Huastecan culture, 4, 125–126, 127, 175

Hudson, Charles, 28, 222

Hugugan Indians, 37, 41

Huiapico Indians, 120, 130

Huicasique Indians, 189

huisache, 117, 275

Hume Indians, 189

hunting: by Antelope Creek people, 188; by Apache Indians, 72, 169, 234; by Capoque Indians, 23; by Cibola Indians, 163; by Conchos Indians, 149, 153; of deer, 123, 127, 149, 153, 157, 199, 250; dogs used in, 258; by Hasinai Caddo, 33, 34, 38, 40, 55, 70–71, 75, 199, 206, 207, 208, 236; by Julime Indians, 157; by Jumano Indians, 77, 127, 152, 161, 164, 188, 237; by La Junta Indians, 161, 183; by La Salle expedition, 32; by Native tribes from Mexico, 242–243; by Plains Indians, 8, 241–242, 292n.16; in prehistoric period, 1–2, 3, 181; of rabbits, 127, 149, 153, 262; by Simaoma Indians, 35; in South Texas, 123, 127–128; subsistence lifestyle of hunter-gatherers, 210, 233–234, 239–240; by Tepehuan Indians, 188, 192, 242; territorial hunting boundaries, 55, 60; of turkeys, 123, 127, 250, 263–264; by Wichita Indians, 169, 192. *See also* bison or buffalo; bow and arrow; deer

huts: of Caddo Indians, 182; of Capoque Indians, 22; of Cauquesi/Caucosi Indians, 88; chief's hut, 59; of Clamcoeh Indians, 91; of Escanjaque Indians, 182; and estimation of encampment populations, 90; of hunter-gatherers, 240; of Jumano Indians, 154; of Karankawa Indians, 98, 291n.11; between Lower Colorado and San Antonio Rivers, 56, 59; mulberry tree bark for, 278; near Paquimé, 143; number of occupants in, 59; of Plains Indians, 182; pole frames of, 56, 90, 240, 291n.11; of Teao Indians, 32. *See also* houses

Huyugan Indians, 45

Ibarra expedition: and bison, 255; map and route of, *10*, 11–12; and Querecho Indians, 165–166, 174; in Trans-Pecos (Study Area 5), 138, 142–143, 174; on trees, 272, 275

Iberville, Pierre Le Moyne d', 282

Ice Age, 2, 256. *See also* Little Ice Age

Ijiaba/Xiabu Indians, *106*, 120, 130, 240

Illinois River, 263

illnesses. *See* diseases

Imhoff, Brian, 189

The Inca (Garcilaso de la Vega), 27, 28, 221–222

indigo. *See* bluewood condalia

Inhame Indians. *See* Injame/Inhame Indians

Injame/Inhame Indians, 189

Iscani/Isconi Indians, 187, 189

Isucho Indians, 157, 164

jackrabbits. *See* rabbits

jadeite, 125

jaguars, 4, 71, 123, 248, 260

jaguarundi, 4, 248, 256

Jaramillo, Juan, 173–174

javelinas, 3, 125, 127, 247, 260–261

Jeapa Indians, 117, 130, 131, 132, 135

Jediondo/Gediondo Indians, 157, 164, 184–185, 191, 192

Jeniocane Indians, 117, 130

Joboso Indians. *See* Toboso Indians

John, Elizabeth, xi–xii

Johnson, LeRoy, 61

Johnson, Marshall C., 266, 268, 279

Jojane Indians. *See* Yojuane Indians

Jolliet, Louis, 200, 283

Jones, Oakah L., 299n.44

Jornada del Muerto (Dead Man's March), 179–180

Josephe (Indian), 155–156

Joutel, Henri: on animals, 53, 86, 90, 100, 252, 254–257, 259, 261; on bison, 53, 86, 90, 99, 100, 256; and Colorado River as boundary, 19, 55, 60, 71; on fish, 259; on food, 268, 301n.30; at Fort St. Louis, 56, 200; on La Salle expedition, 28–34, 55–61, 86–91, 104, 223; on maize cultivation, 277; and Mississippi River, 196, 204; on Native tribes, 31, 38–46, 55–57, 60–61, 66, 73–81, 87–91, 98, 99,

101–102, 196, 202–205, 211–216, 239; in Northeast Texas, 196, 202–206; on plants and trees, 153, 239, 267, 269, 270, 272–274, 278–280, 282–284; publication of journal by, 16, 231–232, 291n.3; on religious practices of Native tribes, 246; on tobacco, 284; on trade networks, 236; on warfare between Flatheads and other Indian tribes, 244. *See also* La Salle expedition

Joyvan Indians. *See* Yojuane Indians

Juama Indians, 189

Julime Indians, 157, 159, 161, 163–167

Jumano Indians: allies of, 32, 41–42, 45, 67, 76, 77, 102, 161, 191, 201, 203, 244; and Cabeza de Vaca expedition, 154; clothing of, 152; as Cow People, 140; and De León expedition, 120; enemies of, 76, 161; and Espejo expedition, 150–151, 152, 154, 164; and Géry's capture by De León, 240; and Hasinai Caddo, 42, 156, 159, 161, 166, 201, 210, 212–213, 236, 244; and horses, 32–33, 153, 201, 237, 260; and horticulture, 160; houses and huts of, 154, 164; hunting by, 77, 127, 152, 161, 164, 188, 237; and La Salle expedition, 30, 32, 201, 213; location of, *136*, 137; and Mendoza expedition, 139, 156–157, 191; Muruam boys as captives of, 67, 78; painted faces of, 154; Sabeata as chieftain of, 62, 77, 156–159, 166; and Salinas Varona expedition, 68, 69, 81, 134, 207; as Spanish scouts in search of French colony, 61–63, 93, 163, 166; and Terán expedition, 35, 66–67, 122, 243; trade by, 77, 153, 154, 236, 260; travel by, 57, 124, 127, 161; warriors of, and Salinas Varona expedition, 68, 81; and weapons, xii

Jume/Jumene Indians, 117, 130–131

juniper trees, 155, 180

Kabaye Indians, 42, 76

Kannehouan Indians, 77. *See also* Cantona Indians

Kanoatinno Indians. *See* Canoatinno/Cannohatinno/Kanoatinno Indians

Kanoatinoa Indians. *See* Quansatinno Indians

Kansas: bison in, 255; Coronado expedition in, 170, 171, 173, 174, 192, 198; and

cosmopolitan nature of Texas tribes, 9; horticulture in, 169, 182, 183, 190, 268, 276; Native tribes in, 169, 173, 191; Oñate expedition in, 181, 183, 191; plants and trees in, 174, 273, 277, 282; rabbits in, 262. *See also* Quivira, Kansas

Karankawa Indians: and Alarcón expedition, 72; allies of, 100; and arrow shafts, 270; cannibalism by, 92, 225, 231; canoes of, 98; clothing of, 98; as cosmopolitan, 100; and De León expedition, 75, 94; destruction of Fort St. Louis by, 62, 63; enemies of, 60, 67, 100, 225; food of, 54; French children as captives of, 65, 67–68; and Hasinai Caddo, 214, 236, 244; and horses, 102, 214; huts of, 98, 291n.11; language of, 84; location and boundaries of, 25, 49–50, *82*, 83–85, 100, 103, 228; and Muruam Indians, 67; name of, 100; physical appearance of, 98; raids on Caddo Indians by, 214, 244; revolt of, at La Bahía mission, 100, 101; Rivera on, 83, 292n.2; travel by, 83–84

Karankawan language, 84

Kebaye Indians. *See* Kabaye Indians

Kemahopiheim Indians, 42

Keremen Indians, 42

Kiabaha Indians, 42

Kiowa/Quataquois Indians, 214

Kirona Indians, *18*, 30, 42

Klein, Richard G., 1, 225, 249

Knight, Vernon James, Jr., 39, 211

Koienkahe Indians, 42

Komkome Indians, 42

Konkone Indians. *See* Komkome Indians

Korimen Indians, 42

Kotter, Steven M., 31

Kourara Indians. *See* Quara Indians

Kouyam Indians, 42

Krieger, Alex D., 39, 74, 101, 111, 113, 128, 139–142, 154, 162, 230, 294n.8, 295n.3

Kuasse Indians, 60, 77

La Bahía presidio/mission, 100, 101, 226, 228

Lafora, Nicolás de, 46, 83, 144, 228–229, 230

Lago Santa María, 155

Laguna Guzmán, 155

Laguna Indians, 268, 273, 276, 277, 281

La Harpe, Bérnard de: on animals, 210, 252, 253, 256, 263; and calumet ceremony, 209–210; on Native tribes, 209–214, 216–217, 301n.46; in Northeast Texas (Study Area 7), 208, 209–214, 216–217; in Upper Texas Coast (Study Area 8), 220, 226

La Junta Indians: allies of, 140; and bison hides, 140; and Cabeza de Vaca's expedition, 11, 138, 139–140, 151, 154, 237; and Casas Grandes, 144; and Catholic missionaries, 159–160, 201; and Chamuscado expedition, 138, 146–147; clothing of, 139–140, 150; and cotton goods, 271; and drought, 54, 140; food of, 140, 267; granaries of, 284; and horticulture, 140, 146, 161, 183, 234, 237, 267, 268, 276; houses of, 139, 146–147, 150; hunting by, 161, 183; language of, 146, 162; and Mendoza expedition, 139, 201; and mesquite, 277; mural painting by, 143; physical appearance of, 146; and Pueblo Indians, 237; and trade, 6–7, 147, 161, 236, 237; tribes included in, 160; weapons of, 146

languages: Atakapan language, 231; Aztec language, 134; Cabeza de Vaca on, 241; Caddoan language, 195, 244; of Central Texas Coast tribes, 241; Géry's knowledge of Native languages, 118; of Han Indians, 220; of hunter-gatherers, 239; Karankawan language, 84, 98; of La Junta Indians, 146, 162; of Northeast Texas tribes, 199; of Nuevo León and Coahuila tribes, 124; of Plains Indians, 148; of Pueblo Indians, 148; Sanan language, 61; of Trans-Pecos tribes, 140, 146, 148, 150, 151. See also sign language

Larios, Fray Juan, 109, 116–117, 275

La Salle, Nicolas de, 213, 269, 274, 275, 300–301n.25

La Salle expedition: and alligators and crocodiles, 31, 252; attacks and threats against, by Matagorda Bay Indians, 87, 89, 91; and birds, 254, 255, 262; and bison, 29, 31, 32, 53, 86, 90, 99, 100, 256; and cannibalism by Native tribes, 225; in Central Texas Coast (Study Area 3), 82, 84, 86–91; and death of La Salle,

196, 202; and deer, 32, 257; deserters from, 201; and dogs, 258; first encounter with Natives by, 29; and Flathead tribes, 33, 37, 77, 103, 289n.30; food for, 59, 274; and Fort St. Louis, 10, 13, 21, 30, 52, 56, 84; and Garcitas Creek fort and colony, 64, 84; and Hasinai Caddo, 21, 32, 40, 45, 89; and horses, 33, 89, 104, 202, 260; hunting by, 32; illness of La Salle, 201; in Lower Brazos River to Lower Colorado River (Study Area 1), 28–34, 223; in Lower Colorado River to San Antonio River (Study Area 2), 48, 52, 55–61, 65; on maize (corn), 30, 276–277; maps and route of, 10, 13, 18, 21, 48; and Mississippi River expedition, 28, 37, 52, 86, 200, 222; Native American captive of, 90; and Native tribes, 30, 32–33, 39–40, 42–46, 56–57, 74, 76–77, 79, 87–88, 101–102, 104, 159, 196, 200–206, 211–216, 258; in Northeast Texas (Study Area 7), 194, 196, 200–206, 215; peace between Native tribes and, 90–91, 101, 104; publication on, 16; ships of, 86–87, 93, 202; in South Texas (Study Area 4), 109, 117; trade by, 59; in Trans-Pecos (Study Area 5), 139; on trees and plants, 33–34, 267–270, 272–274, 278–280, 282–284; and turkeys, 32, 263; in Upper Texas Coast (Study Area 8), 220, 222–223; and Wichita slaves, 173, 192; and wildlife, 32, 252, 261. See also Joutel, Henri

Last Glacial Maximum, 2

Las Víboras River, 146, 153

Late Caddoan period, 300n.10, 301n.46

laurel trees, 275

Lavaca Bay, 84

Lavaca River: convergence of Navidad River and, 90, 99; and De León expedition, 96; distance between Garcitas Creek and, 95–96; and La Salle expedition, 90, 99; location of, 50, 82, 84; and Martínez, 95–96; Native tribes near, 74, 79; plants along, 270

LeBlanc, Steven A., 7, 188, 238–239, 287n.38, 299n.38

lechuguilla, 114, 157

Lekson, Stephen H., 286n.30

Mamitte Indians, 163, 164, 165
mammals. *See* animals
mammoths, 3, 247
Manam Indians, 61, 66, 77
Mandone Indians, 66–67
Manosprieta Indians, 116, 131
Manso Indians, 179
Manzano Mountains, 149
Mapimi, Mexico, 283
margay, 4, 256
Margry, Pierre, 79, 232
Mariame Indians: and Cabeza de Vaca
    expedition, 53, 77, 85–86, 110, 139; ene-
    mies of, 78; location of, 77; and prickly
    pear fields, 54–55, 78, 110; Spaniards
    held as slaves by, 85–86; trade by, 54–55;
    and Yguase Indians, 81
marine shells. *See* shells
Marquette, Jacques, 200, 283
marriage of Capoque Indians, 22, 24
Marshall, Lynn, 266, 268, 279
Martín, Hernán, 190
Martínez, Francisco: in Central Texas
    Coast (Study Area 3), 52, 67–68, 84–85,
    95–97; on cottonwood trees, 272; and
    rescue of French survivors from Fort
    St. Louis, 52, 67–68, 95–97, 99, 288n.61
Massanet, Fray Damián: in Central Texas
    Coast (Study Area 3), 95, 103; on food,
    301n.30; on Géry, 130, 131, 133; in Lower
    Colorado River to San Antonio River
    (Study Area 2), 49, 61, 62, 64–67, 69,
    74–80; and Native tribes, 44, 122, 128–
    135, 159, 206, 239; in Northeast Texas
    (Study Area 7), 206; in South Texas
    (Study Area 4), 120, 122; on trees, 272
mastodons, 3, 247
Matagorda Bay: and Aguayo expedition,
    85; and Alarcón expedition, 72, 85, 209;
    alligators on, 252; archeological study
    of, 99–100; and Cabeza de Vaca expe-
    dition, 26, 85; and De León expedition,
    119; Dorantes party at, 24, 26; entrance
    to, 24, 86, 119; and La Salle expedition,
    30, 86, 87, 119, 223; map location of, *18,
    48, 82;* Martínez at, 67–68; name of, as
    Espiritu Santo, 24, 26, 85; Native tribes
    along, 26, 53, 84, 85, 87, 100; plants near,
    269, 274, 284; and Rívas expedition, 93;
    rivers and creeks flowing into, 24, 50;

and Terán expedition, 122. *See also* Fort
    St. Louis
Matagorda Island, 87
Maye Indians, 214
Mayeye Indians, *18,* 31, 36, 42, 47
Mayo, Casica, 150
McKusick, Charmion, 175
medar. *See* persimmon trees
medicinal herbs, 91
Medieval Warm Period, 7, 107–108, 186–
    188, 210, 233, 238–239, 272, 287n.38,
    287n.40, 291n.1, 299n.42, 303n.1
Medina River, 50, 132, 272
Meghey Indians. *See* Mayeye Indians
melons, 153, 208, 236. *See also*
    watermelons
Membré, Zénobe: on bison, 86; and La
    Salle discovery expedition down Mis-
    sissippi River, 86; on plants and trees,
    267, 268, 274, 278, 279, 282, 283
Mendica Indians, *18,* 26, 31, 43
Mendoza expedition: on animals, 185,
    253, 256, 257; attack against, by Native
    tribes, 166, 186, 188, 190, 191–192, 242;
    and bison, 184, 185–186, 187, 256; and
    Edwards Plateau, 163, 164, 165, 166, 167,
    170, 184–185; and fish, 259; guides for,
    139; map and route of, *10,* 13; and Native
    tribes, 67, 76, 139, 156–157, 162–167, 184–
    187, 189–191, 201; on plants and trees,
    185, 267, 270, 272, 274, 277, 278, 280,
    282; publications on, 15, 16; in Southern
    Plains (Study Area 6), *168,* 170, 184–187,
    188; in Trans-Pecos (Study Area 5), *136,*
    139, 156–157, 201
Meraquaman Indians, 43
mescal, 146, 149
Mescalero Apache, 137
Mescal/Mixcal Indians: and De León
    expedition, 43, 69, 78, 120, 131; and
    Espinosa expedition, 36, 43, 47; and
    Géry, 131, 240; between Lower Brazos
    and Lower Colorado Rivers, 35, 36, 43,
    46, 47; and Salinas Varona expedition,
    46, 68, 80, 122, 243; and Terán expedi-
    tion, 122
mesquite: and Antelope Creek People,
    238; mesquite beans as food source,
    146, 177, 277, 283; in prehistoric period,
    3; in Southern Plains, 177; in South

Texas, 117, 123, 127; in Trans-Pecos, 146, 151, 152, 155, 157
Mesquite Indians: Catholic missions for, 160; and Espinosa expedition, 43, 46, 123; language of, 61; location of, 160, 165; and Ramón Indians, 36; Retis on, 43
metropolitan areas. *See* Cahokia; Casas Grandes; houses; Paquimé, Mexico; Quivira, Kansas; villages and towns
Meunier, Pierre, 56, 87, 95, 96, 102, 206
Mexico. *See specific locations*
Mezquía, Father, 266
Middle Archaic period, 4–5, 210
Middle Onion Creek Valley site, 35
military expeditions. *See* warfare
Mimbres Valley, 6
Minet, Jean, 103
Minime, Gabriel. *See* Barbier, Gabriel Minime, Sieur de
mining, 113, 117, 139, 144–145, 175–176
missionaries. *See* Catholic missionaries
Mission River, 84
Mississippian tribes, 7, 112, 183, 197–198, 199, 210, 235, 237
Mississippi mound builders, 5, 6
Mississippi River: animals along, 253, 256, 263; birds along, 254, 255; and Cabeza de Vaca expedition, 220; Cahokia on, 6, 234–235; and De Soto expedition, 197; fishing in, 259; Joutel's travel on, 204; La Salle's discovery expedition down, 28, 37, 52, 86, 200, 222; maize cultivation along, 275, 276–277; and Moscoso expedition, 27, 196, 199–200, 221; Native tribes along, 7, 60, 203, 216, 221; plants and trees along, 267, 269, 272–274, 277–280, 282–284; rivers flowing into, 196; warfare between Native tribes on east and west sides of, 236, 244; watermelon cultivation along, 284
Missouri, 9
Missouri River, 173, 268, 278, 280
Mixcal Indians. *See* Mescal/Mixcal Indians
Momon Indians, 131
Monclova, Mexico, 43, 116, 118, 119, 122, 138, 155, 176
Monterrey, Mexico, 9, 13, 114, 115, 280
Montezuma, 144

Montoya, Fray Juan de, 12, 178
Monument Hill, 20, 50, 95
Moore, Edward C., 39, 211
Morenger, Crevel, 86–89
Morlete, Juan, 178
Moscoso expedition: attacks by Native tribes on, 221; boats of, 27, 221–222; in Central Texas Coast (Study Area 3), 86; and death of De Soto, 21, 26; food for, 27, 28, 199, 222; and Hasinai Caddo, 26–27, 55, 271; and horticulture, 33, 276; in Lower Brazos River to Lower Colorado River (Study Area 1), 26–28; map and route of, *10, 18,* 21, 28, 221; and Native tribes, 196, 198–200, 213, 214, 215–216, 222, 239; in Northeast Texas (Study Area 7), *194,* 196, 197–200, 215–216; publications on, 287n.44; and retainer sacrifice by Native tribes, 245; and trade, 27, 127, 198–199, 222, 229; in Upper Texas Coast (Study Area 8), 11, 27–28, 220, 221–222, 229; warfare between Indians and, 198
mound builders, 5, 6, 197, 210, 230, 235, 300n.4
Moundville, 235
mountain lions. *See* cougars
mulberry trees, 33–34, 97, 123, 185, 277–278, 279
mural paintings, 143, 254, 296n.9
Muruam Indians, 53, 66, 67, 70, 78, 100
musical instruments, 2, 91, 98, 111, 116, 124, 147, 150, 246, 249. *See also* dancing and singing
Mustang Island, 84

Naaman Indians, 65, 66, 74, 78
Naansi Indians, 214
Nabedache Indians, 214, 215
Nabiri Indians, 214
Nacacahoz Indians, 214
Nacao/Nacau Indians, 214
Nacassa Indians, 214
Nacodissy Indians, 214
Nacodoche Indians, 214
Nacogdoches mission, 227, 228
Nacoho Indians, 214
Nacono Indians, 214, 215
Nadaco Indians, 214
Nadadores River, 117, 277

Nadaho Indians, 214
Nadamin Indians, 214
Nadatcho Indians, 214
Nadeicha Indians, 215
Naguatex Indians, 198, 215
Nahacassi Indians, 215
Nanatsoho Indians, 209, 215
Nardichia Indians, 215
Narváez expedition, xii, 15, 20–22, 52, 53, 84, 139, 154
Nasayaya Indians, 215
Nasitti Indians, 215
Nasoni/Assoni/Nassoni Indians, *194*, 202, 209, 215, 258, 268
Nastchez/Natsoho Indians, 215
Natachitoche Indians, 215
Natchez Indians, 213, 216, 278
Native peoples: and agricultural revolution, 4–5; Classic period of, 5–8, 235; and climate change, 2, 4, 7–8, 287n.38; common traditions in Texas Indian cultures, 243–247; cultural continuity of, 248–250; depopulation of, xi, xii, 12; diversity of Texas Indian cultures, 233–243; earliest culture of, 1–2; in 1500s–1600s AD, 8–13; horticultural lifestyle of, 233, 234–239, 248; immigration of, to the Americas, 1, 285n.1; and mound building, 5, 6; in 900 AD, 5–8; nomadic lifestyle of bison hunters, 234; semisedentary lifestyle of, 233; in 7000 BC, 4–5; subsistence lifestyle of hunter-gatherers, 233–234, 239–240, 249; in 12,000 BC, 2–4. *See also specific tribes and geographic regions*
Native Study Area 1. *See* Lower Brazos River to Lower Colorado River (Study Area 1)
Native Study Area 2. *See* Lower Colorado River to San Antonio River (Study Area 2)
Native Study Area 3. *See* Central Texas Coast (Study Area 3)
Native Study Area 4. *See* South Texas (Study Area 4)
Native Study Area 5. *See* Trans-Pecos (Study Area 5)
Native Study Area 6. *See* Southern Plains (Study Area 6)

Native Study Area 7. *See* Northeast Texas (Study Area 7)
Native Study Area 8. *See* Upper Texas Coast (Study Area 8)
Natschita/Natchitta/Natchitoche/Natshito Indians, 205, 209, 215, 217
Natsoho Indians. *See* Nastchez/Natsoho Indians
Natsshostanno Indians, 215
Navasota River: and Cabeza de Vaca expedition, 24; cane brakes near, 270; crossing area of, 208; and La Salle expedition, 32; map location of, *18;* trees near, 271, 278
Navidad River: convergence of Lavaca River and, 90, 99; location of, 50, 84; trees along, 267, 272, 273
Neanderthal, 2, 25, 240, 247
Nechaui Indians, 215
Neche Indians, 215
Neches River, *194*, 214, *218*, 228, 253, 280
Neihahat Indians, 215
Newcomb, William W., Jr., 53, 74, 189, 190, 191, 220, 291n.3, 291n.11
New Mexico: animals in, 253–254, 256, 257, 260, 262; banishment of Castaño from, 178–179; banishment of Oñate from, 183–184; birds in, 254; Bonilla in, 155–156; Castaño de Sosa expedition in, 138, 155, 176, 178; ceramics in, 6; Chaco Canyon in, 6, 8, 235; Chamuscado expedition in, 138, 145, 148–149, 152, 174–175; climate change in, 188; Coronado in, 170, 171, 191, 255; deaths of Franciscan priests in, 145, 149, 175; Espejo expedition in, 151–152, 155, 175; horticulture in, 146, 148, 155, 169, 173, 175, 180, 183, 268, 276, 284; Oñate expedition in, 138, 156, 179; peyote in, 281; plants and trees in, 266, 279, 282, 284; Pueblo revolt (1680) in, 13, 201; Spanish colonization of, 12, 138–139, 155–156, 178–179; tobacco in, 283–284; trade by Native tribes in, 6; turkeys in, 175; winter weather of, 151–152, 171; writings on, 12; Zaldívar's expedition in, 16. *See also* Pueblo Indians
Nisohone Indians, 215
Niza, Fray Marcos de, 294n.7

Nondaco/Nondacao Indians, *194*, 215–216
nopal. See prickly pear
Norteños, 209, 301n.46
Northeast Texas (Study Area 7): Aguayo
    expedition in, *194*, 209; Alarcón expe-
    dition in, *194*, 209; boundaries of, 195;
    counties in, 195, 299n.2; De León ex-
    pedition in, *194*, 196, 206; horticulture
    in, 196, 204, 206, 215; La Harpe in, 208,
    209–214, 216–217; La Salle expedition
    in, *194*, 196, 200–206, 215; maps of, *14*,
    195; Moscoso expedition in, *194*, 196,
    197–200, 215–216; Native tribes in, *194*,
    195, 210–217; Ramón and Espinosa ex-
    pedition in, 36, *194*, 208, 214, 215; rivers
    in, 195–196; Salinas Varona expedition,
    194, 207; Terán expedition in, *194*, 207;
    trees in, 196
North Llano Draw, 282
Nouista Indians, 216
Novrach Indians, 189
Nueces River: and Alarcón expedition,
    124; crossing area for, 108; and De
    León expedition, 34, 62, 121, 280; and
    Espinosa expedition, 34; javelinas near,
    260; map location of, *106;* mouth of,
    84; prickly pear near, 110; rivers com-
    prising Nueces River system, 107; trees
    along, 280
Nueva Vizcaya, Mexico, 61, 102, 134, 158,
    160, 191–192, 242, 284
Nuevo León, Mexico: animals in, 71, 253,
    256, 257, 260, 263; birds in, 112, 147, 254,
    261–262; bison herds in, 71; Carvajal in,
    113; Chapa on, 12, 108, 113–115, 131, 192;
    and Coronado expedition, 199; De León
    (the elder) on, 12, 124–125, 178–179, 245;
    European diseases impacting Native
    Americans in, 108, 124; Indian raids on
    Spanish settlements in, 129, 130, 134, 177,
    192, 259; Native tribes in, 124, 131, 132,
    140, 177; plants and trees in, 126, 267,
    269, 271–273, 275, 278, 280; silver min-
    ing in, 175–176; song-dances by Native
    tribes in, 247; trade routes in, 175, 267
nut trees, 157, 182, 185, 279–282

oak trees: Post Oak Belt, 19, 20, 32, *48*,
    49, 50, 51, 71, 195, 260; in prehistoric

period, 3; in Southern Plains, 182; in
    South Texas, 123, 127; Spanish and
    French explorers on, 123, 278; in Trans-
    Pecos, 152, 157
Oakville Escarpment, 19, 20, *48*, 50–51
Oaxaca, Mexico, 261
Obayo Indians, 116
Obregón, Baltasar de: on animals, 253,
    255, 257; on Jumano Indians, 165; on
    Paquimé, 11, 138, 142–143, 163, 166, 174;
    on Querecho Indians, 165–166, 174, 180,
    192, 244; on Río Casas Grandes people,
    154; in Trans-Pecos (Study Area 5),
    142–143; on trees and plants, 272, 273,
    275, 282, 284; on Vaqueros, 192
obsidian, 125, 173
Ocana/Ocane/Acani Indians, *106*, 117, 122,
    131, 189
Ocare Indians, 131
ocelots, 4, 248, 256, 260
Odoesmade Indians, 131
Ohio River, 204
Ointemarhen Indians, 43
Ojibwa Indians, 268
Oklahoma: antelope in, 252; bison in, 255,
    256; climate change in, 188; gathering of
    Native tribes in, 209–210; horticulture
    in, 169, 190, 276; Native tribes in, 35,
    169, 172, 195, 208, 213, 214; rivers in, 169;
    Spiro in, 235
Oliver, Alice W., 98
Omenaosse Indians, 43
Onapiem Indians, 60, 78
Oñate expedition: and bison herds, 180–
    182; criminal charges against Oñate for
    abuses against Pueblo Indians, 183–184;
    and Native tribes, 181–183; in New
    Mexico, 138, 156, 179, 180; number of
    colonists with, 179; to Quivira, Kansas,
    181, 183, 191; route of, 12; in Southern
    Plains (Study Area 6), 156, *168*, 170,
    179–184; in Trans-Pecos (Study Area 5),
    138–139, 156
Onion Creek, 34, 50, 71, 72, 185
O'pata Indians, 141
Opelousa Indians, *218,* 231
opossum, 261
Opoxme/Oposme Indians, 160, 165
Orancho Indians, 189

Orcan Indians, 60, 78
Orcoquiza/Arcoquisa/Akokisa Indians, 19, 40–41, *218*, 219, 220, 228, 230, 239
Orcoquizá Presidio, 228, 229
Orobio y Basterra, Joachín de, 19, 40–41, *218*, 220, 226–228, 229, 231
Ororoso Indians, 157, 165
Osage/Anahons Indians, 205, 209, 216, 269
osage orange. *See* bois d'arc
Osatayolida/Osatayogligla Indians, 165
Otermín, Antonio de, 156
Otomi Indians, 114, 131
Otomoaco Indians, 150–152, 154, 160, 162, 165, 166. *See also* Jumano Indians
Ouachita River, 203, 260
Oviedo y Valdez, Gonzalo Fernández de: on animals, 261; on Cabeza de Vaca expedition, 15, 110–113, 141, 287n.42, 293–294n.3; in Lower Brazos River to Lower Colorado River (Study Area 1), 22–24; in Lower Colorado River to San Antonio River (Study Area 2), 52, 53, 77, 81; on number of bowmen, 302n.4; on plants, 266; on sand mounds at entrance to Matagorda Bay, 86, 293n.9; in South Texas (Study Area 4), 110–113; on winter weather, 220–221
Oyster Creek, 20, 24, 228

Paac Indians, 122, 131
Pacausin/Pacuachiam Indians, *106*, 131
Pachal Indians. *See* Patchal/Pachal Indians
Pachaque Indians, 117, 129, 131
Pachina Indians, 227–228, 231
Pacoche Indians. *See* Pacuache/Pacoche Indians
Pacpul Indians, 78, 94, 103, 122, 131
Pacuache/Pacoche Indians, 68, *106*, 122–124, 131, 134
Pacuachiam Indians. *See* Pacausin/Pacuachiam Indians
Pacuasim/Paquasin Indians, 46, 123, 131
Pagaiame Indians, 189
Paiabuna Indians, 189
Paillaille Indians. *See* Payaya/Peyaye Indians
Pajarito Indians, 120, 131
Palakea Indians, 44

Palaquechare Indians: allies of, 41–42; enemies of, 33, 77, 88; and Flathead tribes, 103; and Hasinai Caddo, 236; horticulture by, 33, 268; and La Salle expedition, 32–33, 41–42, 43–44, 77, 88; location of, *18*, 43–44
Palaquesson Indians, 44
Palcedo Creek, 94
Paleo-Indians, 3
palm trees, 123, 278–279
Palona Indians, 44
Pamai Indians. *See* Pamaya/Pamai Indians
Pamaya/Pamai Indians, 36, 43, 44, 122, 132
Pampopa Indians, 44, 70, 123
Panaa Indians, 120, 132
Panac Indians. *See* Papanac/Panac Indians
Panasiu Indians, 66, 78
Panequo Indians, 60, 66, 78
panthers. *See* cougars
Pánuco, Mexico, 23, 24, 53, 139, 175–176, 200, 221
Paouite Indians. *See* Tamerlouan Indians
Papanac/Panac Indians, *106*, 122, 132
Papane Indians, 189
Paquachiam Indians, 132
Paquasin Indians. *See* Pacuasim/Paquasin Indians
Paquimé, Mexico, 6, 11, 112, 138, 141–144, 163, 166, 174. *See also* Casas Grandes
Parchaca/Parchaque Indians, 122, 132
Pardiñas, Juan Isidro de, 93
Parral, Mexico: horticulture in, 153; revolt of Native tribes (1684) in, 163, 164, 165, 167, 186. *See also* Chihuahua, Mexico
parrots and parrot feathers: and Casas Grandes, 142, 144, 261; in Cuba, 262; gift of feathers from Otermín to Native leaders, 156, 175; in Mexico, 112, 147, 261; in South Texas, 124; Spanish and French explorers on, 261–262; trade of, 7, 112, 114, 127, 147, 175
Passaguate/Pazaguante Indians, 150, 153, 161, 165
Pastaloca Indians, 122, 132
Pastia/Paxti Indians, *106*, 132
Pataguaque Indians, 117, 132
Pataguo/Patavo Indians, 122, 123, 132
Pataoo Indians, 120, 132
Patarabuey Indians, 160, 165. *See also* Jumano Indians

Pojue Indians, 189
Polacme Indians, 160, 165
Polvo site, 296n.9
pomegranate trees, 204, 222, 236, 282–283
poplar trees, 35, 155
population centers. *See* Cahokia; Casas
    Grandes; houses; Paquimé, Mexico;
    Quivira, Kansas; villages and towns
Posada, Alonso de, 190
Post Oak Belt, 19, 20, 32, *48*, 49, 50, 51, 71,
    195, 260
potatoes, 224
pottery. *See* ceramics
Poxalma/Poxsalme/Posalme Indians, 160,
    165
prairie chickens, 124, 125
prickly pear: and Conchos Indians, 146;
    and feast on prickly pear tuna, 54–55,
    78, 110, 244; and Mariame Indians,
    54–55, 78, 110; and People of the Figs,
    132–133; in prehistoric period, 3; in
    South Texas, 123; Spanish and French
    explorers on, 116, 123, 283, 284
pronghorn antelopes. *See* antelopes
Pucha Indians, 189
Pueblo, Mexico, 282
Pueblo Indians: and Apache Indians, xii;
    and Cabri Indians, 146; and Chamus-
    cado expedition, 148–149; clothing of,
    146, 155; compared with Aztecs, 148–
    149; and Coronado expedition, 191;
    and cotton, 173, 175, 191, 237, 271; crimi-
    nal charges against Oñate for abuses
    against, 183–184; and dogs, 148, 175, 191;
    and Espejo expedition, 152, 155; food of,
    148, 206; and Hasinai Caddo, 236; and
    horticulture, 146, 148, 155, 169, 173, 175,
    180, 191, 237, 268; houses of, 146, 148,
    150, 152, 155, 173, 175, 191; influences of
    Mexican culture on, 155; and La Junta
    Indians, 237; language of, 148; location
    of, 8; music and dances of, 155; and
    pine trees, 281; and Querecho Indians,
    173–174; revolt of (1680), 13, 201; trade
    and travel by, 148, 169, 172, 173, 180;
    and turkeys, 148, 152, 175, 191; warfare
    between Castaño de Sosa expedition
    and, 178
Puguahiane Indians, 189

Pujai Indians, 133
Pulcha Indians, 189
Pulique Indians, 160, 165
pumas. *See* cougars
pumpkins, 160, 161, 175

quail, 100, 124, 182
Quanoatinno Indians. *See* Quansatinno
    Indians
Quansatinno Indians, 79
Quapaw Indians. *See* Acansa Indians
Quara Indians, 79
Quataquois Indians. *See* Kiowa/Quata-
    quois Indians
Quem Indians, 79–80, 94, 103, 122, 131, 133
Querecho Indians: and Coronado expedi-
    tion, 12, 171, 173–174, 191, 244; dancing
    and singing by, 143, 174; and dogs, 171,
    174, 180, 191, 258; enemies of, 171, 192;
    and flint tools, 191; map location of, *168*;
    Obregón on, 138, 143, 165–166, 180, 244,
    255; sign language by, 171, 174, 177, 191
Quevene Indians: and Cabeza de Vaca
    expedition, 26, 44–45, 53, 85, 103–104;
    and Dorantes, 86; location of, *82*, 85;
    murder of Spaniards by, 26, 85; threats
    against Cabeza de Vaca by, 26, 85;
    warfare between Deaguane/Doguene
    Indians and, 25–26, 41, 44–45, 85, 103,
    104; and woman as peace negotiator, 26
Quezale Indians, 116
Quicasquiri Indians. *See* Wichita Indians
Quicuchabe Indians, 157, 166
Quinapisa Indians, 258
Quinet Indians, 102, 104
Quiouaha Indians, 216
Quisaba Indians, 189
Quitaca Indians, 157, 166
Quitman Mountains, 272
Quitole Indians, 110, 133
Quivira, Kansas, 11, 156, 170–173, 181, 183,
    191, 273, 276, 282
Quoaque Indians, 104. *See also* Coco
    Indians
Quouan Indians, 45

rabbits: hunting of, 127, 149, 153, 248, 262;
    in modern-day Texas, 250; in prehis-
    toric period, 3; in Southern Plains, 182;

in South Texas, 124, 125, 127; Spanish
and French explorers on, 100, 262, 266;
in Trans-Pecos, 141
raids: for horses, 67, 69, 70, 114–115, 121–
122, 214, 227, 229, 259; for slaves, xii, 33,
37, 67, 69, 92, 114, 117, 129, 173, 203, 244,
290n.31, 300n.23; on Spanish settlements by Native tribes, 67, 129, 130, 134,
158, 167, 177, 192, 259
Ramón expedition: in Lower Brazos
River to Lower Colorado River (Study
Area 1), 18, 44, 45, 47, 72; in Lower
Colorado River to San Antonio River
(Study Area 2), 52; and Native tribes,
44, 45, 47, 214, 215; in Northeast Texas
(Study Area 7), 36, *194*, 208, 214, 215;
publication on, 16, 288n.64; purpose
of, 13; in South Texas (Study Area 4),
106, 123
Raya Indians, 145–146, 161, 166
red ocher, 2, 25, 240, 247, 249
Red River: bears near, 253; as boundary
of Northeast Texas, 195–196; crossing
area on, 207; location of, *10, 168,* 169,
194; and Moscoso expedition, 196, 215;
Native tribes near, 35, 36, 198, 202–203,
205, 206, 208, 209, 215, 216–217, 228;
plants near, 269; river flowing into, 196;
turkeys near, 263
religious beliefs and practices: and afterlife, 245–246; burial practices, 2, 22, 127,
235, 240, 246; ceremonial song-dances,
124, 127, 246–247, 281; human and
animal spirits, 245; and peyote, 124, 127,
247, 280–281; rejection of Catholic faith
by Native tribes, 207; retainer sacrifice,
235, 245; and rock art, 127, 247, 248–
249; and shamans, 22, 126, 127, 225, 240,
246, 247; worship of sun, 61, 197, 235.
See also cannibalism
Retana, Juan Fernández de, 62, 157–158,
163, 164
Retis, Don Juan Antonio de Trasviña y, 43,
159–160, 162–167
Rey, Agapito, 162, 189
Ribas, Fray Andrés Pérez de: on animals,
252, 253, 254, 256, 257, 260, 263; on
birds, 261; on maize cultivation, 276;
on Native tribes, 162, 166; on peyote,

281; on song-dances of Native tribes,
247; travels and missionary work of,
in northern Mexico, 12; on trees and
plants, 266, 268, 271, 273, 277, 284
Richard Beene site, 252, 256, 257, 262, 269
Ricklis, Robert A., 25, 61, 83, 85, 103, 125–
126, 291n.3
Río Casas Grandes people: and Cabeza de
Vaca expedition, 138, 141–142, 148, 154;
and Ibarra expedition, 11; and maize
cultivation, 140, 276; and Paquimé, 6,
112, 163; and peyote, 281; and plants and
trees, 267, 272, 273, 284; and trade, 127,
147, 198
Río Conchos: and Chamuscado expedition, 138, 145–146, 174; and Espejo
expedition, 149, 152–153, 175; fish in,
259; horticulture along, 150, 276, 284;
map location of, *10, 136;* and Mendoza
expedition, 157; mining near headwaters of, 144–145; Native tribes along,
137, 145–146, 160–161, 163, 164, 166, 184,
189–191; rabbits along, 262; and Retis
expedition, 160; trees along, 280
Río del Carmen, 148
Río de los Nadadores. *See* Nadadores
River
Río de Pánuco, 222
Rio Grande: and Aguayo expedition, 124;
birds along, 254–255, 261, 262; bison
along, 255; as boundary of South Texas
(Study Area 4), 107; as boundary of
Trans-Pecos (Study Area 5), 137; and
Cabeza de Vaca expedition, 11, 111, 138,
140–141, 154, 176; and Chamuscado
expedition, 147–148, 174–175; crossing areas for, 34, 69, 108, 116, 120, 121,
130–134, 138, 140–141, 154, 156, 179; and
De León expedition, 62, 65–66, 69, 120,
121; and Espejo expedition, 151–152,
154–155; and Espinosa expedition, 34;
fish in, 259; horticulture along, 150; ice
and snow on, 297n.2; javelinas near,
260; and La Salle expedition, 30; maize
cultivation along, 276; map location of,
10, 106, 136, 168; and Mendoza expedition, 139, 156–157, 184; Native tribes
along, 8, 69, 76, 78, 120, 130–133, 137,
140–142, 160, 166, 169, 191, 203; and

aries of, 107; Cabeza de Vaca expedition in, *106,* 109, 110–113; Castaño de Sosa expedition in, 109; climate change in, 107–108, 113, 116, 117, 124, 126; cosmopolitan lifeways of Native tribes in, 114, 123, 127–128; counties in, 107, 293n.1; De León expedition in, *106,* 117–122; encampments of Native tribes in, 118–121, 240; Espinosa expedition in, *106,* 123; La Salle expedition in, 109; maps of, *14, 106;* Native trails through, 108–109; Native tribes in, *106,* 108, 109, 110, 116–122, 127–135; Peñasco de Lozano in, 109, 116; Ramón expedition in, *106,* 123; regional histories and archeological overviews of, 124–126; rivers and river crossings in, 107, 108; Salinas Varona expedition in, *106,* 122; Spanish military expeditions against Cacaxtle Indians in, 12–13, 69, 115–116, 129, 134; Terán expedition in, *106,* 122, 128; trees in, 123, 127

Spanish Colonization Laws, 144

Spanish expeditions: animals reported by, 251–263; diaries from, 9, 11; map of expedition routes of, *10;* overview of, 11–14; publications on, 15–16; on trees and other plants, 265–284. *See also specific expeditions*

spear thrower (atlatl) and dart points, 3, 125, 126, 127, 146, 221, 248, 249

Spichehat Indians, 45

spiritual beliefs and practices. *See* religious beliefs and practices

Spiro, 235

squash: and Antelope Creek People, 238; as food, 152; and Hasinai Caddo, 206, 235; and La Junta Indians, 146, 161, 237, 276; and population centers generally, 6; and Pueblo Indians, 146, 148, 155, 169, 173, 175, 180, 191, 268; at Quivira, Kansas, 191; in Trans-Pecos, 149, 150, 152, 153; and Wichita Indians, 169, 183

squirrels, 100

Suajo Indians, 157, 166

sumac trees, 174

Suma Indians: compared with Arcos Fuertes Indians, 185, 190; enemy of, 162; location of, *136,* 137, 151, 160, 281; and Mendoza expedition, 157, 166; and

peyote, 281; raids against Spanish settlements in, 167; and Retis expedition, 160; and Rivera expedition, 143

sunflowers, 197, 208, 210, 235, 238

Susola Indians, 54, 80, 110, 129, 133

Swanton, John R., 219, 230, 231

Tacame Indians, 80

Taensa Indians: and Caddo Indians, 7; enemies of, 216; horticulture by, 235–236; houses of, 205; and La Salle expedition, 216; and plants and trees, 153, 269, 278, 279, 282; slave raids on, 203, 300n.23; and Tonty, 205

Tahiannihouq Indians, 216

Talon, Jean, 96, 100, 101

Talon, Jean-Baptiste, 80, 91–92, 104, 225, 239, 270

Talon, Pierre, 56, 77, 80, 91–92, 104, 206, 239, 270

Talon children, 94–97

Tama (Caddoan leader), 227

Tamaroa Indians, 173

Tamaulipas, Mexico: alligators near, 252; Carvajal in, 113; maize cultivation in, 275; Native tribes in, 129; parrots in, 112, 147, 175, 261; and Rívas expedition, 92; and trade, 7, 175

Tamaulipas Mountains, 114, 176

Tamerlouan Indians, 80

Tamireguan Indians, 120, 133

Tancaouse Indians. *See* Tonkawa Indians

Taneaho Indians, 216

Tanico/Tonica/Tunica Indians, 203, 204, 216, 300–301n.25

Tankersley, Kenneth B., 249

Tanpachoa Indians, 151, 160, 166

Tanquinno Indians, 216

Taovaya/Toayas/Tawehash Indians, 209–210, 216

Taraha Indians, 44, 45

Taraumara Indians, 166

Tattersall, Ian, 1, 2, 249

tattoos, 88, 92, 205, 249, 250

Tawakoni/Toucara Indians, 209, 216

Tawehash Indians. *See* Taovaya/Toayas/Tawehash Indians

Taylor, Allan R., 240–241, 292n.16

Tchanhe Indians, 216

Torreón, Mexico, 280
Totame Indians, 160, 167
Toucara Indians. *See* Tawakoni/Toucara
    Indians
towns. *See* houses; villages and towns
Toyah Creek, 152
Toyah Lake, 152
Toyal Indians. *See* Tojal/Toyal Indians
trade: by Acansa Indians, 204; by Ante-
    lope Creek People, 238; by Bidai
    Indians, 228; of bison hide and meat,
    54, 148, 177, 234; of bows, 205, 269,
    300n.24; and Cabeza de Vaca expedi-
    tion, 23, 24–25, 111–112, 142, 198, 221,
    261, 271; by Caddohadacho Indians,
    205, 269; by Casas Grandes people, 6–7,
    111–112, 142, 147, 172–173, 192, 198, 237;
    by Cibola Indians, 163; of copper goods,
    6, 7, 112, 141, 142, 147, 172–173, 198, 199,
    202, 294nn.9–10; of cotton goods, 112,
    127, 140, 142, 147, 148, 198, 199, 201;
    evidence of long-distance trade, 125;
    French traders, 227–230; of fruit trees
    and other plants, 204, 236, 301n.31; for
    guns from French traders, 227, 229,
    230; by Hasinai Caddo, 26–27, 35, 37,
    195, 198, 201, 207–208, 210, 227, 235, 271;
    between Huastecan culture and Native
    tribes of South Texas, 125–126, 127, 128;
    by Jumano Indians, 77, 153, 154, 236,
    260; and La Junta Indians, 6–7, 147, 161,
    236, 237; and La Salle expedition, 59;
    by Mariame Indians, 54; and Moscoso
    expedition, 27, 127, 198–199, 222, 229;
    by Plains Indians, 241; by Pueblo Indi-
    ans, 148, 169, 172, 173, 180; and Ramón
    expedition, 36–37; of scarlet macaw
    parrots and feathers, 7, 112, 114, 127, 147,
    175; and sign language, 240–241; by
    Simaoma Indians, 35; by Toho Indians,
    35; and trade grounds and trade fairs,
    158, 207–208, 243; traditional trade
    items, 6–7, 25, 27, 111–112, 142, 147, 151,
    154, 180, 201, 237, 261, 269; by Vaquero
    Indians, 180; by Wichita Indians, 183,
    192. *See also* cosmopolitan lifeways;
    trade routes and travel corridors
trade routes and travel corridors: Bidai
    Trail in Upper Texas Coast, *218,* 226,

227, 228, 230–231; Camino Real, xi, 50,
    227, 260, 283; in Chihuahua, Mexico,
    114, 208, 267, 271; and common tra-
    ditions in Texas Indian cultures,
    243–245; crossing Texas generally, xi,
    6–7, 204; Joutel on, 204, 236; of Native
    tribes along lower Brazos River valley,
    290n.32; in Northeast Texas, 198–199,
    201, 204; in Nuevo León, Mexico, 175,
    267; in Southern Plains, 173, 179–180;
    in South Texas, 111, 127, 236; in Trans-
    Pecos, 147, 151. *See also* cosmopolitan
    lifeways
Trans-Pecos (Study Area 5): bison in, 138,
    143, 149, 150, 152, 157, 192; Bonilla in,
    155–156; boundaries of, 137; Cabeza de
    Vaca expedition in, *136,* 138, 139–142,
    170; Castaño de Sosa expedition in,
    138, 155; Chamuscado expedition in,
    136, 138, 145–149, 174–175; cosmopoli-
    tan lifeways of Native tribes in, 159,
    161, 244; counties in, 137; drought in,
    140; Espejo expedition in, *136,* 149–155;
    horticulture in, 140, 146, 148, 150, 151,
    157, 160, 161, 163, 164, 234, 268; Ibarra
    expedition in, 138, 142–143, 174; La Salle
    expedition in, 139; maps of, *14, 136;*
    Mendoza expedition in, *136,* 139, 156–
    157, 201; Native tribes in, *136,* 137, 157,
    159–167; Oñate expedition in, 138–139,
    156; Retana in, 62, 157–158; Retis in,
    159–160; Rivera expedition in, 143–144;
    rivers in, 137; Rubí in, 144; Sabeata in,
    156–159, 166; topography of, 137; trees
    in, 152, 155, 157. *See also* Big Bend
travel corridors and trade routes. *See*
    trade routes and travel corridors
travel time and distances, 57, 111, 141, 153–
    155, 199, 202–203, 227, 294n.5
trees: in Louisiana, 273, 278, 280, 282; in
    prehistoric period, 3; in South Texas,
    117, 123, 127; Spanish and French expe-
    ditions on, 265–284; trade of fruit trees,
    204, 236, 301n.31; in Trans-Pecos, 152,
    155, 157. *See also specific types of trees*
Tres Palacios Bay, 97
Trinity Bay, 220, 228
Trinity River: and Alarcón expedition,
    209; alligators in, 252; bears along, 253;

and Bellisle, 224; cane near, 270; and La Salle expedition, 202; location of, *194, 196, 218;* Native tribes along, 19, 212, 213; trees near, 271, 280

Tsepcoen Indians, 60

Tseperen Indians, 81

Tserabocherete Indians, 60, 81

Tunica Indians. *See* Tanico/Tonica/Tunica Indians

turkeys: and Casas Grandes, 237; Conchos Indians on, 155; and De León expedition, 34; and Espinosa expedition, 123; hunting of, 123, 127, 250, 263–264; and La Salle expedition, 32, 100, 263; in Northeast Texas, 210; in prehistoric period, 3; and Pueblo Indians, 148, 152, 175, 191; in Southern Plains, 182, 185; in South Texas, 123, 124, 127; Spanish and French explorers on, 262–263

Turner, Ellen Sue, 303n.18

Turpin, Solveig A., 125, 126, 247

turquoise, 127, 141, 142, 147, 180, 198, 199, 201, 237, 238, 249.

turtles, 100, 117

Tusonibi Indians, 35, 36, 46, 47, 70

Tyakappan Indians, 44, 46

Tyler, Ron, 74

Unofita Indians, 189

Upper Texas Coast (Study Area 8): Bellisle in, *218,* 220, 223–226; bison in, 224–225, 230; boundaries of, 219; Cabeza de Vaca expedition in, 11, *218,* 219–221; counties in, 219, 302n.2; horticulture in, 222, 229, 230; La Harpe in, 220, 226; La Salle expedition in, 220, 222–223; maps of, *14, 218;* Moscoso expedition in, 11, 27–28, 220, 221–222, 229; Native tribes in, 219, 227–228, 230–232; Orobio y Basterra in, *218,* 220, 226–228, 229; Rubí in, 220, 228–229

Vanca/Vauca Indians, 122, 134

Vaquero Indians, *168,* 180, 181, 190, 192

Varga site, 270, 277, 278, 279, 282

Vauca Indians. *See* Vanca/Vauca Indians

Vidai Indians. *See* Bidai/Bobida Indians

villages and towns, 5–6, 234–235, 267–268. *See also* Cahokia; Casas Grandes; houses; Paquimé, Mexico; Quivira, Kansas

Villar de Francos, Don Juan Isidro de Pardiñas, 163

vultures, 3

Waco/Honecha Indians, 209, 217

Wade, Mariah F., 162, 189, 274, 281, 299n.38

walnut trees, 155

warfare: among Anasazi, 188; between Atayo and Susola Indians, 129, 133; attacks against Spaniards by Trans-Pecos Indians, 166; and Caddo Indians, 209, 244; between Caux and Tojal Indians, 225; and climate change, 188, 237, 238; between Deaguane and Quevene, 25–26, 41, 44–45, 85, 104; between Escanjaque and Wichita Indians, 182; against Flathead tribes, 60, 88, 103, 203, 244; between Gavilan Indians and Retana, 164; against La Salle expedition, 87, 89, 91; between Moscoso expedition and Indians, 198; between Native tribes on east and west sides of Mississippi River, 236, 244; against Rívas expedition, 93; Salineros' attacks against Mendoza expedition, 166, 186, 188, 242; between Southern Plains Indians and Spanish troops, 190, 191; between South Texas Native tribes, 117, 131, 132, 135; between Spanish troops and Cacaxtle Indians, 13, 69, 115–116, 129, 134; between Tamerlouan and Toho Indians, 80; and Tanpachoa Indians, 151; and war cry, 89

watermelons, 113–114, 153, 160, 161, 204, 206, 236, 284

water supply, 96, 143

Watson Brake site, 258, 259, 262, 263, 267

weapons. *See* bow and arrow; spear thrower (atlatl) and dart points; warfare

weather. *See* climate change

Weddle, Robert S., 101

Weinstein, Richard A., 99–100

West Indies, 84, 203, 261, 283

wheat, 160

whistling, 150, 151

White, Randall, 303–304n.19

Wichita Indians: allies of, 192; and Coronado expedition, 192, 198; and fruit, 277, 282; and horticulture, 169, 183, 190, 192, 268; houses of, 182–183, 192; hunting by, 169, 192; and La Harpe expedition, 209, 217; La Salle expedition and Wichita slaves, 173, 192; location of, 172, *194*, 196; in Quivira, Kansas, 191; trade by, 183, 192; and warfare, 182
Wichita River, *168, 194*
wildcats. *see* bobcats
wildlife. *See* animals *and specific animals*
willow trees, 117, 127, 284
Wolf Indians, 225
wolves, 3, 178, 247, 263

Xaeser Indians, 117, 134
Xana Indians. *See* Sana Indians
Xarame Indians, 36, 43, 47, 70, 123. *See also* Chaularame Indians
Xiabu Indians. *See* Ijiaba/Xiabu Indians
Xoman Indians, 117, 133, 134

Yatisi/Yatasi Indians, 209, 217
Yazoo River, 204, 300–301n.25
Yegua Creek, *18*, 20
Yeripiama Indians, 43, 47. *See also* Ervipiame Indians

Ygodsa Indians. *See* Deadose/Ygodsa Indians
Yguase/Yguaze Indians, 53, 81, 110, 129, 134
Ylame Indians, 157, 167
Yojane Indians. *See* Yojuane Indians
Yojuane Indians: enemies of, 35; and Espinosa expedition, 35, 36, 47, 70, 81; and La Harpe, 217; location of, 36, 46, 47, 81, 217; and Rivera expedition, 36
Yorca Indians. *See* Yorica/Yorca Indians
Yorica/Yorca Indians, *106*, 117, 122, 131, 132, 134–135
Yoyehi Indians, 189
Yscani/Ascanis Indians, 209, 217
Yucatan Peninsula, 4
yucca, 114, 123, 284
Yurbipame Indians. *See* Yeripiama Indians
Yurbipane Indians, 117, 135

Zacatecas, Mexico, 115
Zacatil Indians, 135
Zaldívar, Vicente de: bison-hunting expedition by, 12, 138, 170, 180–181; on dog train, 258; guides for, 180; publication of texts by, 15–16; in Southern Plains (Study Area 6), 12, *168*, 170, 180–181
Zavala, Don Martín de, 113